READINGS IN GLOBAL HISTORY
Volume 1

Revised printing
Second Edition

Anthony Snyder
Sherri West
Brookdale Community College

KENDALL/HUNT PUBLISHING COMPANY
4050 Westmark Drive   P.O. Box 1840   Dubuque, Iowa 52004-1840

Cover image courtesy of PhotoDisc.

Copyright © 1992, 1997, 2001 by Kendall/Hunt Publishing Company

Library of Congress Catalog Card Number: 2008931933

ISBN 978-0-7575-5320-2

Printed in the United States of America
20   19   18   17   16   15   14   13   12   11

Contents

Acknowledgments

We would like to thank Jess Le Vine, Laura Neitzel, George Reklaitis, and Jane Scimeca, our colleagues in world history at Brookdale, for sharing their suggestions for this new edition. Also, our adjunct instructors have been helpful in advising us on various aspects of this reader. Finally, our thanks go to our students for whom we have labored on this book and from whom we have received invaluable information as to its strengths and weaknesses—we owe them a debt of gratitude.

Anthony W. Snyder
Sherri L. West

1

Geologic Time and Human History

In this selection, Carl Sagan proposes that we look at the expanse of time since the "Big Bang" as a single year.

Discussion Questions

1. According to the perspective presented by Sagan, how significant are human beings in the history of the universe?

2. If the month of December were expanded to become a whole year, how would that perspective change? Where would modern civilization fit in?

The Dragons of Eden

The world is very old, and human beings are very young. Significant events in our personal lives are measured in years or less; our lifetimes in decades; our family genealogies in centuries; and all of recorded history in millennia. But we have been preceded by an awesome vista of time, extending for prodigious periods into the past, about which we know little—both because there are no written records and because we have real difficulty in grasping the immensity of the intervals involved.

Yet we are able to date events in the remote past. Geological stratification and radioactive dating provide information on archaeological, paleontological and geological events; and astrophysical theory provides data on the ages of planetary surfaces, stars, and the Milky Way Galaxy, as well as an estimate of the time that has elapsed since that extraordinary event called the Big Bang—an explosion that involved all of the matter and energy in the present universe. The Big Bang may be the beginning of the universe, or it may be a discontinuity in which information about the earlier history of the universe was destroyed. But it is certainly the earliest event about which we have any record.

The most instructive way I know to express this cosmic chronology is to imagine the fifteen-billion-year lifetime of the universe (or at least its present incarnation since the Big Bang) compressed into the span of a single year. Then every billion years of Earth history would correspond to about twenty-four days of our cosmic year, and one second of that year to 475 real revolutions of the Earth about the sun.

[Following] I present the cosmic chronology in three forms: a list of some representative pre-December dates; a calendar for the month of December; and a closer look at the late evening of New Year's Eve. On this scale, the events of our history books—even books that make significant efforts to deprovincialize the present—are so compressed that it is necessary to give a second-by-second recounting of the last seconds of the cosmic year. Even then, we find events listed as contemporary that we have been taught to consider as widely separated in time. In the history of life, an equally rich tapestry must have been woven in other periods—for example, between 10:02 and 10:03 on the morning of April 6th or September 16th. But we have detailed records only for the very end of the cosmic year.

The chronology corresponds to the best evidence now available. But some of it is rather shaky. No one would be astounded if, for example, it turns out that plants colonized the land in the Ordovician rather than the Silurian Period; or that segmented worms appeared earlier in the Precambrian Period than indicated. Also, in the chronology of the last ten seconds of the cosmic year, it was obviously impossible for me to include all significant events; I hope I may be excused for not having explicitly mentioned advances in art, music and literature or the historically significant American, French, Russian and Chinese revolutions.

The construction of such tables and calendars is inevitably humbling. It is disconcerting to find that in such a cosmic year the Earth does not condense out of interstellar matter until early

September; dinosaurs emerge on Christmas Eve; flowers arise on December 28th; and men and women originate at 10:30 p.m. on New Year's Eve. All of recorded history occupies the last ten seconds of December 31; and the time from the waning of the Middle Ages to the present occupies little more than one second. But because I have arranged it that way, the first cosmic year has just ended. And despite the insignificance of the instant we have so far occupied in cosmic time, it is clear that what happens on and near Earth at the beginning of the second cosmic year will depend very much on the scientific wisdom and the distinctly human sensitivity of mankind.

PRE-DECEMBER DATES	
Big Bang	January 1
Origin of the Milky Way Galaxy	May 1
Origin of the solar system	September 9
Formation of the Earth	September 14
Origin of life on Earth	~September 25
Formation of the oldest rocks known on Earth	October 2
Date of oldest fossils (bacteria and blue-green algae)	October 9
Invention of sex (by microorganisms)	~November 1
Oldest fossil photosynthetic plants	November 12
Eukaryotes (first cells with nuclei) flourish	November 15
~ = *approximately*	

COSMIC CALENDAR DECEMBER

SUNDAY	MONDAY	TUESDAY	WEDNESDAY	THURSDAY	FRIDAY	SATURDAY
–	1	2 Significant oxygen atmosphere begins to develop on Earth.	3	4	5 Extensive vulcanism and channel formation on Mars.	6
7	8	9	10	11	12	13
	15	16 First worms.	17 Precambrian ends. Paleozoic Era and Cambrian Period begin. Invertebrates flourish.	18 First oceanic plankton. Trilobites flourish.	19 Ordovician Period. First fish, first vertebrates.	20 Silurian Period. First vascular plants. Plants begin colonization of land.
21 Devonian Period begins. Animals begins colonization of land.	22 First amphibians, first winged insects.	23 Carboniferous Period. First trees. First reptiles.	24 Permian Period begins. First dinosaurs.	25 Paleozoic Era ends. Mesozoic Era begins.	26 Triassic Period. First mammals.	27 Jurassic Period. First birds.
28 Cretaceous Period First flowers. Dinosaurs Become extinct.	29 Mesozoic Era ends. Cenozoic Era and Tertiary Period begin. First cetaceans First primates.	30 Early evolution of frontal lobes in the brains of primates. First hominids. Giant mammals flourish.	31 End of the Pliocene Period. Quaternary (Pleistocene and Holocene) Period. First humans.			

DECEMBER 31

Origin of Proconsul and Ramapithecus, probable ancestors of apes and men	-1:30 p.m.
First humans	-10:30 p.m.
Widespread use of stone tools	11:00 p.m.
Domestication of fire by Peking man	11:46 p.m.
Beginning of most recent glacial period	ll:56 p.m.
Seafarers settle Australia	11:58 p.m.
Extensive cave painting in Europe	ll:59 p.m.
Invention of agriculture	11:59:20 p.m.
Neolithic civilization; first cities	11:59:35 p.m.
First dynasties in Sumer, Ebla and Egypt; development of astronomy	11:59:50 p.m.
Invention of the alphabet; Akkadian Empire	11:59:51 p.m.
Hammurabic legal codes in Babylon; Middle Kingdom in Egypt	11:59:52 p.m.
Bronze metallurgy; Mycenaean culture; Trojan War; Olmec culture; invention of the compass	11:59:53 p.m.
Iron metallurgy; First Assyrian Empire; Kingdom of Israel; founding of Carthage by Phoenicia	11:59:54 p.m.
Asokan India; Ch'in Dynasty China; Periclean Athens; birth of Buddha	11:59:55 p.m.
Euclidean geometry; Archimedean physics; Ptolemaic astronomy; Roman Empire; birth of Christ	11:59:56 p.m.
Zero and decimals invented in Indian arithmetic; Rome falls; Moslem conquests	11:59:57 p.m.
Mayan civilization; Sung Dynasty China; Byzantine empire; Mongol invasion; Crusades	11:59:58 p.m.
Renaissance in Europe; voyages of discovery from Europe and from Ming Dynasty China; emergence of the experimental method in science	11:59:59 p.m.

2

Paleolithic Society: The Kung

In the following selection, L. S. Stavrianos describes the lifestyle of the Kung people who live in the Kalahari desert of southern Africa. He argues that the life of these people is representative of the paleolithic age, past and present.

Discussion Questions

1. Can the Kung legitimately be labeled "primitives" or "savages?"

2. Are there any ways in which Kung life is superior to ours today?

3. How is the "communalism" of the Kung manifested?

4. In what ways have the strengths of Kung society become weaknesses in modern times? Do the Kung have a future?

The Kung

Since human behavior, unlike bones, does not become fossilized, anthropologists must rely mainly on contemporary food gatherers when they seek to determine the nature of Paleolithic society. But can we assume that our Paleolithic ancestors had the same social organization as today's food gatherers, simply because they, too, lived off the bounty of nature rather than producing their own food. Anthropologists believe the assumption can be made because of the basic similarity of all food-gathering societies today, regardless of whether they are located in the Arctic or the Amazon, the deserts of Australia or southern Africa.

The remarkably similar ways in which all kinship societies function despite the radically different environments they inhabit suggests that the determining factor in their lives is the limited set of alternatives open to food gatherers, regardless of their geographic location or the period in which they thrive. All peoples living off the land face basically similar problems and so evolve roughly similar social institutions. Probably the principal difference between Paleolithic food gatherers and those of today is that the latter have been driven into undesirable peripheral regions—deserts and jungles, for example—where they are subsisting under the most difficult of conditions. Their Paleolithic ancestors, by contrast, had access to the entire globe, including the fertile regions with hospitable climates that are now populated by more numerous and more powerful agricultural and industrial peoples. Consequently, the food-gathering societies observed by anthropologists today cannot be considered ideal representatives

of their genre; rather they are societies that have somehow survived against overwhelming odds, are now hanging on under the most adverse and stressful conditions, and face the prospect of an even less favorable future.

Given these dismal circumstances, it is all the more significant that anthropologists in recent years have found it necessary to abandon the traditional Hobbesian view of food-gathering life as "solitary, poor, nasty, brutish, and short." Today each one of these adjectives has been replaced by its exact opposite. Food-gathering society is now viewed as "the original affluent society," whose members work "bankers' hours" and enjoy healthy diets, economic security, and a warm social life. This reappraisal is based on studies of surviving bands on all continents, the most detailed being those of the Kung group of the Bushmen living in the Kalahari Desert of southern Africa. Since 1963 the Kung have been carefully studied by anthropologists, archaeologists, linguists, psychologists, and nutritionists. Their findings jibe with those from other continents, and together yield a revealing and significant insight into the mode of life that prevailed during more than 95 percent of human history.

One surprising revelation to emerge from studies of the Kung is how abundant and reliable are their food supplies, despite an unfavorable environment. This is due in part to their extraordinary knowledge of their home territory and all its plant and animal life. Although these nomads cannot read or write, they can learn and remember—so much so that it is estimated that their fund of information, transmitted

From *Lifelines from Our Past* by Leften S. Stavrianos. Copyright © 1989 by L.S. Stavrianos. Used by permission of Pantheon Books, a division of Random House, Inc.

orally from generation to generation, would fill thousands of volumes.

The Kung use no less than five hundred species of plants and animals as food, or for medical, cosmetic, toxic, and other purposes. Between 60 and 80 percent of Kung food is obtained by the women, who gather plants (bulbs, beans, roots, leafy greens, berries and nuts, especially the all-important mongongo fruit and nut) as well as small mammals, tortoises, snakes, caterpillars, insects, and bird eggs. Although Westerners are culturally programmed to reject most of these food sources, the fact is that beetle grubs, caterpillars, bee larvae, termites, ants, and cicadas, all of which are eaten today by gatherers, are highly nutritious. Termites, for instance, are about 45 percent protein, a higher proportion than that found even in protein-rich dried fish. Men contribute to the Kung diet by hunting animals, snaring birds, and extracting honey from beehives. The diversity of these food sources ensures a year-round reliable supply of food even under the most adverse climatic conditions, in contrast to agriculturists, who must depend on the few crops they grow, and therefore are vulnerable to droughts, frosts, floods, and pests. In fact, anthropologists noted that during a serious drought in the summer of 1964, the Kung food supply remained as plentiful as usual, while the neighboring Bantu farmers starved. To feed their hungry families, Bantu women joined their Kung sisters in their foraging expeditions.

Not only abundant and dependable, the Kung food supply also constitutes an exceptionally healthy diet. It is low in salt, saturated fats, and carbohydrates, high in polyunsaturated oils, roughage, vitamins, and minerals. This diet, together with the Kung's physically active and relatively tension-free life-style, helps explain their low incidence of high blood pressure, hypertensive heart disease, high cholesterol, obesity, varicose veins, and stress-related diseases such as ulcers and colitis. The life

expectancy of Kung adults is greater than that in many industrialized countries. On the other hand, the Kung are more vulnerable to infant mortality, malaria, and respiratory infections, as well as to a high death rate from accidents due to the absence of doctors and hospitals. Western scientists who observed Kung communities found that about one-tenth of the total population was over sixty years old, or roughly the same percentage as in those agricultural and industrialized societies with customary medical-care systems.

It is equally significant that the Kung are able to carry on their hunting and gathering with much less labor than is exacted today from workers in agricultural and industrial societies. The forty-hour week, which was won only after long and bitter struggle, would be considered inhuman by the Kung of both sexes. They devote fifteen to twenty hours a week to gathering and hunting, leaving the rest of the week free for resting, playing games, chatting, sharing the pipe, grooming each other, and visiting friends at nearby camps. Since the necessary food supplies can be obtained with a relatively small labor investment, young people are not required to work. Not until their mid-teens do girls join their mothers foraging, and boys their fathers hunting. At the campsite, work is shared along traditional gender lines, women being responsible for child care, cooking the vegetables and small game, serving the food, washing utensils, and cleaning the fireplaces, while men collect firewood, butcher the game, cook the meat, and make the tools.

The underlying communalism of Kung kinship society is evident in the sharing of property. Each Kung band collectively "owns" about twenty-five square miles of surrounding land, this being the maximum that is logistically manageable. If any band experiences a temporary food shortage, it is expected to ask permission to gather food in a neighboring tract. Permission usually is given, with the understanding that the favor will be reciprocated if the occasion arises. Perishable foods, whether meat or plants, are shared by all band members, but tools and clothes are the private property of the owner.

Communalism extends from property sharing to the Kung's carefully regulated social behavior. If a hunter, for instance, is exceptionally successful and returns repeatedly with much game, measures are taken to dampen any tendency toward conceit or any desire to lord it over others. "We refuse one who boasts," explains a band member, "for someday his pride will make him kill somebody. So we always speak of his meat as worthless . . . `you mean to say you have dragged us all the way out here to make us cart home your pile of bones.' . . . In this way we cool his heart and make him gentle." After a run of successful hunts, the rising star finds it politic to ward off possible envy or resentment by retiring into inactivity and enjoying the benefits of the reciprocal obligations he has accumulated. In this way, the Kung preserve band harmony by alternating periods of hunting and credit accumulation with periods of quiescence, when hearts can "cool" and hunters are made "gentle."

Finally, Kung social life is exceptionally rich and satisfying. Huts are so small that they serve only for sleeping. Fires burn in front of each hut door, and all doors face toward a large communal space. The emphasis then is entirely on the band's common social life. Individuals seek not privacy but companionship. Two-thirds of their waking hours are spent visiting or being visited by friends and relatives from other bands. An anthropologist observer notes that the Kung "must be among the most talkative people in the world." The talk is about the day's experiences hunting and gathering, about food distribution, gift giving, and much-savored gossip and scandal. Music and dancing are also important band activities, as are initiation rites accompanied by myths and legends passed down through the generations. This interweaving of art, religion, entertainment, and education constitutes the basis for band tradition and cultural continuity. "Their life is rich in human warmth and aesthetic experience," concludes an observer, "and offers an enviable balance of work and love, ritual and play."

The Kung way of life is not only "enviable," but also inherently stable, or at least it was so until recent times. It is a society in equilibrium—an equilibrium that prevails not only between individuals, but also between those individuals and their environment. Basic needs are satisfied in a nonexploitative fashion. Personal conflicts of course abound, but not institutional ones. In fact, as anthropologist Stanley Diamond concludes about food-gathering societies in general, "revolutionary activity is, insofar as I am aware, unknown. It is probably safe to say that there has never been a revolution in a primitive society."

Not only the concept of revolution but that of reform, too, is alien to such a society, and naturally so, since prehistoric peoples assumed that after the creation of themselves, their culture, and their habitat, equilibrium simply continued and was destined to continue. What need was there to criticize their culture or to try to change it? Parents trained their children to do what they themselves did. Education was a mechanism for preserving, not for altering their world.

Despite its past stability, Kung society today is fragile, if not rapidly disintegrating, as are other food-gathering societies throughout the world. Having existed for many millennia, all are now crumbling and face a bleak future. Inherently well balanced and self-perpetuating as long as they were left alone, these societies could not continue to exist in isolation once agriculture appeared about 10,000 B.C. The impact of agriculturists on food-gathering peoples is all too apparent today in southern Africa. The Kung have contact with neighboring Bantu farmers, whose mode of life they envy.

They covet their domesticated animals, their ready supply of meat, milk, and vegetables, the colorful dresses of Bantu women, and above all, their seductive alcohol and tobacco. Therefore, the Kung take menial, poor-paying jobs in order to earn money to buy these desired goods.

Contacts with the nonfood-gathering world have created serious problems for the Kung. These include the coming of venereal and other diseases, as well as the contamination of the Kung's springs by the cattle and goats of the Bantu. The grazing of Bantu livestock has also had the effect of denuding the terrain of plants on which the Kung have depended, as well as frightening off their wild game. Not only are the Kung being reduced to the status of virtual beggars and hangers-on in Bantu villages, but even worse is their absorption into the military machine of South Africa. Today almost half the Kung adults are employed in one capacity or another at South African military installations. At the same time, the authorities have issued licenses for the opening of local liquor stores, so that the Kung can use their newfound wealth to purchase Johnnie Walker Scotch and cigarettes. What is happening to the Kung is also happening to the Eskimos in the Arctic, to the Native Americans on reservations in the United States and Canada, and to the aborigines in Australia.

Despite an antiquity that no other social system can remotely approach, all food-gathering societies have always faced the problem of what has been aptly defined as "the imminence of diminishing returns." After several weeks or possibly months in one location, food resources are depleted and a band must move on to a new site. Hence, the constant nomadism, and the lack of any incentive either to build up food reserves beyond a certain minimal point or to construct substantial housing. Generally, only enough food is collected to meet the needs of the moment, and the birth rate must necessarily be kept low since too short an interval between births would create unmanageable problems for the mother. Two infants could neither be so easily breast-fed nor carried during foraging expeditions or treks from camp to camp.

In fact, the unpleasant but inescapable task of population control forced parents in many food-gathering societies to endure long periods of sexual abstinence after the birth of a baby. In others, an infant born too soon after its sibling or together with a twin, might be exposed to the elements, while old people might voluntarily end their lives lest they become too much of a drain on food supplies or too much of a burden on the community during migrations. Peter Freuchen, who lived for decades with the Eskimos, has described the poignant yet dignified suicide of an aged grandmother who could no longer keep up with her band, and whose aching bones and wheezing lungs made life a burden for herself and for her kin. Freuchen concludes that suicides are common when, as the Eskimos express it, "life is heavier than death; [when] old men and women are burdened with the memories of their youth, and can no longer meet the demands of their reputation. . . . Fear of death is unknown . . . they merely say that death can be either the end of it all or a transition into something new, and that in either case there is nothing to fear."

The end result has been an extraordinarily stable mode of life with a built-in equilibrium, but also with a built-in Achilles' heel. The population of any food-gathering society was bound to remain sparse since far fewer of them could support themselves in a given area than could food producers. Consequently, once agriculture made its appearance, the food gatherers, unable to hold their own, were pushed aside by sheer weight of numbers, an encounter between two ways of life made all the more unequal by the allure of alcohol and nicotine, and by the material plenty of cultivated fields.

Equally lethal today has been the essential incompatibility between the cooperative, nonaggressive food-gathering way of life, and the competitive, acquisitive, consumer-oriented ethos of much of the twentieth-century world. "It is almost a contest of values," concludes an anthropologist analyzing the current situation on the Crow Indian Reservation in Montana. "The Crow believe in sharing wealth, and whites believe in accumulating wealth. . . . As a consequence the Crow have been paying a very heavy price for adhering to their traditional outlook." That price includes an unemployment rate on the reservation of 85 percent, and a death rate from alcohol abuse eleven times higher than the national average. Analogous patterns prevail among native populations on all continents. As a result, while only ten thousand years ago, food gatherers made up 100 percent of the five million human beings who then inhabited the globe, today they number far less than 1 million out of a total world population of 5 billion.

3

Drudge on the Hide

Stone Age depictions of human societies are replete with assumptions about lives and values that are echoes of our own. This reading attempts to expose some of the ways that attitudes toward gender have been used to perpetuate stereotypes of men and women living in hunting and gathering societies, particularly focusing on the role of women.

Discussion Questions

1. How does this reading complement that of Genesis and the Kung in its description of the role of women?

2. Was prehistory (hunting and gathering) largely a "guy thing?"

3. What is the "drudge on the hide" image meant to reflect? Look at the images in your text and online. Are these same images of women in hunting and gathering societies still being projected, or have times and sensibilities changed?

The Drudge-on-the-Hide

Most of us would question a museum display with a heading that read: "In the Stone Age, men hunted, made tools and houses, created art, and performed rituals. Women stayed home, held babies, and scraped hides. Old people and children just hung out because they weren't useful, like men." Yet depiction of prehistoric life that accompany many displays and that appear in books convey that impression. This raises an intriguing question: our knowledge of Stone Age prehistory and the diversity of gender roles among modern foragers has grown during this century—why have visual artists failed to keep pace?

I recently studied 135 drawings of Cro-Magnon people in books intended for the general public. Stereotypical portrayals of men and women prevail. Man-the-Hunter and Man-the-Toolmaker, fit and in their prime, predominate. Women, unless young, decorative, and unclothed, work on hides and appear in the background along with the useless children and old folks. Woman as hide-worker is an extraordinarily potent symbol of primordial womanhood and female labor. I call her the Drudge-on-the-Hide. On her hands and knees, scraping a bloody hide, she is part of the scenery, doing dull and nasty work. To make matters worse, the Drudge is seldom shown using scraping tools, which makes her look not only irrelevant but incompetent. Hides are never stretched on frames, and women never work sitting or standing. They crouch or kneel, confronting the hide with, at best, a flake of stone. The image of a woman crouched on all fours conveys subservience and animality, with sexual overtones. Remember the rape scenes in Quest for Fire and Clan of the Cave Bear? Both feature unwilling female victims crouched on all fours, a blatant evocation of the Drudge's animality.

And what about the men? Consumed with hunting, toolmaking, and performing rituals, they never hold a baby, make ornaments, or, heaven forfend, relax. Do artists creating dioramic representations of early humans deliberately select subjects and viewpoints that marginalize women, children, and the elderly? Or do some of them, by following long-entrenched iconographic conventions, simply re-create prehistoric social conventions they themselves might, upon further reflection, call into question? I suspect that the latter is the case.

Those most responsible for these distorted images are scientific experts—people like me. We rush to correct an anachronistic tool or wrong-shaped skull in such renderings, but remain blind to the cultural messages these images send. We have not challenged artists on scientific grounds, nor have we offered alternative visions. Highly creative and more probable images have been created by French illustrator Vèronique Ageorges and former Smithsonian artist John Gurche, both of whom are well versed in archaeology and physical anthropology. Their "ancestors" include capable elders, active children, and strong women who create rock art, dance, make tools, and forage away from camp. Their men sometimes wear ornaments, smile, even sit idle.

The challenge for illustrators and experts is not to produce politically correct, quota-system illustration, e.g., Guys-on-Hides. Instead, we need to re-envision our ancestors, to think of prehistory as more than a repetitive set of "guy things." This requires knowledge of archaeological and fossil evidence, and an understanding of anthropology, ecology, and other relevant fields. Illustrations that reveal learned speculation about the past will stimulate rather than stultify. One such illustration by Ageorges had a profound effect on me. A handsome, slightly weathered Cro-Magnon couple sit at a fire. He gnaws on a roast rib. She squats at the fire cutting rib meat with a flint knife. Her muscular arms are bare and flexed, her brow a little furrowed as she speaks. Her face and arms suggest a world of strong women. I like that. Women had to be strong to survive in those times. If they had been as abject as the Drudge, we never would have made it out of the Stone Age. A creative illustrator can make this point with a few strokes of the brush.

4

The Neolithic Revolution: The Fertile Crescent

FERTILE CRESCENT

Founder Crops (Food Package):

Cereals: Emmer wheat, Einkorn wheat, barley
Pulses: lentil, pea, chickpea, bitter vetch (type of bean)
Fiber: flax

[The Fertile Crescent has 32/56 prize wild grasses which have large seeds; other Mediterranean climate areas have few]

Domesticated Large Animals:

Goat, sheep, pig, cow

This bundle of crops and animals met humanity's basic needs:

Carbohydrates, protein, fat, clothing, traction and transport

This gave the Fertile Crescent a big lead in advanced technology, complex political organization and epidemic diseases.

Adapted from *Guns, Germs & Steel* by Jared Diamond, WW Norton Company, New York.

5

The Rise of Civilization: Genesis

The following passages from the Book of Genesis can be viewed from several perspectives. For the religious fundamentalist, Genesis is taken literally as the actual story of the creation of the universe and humankind. For the mythologist, Genesis represents a Bronze Age creation myth, on a parallel with those found in many early societies. The sociologist-anthropologist, as suggested in the accompanying reading, finds in Genesis an explanation for patriarchy, or the subordination and devaluation of women to men. The historian may see Genesis as a lament, the story of a lost age of simplicity, innocence and even perfection, and, in miniature, the story of the rise of civilization.

Discussion Questions

1. What picture of human existence before the "fall" is presented in the passages from Genesis and in the accompanying reading?

2. Does the author of Genesis think that the changes that took place after the "fall" were good of bad? (Does the author seem to believe in what we call the idea of "progress?")

3. What does the story of Cain and Abel represent historically?

4. What aspects of "civilization" are presented in the selection?

5. If agriculture, or "women's work" was so productive, why were women castigated rather than praised for its creation?

6. Why is Eve the "bad guy" in the book of Genesis?

7. What explanations for the rise of patriarchy are presented in the readings? Do you find them convincing?

Genesis: Chapter 3

Now the serpent was more subtil than any beast of the field which the Lord God had made. And he said unto the woman, Yea, hath God said, Ye shall not eat of every tree of the garden?

2. And the woman said unto the serpent, We may eat of the fruit of the trees of the garden:

3. But of the fruit of the tree which is in the midst of the garden, God hath said, Ye shall not eat of it, neither shall ye touch it, lest ye die.

4. And the serpent said unto the woman, Ye shall not surely die:

5. For God doth know that in the day ye eat thereof, then your eyes shall be opened, and ye shall be as gods, knowing good and evil.

6. And when the woman saw that the tree *was* good for food, and that it *was* pleasant to the eyes, and a tree to be desired to make *one* wise, she took of the fruit thereof, and did eat, and gave also unto her husband with her; and he did eat.

7. And the eyes of them both were opened, and they knew that they *were* naked; and they sewed fig leaves together, and made themselves aprons.

8. And they heard the voice of the Lord God walking in the garden in the cool of the day; and Adam and his wife hid themselves from the presence of the Lord God amongst the trees of the garden.

9. And the Lord God called upon Adam, and said unto him, Where *art* thou?

10. And he said, I heard thy voice in the garden, and I was afraid, because I was naked; and I hid myself.

11. And he said, Who told thee that thou *wast* naked? Hast thou eaten of the tree, whereof I commanded thee that thou shouldest not eat?

12. And the man said, The woman whom thou gavest *to be* with me, she gave me of the tree, and I did eat.

13. And the Lord God said unto the woman, What *is* this *that* thou hast done? And the woman said, The serpent beguiled me, and I did eat.

14. And the Lord God said unto the serpent, Because thou hast done this, thou art cursed above all cattle, and above every beast of the field; upon thy belly shalt thou go, and dust shalt thou eat all the days of thy life:

15. And I will put enmity between thee and the woman, and between thy seed and her seed; it shall bruise thy head, and thou shalt bruise his heel.

16. Unto the woman he said, I will greatly multiply thy sorrow and thy conception; in sorrow thou shalt bring forth children; and thy desire *shall be* to thy husband, and he shall rule over thee.

17. And unto Adam he said, Because thou hast harkened unto the voice of thy wife, and hast eaten of the tree, of which I commanded thee, saying, Thou shalt not eat of it: cursed *is* the ground for thy sake; in sorrow shalt thou eat *of* it all the days of thy life;

18. Thorns also and thistles shall it bring forth to thee; and thou shalt eat the herb of the field;

19. In the sweat of thy face shalt thou eat bread, till thou return unto the ground; for

out of it wast thou taken: for dust thou *art*, and unto dust shalt thou return.

20. And Adam called his wife's name Eve; because she was the mother of all living.

21. Unto Adam also and to his wife did the Lord God make coats of skins, and clothed them.

22. ¶And the Lord God said, Behold, the man is become as one of us, to know good and evil: and now, lest he put forth his hand,

and take also of the tree of life, and eat, and live for ever:

23. Therefore the Lord God sent him forth from the garden of Eden, to till the ground from whence he was taken.

24. So he drove out the man; and he placed at the east of the garden of Eden Cherubims, and a flaming sword which turned every way, to keep the way of the tree of life.

Genesis: Chapter 4

And Adam knew Eve his wife; and she conceived, and bare Cain, and said, I have gotten a man from the Lord.

2. And she again bare his brother Abel. And Abel was a keeper of sheep, but Cain was a tiller of the ground.

3. And in process of time it came to pass, that Cain brought of the fruit of the ground an offering unto the Lord.

4. And Abel, he also brought of the firstlings of his flock and of the fat thereof. And the Lord had respect unto Abel and to his offering:

5. But unto Cain and to his offering he had not respect. And Cain was very wroth, and his countenance fell.

6. And the Lord said unto Cain, Why art thou wroth? and why is thy countenance fallen?

7. If thou doest well, shalt thou not be accepted? and if thou doest not well, sin lieth at the door. And unto thee *shall be* his desire, and thou shalt rule over him.

8. And Cain talked with Abel his brother: and it came to pass, when they were in the field, that Cain rose up against Abel his brother, and slew him.

9. ¶And the Lord said unto Cain, Where is Abel thy brother? And he said, I know not: *Am* I my brother's keeper?

10. And he said, What has thou done? the voice of thy brother's blood crieth unto me from the ground.

11. And now *art* thou cursed from the earth, which hath opened her mouth to receive thy brother's blood from thy hand;

12. When thou tillest the ground, it shall not henceforth yield unto thee her strength; a fugitive and a vagabond shalt thou be in the earth.

13. And Cain said unto the Lord, My punishment *is* greater that I can bear.

14. Behold, thou hast driven me out this day from the face of the earth; and from thy face shall I be hid; and I shall be a fugitive and a vagabond in the earth; and it shall come to pass, *that* every one that findeth me shall slay me.

15. And the Lord said unto him, Therefore whosoever slayeth Cain, vengeance shall be taken on him sevenfold. And the Lord set a mark upon Cain, lest any finding him should kill him.

16. ¶And Cain went out from the presence of the Lord, and dwelt in the land of Nod, on the east of Eden.

17. And Cain knew his wife; and she conceived, and bare Enoch: and he builded a city, and called the name of the city, after the name of his son, Enoch.

18. An unto Enoch was born Irad: and Irad begat Mehujael: and Mehujael begat Methusael: and Methusael begat Lamech.

19. ¶And Lamech took unto him two wives: the name of the one *was* Adah, and the name of the other Zillah.

20. And Adah bare Jabal: he was the father of such as dwell in tents, and *of such as have* cattle.

21. And his brother's name *was* Jubal: he was the father of all such as handle the harp and organ.

22. And Zillah, she also bare Tubalcain, an instructer of every artificer in brass and iron: and the sister of Tubalcain *was* Naamah.

Women in Genesis

 My revisionist take on Genesis is grounded in the now widely accepted belief of scholars that women invented agriculture. Women, it is known, were the ones responsible for plant food in earlier hunter-gatherer societies. The myths of numerous cultures attribute the teaching to men of how to grow food to a goddess. In Greek mythology, for example, Demeter is the teacher of planting arts. The book of Genesis can be read as another version of this story.

Let's go back 10,000 years to pick up the story. Women had developed the practice of intentional production of food, according to such scholars as sociologist Elise Boulding and anthropologist Margaret Ehrenberg. The attractions were irresistible—a more plentiful and healthy diet, the ability to stockpile foods for periods of drought and so on. But for men, agriculture ultimately showed itself to be a Faustian bargain. When people could produce all the food—both meat (through herding) and plant—that they needed, the principal male role of hunter was largely devalued. Eventually, men were obliged to take up the "women's work" of farming. Yet farming seemed both less "manly" and harder work than hunting.

Once agriculture was well established, it was not possible for human society to go back to hunting and gathering. Populations had grown sufficiently large that they were dependent on continued farming. The oral stories of hunter-gatherer life gave that pre-agricultural time the appearance of a lost paradise. Men in the golden age, it seemed, had been able to walk about, easily finding food, without work. And who was responsible for losing this paradise? The women who had tempted men with the knowledge of how to grow food, of course.

If this story sounds familiar, it is with good reason. It is a rough summary of the first four chapters of Genesis.

From *Washington Post*, November 3, 1996 by Robert S. McElvaine. Copyright © 1996 by RobertMcElvaine. Reprinted by permission of the author.

The first chapter tells of the creation of a self-propagating pre-agricultural paradise in which humans had everything they needed, without work. Eden, in this reading, is the long-gone life of the hunter-gatherers, where there was no agriculture and people lived well merely by picking the fruit from trees whenever they so desired. While this certainly was an idealization of hunting and gathering, the onset of agriculture did require far greater discipline and harder and more consistent work than had hunting and gathering.

If women had invented agriculture and were still associated with it in the minds of men at the time that Genesis was composed, then castigating Eve makes a certain amount of sense. The "sin" of acquiring knowledge is what brought about the end of this way of life and obliged man to work by the sweat of his brow to obtain food. Genesis 3:17-19 is eloquent about the unpleasantness of this new way of life:

Cursed is the ground because of you; in toil you shall eat of it all the days of your life; thorns and thistles it shall bring forth to you; and you shall eat the plants of the field. In the sweat of your face you shall eat bread.

Genesis 3:23 makes the equation of expulsion from Eden and the beginning of agriculture even explicit:

Therefore the Lord God sent him forth from the Garden of Eden to till the ground from which he was taken.

One of the changes that the invention of agriculture produced was the placing of a premium on a growing population, which meant that women were obliged to spend more of their lives in child-bearing. Ultimately, the combination of women ceasing to be major producers (as men replaced them in farming) and becoming more fully occupied as reproducers helped to subordinate women more fully to men. All of this is reflected in Genesis 3:16:

To the woman he said, `I will greatly increase your toil and your pregnancies; Along with travail shall you beget children. For to your man is your desire, And he shall predominate over you.'

The people who told the stories that were compiled in Genesis, it seems, knew a great deal about human prehistory and what agriculture had wrought. Unfortunately the Hebrews' allegory of the transformation from the natural "paradise" of the hunter-gatherer to the troubled surplus of the agricultural warrior has been taken too literally by the faithful. If we understand the imagery of Genesis, in light of what we now know about the earliest human societies, the Adam and Eve story reemerges as an exaggerated, but not wholly inaccurate, assessment of prehistory. Now it is time that we consider the impact that it has had on our ideas about women and men. Hell hath no fury like a man devalued.

6

The Code of Hammurabi

Hammurabi was the ruler of Babylonia around 1792–1750 BC. His code of laws was discovered in 1902 and is the oldest of its type in existence. Drawn from earlier Sumerian and Semitic laws, the emphasis is clearly on retribution rather than forgiveness. Yet it did provide a legal standard of behavior for all members of Babylonian society to replace the more haphazard practices of the past.

Discussion Questions

1. In this code are all people equal under the law?

2. What does the code tell us about the structure of Babylonian society?

3. Would you describe Babylonia as a society where people had "rights"?

4. Why do you think so much emphasis is put on physical punishments?

5. Do you think that a law code like this would make people become morally and ethically good?—Or would it simply encourage them to avoid being punished?

The Code of Hammurabi

1. If a man has accused another of laying a *nêrtu* (death spell?) upon him, but has not proved it, he shall be put to death.

2. If a man has accused another of laying a *kispu* (spell) upon him, but has not proved it, the accused shall go to the sacred river, he shall plunge into the sacred river, and if the sacred river shall conquer him, he that accused him shall take possession of his house. If the sacred river shall show his innocence and he is saved, his accuser shall be put to death. He that plunged into the sacred river shall appropriate the house of him that accused him.

3. If a man has borne false witness in a trial, or has not established the statement that he has made, if that case be a capital trial, that man shall be put to death.

8. If a patrician has stolen ox, sheep, ass, pig, or sheep, whether from a temple, or a house, he shall pay thirtyfold. If he be a plebeian, he shall return tenfold. If the thief cannot pay, he shall be put to death.

14. If a man has stolen a child, he shall be put to death.

15. If a man has induced either a male or female slave from the house of a patrician, or plebeian, to leave the city, he shall be put to death.

16. If a man has harbored in his house a male or female slave from a patrician's or plebeian's house, and has not caused the fugitive to leave on the demand of the officer over the slaves condemned to public forced labor, that householder shall be put to death.

17. If a man has caught either a male or female runaway slave in the open field and has brought him back to his owner, the owner of the slave shall give him two shekels of silver....

21. If a man has broken into a house he shall be killed before the breach and buried there.

22. If a man has committed highway robbery and has been caught, that man shall be put to death.

23. If the highwayman has not been caught, the man that has been robbed shall state on oath what he has lost and the city or district governor in whose territory or district the robbery took place shall restore to him what he has lost.

24. If a life [has been lost], the city or district governor shall pay one mina of silver to the deceased's relatives.

25. If a fire has broken out in a man's house and one who has come to put it out has coveted the property of the householder and appropriated any of it, that man shall be cast into the self-same fire.

44. If a man has taken a piece of virgin soil to open up, on a three years' lease, but has left it alone, has not opened up the land, in the fourth year he shall break it up, hoe it, and plough it, and shall return it to the owner of the field, and shall measure out ten *GUR* of corn for each *GAN* of land....

108. If the mistress of a beer-shop has not received corn as the price of beer or has demanded silver on an excessive scale, and has made the measure of beer less than the measure of corn, that beer-seller shall be prosecuted and drowned.

109. If the mistress of a beer-shop has assembled seditious slanderers in her house and those seditious persons have not been captured and have not been haled

to the palace, that beer-seller shall be put to death.

110. If a votary, who is not living in the convent, open a beer-shop, or enter a beer-shop for drink, that woman shall be put to death.

111. If the mistress of a beer-shop has given sixty KA of *sakani* beer in the time of thirst, at harvest, she shall take fifty KA of corn.

126. If a man has said that something of his is lost, which is not, or has alleged a depreciation, though nothing of his is lost, he shall estimate the depreciation on oath, and he shall pay double whatever he has estimated.

127. If a man has caused the finger to be pointed at a votary, or a man's wife, and has not justified himself, that man shall be brought before the judges, and have his forehead branded.

128. If a man has taken a wife and has not executed a marriage-contract, that woman is not a wife.

129. If a man's wife be caught lying with another, they shall be strangled and cast into the water. If the wife's husband would save his wife, the king can save his servant.

130. If a man has ravished another's betrothed wife, who is a virgin, while still living in her father's house, and has been caught in the act, that man shall be put to death; the woman shall go free....

132. If a man's wife has the finger pointed at her on account of another, but has not been caught lying with him, for her husband's sake she shall plunge into the sacred river.

133. If a man has been taken captive, and there was maintenance in his house, but his wife has left the house and entered into another man's house; because that woman has not preserved her body, and has entered into the house of another, that woman shall be prosecuted and shall be drowned.

134. If a man has been taken captive, but there was not maintenance in his house, and his wife has entered into the house of another, that woman has no blame.

135. If a man has been taken captive, but there was no maintenance in his house for his wife, and she has entered into the house of another, and has borne him children, if in the future her [first] husband shall return and regain his city, that woman shall return to her first husband, but the children shall follow their own father.

136. If a man has left his city and fled, and, after he has gone, his wife has entered into the house of another; if the man return and seize his wife, the wife of the fugitive shall not return to her husband, because he hated his city and fled.

137. If a man has determined to divorce a concubine who has borne him children, or a votary who has granted him children, he shall return to that woman her marriage-portion, and shall give her the usufruct of field, garden, and goods, to bring up her children. After her children have grown up, out of whatever is given to her children, they shall give her one son's share, and the husband of her choice shall marry her.

138. If a man has divorced his wife, who has not borne him children, he shall pay over to her as much money as was given for her bride-price and the marriage-portion which she brought from her father's house, and so shall divorce her.

139. If there was no bride-price, he shall give her one mina of silver, as a price of divorce.

140. If he be a plebeian, he shall give her one-third of a mina of silver.

141. If a man's wife, living in her husband's house, has persisted in going out, has acted the fool, has wasted her house, has

belittled her husband, he shall prosecute her. If her husband has said, "I divorce her," she shall go her way; he shall give her nothing as her price of divorce. If her husband has said, "I will not divorce her," he may take another woman to wife; the wife shall live as a slave in her husband's house.

142. If a woman has hated her husband and has said, "You shall not possess me," her past shall be inquired into as to what she lacks. If she has been discreet, and has no vice, and her husband has gone out, and has greatly belittled her, that woman has no blame, she shall take her marriage-portion and go off to her father's house.

143. If she has not been discreet, has gone out, ruined her house, belittled her husband, she shall be drowned.

152. From the time that woman entered into the man's house they together shall be liable for all debts subsequently incurred.

153. If a man's wife, for the sake of another, has caused her husband to be killed, that woman shall be impaled.

154. If a man has committed incest with his daughter, that man shall be banished from the city.

155. If a man has betrothed a maiden to his son and his son has known her, and afterward the man has lain in her bosom, and been caught, that man shall be strangled and she shall be cast into the water.

156. If a man has betrothed a maiden to his son, and his son has not known her, and that man has lain in her bosom, he shall pay her half a mina of silver, and shall pay over to her whatever she brought from her father's house, and the husband of her choice shall marry her.

157. If a man, after his father's death, be caught in the bosom of his mother, they shall both of them be burnt together.

158. If a man, after his father's death be caught in the bosom of his step-mother who has borne children, that man shall be cut off from his father's house.

159. If a man, who has presented a gift to the house of his prospective father-in-law and has given the bride-price, has afterward looked upon another woman and has said to his father-in-law, "I will not marry your daughter"; the father of the girl shall keep whatever he has brought as a present.

160. If a man has presented a gift to the house of his prospective father-in-law, and has given the bride-price, but his comrade has slandered him and his father-in-law has said to the suitor, "You shall not marry my daughter," [the father] shall return double all that was presented to him. Further, the comrade shall not marry the girl.

162. If a man has married a wife, and she has borne him children, and that woman has gone to her fate, her father shall lay no claim to her marriage-portion. Her marriage-portion is her children's only.

165. If a man has presented field, garden, or house to his son, the first in his eyes, and has written him a deed of gift; after the father has gone to his fate when the brothers share, he shall keep the present his father gave him, and over the above shall share equally with them in the goods of his father's estate.

166. If a man has taken wives for the other sons he had, but has not taken a wife for his young son, after the father has gone to his fate, when the brothers share, they shall set aside from the goods of their father's estate money, as a bride-price, for their young brother, who has not married a wife, over and above his share, and they shall cause him to take a wife.

167. If a man has taken a wife, and she has borne him children and that woman has gone to her fate, and he has taken a second wife, and she also has borne children;

after the father has gone to his fate, the sons shall not share according to mothers, but each family shall take the marriage-portion of its mother, and all shall share the goods of their father's estate equally.

168. If a man has determined to disinherit his son and has declared before the judge, "I cut off my son," the judge shall inquire into the son's past, and, if the son has not committed a grave misdemeanor such as should cut him off from sonship, the father shall not disinherit his son....

170. If a man has had children borne to him by his wife, and also by a maid, if the father in his lifetime has said, "My sons," to the children whom his maid bore him, and has reckoned them with the sons of his wife; then after the father has gone to his fate, the children of the wife and of the maid shall share equally. The children of the wife shall apportion the shares and make their own selections.

175. If either a slave of a patrician, or of a plebeian, has married the daughter of a free man, and she has borne children, the owner of the slave shall have no claim for service on the children, of a free woman...

177. If a widow, whose children are young, had determined to marry again, she shall not marry without consent of the judge. When she is allowed to remarry, the judge shall inquire as to what remains of the property of her former husband and shall intrust the property of her former husband to that woman and her second husband. He shall give them an inventory. They shall watch over the property, and bring up the children. Not a utensil shall they sell. A buyer of any utensil belonging to the widow's children shall lose his money and shall return the article to its owners....

185. If a man had taken a young child, a natural son of his, to be his son, and has brought him up, no one shall make a claim against that foster child.

186. If a man has taken a young child to be his son, and after he has taken him, the child discovers his own parents, he shall return to his father's house....

188, 189. If a craftsman has taken a child to bring up and has taught him his handicraft, he shall not be reclaimed. If he has not taught him his handicraft, that foster child shall return to his father's house.

192. If the son of a palace favorite or the son of a vowed woman has said to the father that brought him up, "You are not my father," or to the mother that brought him up, "You are not my mother," his tongue shall be cut out.

193. If the son of a palace favorite or the son of a vowed woman has come to know his father's house and has hated his father that brought him up, or his mother that brought him up, and shall go off to his father's house, his eyes shall be torn out.

195. If a son has struck his father, his hands shall be cut off.

7

Civilization: Curse or Blessing?

The following selection looks at the emergence of civilization from both positive and negative perspectives.

Discussion Questions

1. What did humankind gain and lose through the development of civilization?

2. Does the emergence of civilization constitute progress as we define it today?

3. Taking into consideration all the pluses and minuses of civilization, do you think humans came out ahead, fell behind or it was a tie?

In all civilizations there have been poets and thinkers who have looked to the past with longing. They have regarded prehistoric man as the "noble savage," untainted by the corrupting influence of civilization. Long ago, "in the beginning," during that wonderful first chapter of human existence, there was paradise on earth. In the Hindu epics there are passages extolling an idyllic past in which castes were absent and man could enjoy life in freedom and security. Likewise Hesiod, an eighth-century-B.C. Greek poet, described a Golden Age of long ago and then traced man's declining fortunes through the Silver and Iron ages to the deplorable present in which the author lived.

This concept of original bliss had some basis in historical fact. So far as economic and social relationships were concerned, the tribal peoples before the advent of civilization had enjoyed free and equal access to the natural resources necessary for livelihood. Economic equality and social homogeneity had been the hallmark of their Neolithic villages. But when the tribal peoples became peasants they no longer had free access to land and they no longer enjoyed the full product of their labor. Their specific obligations varied from region to region, but the net result was everywhere the same. After making the payments required by the state, the priest, the landlord, and the money lender, they were left almost invariably with only enough for sheer existence. In contrast to the egalitarianism of the Paleolithic hunting bands and the Neolithic villages, all the ancient civilizations divided people into haves and have-nots.

What this meant in human terms was expressed as early as the third millennium B.C. by an Egyptian father sending his son to school. He tried to convince his son to study hard and urged him to compare the wretchedness of both

peasants and workers with the blessings of learned scribes and officials.

"Put writing in your heart that you may protect yourself from hard labor of any kind and be a magistrate of high repute. The scribe is released from manual tasks; it is he who commands.... Do you not hold the scribe's palette? That is what makes the difference between you and the man who handles an oar.

I have seen the metal-worker at his task at the mouth of his furnace, with fingers like a crocodile's. He stank worse than fish-spawn. ... The stonemason finds his work in every kind of hard stone. When he has finished his labors his arms are worn out, and he sleeps all doubled up until sunrise. His knees and spine are broken. . . . The barber shaves from morning till night; he never sits down except to meals. He hurries from house to house looking for business. He wears out his arms to fill his stomach, like bees eating their own honey.... The farmer wears the same clothes for all times. His voice is as raucous as a crow's. His fingers are always busy, his arms are dried up by the wind. He takes his rest—when he does get any rest—in the mud. If he's in good health he shares good health with the beasts; if he is ill his bed is the bare earth in the middle of his beasts. ...

Apply your heart to learning. In truth there is nothing that can compare with it. If you have profited by a single day at school it is a gain for eternity.

The coming of civilization brought drastic change in political relationships as well as economic. The Neolithic villages had been subject to only a few controls, whether internal or external. But tribal chiefs and elders now were replaced by a king or emperor, and by an ever-present bureaucracy, including palace functionaries, provincial and district officials, judges, clerks, and accountants. Working

L. S. Stavrianos, *A Global History*: From Prehistory to the Present, 5e, © 1991, pp. 171–174, 281–282, 321–322. Reprinted by permission of Prentice Hall, Englewood Cliffs, New Jersey.

closely with this imperial administration was the ecclesiastical hierarchy that was also an essential feature of civilization. In place of the former shaman who had been a "leisure-time specialist," there was the priest, a "fulltime specialist." Now it was possible to develop an official theology and a priestly hierarchy. Both the theology and the hierarchy served to buttress the existing social order. They gave political institutions and leaders divine sanction and attributes. For example, the Egyptian pharaoh was not only the ruler of his country but also the "living god." This coupling of divine and secular authority provided most powerful support for the status quo. It was a rare individual who dared risk both swift punishment in this life and everlasting punishment in the afterlife.

The transformation of culture wrought by civilization was fundamental and enduring. The culture of Neolithic villages had been autonomous and homogeneous. All members had shared common knowledge, customs, and attitudes and had not depended on outside sources for the maintenance of their way of life. But with civilization, a new and more complex society emerged. In addition to the traditional culture of the village agricultural people, there was now the new culture of the scribes, who knew the mysterious art of writing, of the priests, who knew the secrets of the heavens, of the artists, who knew how to paint and carve, and of the merchants, who exchanged goods with lands beyond deserts and seas. So there was no longer a single culture. Instead there developed what has been called high culture and low culture. The high culture was to be found in the schools, temples, and palaces of the cities; the low culture was in the villages. The high culture was passed on in writing by philosophers, theologians, and literary men; the low culture was passed on by word of mouth among illiterate peasants.

The high and low cultures of the various civilizations differed in details but were all similar in essentials. They were all based on "sacred books," such as the Indian Vedas, the Buddhist Canon, the Chinese Classics, and the Christian Old and New Testaments. Since these texts were the basis of knowledge, they dominated education. Anyone who wished to get ahead had to memorize large portions of them. The sacred books also were used to enforce loyalty and obedience. Repudiation of official teachings or challenge to the social order were branded as crimes punishable in this world and in the next. The "hells" which were so prominent in all high cultures were eternal concentration camps for those who dared resist their secular or religious leaders.

The low cultures of all civilizations also were essentially the same. Peasants everywhere had a considerable body of factual information concerning the care of animals and plants. They all regarded hard work as a virtue and looked down upon town people as weaklings who tired easily. All peasants also had a common passion to own a plot of land, a few animals, and the simple tools of field and shop. These meant independence and security, and to attain them all peasantries stubbornly resisted, and still resist, intervention, whether by a landlord or by today's government-run collective. The "rugged individualism" of the peasant was balanced, however, by the communal life and relationships of the village. The good neighbor was always ready to offer aid and sympathy when needed, as well as to participate in house raisings, warmings, harvest festivals, and other community affairs.

Relations between the high and low cultures usually were strained. On the one hand, the peasants felt superior, regarding country life and agricultural work as morally "good," in contrast to urban life and professions. On the other hand, the peasants were economically and politically subject to the city. The landlords, the tax collectors, the church officials, and the soldiers all came from the city. Their arrogance and arbitrariness made it crystal clear who were the rulers and who the ruled. Whereas the elite viewed their rich life as the product of their own superior mental and moral qualities, their good life was actually made possible by the exploitation of the peasantry. Inevitably, in the course of millennia, the peasants internalized the attitudes of the elite towards them and became servile and obsequious.

It is clear that the coming of civilization was a setback for equality between human beings. Yet civilization also brought great gains and achievements. Viewed in the light of historical perspective it was a major step forward despite all the injustice and exploitation. In this respect it resembled the industrial revolution, which at first caused painful social disruption and human suffering, but which in the long run decisively advanced human productivity and well-being. So it was with the coming of civilization. The average Neolithic tribe member probably led a more rounded and satisfying life than the average peasant or urban worker. But precisely because tribal culture was comfortable and tension-free, it was also relatively unproductive. The demands of the tax collector, the priest, and the landowner were harsh, but they were also effective in stimulating output. Positive proof of this enhanced productivity can be seen in the enormous population increase in the agrarian river valleys. Living standards also rose along with population figures. Certainly the monarchs and the top officials, both secular and ecclesiastical, enjoyed a variety of food and drink, along with richness in clothing and housing, that no tribal chieftain could ever have imagined. The new middle classes—merchants, scribes, lower officials, and clergy—also were able to lead lives that probably were as pleasant and refined as those enjoyed by their counterparts today. Even the masses may in some cases have been better off in the material sense, if not the psychosocial.

Civilization, with the new art of writing, made it possible to accumulate more and more knowledge and transmit it to successive generations. Various sciences, including mathematics, astronomy, and medicine, were able to take root and to flourish. Also the appearance of wealthy upper classes gave opportunities for the creativity of architects, sculptors, painters, musicians, and poets. The results of this creativity we can see today in masterpieces such as the Parthenon, the Taj Mahal, and the Notre Dame Cathedral.

These precious gains benefitted the few much more than the many, who, in the final analysis, bore the costs of the high culture. But the important point insofar as the whole history of humanity is concerned is that the advances were made. And it was these advances, accumulating through the millennia, that finally allowed us to gain such mastery over nature and to attain such productivity through science and technology, which today benefit the many along with the few.

It is true that many millions of people are still illiterate, diseased, and hungry. But that condition is very different from the mid-fourteenth century when a third to a half of Europe's total population was wiped out by the Black Death. It is different also from 1846, when a million Irish died of hunger because of the potato blight, and from 1876, when five million Indians starved to death when their crops failed. These victims of plague and famine could not possibly have been saved because the people of those times lacked the necessary knowledge.

Today we have that knowledge, and therefore we have the potential to free ourselves from millennia-old scourges. It is tragic that the potential has not yet been realized, but the fact remains that it does exist. And it exists because of the advances made possible in the past by the different civilizations of the human race. Therefore—to answer the question, has civilization been a curse or a blessing?—in the past it has been both. What it will be in the future depends on whether the knowledge accumulated from past civilizations is used for destructive or constructive purposes.

8

Civilization: Cultural Diffusion

How much of any culture is owed to its own originality and inventiveness? This is the question sociologist Ralph Linton discusses in the following selection.

Discussion Questions

1. Why does Linton believe that cultural diffusion is responsible for most of the greatest advances in history?

2. Is it possible for anyone to say they are 100% American, or 100% anything for that matter?

We have seen in the previous chapter how the particular culture within which any inventor works directs and circumscribes his efforts and determines whether his inventions will be socially accepted. Because of this the number of successful inventions originating within the confines of any one linked society and culture is always small. If every human group had been left to climb upward by its own unaided efforts, progress would have been so slow that it is doubtful whether any society by now would have advanced beyond the level of the Old Stone Age. The comparatively rapid growth of human culture as a whole has been due to the ability of all societies to borrow elements from other cultures and to incorporate them into their own. This transfer of culture elements from one society to another is known as *diffusion*. It is a process by which mankind has been able to pool its inventive ability. By diffusion an invention which has been made and socially accepted at one point can be transmitted to an ever-widening group of cultures until, in the course of centuries, it may spread to practically the whole of mankind.

Diffusion has made a double contribution to the advance of mankind. It has stimulated the growth of culture as a whole and at the same time has enriched the content of individual cultures, bringing the societies which bore them forward and upward. It has helped to accelerate the evolution of culture as a whole by removing the necessity for every society to perfect every step in an inventive series for itself. Thus a basic invention which has been made at one point will ultimately be brought to the attention of a great number of inventors and its potentialities for use and improvement thoroughly explored. As more minds are put to work upon each problem the process of culture advance is accelerated. The rapidity of progress during the past century is certainly due in large part to the development of means for easy and rapid communication plus techniques for ensuring to the inventor the economic rewards of his labors. Patents have made secrecy unnecessary. They impose a temporary tax upon the use of inventions but make the idea available to all. Any invention which is made at the present time is promptly diffused over a wide area and becomes part of the store of knowledge available to hundreds of inventors. Prior to the development of the present conditions it took centuries for any new element of culture to diffuse over the same territory to which it is now extended in a few months or years.

The slow cultural advance of societies which are left to their own abilities is well illustrated by the conditions in isolated human groups. Perhaps the outstanding example is the Tasmanians. These people were cut off from the rest of mankind at least 20,000 years ago. When they reached their island they seem to have had a culture which, in its material development at least, correspond roughly to that of Europe during the Middle Paleolithic. They were still in this stage when Europeans first visited them during the eighteenth century. During the long period of isolation they had no doubt made some minor advances and improvements, but their lack of outside contacts was reflected in a tremendous culture lag. To cite a much less extreme example, the culture of some of our own isolated mountain communities still corresponds in many respects to that of the pioneers of a century ago. The first settlers of these isolated regions brought this culture with them, and their unaided efforts have contributed little to it. In general, the more opportunities for

borrowing any society has the more rapid its cultural advance will be.

The service of diffusion in enriching the content of individual cultures has been of the utmost importance. There is probably no culture extant to-day which owes more than 10 per cent of its total elements to inventions made by members of its own society. Because we live in a period of rapid invention we are apt to think of our own culture as largely self-created, but the role which diffusion has played in its growth may be brought home to us if we consider the beginning of the average man's day. The locations listed in the following paragraphs refer only to the origin points of various culture elements, not to regions from which we now obtain materials or objects through trade.

Our solid American citizen awakens in a bed built on a pattern which originated in the Near East but which was modified in Northern Europe before it was transmitted to America. He throws back covers made from cotton, domesticated in India, or linen, domesticated in the Near East, or wool from sheep, also domesticated in the Near East, or silk, the use of which was discovered in China. All of these materials have been spun and woven by processes invented in the Near East. He slips into his moccasins, invented by the Indians of the Eastern woodland, and goes to the bathroom, whose fixtures are a mixture of European and American inventions, both of recent date. He takes off his pajamas, a garment invented in India, and washes with soap invented by the ancient Gauls. He then shaves, a masochistic rite which seems to have been derived from either Sumer or ancient Egypt.

Returning to the bedroom, he removes his clothes from a chair of southern European type and proceeds to dress. He puts on garments whose form originally derived from the skin

Ralph Linton, *The Study of Man*, © 1936, pp. 324–327. Reprinted by permission of Prentice-Hall, Inc., Englewood Cliffs, NJ.

clothing of the nomads of the Asiatic steppes, puts on shoes made from skins tanned by a process invented in ancient Egypt and cut to a pattern derived from the classical civilizations of the Mediterranean, and ties around his neck a strip of bright-colored cloth which is a vestigial survival of the shoulder shawls worn by the seventeenth-century Croatians. Before going out for breakfast he glances through the window, made of glass invented in Egypt, and if it is raining puts on overshoes made of rubber discovered by the Central American Indians and takes an umbrella, invented in southeastern Asia. Upon his head he puts a hat made of felt, a material invented in the Asiatic steppes.

On his way to breakfast he stops to buy a paper, paying for it with coins, an ancient Lydian invention. At the restaurant a whole new series of borrowed elements confronts him. His plate is made of a form of pottery invented in China. His knife is of steel, an alloy first made in southern India, his fork a medieval Italian invention, and his spoon a derivative of a Roman original. He begins breakfast with an orange, from the eastern Mediterranean, a cantaloupe from Persia, or perhaps a piece of African watermelon. With this he has coffee, an Abyssinian plant, with cream and sugar. Both the domestication of cows and the idea of milking them originated in the Near East, while sugar was first made in India. After his fruit and first coffee he goes on to waffles, cakes made by a Scandinavian technique from wheat domesticated in Asia Minor. Over these he pours maple syrup, invented by the Indians

of the Eastern woodlands. As a side dish he may have the egg of a species of bird domesticated in Indo-China, or thin strips of the flesh of an animal domesticated in Eastern Asia which have been salted and smoked by a process developed in northern Europe.

When our friend has finished eating he settles back to smoke, an American Indian habit, consuming a plant domesticated in Brazil in either a pipe, derived from the Indians of Virginia, or a cigarette, derived from Mexico. If he is hardy enough be may even attempt a cigar, transmitted to us from the Antilles by way of Spain. While smoking he reads the news of the day, imprinted in characters invented by the ancient Semites upon a material invented in China by a process invented in Germany. As he absorbs the accounts of foreign troubles be will, if he is a good conservative citizen, thank a Hebrew deity in an Indo-European language that he is 100 per cent American.

The foregoing is merely a bit of antiquarian virtuosity made possible by the existence of unusually complete historic records for the Eurasiatic area. There are many other regions for which no such records exist, yet the cultures in these areas bear similar witness to the importance of diffusion in establishing their content. Fairly adequate techniques above been developed for tracing the spread of individual traits and even for establishing their origin points, and there can be no doubt that diffusion has occurred wherever two societies and cultures have been brought into contact.

9

Theories of History: Racism

Many theories have been developed to explain the course of history. In pre-modern societies religion often played this role. In the modern era, more À ÀscientificÀÀ theories have been proposed, such as Marxism, which attempted to see history as the working out of economic forces. Another type of theory has tended to see human biological characteristics as the determinants of history and the destiny of human societies. Toward the end of the 19th century, especially as a consequence of Darwinism, a number of individuals saw racial qualities as the major force in history.

The following two selections deal with the issue of race and its role in history. *Racial Odyssey* is an attempt to discuss race as a scientific concept and its possible role in human evolution. *Races in History* takes up the question of how we can account for the relative "success" or "failure" of different societies in history and whether race has anything to do with it.

Discussion Questions

1. Is there such a thing as "race?" How can we identify specific "races?"

2. Where do races come from? Are they static and fixed for all time? Is there such a thing as a pure "race?"

3. Once we have identified specific "races," what do we have? What do we know? How should this information be used?

4. Has anything positive ever come out of identifying "races?"

5. Can you think of any specific ways that identifying "races" has been damaging?

6. Can the concept of "race" help us to understand why some societies are (or were) more advanced than others at particular times in history?

Racial Odyssey

Mixing, migrating, adapting, emerging anew—are all part of the great drama in which diversity is the key to long-term survival.

The human species comes in an artist's palette of colors: sandy yellows, reddish-tans, deep browns, light tans, creamy whites, pale pinks. It is a rare person who is not curious about the skin colors, hair textures, bodily structures and facial features associated with racial background. Why do some Africans have dark brown skin, while that of most Europeans is pale pink? Why do the eyes of most "white" people and "black" people look pretty much alike but differ so from the eyes of Orientals? Did one race evolve before the others? If so, is it more primitive or more advanced as a result? Can it be possible, as modern research suggests, that there is no such thing as a pure race? These are all honest, scientifically worthy questions. And they are central to current research on the evolution of our species on the planet Earth.

Broadly speaking, research on racial differences has led most scientists to three major conclusions. The first is that there are many more differences among people than skin color, hair texture and facial features. Dozens of other variations have been found, ranging from the shapes of bones to the consistency of ear wax to subtle variations in body chemistry.

The second conclusion is that the overwhelming evolutionary success of the human species is largely due to its great genetic variability. When migrating bands of our early ancestors reached a new environment, at least a few already had physical traits that gave them an edge in surviving there. If the coming centuries bring significant environmental changes, as many believe they will, our chances of surviving them will be immeasurably enhanced by our diversity as a species.

There is a third conclusion about race that is often misunderstood. Despite our wealth of variation and despite our constant, everyday references to race, no one has ever discovered a reliable way of distinguishing one race from another. While it is possible to classify a great many people on the basis of certain physical features, there are no known features or groups of features that will do the job in all cases.

Skin color won't work. Yes, most Africans from south of the Sahara and their descendants around the world have skin that is darker than that of most Europeans. But there are millions of people in India, classified by some anthropologists as members of the Caucasoid, or "white," race who have darker skins than most Americans who call themselves black. And there are many Africans living in sub-Sahara Africa today whose skins are no darker than the skins of many Spaniards, Italians, Greeks or Lebanese.

What about stature as a racial trait? Because they are quite short, on the average, African Pygmies have been considered racially distinct from other dark-skinned Africans. If stature, then, is a racial criterion, would one include

From Boyce Rensberger, "Racial Odyssey," *Science Digest,* New York, Jan/Feb 1981, pp. 50-57, 135-136. Reprinted with permission of the author.

in the same race the tall African Watusi and the Scandinavians of similar stature?

The little web of skin that distinguishes Oriental eyes is said to be a particular feature of the Mongoloid race. How, then, can it be argued that the American Indian, who lacks this epicanthic fold, is Mongoloid?

Even more hopeless as racial markers are hair color, eye color, hair form, the shapes of noses and lips or any of the other traits put forth as typical of one race or another.

No Norms

Among the tall people of the world there are many black, many white and many in between. Among black people of the world there are many with kinky hair, many with straight or wavy hair, and many in between. Among the broadnosed, full-lipped people of the world there are many with dark skins, many with light skins and many in between.

How did our modern perceptions of race arise? One of the first to attempt a scientific classification of peoples was Carl von Linnè, better known as Linnaeus. In 1735, he published a classification that remains the standard today. As Linnaeus saw it there were four races, classifiable geographically and by skin color. The names Linnaeus gave them were *Homo sapiens Africanus nigrus* (black African human being), *H. sapiens Americanus rubescens* (red American human being), *H. sapiens Asiaticus fuscusens* (brownish Asian human being), and *H. sapiens Europaeus albescens* (white European human being). All, Linnaeus recognized, were members of a single human species.

A species includes all individuals that are biologically capable of interbreeding and producing fertile offspring. Most matings between species are fruitless, and even when they succeed, as when a horse and a donkey interbreed and produce a mule, the progeny are sterile. When a poodle mates with a collie,

however, the offspring are fertile, showing that both dogs are members of the same species.

Even though Linnaeus' system of nomenclature survives, his classifications were discarded, especially after voyages of discovery revealed that there were many more kinds of people than could be pigeonholed into four categories. All over the world there are small populations that don't fit. Among the better known are:

- The so-called Bushmen of southern Africa, who look as much Mongoloid as Negroid.
- The Negritos of the South Pacific, who do look Negroid but are very far from Africa and have no known links to that continent.
- The Ainu of Japan, a hairy aboriginal people who look more Caucasoid than anything else.
- The Lapps of Scandinavia, who look as much like Eskimos as like Europeans.
- The aborigines of Australia who often look Negroid but many of whom have straight or wavy hair and are often blond as children.
- The Polynesians, who seem to be a blend of many races, the proportions differing from island to island.

To accommodate such diversity, many different systems of classification have been proposed. Some set up two or three dozen races. None has ever satisfied all experts.

Classification System

Perhaps the most sweeping effort to impose a classification upon all the peoples of the world was made by the American anthropologist Carleton Coon. He concluded there are five basic races, two of which have major subdivisions: Caucasoids; Mongoloids; full-size Australoids (Australian aborigines); dwarf Australoids (Negritos—Andaman Islanders and similar peoples); full-size Congoids (African Negroids); dwarf Congoids (African Pygmies); and Capoids (the so-called Bushmen and Hottentots).

In his 1965 classic, *The Living Races of Man*, Coon hypothesized that before A.D. 1500 there were five *pure* races—five centers of human population that were so isolated that there was almost no mixing.

Each of these races evolved independently, Coon believed, diverging from a *pre-Homo sapiens* stock that was essentially the same everywhere. He speculated that the common ancestor evolved into *Homo sapiens* in five separate regions at five different times, beginning about 35,000 years ago. The populations that have been *Homo sapiens* for the shortest periods of time, Coon said, are the world's "less civilized" races.

The five pure races remained distinct until A.D. 1500; then Europeans started sailing the world, leaving their genes—as sailors always have—in every port and planting distant colonies. At about the same time, thousands of Africans were captured and forcibly settled in many parts of the New World.

That meant the end of the five pure races. But Coon and other experts held that this did not necessarily rule out the idea of distinct races. In this view, there *are* such things as races; people just don't fit into them very well anymore.

The truth is that there is really no hard evidence to suggest that five or any particular number of races evolved independently. The preponderance of evidence today suggests that as traits typical of fully modern people arose in any one place, they spread quickly to all human populations. Advances in intelligence were almost certainly the fastest to spread. Most anthropologists and geneticists now believe that human beings have always been subject to migrating and mixing. In other words, there probably never were any such things as pure races.

Race mixing has not only been a fact of humanity but is, in this day of unprecedented global mobility, taking place at a more rapid rate than ever. It is not farfetched to envision the day when, generations hence, entire "complexion" of major population centers will be different. Meanwhile, we can see such changes taking place before our eyes, for they are a part of everyday reality.

Hybrid Vigor

Oddly, those who assert scientific validity for their notions of pure and distinct races seem oblivious of a basic genetic principle that plant and animal breeders know well: too much inbreeding can lead to proliferation of inferior traits. Crossbreeding with different strains often produces superior combinations and "hybrid vigor."

The striking differences may very well be a result of constant genetic mixing. And as geneticists and ecologists know, in diversity lies strength and resilience.

To understand the origin and proliferation of human differences, one must first know how Darwinian evolution works.

Evolution is a two-step process. Step one is mutation; somehow a gene in the ovary or testes of an individual is altered, changing the molecular configuration that stores instructions for forming a new individual. The children who inherit that gene will be different in some way from their ancestors.

Step two is selection: for a racial difference, or any other evolutionary change to arise, it must survive and be passed through several generations. If the mutation confers some disadvantage, the individual dies, often during embryonic development. But if the change is beneficial in some way, the individual should have a better chance of thriving than relatives lacking the advantage.

Natural Selection

If a new trait is beneficial, it will bring reproductive success to its bearer. After several generations of multiplication, bearers of the new trait may begin to outnumber nonbearers. Darwin called this natural selection to distinguish it from the artificial selection exercised by animal breeders.

Skin color is the human racial trait most generally thought to confer an evolutionary advantage of this sort. It has long been obvious in the Old World that the farther south one goes, the darker the skin color. Southern Europeans are usually somewhat darker than northern Europeans. In North Africa, skin colors are darker still and, as one travels south, coloration reaches its maximum at the Equator. The same progression holds in Asia, with the lightest skins to the north. Again, as one moves south, skin color darkens, reaching in southern India a "blackness" equal to that of equatorial Africans.

This north-south spectrum of skin color derives from varying intensities of the same dark brown pigment called melanin. Skin cells simply have more or less melanin granules to be seen against a background that is pinkish because of the underlying blood vessels. All races can increase their melanin concentration by exposure to the Sun.

What is it about northerly latitudes in the Northern Hemisphere that favors less pigmentation and about southerly latitudes that favors more? Exposure to intense sunlight is not the only reason why people living in southerly latitudes are dark. A person's susceptibility to rickets and skin cancer, his ability to withstand cold and to see in the dark may also be related to skin color.

The best-known explanation says the body can tolerate only a narrow range of intensities of sunlight. Too much causes sunburn and cancer, while too little deprives the body of vitamin D, which is synthesized in the skin under the influence of sunlight. A dark complexion protects the skin from the harmful effects of intense sunlight. Thus, albinos born in equatorial regions have a high rate of skin cancer. On the other hand, dark skin in northerly latitudes screens out sunlight needed for the synthesis of vitamin D. Thus, dark-skinned children living in northern latitudes had high rates of rickets—a bone-deforming disease caused by a lack of vitamin D—before their milk was routinely fortified. In the sunny tropics, dark skin admits enough light to produce the vitamin.

Recently, there has been some evidence that skin colors are linked to differences in the ability to avoid injury from the cold. Army researchers found that during the Korean War blacks were more susceptible to frostbite than were whites. Even among Norwegian soldiers in World War II, brunettes had a slightly higher incidence of frostbite than did blonds.

Eye Pigmentation

A third link between color and latitude involves the sensitivity of the eye to various wavelengths of light. It is known that dark-skinned people have more pigmentation in the iris of the eye and at the back of the eye where the image falls. It has been found that the less pigmented the eye, the more sensitive it is to colors at the red end of the spectrum. In situations illuminated with reddish light, the northern European can see more than a dark African sees.

It has been suggested that Europeans developed lighter eyes to adapt to the longer twilights of the North and their greater reliance on firelight to illuminate caves.

Although the skin cancer-vitamin D hypothesis enjoyed wide acceptance, it may well be that resistance to cold, possession of good night vision and other yet unknown factors all played roles in the evolution of skin colors.

Most anthropologists agree that the original human skin color was dark brown, since it is fairly well established that human beings evolved in the tropics of Africa. This does not, however, mean that the first people were Negroids whose descendants, as they moved north, evolved into light-skinned Caucasoids. It is more likely that the skin color of various populations changed several times from dark to light and back as people moved from one region to another. Consider, for example, that long before modern people evolved, *Homo erectus* had spread throughout Africa, Europe and Asia. The immediate ancestor of *Homo sapiens, Homo erectus*, was living in Africa 1.5 million years ago and in Eurasia 750,000 years ago. The earliest known forms of *Homo sapiens* do not make their appearance until somewhere between 250,000 and 500,000 years ago. Although there is no evidence of the skin color of any hominid fossil, it is probable that the *Homo erectus* population in Africa had dark skin. As subgroups spread into northern latitudes, mutations that reduced pigmentation conferred survival advantages on them and light skins came to predominate. In other words, there were probably black *Homo erectus* peoples in Africa and white ones in Europe and Asia.

Did the black *Homo erectus* populations evolve into today's Negroids and the white ones in Europe into today's Caucasoids? By all the best evidence, nothing like this happened. More likely, wherever *Homo sapiens* arose it proved so superior to the *Homo erectus* populations that it eventually replaced them everywhere. If the first *Homo sapiens* evolved in Africa, they were probably dark skinned; those who migrated northward into Eurasia lost their pigmentation. But it is just as possible that the first *Homo sapiens* appeared in northern climes, descendants of white-skinned *Homo erectus*. These could have migrated southward toward Africa, evolving darker skins. All modern races, incidentally, arose long after the brain had reached its present size in all parts of the world.

North-south variations in pigmentation are quite common among mammals and birds. The tropical races tend to be darker in fur and feather, the desert races tend to be brown, and those near the Arctic Circle are lighter colored.

There are exceptions among humans. The Indians of the Americas, from the Arctic to the southern regions of South America, do not conform to the north-south scheme of coloration. Though most think of Indians as being reddish-brown, most Indians tend to be relatively light skinned, much like their presumed Mongoloid ancestors in Asia. The ruddy complexion that lives in so many stereotypes of Indians is merely what years of heavy tanning can produce in almost any light¬skinned person. Anthropologists explain the color consistency as a consequence of the relatively recent entry of people into the Americas—probably between 12,000 and 35,000 years ago. Perhaps they have not yet had time to change.

Only a few external physical differences other than color appear to have adaptive significance. The strongest cases can be made for nose shape and stature.

What's in a Nose

People native to colder or drier climates tend to have longer, more beakshaped noses than those living in hot and humid regions. The nose's job is to warm and humidify air before it reaches sensitive lung tissues. The cooler or drier the air is, the more surface area is needed inside the nose to get it to the right temperature or humidity. Whites tend to have longer and beakier noses than blacks or Orientals. Nevertheless, there is great variation within races. Africans in the highlands of East Africa have longer noses than Africans from the hot, humid lowlands, for example.

Stature differences are in the tendency for most northern peoples to have shorter arms, legs and torsos and to be stockier than people from the tropics. Again, this is an adaptation to heat or cold. One way of reducing heat loss is to have less body surface, in relation to weight or volume, from which heat can escape. To avoid overheating, the most desirable body is long limbed and lean. As a result, most Africans tend to be lankier than northern Europeans. Arctic peoples are the shortest limbed of all.

Hair forms may also have a practical role to play, but the evidence is weak. It has been suggested that the more tightly curled hair of Africans insulates the top of the head better than does straight or wavy hair. Contrary to expectation, black hair serves better in this role than white hair. Sunlight is absorbed and converted to heat at the outer surface of the hair blanket; it radiates directly into the air. White fur, common on Arctic animals that need to absorb solar heat, is actually transparent and transmits light into the hair blanket allowing the heat to form within the insulating layer, where it is retained for warmth.

Aside from these examples, there is little evidence that any of the other visible differences among the world's peoples provide any advantage. Nobody knows, for example, why Orientals have epicanthic eye folds or flatter facial profiles. The thin lips of Caucasoids and most Mongoloids have no known advantages over the Negroid's full lips. Why should middle-aged and older Caucasoid men go bald so much more frequently than the men of other races? Why does the skin of Bushmen wrinkle so heavily in the middle and later years? Or why does the skin of Negroids resist wrinkling so well? Why do the Indian men in one part of South America have blue penises? Why do Hottentot women have such unusually large buttocks?

There are possible evolutionary explanations for such apparently useless differences.

One is a phenomenon known as sexual selection. Environmentally adaptive traits arise, Darwin thought, through natural selection—the environment itself chooses who will thrive or decline. In sexual selection, which Darwin also suggested, the choice belongs to the prospective mate.

In simple terms, ugly individuals will be less likely to find mates and reproduce their genes than beautiful specimens will. Take the blue penis as an example. Women might find it unusually attractive or perhaps believe it to be endowed with special powers. If so, a man born with a blue penis will find many more opportunities to reproduce his genes than his ordinary brothers.

Sexual selection can also operate when males compete for females. The moose with the larger antlers or the lion with the more imposing mane will stand a better chance of discouraging less well-endowed males and gaining access to females. It is possible that such a process operated among Caucasoid males, causing them to become markedly hairy, especially around the face.

Attractive Traits

Anthropologists consider it probable that traits such as the epicanthic fold or the many regional differences in facial features were selected this way.

Yet another method by which a trait can establish itself involves accidental selection. It results from what biologists call genetic drift.

Suppose that in a small nomadic band a person is born with perfectly parallel fingerprints instead of the usual loops, whirls or arches. That person's children would inherit parallel fingerprints, but they would confer no survival advantages. But if our family decides to strike out on its own, it will become the founder of a new band consisting of its own descendants, all with parallel fingerprints.

Events such as this, geneticists and anthropologists believe, must have occurred many times in the past to produce the great variety within the human species. Among the apparently neutral traits that differ among populations are:

Ear Wax—There are two types of ear wax. One is dry and crumbly and the other is wet and sticky. Both types can be found in every major population, but the frequencies differ. Among northern Chinese, for example, 98 percent have dry ear wax. Among American whites, only 16 percent have dry ear wax. Among American blacks the figure is 7 percent.

Scent Glands—As any bloodhound knows, every person has his or her own distinctive scent. People vary in the mixture of odoriferous compounds exuded through the skin—most of it coming from glands called apocrine glands. Among whites, these are concentrated in the armpits and near the genitals and anus. Among blacks, they may also be found on the chest and abdomen. Orientals have hardly any apocrine glands at all. In the words of the Oxford biologist John R. Baker, "The Europids and Negrids are smelly, the Mongolids scarcely or not at all." Smelliest of all are northern European, or so-called Nordic, whites.

Body odor is rare in Japan. It was once thought to indicate a European in the ancestry and to be a disease requiring hospitalization.

Blood Groups—Some populations have a high percentage of members with a particular blood group. Americans are overwhelmingly group O—100 percent in some regions. Group A is most common among Australian aborigines and the Indians in western Canada. Group B is frequent in northern India, other parts of Asia and western Africa. Advocates of the pure-race theory once seized upon blood groups as possibly unique to the original pure races. The proportions of groups found today, they thought, would indicate the degree of mixing. It was subsequently found that chimpanzees, our closest living relatives, have the same blood groups as humans.

Taste—PTC (phenylthiocarbamide) is a synthetic compound that some people can taste and others cannot. The ability to taste it has no known survival value, but it is clearly an inherited trait. The proportion of persons who can taste PTC varies in different populations: 50 to 70 percent of Australian aborigines can taste it, as can 60 to 80 percent of all Europeans. Among East Asians, the percentage is 83 to 100 percent, and among Africans, 90 to 97 percent.

Urine—Another indicator of differences in body chemistry is the presence of a compound known as BAIB (beta-amino-isobutyric acid) in urine. Europeans seldom excrete large quantities but high levels of excretion are common among Asians and American Indians. It has been shown that the differences are not due to diet.

No major population has remained isolated long enough to prevent any unique genes from eventually mixing with those of neighboring groups. Indeed, a map showing the distribution of so-called racial traits would have no sharp boundaries except for coastlines. The intensity of a trait such as skin color, which is controlled by six pairs of genes and comes therefore in many shades, varies gradually from one population to another. With only a few exceptions, every known genetic possibility possessed by the species can be found to some degree in every sizable population.

Ever-changing Species

One can establish a system of racial classification simply by listing the features of populations at any given moment. Such a concept of race is, however, inappropriate to a highly mobile and ever-changing species such as *Homo sapiens*. In the short view, races may seem distinguishable, but in biology's long haul, races come and go. New ones arise and blend into neighboring groups to create new and racially stable populations. In time, genes from these groups flow into other neighbors, continuing the production of new permutations.

Some anthropologists contend that at the moment American blacks should be considered a race distinct from African blacks. They argue that American blacks are a hybrid of African blacks and European whites. Indeed, the degree of mixture can be calculated on the basis of a blood component known as the Duffy factor.

In West Africa, where most of the New World's slaves came from, the Duffy factor is virtually absent. It is present in 43 percent of whites. From the number of American blacks who are now "Duffy positive" it can be that whites contributed 21 percent of the genes in the American black population. The figure is higher for blacks in northern and western states and lower in the South. By the same token, there are whites who have black ancestors. The number is smaller because of the tendency to identify a person as black even if only a minor fraction of his ancestors were originally from Africa.

The unwieldiness of race designations is also evident in places such as Mexico where most of the people are, in effect, hybrids of Indians (Mongoloid by some classifications) and Spaniards (Caucassoid). Many South American populations are tri-hybrids—mixtures of Mongoloid, Caucasoid and Negroid. Brazil is a country where the mixture has been around long enough to constitute a racially stable population. Thus, in one sense, new races have been created in the United States, Mexico and Brazil. But in the long run, those races will again change.

Sherwood Washburn, a noted anthropologist, questions the usefulness of racial classification: "Since races are open systems which are intergrading, the number of races will depend on the purpose of the classification. I think we should require people who propose a classification of races to state in the first place why they wish to divide the human species."

The very notion of a pure race, then, makes no sense. But, as evolutionists know full well, a rich genetic diversity within the human species most assuredly *does*.

Races in History

When the Western Europeans began their voyages of exploration, they found peoples scattered around the world and living at very different levels of development. The Chinese, for example, had a civilization that was so wealthy, sophisticated, and well governed that many of the early European visitors considered it superior to their own. Other overseas people were naked, nomadic food gatherers whom the Europeans looked down upon as barely human. So they pushed them aside into deserts or jungles, or enslaved them, or hunted them down and exterminated them. In doing these things, the Europeans justified their actions on the ground that they were a superior people bringing the light of their superior civilization to the inferior (and therefore backward) peoples of the world.

This argument raises a question which is still a matter of dispute today. Are the various human races genetically equal, or are some inherently superior, and others inferior? The great majority of scientists, though not all, agree that races are genetically equal. Typical is the statement issued at an international conference of physical anthropologists and geneticists in September 1952:

"Available scientific knowledge provides no basis for believing that the groups of mankind differ in their innate capacity for intellectual and emotional development. . . . Genetic differences are of little significance in determining the social and cultural differences between different groups of men."

If genes do not explain the great differences that European explorers found overseas, then what does? The distinguished anthropologist, Franz Boas, has offered a theory that seems to mesh with actual historical experience.

"The history of mankind proves that advances of culture depend upon the opportunities presented to a social group to learn from the experience of their neighbors. The discoveries of the group spread to others and, the more varied the contacts, the greater the opportunities to learn. The tribes of simplest culture are on the whole those that have been isolated for very long periods and hence could not profit from the cultural achievements of their neighbors."

In other words, the key to different levels of human development has been accessibility. Those with the most opportunity to interact with other people have been the most likely to forge ahead. Indeed they were driven to do so, for there was selective pressure as well as opportunity. Accessibility involved the constant threat of assimilation or elimination if opportunity was not grasped. By contrast, those who were isolated received neither stimulus nor threat, were free from selective pressure, and thus could remain relatively unchanged through the millennia without jeopardizing their existence.

If this hypothesis is applied on a global scale, the remote Australian Aborigines should have been the most culturally retarded of all major groups; next, the American Indians in the New World; then the Negroes of sub-Saharan Africa; and finally—the least-retarded, or the most-advanced—the various peoples of Eurasia who were in constant and generally increasing contact with each other. This, of course, is precisely the graduation of culture levels found by the European discoverers after 1500. The Australian aborigines were still at the Paleolithic food-gathering stage; the American Indians varied from the Paleolithic tribes of California to the impressive civilizations of Mexico, Central America, and Peru; the African Negroes presented comparable diversity, though their overall level of development was higher; and finally, at quite another level, there were the highly advanced and sophisticated civilizations found in Eurasia—the Moslem in the Middle East, the Hindu in South Asia, and the Confucian in East Asia.

We may conclude, then, that the Western domination of the globe after 1500 did not mean Western genetic superiority. It meant only that, at that period of history, the Western Europeans were in the right place at the right time. At other periods of history the situation was very different. For example, at the time of the classical civilizations it was the people of the Mediterranean who were in the center of things and who, therefore, were the most accessible and most developed. By contrast, the Northern Europeans were then on the periphery, and therefore isolated and underdeveloped. Thus we find Cicero writing to a friend in Athens in the first century B.C.: "Do not obtain your slaves from Britain because they are so stupid and so utterly incapable of being taught that they are not fit to form a part of the household of Athens."

Likewise, during the period of the medieval civilizations, the Mediterranean was still the center, and Northern Europe, still an isolated region of backward peoples. Thus a Moslem in Toledo Spain, wrote in the eleventh century: "Races north of the Pyrenees are of cold temperament and never reach maturity; they are of great stature and of a white color. But they lack all sharpness of wit and penetration of intellect."

Both Cicero and the Toledo Moslem seemed in their times to have been justified in looking down on Northern Europeans as "stupid" and lacking in "wit" and "intellect." But Nordic "backwardness" in classical and medieval times had no more to do with genes than did the "backwardness" of Africans, or American Indians, or Australian aborigines in the times of the discoveries—or than does the "backwardness" of the underdeveloped peoples of the world today.

10

Civilization: The "Retarding Lead"

Why civilizations rise and fall is the subject of this reading. Is it as a result of "imperial overstretch" as with the Roman or the Hellenistic Empires, whose desire for more led them to stretch their resources too thinly? Or were more subtle, but equally important, forces as work? The author's contention is that no society can remain in the lead if it is not willing to change, something that most successful societies have great trouble doing. With the attitude that, "if it ain't broke, don't fix it," many civilizations have seen their leading position in the world evaporate, thus raising questions not only about the decline of civilization, but also about the meaning of progress.

Discussion Questions

1. What is meant by the law of the "retarding lead?"

2. The reading says that "in history nothing fails like success?" What does this mean?

3. Does the author imply that all civilizations are doomed? What escape can there be from this fate? Has any civilization escaped?

4. Is "progress" the enemy of civilization? Is it possible to be too successful?

5. Can the concept of the "retarding lead" be related to the current debate over America's position in the world?

The most surprising and significant development during the thousand years of Eurasian medieval history was the rise of western Europe from poverty and obscurity. During most of this period from roughly 500 to 1500, the West was the underdeveloped region of Eurasia. We have seen that this underdevelopment proved an advantage in contrast to the development of China, which acted as a brake on that country. The Chinese enjoyed a sophisticated culture, advanced crafts, large-scale commerce, an efficient bureaucracy based on merit, and the creed of Confucianism that provided social cohesion and intellectual rationale. Very naturally, the Chinese considered their civilization to be superior to any other and regarded foreigners as "barbarians." When the first Westerners appeared on their coasts, the Chinese assumed there was nothing important they could learn from those peculiar "long-nosed barbarians."

This attitude, understandable though it was, left the Chinese unchanging during a time of great change. By contrast, the Western Europeans, precisely because of their relative backwardness, were ready and eager to learn and to adapt. They took Chinese inventions, developed them to their full potential, and used them for overseas expansion. This expansion, in turn, triggered more technological advances and institutional changes. The end result was the transition from medieval to modern civilization, with the Europeans serving as the pioneers and the beneficiaries.

This was not the first time that a backward, peripheral region had led in the transition from one historical era to another. During the period of the ancient civilizations (3500-1000 B.C.), the Middle East had functioned as the developed core that made the basic innovations in agriculture, metallurgy, writing, and urban life. But this highly developed center fell behind during the transition from the ancient to the classical civilizations. It was the peripheral and comparatively backward regions of China, India, and Europe that pioneered in the creative innovations of the Classical Age, including effective exploitation of iron metallurgy, coinage, and the alphabet, as well as the new religions of Confucianism, Hinduism, and Christianity.

This pattern suggests that in history, nothing fails like success. Anthropologists refer to this as the Law of Retarding Lead, which holds that the best-adapted and most-successful societies have the most difficulty in changing and retaining their lead in a period of transition. And conversely, the backward and less-successful societies are more likely to be able to adapt and to forge ahead.

The significance of this law is obvious for us today, when the West—the heir of medieval Western Europe—no longer represents an underdeveloped region of Eurasia but rather the most highly developed part of the globe. Furthermore we are living in an age of transition when the tempo of history has speeded up immensely in comparison with the Middle Ages. In such a period of constantly accelerating change, adaptability is the key to personal and national success or perhaps we should say, personal and national survival. President Lyndon B. Johnson summarized it best with this warning to his fellow Americans: "We must change to master change."

L. S. Stavrianos, *A Global History*: From Prehistory to the Present, 5e, © 1991, pp. 171–174, 281–282, 321–322. Reprinted by permission of Prentice Hall, Englewood Cliffs, New Jersey.

11

Characteristics of Traditional Societies

In World Civilization I you will be studying the major traditional societies of the world from a number of different perspectives. In this and the following readings, you are going to examine the chief characteristics of their social institutions and values. The following general list will help you better understand the readings in the text and this book related to this topic. You will quickly discover that traditional societies are in many ways very different from modern ones and one of your major goals will be to discover why they held their particular values and, by inference, why we moderns don't.

1. **There is no idea or ideal of progress.** This does not mean that traditional societies did not in fact progress—they did—all of them show impressive advance¬ments in the arts, technology, science, political organi¬zation, etc. What is missing is the idea that progress is usually (or always) good or desireable and a veritable duty or obligation of man. What is also missing is the idea that history shows that progress is a fact.

2. Generally speaking, traditional societies have only (judged by our modern circumstances) limited technology available to them. But this technology is sufficient to produce those foods and materials necessary for survival and quite a bit more (especially for some groups). In any case, technology is not so advanced and advancing that significant and permanent change is visible from genera¬tion to generation. **Traditional societies are not technology driven** and technology has no ideological value; technology is used to make society function better, not to change its values or relationships.

3. The lack of an ideal of progress and of rapid technological change leads people to believe that **life will be pretty much the same from age to age** and that **values need not change** to fit particular circumstances or periods of history.

46

4. **All traditional societies are agricultural**—the vast majority of the population must toil in the fields not only to support themselves but also support the minority which does the other tasks of a civilized society. Wealth is usually equivalent to the ownership of productive land (which is a limited commodity) and this limits the number of people who can be "well off." This usually necessitates a very conservative and frugal out¬look for most people.

5. Because of the limited nature of wealth, **traditional societies are "Dual-Culture Societies."** There exists an elite which, because of its near monopolization of surplus wealth, political power, etc., lives in a different realm of culture than the average person (mostly farmers). The elite alone participates in and creates the highest elements of culture such as in the arts, science, literature, philosophy, and most of the aspects of religion. Travel, leisure, elegance and luxury in all their forms belong to this elite. They may speak a different dialect or even a different language and may be the only literate element in society. Their culture alone is not limited to certain localities, but is the dominant culture of the society as a whole (sometimes called the "Great Tradition") and transcends parochial cultures.

6. For most people **life is dealt with exclusively on a local basis**. Seldom do people move from where they were born. The goal is local self-sufficiency; most people consume what they produce and produce what they consume. Also, the family, clan, caste or village is the normal agency of social control. Traditional societies are "self-policing," i.e. people try to handle their own problems locally rather than resorting to outsiders or a higher authority. The central government is a feature of the elite culture, not that of the average person.

7. **There is no ethic of social mobility**—occupation and status are determined almost exclusively by birth not choice. The circumstances of birth are not seen as the result of chance, but rather as part of some cosmic order of which all individuals are a part. People's lives are comprised mostly of duties, responsibilities and obliga¬tions not freedoms, liberties or rights. Limited wealth means limited opportunity. Traditional societies believe **there is a way things are meant to be**—and people should fit into this "way," not rebel against it.

8. **The group is more important than the individual.** Individuals identify almost exclusively with their family, clan or caste; they do not see themselves as having an independent destiny apart from the group. Traditional societies are therefore **collectivistic rather than individualistic**.

12

India: The Family

The family is a key institution in all traditional societies; in India it is closely linked to caste and all that that implies. The family is responsible for passing the *dharma* of the caste on to another generation and thus for helping to preserve the social order as a whole. Unlike China, therefore, the family has to share its prerogatives with another major social body. The following selection discusses many aspects of family life in India.

Discussion Questions

1. How does the size of the typical Indian family differ from that of the typical American today? What are the advantages and disadvantages of each?

2. How is property viewed in the Indian family?

3. Would you describe the Indian family as democratic?

4. Do traditional Indians look on marriage more seriously than modern Americans?

5. What are the differences between the status of males and females within the family?

6. How do traditional Indians and modern Americans differ in their view of children? What are the comparative advantages of both?

The Joint Family

The family in India generally consists of parents, their married sons with their wives and children, all married children, and sometimes other dependents such as aged parents, uncles, cousins, nephews, and brothers. This kind of family is commonly called a joint family because the family members join together in eating, in worshipping, and in holding property.

The average number of persons living in an Indian family is about six or seven, though in any given family there may be as many as fifty or more members and as few as two.

Common Property and Worship

Ancestral, and generally immovable, property is held in common. Family members are supposed to pool their resources and income, thus creating a common fund out of which each is given what is required for living purposes. The head of the family, generally the oldest male, is responsible for the supervision of the common property and finances. He does receive advice as to the disposition of the common property from other family members, especially the adult males. Though extremely powerful, he is restrained by sacred law and custom from making any use of the common property that might impoverish his descendants or the present individuals in the family.

From the earliest times provision has been made for the division of the common family property. In such close association of several families, quarrels, jealousies, suspicions, and envious comparisons are bound to arise, which may eventually culminate in demands to divide the family property among the members. When such divisions occur, the families split into individual units and become the creators of new joint families.

Individuals within the family may sometimes own property in their own right. Gifts, personal earnings, and jewelry may belong exclusively to the individual and not be included in the common fund. The jewelry that a bride has received from her parents and others customarily remains her personal property and cannot be taken from her.

Males of the joint family worship together. Sons, grandsons, great-grandsons, and others join together in commemorating their ancestors in a religious ceremony called Sraddha. This ceremony is extremely old and is similar to Chinese ancestor worship in that it links the living and the dead. Sraddha is another method of determining membership in a family group. Those entitled to participate in this ceremony by offering rice-balls are regarded as genuine members of the family.

Headship and Responsibility

When the oldest male is too old or handicapped to remain as head, his eldest son assumes his position. If the grandmother is still alive, she often exerts tremendous influence, holding more authority than her eldest son and his wife, though technically and formally the headship descends in the male line.

Although the head of an Indian family carries great authority, he also bears great responsibility. From early childhood the individual has found

Excerpts pp. 102–107 from *The Asians* by Paul Thomas Welty. Copyright © 1976 by J.B. Lippincott Company. Reprinted by permission of Pearson Education, Inc.

his whole being and purpose revolving around family life. He has been indoctrinated with the necessity of preserving and continuing the family line. He finds it almost impossible to escape the dictates of family duty even when this duty conflicts absolutely with his own ambitions. There are several instances of young Indians who gave up promising careers in order to take up family responsibilities. A brilliant young student had a magnificent future in psychology, but he was forced to give it up in order to ensure the future of his family. As the new head of a family he was compelled to undertake a career in business so that the family might have more income. Sacrificing his own future, he thus provided more opportunities for the other members of the family. Another promising young Indian retained his position as a clerk rather than jeopardize his family's financial state by taking time off for future studies.

Marriage and Family

Attitudes and customs with regard to marriage also indicate the importance of the family and the subordination of individual interests to its interests.

Marriage is thought of primarily in terms of protecting and preserving the basic family unit. It is not considered a private affair of romantic passion between two individuals but a family matter in which the individual has little, if any, choice. Traditionally, the bride and bridegroom do not see each other until the marriage ceremony itself. In India, unlike Europe and America, love is supposed to follow rather than precede marriage.

Because marriage is so essential to the preservation of the family, it is looked upon as a serious duty. Hindu parents have an obligation to find suitable mates for their children. Even though the head of the family is not a parent

of the unmarried members, he still bears the responsibility of finding spouses for them.

The force of this obligation is so great that a Hindu family will often go into heavy debt in order to marry off a daughter. The expensive wedding of a high-caste Hindu is borne almost entirely by the bride's family. The social status of the bride's family generally determines the amount of her dowry, and a high-caste son-in-law is a high-priced item. He is expensive because there is no real necessity for him to marry early, whereas Indian girls are generally married off at an early age. In the past it was not uncommon for boys of ten to thirteen years of age to marry girls two or three years younger. In 1929 the Child Marriage Act was passed making it a criminal offense to arrange the marriage of a girl before she was fourteen or a boy before he was eighteen. In 1949 the Child Marriage Restraint Act raised the girls' marriage age from fourteen to fifteen. Many Indians circumvent these marriage laws by betrothing their daughters at an early age. Betrothal is tantamount to marriage. Since unmarried daughters are a continuous drain on the family resources that offers no hope of a return, Indian families are especially eager to marry them off early. The author has conversed with many Asian fathers and prospective fathers on the economic disadvantages of a daughter. A typical conversation with an expectant father might run something like this:

Prospective father: I hope it is a boy.

Author: Why not a girl?

Prospective father: It is better to have a boy. A girl is of little future value to the house. I must feed her, clothe her, take care of her, and then marry her off to another family. Her marriage cost me money too because I must give her a trousseau and make a feast. What do I get in return for all this money I have spent on her! Nothing. She may even come back and ask for more things if the husband's family is poor or stingy. No, I want a boy. He will stay home and work and, when I am old, care for me.

Many modern educated Indians have emphasized the necessity of decreasing the amount of money that is spent for wedding ceremonies, especially among high-caste Indians. The fact that certain wealthy men have agreed to keep the wedding expenses within one year's income of the bride's father gives some indication of the vast amounts that are expended in marriage ceremonies and practices. Among some of the lower castes this situation is reversed, and the bridegroom must pay a dowry to the bride's father.

Since the customs and ceremonies relating to marriage arrangements and weddings are regarded as important to the security of the basic family unit in India, the community demands their continuance, even though these customs place a tremendous financial burden on some families. This is another revealing instance of the importance of the family institution in India. No sacrifice is too great to maintain it.

Marriages in India are usually arranged between families with the help of a middle-man. In India, as in China, these middle-men help families find suitable mates for their children and carry on all the many financial, religious, social, and other negotiations which are necessary to bring the marriage to a successful conclusion. The rise of cities has complicated the task of finding spouses, but the problem is partially met by the newspapers, which carry daily columns of matrimonial advertisements.

Generally speaking, whether the young man or woman is found by means of a middle-man or a newspaper, certain conditions must be met. There is the all-important question of caste. Does the prospective mate belong to a caste into which the boy or girl can marry? What kind of family does the individual come from? Is it respectable? What is its economic condition? A family too rich or, too poor can present complications for the future. Does the family live nearby? Indians,

especially those in villages, prefer the in-laws to live somewhere in the neighborhood. Since the passage of the new laws regarding age, the age of the prospective mates is also an important consideration. All-important is the matter of comparing horoscopes. When a Hindu child is born, the position of the stars is plotted and a horoscope drawn up by an astrologer. Prior to the final decision the horoscopes of the boy and girl are compared by a Brahmin teacher or learned man. If the two horoscopes favor a union between the two young people, the marriage can take place without fear of dire consequences. Finally, financial arrangements must be fixed, including arrangements regarding time and form of payment.

It is only after all these questions have been settled that a marriage can be held. Throughout the negotiations the individuals to be married have usually not been consulted. This is not their affair; this is a family affair. The heads of the two families, with the advice of their wives and other adult members, carry on the negotiations and make the final decision.

Many young modern Indians are following the Western custom of choosing their own wives. However, their number is still small, and the great majority of Indian marriages are being arranged as in the past.

Marriage among Hindus is a tie not easily broken, especially if they belong to the middle or high castes. The high-caste Hindu will do everything possible to prevent the dissolution of a marriage. Such an attitude was especially characteristic of traditional India. Even in the case of a woman caught in adultery, the old Hindus though it better to punish her severely than to divorce her. The stability and permanence of the family is still valued too highly by the majority of Indians to have it broken by divorce.

Nevertheless, the number of divorces is increasing. Separation by divorce was legalized under certain conditions by the Bombay Divorce

Act of 1947. The new proposed Hindu Code Bill allows for divorce proceedings, but divorce remains rare.

Children and the Family

The child is living evidence of the successful continuation of the family. He is the important result of a duty well done. The families who arranged the marriage, the couple who participated in the marriage, have accomplished their aim—the extension of the family by the procreation of children. The child represents a link with the future as well as the past. In the faces of their children the family sees the creators of other families and a long, long line of other generations stretching endlessly into the future. The child is the happiness of the family.

A child is primarily a member of a family and only secondarily the specific off spring of a specific couple. He is responsible to a group, not merely to one or two individuals. For this reason relationships within the family are often quite blurred for the child. If his father has more than one wife, the child might refer to all the wives as mother. He uses the same word for both brothers and paternal cousins. The child might be as close to his aunt as to his real mother, and he looks upon all females as having the same functions in the family. He finds happiness and security within the wide embrace of the large Indian family. Loved and cherished by the entire family, wrapped in great protective layers of affection, he develops a sense of security which never leaves him throughout life. The male child is especially cherished and favored by the Indian family.

At this time the child imbibes a sense of responsibility and obligation toward the family which never really leaves him. It is not uncommon in India, or elsewhere in Asia, to see children of five or six taking care of even younger children. The teaching of the individual's duties with regard to the family starts early, and fundamental to all these duties is the preservation, stability, and continuation of the Indian family.

13

Arranged Marriages

In most traditional societies marriages were arranged by parents for their children; parents considered this one of their most important obligations. In modern societies marriage is usually based (or is supposed to be based) on romantic love. The following selection, *No More MoonJune: Love's Out* is a contemporary analysis of these different types of marriages—and not to the advantage of the modern view.

Discussion Questions

1. Is romantic love an instinct or learned behavior? Where does the author say it came from?

2. What is wrong with romantic love as the basis of marriage?

3. What are the arguments in favor of arranged marriages? Would you trust your parents to select a spouse for you? Why or why not?

4. Why did traditional societies rely on arranged marriages? Could they have functioned as well on marriages based on romantic love?

5. Why do modern societies rely on romantic love? Is it a success or a failure?

No More MoonJune: Love's Out

Romantic love is a supreme fiction, marriage for love the consequence of that fiction, and divorce the painful evidence of that initial delusion.

The history of romantic love is the continuing ironic testimony of the power of our minds to mesmerize our bodies, while romantic marriage is the most recent and least successful evolutionary stage in the history of matrimony. Now that the Census Bureau has estimated that more than one in three marriages will end in divorce, it is apparent that the solution to the troubled state of matrimony is a return to the tradition of arranged marriages.

The sentimental sanctity of love was the invention of the Provencal poets of the 12th century, and they saw it as the exotic refinement of a bored aristocracy. Since then, however, love has democratized itself and is no longer the luxury of a courtly minority but the expectation of every man and woman. Indeed, the joys of romantic love are the birthright of every American, for the Framers of the Declaration of Independence declared "the pursuit of happiness" to be the inalienable right of all men and women.

Love, though, is neither a right nor an instinct, but a learned form of behavior; it is not a spontaneous feeling but an artificial ritual. It is a response that we have learned from literature, and its contemporary handmaidens, the news media.

As lovers, we are all actors—we imagine ourselves most spontaneous when we are most imitative. We learn how to love from movies, television, novels, magazines and advertisements. We learn to adore love, to idolize love, to fall in love with love.

To most Americans, love is romantic love. It is a drive or state of tension induced by our prevailing romantic myths. The lover's nourishment is the expectation of bliss. Love is a competitive and covetous game: Competition for a mate brings out the best in an individual. To be alone is not considered a self-imposed choice but evidence of failure in the contest of love.

During the Industrial Revolution, arranged romantic marriages succumbed to individual love matches. The monotony of work and the impersonality of the city led people to escape monotony in personal relations and retreat from impersonality to the "emotional fortress" of marriage. Urbanization caused the "privatization" of marriage so that the intimacy of wedlock became a sanctuary from a world where all intimacy was excluded.

Yet, romantic marriage was the cradle of its own demise. More and more pressure was forced on marriage to be "a haven in a heartless world." As the temptations of the outside world were becoming more varied, the standards of marital fidelity became more exigent. Opportunity multiplies, morality declines: The pressure on marriage increased geometrically. Between 1870 and 1920 the number of divorces multiplied fifteen-fold.

In the past, when society was more structured, married partners were externally oriented, and did not have to rely exclusively on each other for emotional gratification. They could find that elsewhere. Romantic passion had always existed outside of marriage but it had nothing to do with wedlock. Contemporary society forces couples to depend on each other for permanence and stability, functions that were formerly provided by a large familial and social network.

Today, marriage has not lost its function; it suffers from a surfeit of functions. The marriage partner must not only be a lover, but a friend, a colleague, a therapist, and a tennis partner. Indeed, the standards of romantic marriage—unquestioned fidelity and undiminished passion—are merely an ideal to be approximated, not a universal precept to be obeyed.

Traditionally, the selection of mates has been determined by social, political and economic considerations directed either toward establishing new ties or reaffirming old ones. Every arranged marriage was the formation of a new society—a merger of a network of familial and social relationships. Marriage was a duty. Its raison d'etre was procreation. Children were best raised in a congenial home, and a congenial home was best created by a reasonable arrangement between congenial people. Marriage was contracted according to a principle other than the self-interest of the participants, and emotional satisfaction was neither the origin nor purpose of marriage.

The concept of arranged marriage is based on a positive view of human nature. Its guiding principle is that marriage requires a more durable foundation than romantic love, that wisdom is more important in the choosing of a partner than passion, and that everyone can find something to "love, honor, and cherish" in anyone else.

Romantic love, however, is fundamentally narcissistic; we either choose someone who resembles ourself, the self we'd like to be or think we are, or we choose someone who complements us. The former is incestuous, the latter entropic. If love means touching someone outside of ourselves, then romantic love is solipsistic while arranged marriage is altruistic.

Romantic love allows us the reverie of imagining what the other person is like, whereas arranged marriage forces us to acknowledge truly another human being. Instead of falling in love with an ideal-image, an arranged marriage teaches us how to live with an actual individual. The myths of romantic love teach us how to fall in love. Perhaps when marriages are arranged, we will learn how to love.

14

China: Filial Piety

In China there was no question that the most important social institution was the family. Part of its strength was due to the fact that there was no other institution that competed with it for the loyalty of the average Chinese (there were, after all, no public schools, no churches, no castes). Also, the family was idealized in a way not found in most other civilizations; even the government was seen as an extension of the family structure, with the emperor a decidedly paternalistic figure. As the basic building block of society, it was felt that if the family worked the way it should, there would be peace and harmony in the society as a whole. And within the family, the highest virtue was filial piety, or *xiao*, devotion and obedience of children to their parents. To be "unfilial" was about the worst offense in the family situation.

The following reading illustrates filial piety and the obligations children should ideally feel toward parents.

Discussion Questions

1. One of the key figures in the story was Madame Li. What do her activities tell you about the role of women in China? What was her objective?

2. What did Shen-sheng think were his obligations to his father? To himself?

3. How does the modern child's concept of obligations to parents differ from those of Shen-sheng?

4. What does this story tell you about the concept of justice in traditional China? How does it differ from yours? What would you have done in the same situation?

The Death of Prince Shen-sheng

In the fifth year of Duke Hsien's reign (672 B.C.), the Duke attacked Li-jung and acquired Madame Li. Both Madame Li and her younger sister became the Duke's favorites.

In the twelfth year Madame Li gave birth to a son named Hsi-ch'i. The Duke began to think seriously about the possibility of replacing Shen-sheng (the present heir) by Hsi-ch'i as the crown prince.

In the seventeenth year (660 B.C.) the Duke ordered crown prince Shen-sheng to head an army to attack Tung-shan.

"I have several sons," said the Duke to a minister, Li K'e. "I do not know which of them should be designated as my heir apparent." Li K'e did not reply. Later he went to see the crown prince.

"Is it true that I am going to be replaced as the crown prince?" Shen-sheng asked.

"You should do your best while you are commanding the army," said Li K'e. "As long as you believe that you are respectful to your father, why should you be afraid of being replaced? Moreover, a man should be more concerned with his performance as a loyal son than with the possibility, or the lack of it, of being designated as the heir apparent. You will be very safe indeed if you diligently cultivate your virtue and never place any blame on others."

One day in the nineteenth year the Duke told Madame Li privately that he intended to replace Shen-sheng with Hsi-ch'i as the crown prince. "No, you should not," Madame Li protested in tears. "The fact that Shen-sheng is the crown prince is known to all the states throughout the country. Moreover, he is at the head of the army and is very popular with the people. You must not replace the eldest son of a legal wife by the young son of a concubine on my behalf. If you insist on carrying out your plan I will commit suicide."

Despite what she said in front of the Duke, Madame Li secretly sent her agents to spread rumors for the purpose of slandering the crown prince, though outwardly she kept on praising him. She, of course, wanted her own son to be installed as crown prince.

One day in the twenty-first year (656 B.C.) Madame Li told the crown prince that she had dreamed about Madame Chiang, the crown prince's deceased mother, and that he, the crown prince, should proceed to Ch'ufu to offer sacrifices to comfort his deceased mother. After the rituals had been completed, the crown prince brought back the sacrificial meat to his father as tribute. The Duke was then on a hunting trip outside the capital, and Madame Li ordered her servants secretly to place poison in the meat.

Two days later the Duke returned from his hunting trip, and the royal chef presented the sacrificial meat. The Duke was about to eat it when he was stopped by Madame Li. "Since the meat comes from a place far away, it should be tested before you eat it," she said. The Duke threw the meat to the ground, the ground began to bulge. Fed with it, a dog died immediately. Tested on a slave, the slave also dropped dead. "How cruel the crown prince is!" Madame Li said in tears. "He wants to kill his own father whom he is anxious to replace. How can he possibly have mercy on others? You, sir, are

From *The Essence of Chinese Civilization*, by Dun J. Li, editor. Van Nonstrand Reinhold, 1967.

very advanced in years, and yet he cannot wait. The reason he wants to kill his father is because he cannot stand me and my son Hsi-Ch'i. Under the circumstances I and my son can either flee to another country before it is too late, or commit suicide before the crown prince slaughters us with his own hands. Formerly when you wanted to replace him as crown prince, I was strongly opposed to it. Now I know how wrong I was."

As soon as he learned that he had been implicated by Madame Li in the alleged attempt to murder his father, the crown prince fled to Hsinch'eng. Unable to locate the crown prince, the Duke was furious enough to kill the prince's tutor as a substitute.

Someone told the crown prince that the poison was placed by Madame Li and that he should inform his father about his innocence. "My father is very old," said the crown prince. "He needs Madame Li for his old age. Without her he could not eat or sleep well. If I tell him the truth, he will be very angry with her. I cannot bear to see his only comfort taken away from him during his old age." Someone suggested that he should flee to another state. "With a bad reputation such as I have, which state or country will take me in as its guest?" said the crown prince. "The only course open to me is to commit suicide."

In the twelfth month, crown prince Shen-sheng committed suicide at Hsinch'eng.

15

Japan: Group and Rank

The following selection illustrates how Japan exemplifies the characteristics of a traditional society.

Discussion Questions

1. How does the Japanese view of the individual differ from the modern Western view?

2. How does the way a Japanese makes a decision differ from the way you make a decision?

3. What are the advantages of the Japanese approach to individual-group relations?

4. Why do the Japanese put such an emphasis on etiquette in human relations?

The Group

The most important of these is the Japanese sense of the importance of the group. The Japanese have never fully accepted the Western notion that the individual has the right to make up his own mind about his position in society so long as he doesn't injure others. For a Japanese, the group that he belongs to and his position in it determine his status and his value to society, and the individual doesn't count for much.

Early in life the group is the family, and, even as he learns to speak, the young child is forced to recognize clearly his position within it. For instance, there is no way to say just "brother" or "sister" in Japanese. Instead, there are two words for each, depending on whether an elder or younger is meant. A Japanese child learns to address his seniors as "honorable elder brother" or "honorable elder sister," but he calls his juniors more familiarly by name. If he gets into trouble or behaves well outside the home, it is his family that gets the blame or the credit, and later, when he applies for even a simple, temporary job, his family background will be examined very carefully by the prospective employer.

The next group is the school—and it is significant that in Japan one does not ask a child his age but inquires what grade he's in. From junior high school on, students wear uniforms which not only indicate what school they go to but what class they are in. When a young man graduates and goes to work he will probably stay with the same company for his entire career and proudly wear the company's badge in his lapel. Introducing himself, he will give not only his own name but the name of his firm as well.

If he is a factory worker he is reminded of his group affiliation constantly, because he will probably live in a company-owned house, get married in the company's wedding hall, go to a company hospital if he is sick, and take his vacations together with his fellow workers in a company-owned vacation resort at the mountains or the seashore. If he is a farmer or fisherman his loyalty is to his village and its cooperative society; if he is a small businessman he belongs to a local businessmen's association and strictly keeps the shop hours that the association decides on. Even actors and actresses very rarely switch from one movie company or stage production company to another.

An individual Japanese is restricted in what he can do by his group consciousness. He does not feel that he has rights as an individual that go beyond his rights as a member of the group. That is to say, he obeys the group commands not out of fear and not only because he is reluctant to bring any kind of shame upon the group, but because he has been taught and conditioned into believing that the group is more important. The extent of this feeling is hard for a Westerner to appreciate, but a Japanese finds it very difficult to make an unusual decision by himself, or to act alone.

One of the most striking examples of this is in the national Diet, or parliament, where the elected members almost never vote against their party's official position; if they do they are severely criticized and may be kicked out of their party entirely. The Japanese even have a proverb for this process: "The nail that sticks out gets hammered down." The positive side of this lack of individualism is that Japanese find it easy to cooperate with each other.

This attitude toward the individual is common to all Oriental societies. But the Japanese, living in narrow valleys and small plains, developed more of a sense of local loyalty than did the Chinese, for example, on the broad rice plains of the mainland. The traditional Japanese allegiance to clans and local feudal leaders has been transferred in modern times to company, union, religious group, and political faction.

Rank and Etiquette

A Japanese is always conscious of what favors or respect he owes to others and what they owe to him. Everyone's relations with everyone else are precisely defined and recognized and mutual obligations are understood by all. There are very few casual acquaintanceships among the Japanese. If two people are not strangers there is bound to be a definable relationship between them, such as colleague, classmate, customer, teacher, or boss.

The famous politeness of the Japanese is based on this web of relationships. Living so close together in such crowded conditions, the Japanese developed an intricate etiquette that hides real thoughts and emotions and prevents the normal stresses and strains of daily life from growing into outright conflict. Everyone knows the form of etiquette which is due him, and what he must say to others in almost any given circumstance. If these ritual forms are observed everyone "can hold up his face," as the Japanese saying goes, and everyone is more or less satisfied.

The Japanese language not only simplifies this but makes it nearly impossible for even modern Japanese to break out of the system. There are, for instance, more than a dozen words for "you" in Japanese, and the choice between them depends on who is being addressed. This dependence on etiquette has been diminishing in recent years but is still very evident.

Therefore, with guests, friends, associates—anyone to whom they are connected by threads of the web—the Japanese are careful to exchange the proper kind of phrases and measured bows, and the right kind of presents and greeting according to the season and the occasion. But to strangers, other people rushing for seats on a crowded train, for instance, the Japanese can be as rude as anybody. Foreign visitors don't often see this side of the Japanese, however, because the Japanese regard every foreigner in their county as somewhat of a guest.

What all this means is that the Japanese do not believe that all men are created equal. Legally, equality is guaranteed in Japan's constitution and laws, and modern educators try to encourage the idea. But two thousand years of living under a single imperial dynasty (and a tradition of rule by clan chieftains even older than that) have bred into the Japanese a conviction that the natural order of the world is not equality but hierarchy. There have been many historical changes in Japanese society, but the concept that one man is as important as another has never emerged in any era.

In the traditional Japanese scheme of things (which was influenced to a great extent by Chinese society and Confucian philosophy), every person has his place, and his place determines his rights and his duties. In a family, until recently, everyone accepted as natural the privileged role of the oldest son, and many families still do. A factory or office worker would not dream of walking through a door in front of his superior and even today will always address his superior by title (such as "honorable section chief" or "honorable foreman") rather than by name. Democracy is only slowly weakening the idea of status, and easy camaraderie exists only between people who are of the same social or business rank, or who were classmates together. For this reason it is very difficult for Japanese to strike up conversations with strangers. Until they can exchange name cards to learn each other's rank, they literally do not know how to behave to one another, or who should defer to whom, or who should bow more deeply. And it is still very rare for a person to be promoted over the head of a senior just because of superior ability. The gifted individual must play the game and wait his turn. This tends to frustrate many young Japanese, who have been brought up with modern ideas of equality and individualism.

All this does not mean, however, that a Japanese is doomed to live his life in the class to which he is born, as is still true of many Asian countries. Advancement in Japan is through education, and bright Japanese youth from poor families can enter good schools and some day reach important positions.

16

Africa: Systems of Land Tenure

The modern Western concept of private property has not been shared by most people in history. This is especially true when it comes to land. Often it was considered too important a resource to be permitted to be owned and used by individuals for their own "selfish" purposes. The following selection presents an African variation on this theme.

Discussion Questions

1. Who did own land in Africa?

2. How does the traditional African concept of ownership differ from the prevailing modern view?

3. What distinctions are made between things that can be personally owned and used and those that cannot?

4. Can you think of any contemporary parallels to this traditional concept?

The ideas men hold about the land they live on depend largely on how much there is of it and the uses to which it can be put. In Africa there was plenty of land, but few ways of using it, so the ideas concerning the owning and use of land were pretty much the same everywhere.

The most widespread of these ideas was that of communal ownership. Land was not thought of as belonging to persons, but to people; and the people could be the members of a clan, village, tribe, or kingdom. One Nigerian chieftan spoke representatively when he said: "I conceive that land belongs to a vast family of which many are dead, few are living, and countless members are still unborn." Although a person could have the use of a particular piece of land, his rights over it and what he could do with it were limited by other rights over the same piece of land held by other members of his "family." These rights were limited both as to the period of effective occupation and as to transfer and succession. So long as a man worked a piece of land or members of his community worked it for him, it remained in his possession and no one might encroach on it. Should he leave it temporarily, he could, as a rule, take possession of it again on his return. If he did not wish to retain the use of it he might negotiate its transfer to another, receiving in exchange goods or services of some kind. But usually he could not treat it as a salable or a rentable commodity. There was, therefore, no opportunity for land speculation and no incentive to acquire large holdings from which a return might be derived in the form of purchase money or rent. There were no renters and no tenants in the American sense of that term; but a landowner always had plenty of relatives and friends to whom he could loan land in return for help given him in cultivating and reaping crops on his "home farm."

In many areas, customary law limited the extent of land that anyone might hold to the amount he required for the support of himself and his family. The absentee owner was, therefore, a rarity. So too was the compact lot, since in most areas either bush-fallowing or shifting cultivation was the rule and, by the laws of inheritance, good and bad land had to be divided equitably. This almost always meant that a man's holdings consisted of a series of patches scattered over a wide area.

The ideas entertained about useful trees were in several respects similar to those about the land on which they stood. For example, the fruit of the wild palm tree was generally anybody's, but the moment the tree was tapped for wine it became the tapper's. He retained possession of it even though he neglected the land on which it stood—even though he did not own the land on which it stood. Similarly, if a person planted a palm tree, or any other tree of economic importance, the tree belonged to him no matter on whose ground it was planted. To make sure that its ownership was accepted, the planter would probably summon the village elders to witness the planting, especially if the land did not belong to him. In a sense, a tree was more of a property than land, for if a man owned both a tree and the land on which it stood, and he should leave his village, he would not automatically lose his rights over the tree. If he wished, he could even rent out his tree.

Land and trees, then, were regarded in the same light as sunshine and air, as plentiful and necessary, and as things to be enjoyed by all members of the community according to their requirements. In themselves they had little or no value; it was the work which a man, a family or a community put into a piece of land or a tree that gave it its value. Consequently, when a piece of land was transferred from one owner to another, its value was judged to be the value of the standing crop, if any, and of the work which had gone into clearing and breaking the ground for the crop.

From George H. T. Kimble, *Tropical Africa, Vol. I: Land and Livelihood* , pp. 34-35. Copyright 1962 by The 20th Century Fund, New York, NY. Reprinted with permission.

17

Africa: The Ideal Balance and Morality

In traditional societies there was often a clear link between what we would call the economic aspects of society and the morality of that society. The following brief selection provides an example of this in the African context, but it was certainly not unique to Africa.

Discussion Questions

1. What is meant by the idea that "enough is enough?"

2. What is wrong with getting three beehives?

3. What is an underlying reason why modern Western economic and social values are different from these more traditional ones?

African systems of cultivation and cropping are generally well-adapted to produce the means of subsistence with the minimum of labor. And the minimum of labor, no doubt, is what all people have striven for, but especially the Africans with their ethos of "enough is enough."

The ideal balance always supposed enough but not much more: enough for a given community in a given place, taking it for granted that whenever the community grew too large for local sustenance, for the achieved balance, some of its members would find new land elsewhere. This attitude may be miles away from the accumulation drive of our own industrial societies with their drumming emphasis on "more than enough." But it had its own moral consistency. The ideal for most Africans, though not all, has been conformity to the life led by one's fellows, seeking little or no wealth and position in a carefully egalitarian world where personal gain above the level of the accepted norm would be a source of unhappiness or danger, since exceptional achievement could only be at the expense of one's neighbors. This is why exceptional achievement could be interpreted as a sign of social malice; as the working of destructive witchcraft. Among one tribe to find one beehive is good luck, to find two is very good luck, to find three is witchcraft. Whoever failed to live the good life according to the ideal balance, or became the recipient of favors beyond the average, might well be thought to have set himself against the norm.

With them, the difference between good and bad lay in acceptance and rejection of traditions—everyday, practical, all-pervasive—of what seemed to be right and natural. Those very forces which have made for stability among them also tend to hamper any man who tries to remake his life in new ways. Those traits of character which the modern world admires, such as pushing egotism and the desire for personal wealth or power, are precisely the qualities which make some Africans disliked and even feared among their fellows.

Excerpt from *The African Genius* by Basil Davidson, Little Brown & Company, 1969.

18

China: Legalism

One of the most influential political philosophies in Chinese history was Legalism (sometimes called Realism). It was at the height of its influence during the Ch'in dynasty in the 3rd century BC in the reign of Shih Huang-ti (Shihuangdi), the first emperor. This reading summarizes the Legalist position.

Discussion Questions

1. What view of human nature lies at the basis of the Legalist philosophy? Do you think this view is realistic?

2. What are the major principles of the Legalist system?

3. Why might Legalists think that neither Confucianism nor Daoism could possibly form the basis of sound government?

4. Is contemporary American government closer to the Legalist or Confucianist position?

The Legalists and Law

1. Although a very few persons may be found who are naturally altruistic, the great majority of men act only out of self-interest. Therefore, stern punishments are necessary. Law is concerned only with the many who are selfish, not with the insignificant few who are good.

2. A government, if it is to be strong, must destroy factionalism and privilege. Hence it is imperative that it publicize its laws and apply them impartially to high and low alike, irrespective of relationship or rank.

3. Law is the basis of stable government because, being fixed and known to all, it provides an exact instrument with which to measure individual conduct. A government based on li cannot do this, since the li are unwritten, particularistic, and subject to arbitrary interpretation.

4. Because history changes, human institutions must change accordingly. In antiquity people were few and life was easy, but today the growth of population has resulted in a sharpening struggle for existence. Hence the li of the ancients no longer fit modern conditions and should be replaced by a system of law.

5. A state that is strong is one that maintains a single standard of morality and thought for its people. All private standards must be suppressed if they do not agree with the public standard as prescribed by law.

6. Men, being essentially selfish, cannot be induced merely by moral persuasion to act altruistically. Only by playing on their own self-interest can the state induce them to do what it desires. Hence the wise ruler establishes a system of rewards and punishments.

7. The importance of individual capabilities in government is lessened when there is good legal machinery. Thus even a mediocre ruler, provided he keeps to his laws, can have a good administration.

8. Laws that are sufficiently stringent will no longer have to be applied because their mere existence will be enough to deter wrongdoing. Thus, harsh laws, though painful in their immediate effect, lead in the long run to an actual reduction of government and to a society free from conflict and oppression....

Reprinted by permission of the publisher from *Law in Imperial China: Exemplified by 190 Ch'ing Dynasty Cases* (translated from the Hsing-An-Hui_lan), with Historical, Social and Juridical Commentaries by Derk Bodde and Clarence Morris, Cambridge, Mass.: Harvard University Press, Copyright © 1967 by the President and Fellows of Harvard College.

19

China: Confucianism

A number of the key elements of Confucian philosophy are included in the following selections from the *Analects*, the sayings of Confucius collected over the years by his pupils.

Discussion Questions

1. Does Confucius believe in social equality? How or how not?

2. What does Confucius mean by "reciprocity?" How is it similar to or different from the Golden Rule?

3. What would Confucius think about modern American society and values?

4. What, for Confucius, is the best kind of government?

5. Why did he not think that laws and penalties was the way to deal with crime? Was he right?

6. How would Confucius have defended his approach to a Daoist?

Confucius

From the Analects

On Education

23. By nature men are pretty much alike; it is learning and practice that set them apart.
22. In education there are no class distinctions.
29. Shall I teach you what knowledge is? When you know a thing, say that you know it; when you do not know a thing, say that you do not know it. That is knowledge.
32. A young man's duty is to be filial to his parents at home and respectful to his elders abroad, to be circumspect and truthful, and, while overflowing with love for all men, to associate himself with humanity. If, when all that has been done, he has any energy to spare, then let him study the polite arts.

On Reciprocity

40. Tzu Kung asked: "Is there any one word that can serve as a principle for the conduct of life?" Confucius said: "Perhaps the word `reciprocity': Do not do to others what you would not want others to do to you."
43. Behave when away from home as though you were in the presence of an important guest. Deal with the common people as though you were officiating at an important sacrifice. Do not do to others what you would not want others to do to you. Then there will be no dissatisfaction either in the state or at home.
44. The humane man, desiring to be established himself, seeks to establish others; desiring himself to succeed, he helps others to succeed. To judge others by what one knows of oneself is the method of achieving humanity.

On Humanheartedness (Jen)

46. To be able to practice five virtues in the world constitutes humanity; they are courtesy, magnanimity, good faith, diligence, and kindness. He who is courteous is not humiliated, he who is magnanimous wins the multitude, he who is of good faith is trusted by the people, he who is diligent attains his objective, and he who is kind can get service from the people.
53. Riches and honor are what every man desires, but if they can be obtained only by transgressing the right way, they must not be held. Poverty and lowliness are what every man detests, but if they can be avoided only by transgressing the right way, they must not be evaded. If a gentleman departs from humanity how can he be called "gentleman."

54. The resolute scholar and the humane person will under no circumstance seek life at the expense of humanheartedness. On occasion they will sacrifice their lives to preserve their humanity.

On the Gentleman (Chun-tzu) (junzi)

80. The gentleman occupies himself with the Way and not with his livelihood. One may attend to farming, and yet may sometimes go hungry. One may attend to learning and yet may be rewarded with emolument. What the gentleman is anxious about is the Way and not poverty.

82. The way of the gentleman is threefold. Being humane, he has no anxieties; being wise, he has no perplexities; being brave, he has no fear.

84. The gentleman first practices what he preaches and then preaches what he practices.

85. The gentleman reaches upward; the inferior man reaches downward.

86. The gentleman is always calm and at ease; the inferior man is always worried and full of distress.

87. The gentleman understands what is right; the inferior man understands what is profitable.

88. The gentleman cherishes virtues; the inferior man cherishes possessions.

89. The gentleman makes demands upon himself; the inferior man makes demands on others.

90. The gentleman seeks to enable people to succeed in what is good but does not help them in what is evil. The inferior man does the contrary.

91. The gentleman is broad-minded and not partisan; the inferior man is partisan and not broad-minded.

On Government

95. If a ruler himself is upright, all will go well without orders. But if he himself is not upright, even though he gives orders they will not be obeyed.

97. Lead the people by laws and regulate them by penalties, and the people will try to keep out of jail, but will have no sense of shame. Lead the people by virtue and restrain them by the rules of decorum, and the people will have a sense of shame, and moreover will become good.

99. A government is good when those near are happy and those far off are attracted.

101. Tzu Kung asked about government. Confucius said: "The essentials are sufficient food, sufficient troops, and the confidence of the people." Tzu Kung asked: "Suppose you were forced to give up one of these three, which would you let go first?" Confucius said: "The troops." Tzu Kung asked again: "If you were forced to give up one of the two remaining, which would you let go?" Confucius said: "Food. For from old, death has been the lot of all men, but a people without faith cannot survive."

103. To have done nothing and yet have the state well-governed—Shun was the one! What did he do? He merely made himself reverent and correctly occupied his royal seat.

20

China: Daoism

Often seen as the yin to Confucianism's yang, Daoism represents the most significant alternative philosophy in China. Whereas Confucianism tended to stress the place of the individual in a civilized order, Daoism saw the individual as an independent creature with a direct link to the forces of nature.

The two most famous Daoist philosophers were Laozi and Zhuangzi who are represented in the following selections. The first reading, the *Daodejing*, is the classic of Daoist philosophy.

Discussion Questions

1. What is the apparent attitude of Laozi to Confucian philosophy?

2. What alternative does he offer?

3. What does Laozi think is the cause of society's problems?

4. What might Laozi think of the earlier essay, *Civilization: Curse or Blessing?*

5. How would Zhuangzi describe the "good life?"

6. Can you find any similarities between the Daoist and Indian philosophies?

7. How, according to Zhuangzi, have horses and men come to be degraded?

From the *Daodejing* by Laozi

3

Refrain from exalting the worthy,
So that the people will not scheme and contend;
Refrain from prizing rare possessions,
So that the people will not steal;
Refrain from displaying objects of desire,
So that the people's hearts will not be disturbed.
Therefore a sage rules his people thus:
He empties their minds and fills their bellies
He weakens their ambitions and strengthens their bones.
He strives always to keep the people innocent of knowledge and desires, and to keep the knowing ones from meddling. By doing nothing that interferes with anything (wu-wei), nothing is left unregulated.

16

To return to the root is called quietude,
Which is also said to be reversion to one's destiny.
This reversion belongs with the eternal:
To know the eternal is enlightenment;
Not to know the eternal means to run blindly to disaster.

18

It was when the great Tao declined,
That there appeared humanity and righteousness.
It was when knowledge and intelligence arose,
That there appeared much hypocrisy.
It was when the six relations lost their harmony,
That there was talk of filial piety and paternal affection.
It was when the country fell into chaos and confusion,
That there was talk of loyalty and trustworthiness.

19

Banish sageliness, discard wisdom,
And the people will be benefitted a hundredfold.
Banish humanity, discard righteousness,
And the people will return to filial piety and paternal affection.
Banish skill, discard profit,
And thieves and robbers will disappear.

80

Let there be a small country with a few inhabitants. Though there be labor-saving contrivances, the people would not use them. Let the people mind death and not migrate far. Though there be boats and carriages, there would be no occasion to ride them. Though there be armor and weapons, there would be no occasion to display them.

Let the people revert to the practice of ropeknotting (instead of writing), and be contented with their food, pleased with their clothing, satisfied with their houses, and happy with their customs. Though there be a neighboring country in sight, and the people hear each other's cocks crowing and dogs barking, they would grow old and die without having anything to do with each other.

Selections from Zhuangzi

" The life of things passes like a galloping horse. Every movement brings a change, and every hour makes a difference. What is one to do or what is one not to do? Indeed, everything will take its own course. . . ."

"Therefore it has been said that the natural abides within, the artificial without, and virtue resides in the natural. If one knows the course of nature and man, taking nature as the fundamental and abiding by virtue, one may feel free either to proceed or retreat, either to contract or expand, for there is always a return to the essential and to the ultimate."

"What do you mean," inquired the Earl of the River, "by the natural and the artificial?"

"Horses and oxen," answered the Spirit of the Ocean, "have four feet. That is the natural. Putting a halter on a horse's head, a string through a bullock's nose—that is the artificial."

"Therefore it has been said, do not let the artificial obliterate the natural; do not let effort obliterate destiny; do not let enjoyment be sacrificed to fame. Diligently observe these precepts without fail, and thus you will revert to the original innocence."

* * *

How do I know that wanting to be alive is not a great mistake? How do I know that hating to die is not like thinking one has lost one's way, when all the time one is on the path that leads to home? Li Chi was the daughter of the frontier guardsman at Ai. When first she was captured and carried away to Chin, she wept till her dress was soaked with tears. But when she came to the king's palace, sat with him on his couch and shared with him the dainties of the royal board, she began to wonder why she had wept. How do I know the dead do not wonder why they should ever have prayed for a long life? It is said that those who dream of drinking wine will weep when day comes; and that those who dream of weeping will next day go hunting. But while a man is dreaming, he does not know that he is dreaming; nor can he interpret a dream till the dream is done. It is only when he wakes, that he knows it was a dream. Not till the Great Awakening can we know that all this was one Great Dream....

Once Chuang Tzu dreamt that he was a butterfly. He did not know that he had ever been anything but a butterfly and was content to hover from flower to flower. Suddenly he woke and found to his astonishment that he was Chuang Tzu. But it was hard to be sure whether he really was Chuang Tzu and had only dreamt he was a

---

From Arthur Waley, *Three Ways of Thought in Ancient China.*

butterfly, or was really a butterfly, and was only dreaming he was Chuang Tzu.*

* * *

Knowing that there are dishonest people who pry into boxes delve in sacks, raise the lids of chests, to protect their property people provide strong ropes and solid locks; and in the common opinion of the world they act wisely in doing so. But suppose real brigands come. They will snatch up the boxes, hoist the sacks, carry away the big trunks on their backs, and be gone; only too glad the locks are solid and the ropes strong. The sole result of what before seemed wisdom was that the brigands were saved the trouble of packing!**

The Degradation of Horses and Men

Horses have hoofs to carry them over frost and snow; hair, to protect them from wind and cold. They eat grass and drink water, and fling up their heels over the champaign. Such is the real nature of horses. Palatial dwellings are of no use to them.

One day Poh Loh appeared, saying, "I understand the management of horses."

So he branded them, and clipped them, and pared their hoofs, and put halters on them, tying them up by the head and shackling them by the feet and disposing them in stables, with the result that two or three in every ten died. Then he kept them hungry and thirsty, trotting them and galloping them, and grooming, and trimming, with the misery of the tasselled bridle before and the fear of the knotted whip behind, until more than half of them were dead. Nevertheless, every age extols Poh Loh for his skill in managing horses.

Now I regard government of the empire from quite a different point of view.

The people have certain natural instincts;—to weave and clothe themselves, to till and feed themselves. These are common to all humanity, and all are agreed thereon. Such instincts are called "Heaven-sent."

And so in the days when natural instincts prevailed and men moved quietly and gazed steadily. At that time, there were no roads over mountains, nor boats, nor bridges over water. All things were produced, each for its own proper sphere. Birds and beasts multiplied; trees and shrubs grew up. The former might be led by the hand; you could climb up and peep into the raven's nest. For then man dwelt with birds and beasts, and all creation was one. There were no distinctions of good and bad men. Being all equally without knowledge, their virtue could not go astray. Being all equal without evil desires, they were in a state of natural integrity, the perfection of human existence.

But when sages appeared, tripping people over charity and fettering with duty to one's neighbour, doubt found its way into the world. And then with their gushing over music and fussing over ceremony, the empire became divided against itself.

From Mystic, *Moralist and Social Reformer*, translated by Herbert A. Giles, London, 1889
* Arthur Waley, *Three Ways of Thought in Ancient China* , Doubleday Anchor Edition, pp. 115.
** Wm. Theodore de Bary, ed., *Sources of Chinese Tradition* , pp. 79.

Horses live on dry land, eat grass and drink water. When pleased, they rub their necks together. When angry, they turn round and kick up their heels at one other. Thus far only do their natural dispositions carry them. But bridled and bitted, with a plate of metal on their foreheads, they learn to cast vicious looks, to turn the head to bite, to resist, to get the bit out of the mouth or the bridle into it. And thus their natures become depraved,—the fault of Poh Loh.

In the days of Ho Hsu the people did nothing in particular when at rest, and went nowhere in particular when they moved. Having food, they rejoiced; having full bellies, they strolled about. Such were the capacities of the people. But when the sages came to worry them with ceremonies and music in order to rectify the form of government, and dangled charity and duty to one's neighbour before them in order to satisfy their hearts,—then the people began to develop a taste for knowledge and to struggle one with the other in their desire for gain. This was the error of the sages.

21

China: Government and the People

The emperor of China was the Son of Heaven but he was also responsible for how he used his power. Joseph Needham, one of the foremost authorities on Chinese science and culture, outlines the relationship between the emperor and his people.

Discussion Questions

1. What was the Chinese emperor held responsible for?

2. On what conditions did the emperor hold the mandate from Heaven to rule?

3. Was the Chinese ruler subject to a form of "democracy?"

In addition to the respect entertained by the emperor for the people, was the deeply based respect for authority which throughout the ages was felt by them. The Emperor was the Son of Heaven (T'ientzu). He had a mandate from Heaven to rule "all under Heaven;" but this was something very unlike the divine right of kings in Europe. The Emperor's right was conditional. In ancient times he was held personally responsible for the prosperity of the country, in particular for securing the right sort of weather for agriculture. As high priest of the cosmos as well as king, he offered sacrifices on behalf of the whole people, securing the blessing of Heaven not only by them but also by himself behaving in the way which Heaven approved. By Heaven's mandate he ruled as long as his rule was good. But if his rule degenerated, natural calamities such as floods and earthquakes would come as warnings, and rebels would arise to claim the mandate. If there emerged a successful pretender to the throne,

From Joseph Needham, *Within the Four Seas: The Dialogue of East and West* , pp. 41-42. Copyright 1969 by University of Toronto Press, Toronto. Reprinted with permission.

or a new and more powerful dynasty, it was always held that the previous imperial house had forfeited the mandate from Heaven by not behaving in the way appropriate to imperial rule. Thus the dual function of priest and king evoked in the Chinese people a very deeply based respect for authority. It generated the idea that a government is not simply a thing which has been created by a man, not something which has come about because one man is more powerful than another, but that it is part of a certain cosmic order.

22

China: The Civil Service

The "Stars in Heaven" was the term applied to the officials who were part of the Chinese civil service system. Although the examinations used to select officials were initiated during the early Han dynasty in the 2nd century BC, the system evolved over time to absorb the entire government bureaucracy. By the Tang and Song dynasties it reached its full flower, not to be eliminated until the end of the Manchu (Qing) dynasty early in the 20th century (the last examinations were given in 1906). Its embodiment in the Song dynasty has been called the most representative and best functioning governmental system of any traditional society, comparing favorably with the modern American system. This reading describes the internal workings of this most remarkable form of government.

Discussion Questions

1. The Chinese bureaucracy has been called a "meritocracy." What did this mean? How does this aspect of the system compare with the modern American system?

2. How were the officials selected? Would this work in a modern society? Should it?

3. Why was the system designed in the manner it was?

4. Why do you think it lasted as long as it did—over 2100 years?

5. Would you call this a "representative" form of government? Who was represented and who did the representing?

6. What was the relationship between the bureaucracy and the emperor, whom they were supposed to serve?

Both the general administration and the censorial agencies of the traditional government were staffed chiefly with men originally selected for state service on the basis of their individual merits as demonstrated in competitive, public, written examinations, which tested their grasp of classical and historical literature and especially of Confucian philosophical principles, and their ability to apply the precepts and precedents of the past to either timely or timeless political and ethical problems, and to do so in good literary style. Having once entered state service with such a background, they were regularly shifted from one post to another, rated on their performances, and cautiously promoted step by step into steadily more responsible and prestigious echelons of government. They were classical scholars, historians, moralists, poets, essayists, and calligraphers. They were not professional specialists in any particular branch of administration, except as they gained on-the-job experience; and they were not expected to think of themselves as professional bureaucrats. They were genteel, right-minded men, proven so in examinations and in service; and their principal responsibility was to conserve and exemplify the religiophilosophical principles on which Chinese civilization was based. The longevity and the general conservatism of the traditional state system are due primarily to its domination by such men.

The abolition of feudalism in the third century B.C. set the stage for the emergence of this civil service system in Chinese government but did not automatically bring it to full flower. Through the Han era and for some centuries thereafter, the men who dominated the government were in large part direct or indirect representatives of powerful, wealthy "great families" which maintained aristocratic traditions and privileges. Newcomers to the state service were generally appointed on the basis of recommendations submitted by existing officials. But such nominees began to be subjected to qualifying written examinations in the second century B.C., and the notion gradually developed that educational achievement was a better basis for appointment than social status and contacts. In T'ang times, in the eighth century, the full transition from aristocracy to "meritocracy" finally came about, and from then on the typical successful civil servant was the examination graduate.

In its fullest development the civil service examination system functioned as follows. Every year educational intendants representing the provincial governments traveled about their jurisdictions giving examinations to the students in state-supported schools and to private scholars who presented themselves. Those who came up to the educational intendants' standards were given titles certifying them as state-recognized men of talents, or literati. They were thus entitled to wear distinctive costumes, their families were granted certain tax exemptions, they were honored as local heroes, they became confidants and social equals of local officials, their views on private and public matters were heard with respect, and they were sought after as tutors of the next generation.

Passing the local examination qualified a man to participate in provincial-level examinations in competition with candidates from all over the province, often numbering several thousand. These examinations were prepared, proctored, and graded by high-ranking scholar-officials sent out from the central government. The candidates faced a grueling ordeal: three full days of writing examinations, spaced over a week. Those who passed were very few, perhaps one in twenty; and the passers became provincial heroes overnight. They were given new titles, new costumes, and new privileges. They could be considered for low-ranking governmental appointments, and their new status need not be renewed at intervals. They were assured of social and economic success.

To be certain of a fully successful career in government, one more hurdle had to be surmounted. This was an empire-wide metropolitan examination conducted at the national capital several months after the various provincial examinations every third year. It also stretched out over a week, but was even more difficult, and those who passed were still relatively few, totaling two or three or perhaps four hundred. The graduates (generally called *chin-shih*) had a final ordeal, a palace examination presided over by the emperor himself; but this was a brief examination for the sole purpose of ranking all of the *chin-shih* in order of their excellence, and no one failed.

All new *chin-shih*, and especially those who ranked first, second, and third in the final list, were lionized both at court and in their home towns to a degree that even all-American athletes of our time would envy. They had been accepted into the fraternity of supreme literate to whom the state looked for leadership, with prestige and access to power and wealth that no other group in society could aspire to. Winning such status was the ideal goal of every filial son, and having a son or a grandson win such status was the dream of every father.

For all its glory, becoming a *chin-shih* merely opened the door to a civil service career. Graduates became part of the pool of literati from which the Ministry of Personnel called men to fill official vacancies when they occurred. All posts in the officialdom were ranked on a scale of eighteen degrees, ranging

from 9b at the bottom to 1a at the top; and all qualified civil servants were comparably ranked, new graduates naturally falling low in the scale. When a 6b post fell vacant, an unassigned 6b official was assigned to it. His performance was evaluated by his administrative superiors at the end of three, then of six, and finally of nine years on the job; and he was also evaluated irregularly by touring censorial officials. All these evaluations went into the records of the Ministry of Personnel, which retained a man in one post and in one rank up to a maximum of nine years or demoted or promoted him as circumstances warranted. Progress up the ladder of ranks, through a succession of varied posts, was normally slow and erratic, so that those few officials who ultimately emerged into the top echelon of highest ranking officials who were the executive advisers to the throne ordinarily attained such distinction when they were full of years and experience, widely acclaimed for their erudition and probity, and sufficiently awesome to deserve respect and deference from even the most arrogant emperor.

The great prestige of the civil officialdom throughout the last millenium of the empire was based in considerable part on the traditional Chinese respect for learning, but it also derived from very real power exercised by the officialdom. The civil service was largely self-regulating. It conducted its own recruitment examinations. Although all appointments within the service were made by the emperor, he was customarily bound to accept nominations from the Ministry of Personnel or, in the case of very high-ranking posts to choose one of two or three qualified men nominated by the Ministry. Moreover, although the emperor established state policies, the size of the empire and the complexity of its affairs made him almost totally dependent on the factual information and recommendations provided by the officialdom, which thus tended to limit the alternatives among which the emperor could choose in his policy decisions. The fact that the emperor, as Son of Heaven, had unchallengeable power to punish any official on any pretext in any way was, to be sure, a restraint on the officialdom's sense of independence. But, on the other hand, emperors of the most despotic inclinations had to realize that there were clear limits beyond which they dared not antagonize the officialdom or any substantial segment of it. The civil service, in short, had become a relatively autonomous and self-perpetuating power bloc in the state system. The emperor had no choice but to share his power with it and to accept the principles on which it insisted the state must function.

23

China: The Four Classes

In this selection, Dun J. Li describes the class structure of China as it was traditionally conceived under the auspices of a Confucian valuation system.

Discussion Questions

1. How did the Chinese class structure differ from the modern American one? Do you think it was better?

2. Why did the Chinese value scholars so highly? Do we today?

3. Are merchants as contemptible as this structure implies? Where do they rank in our society? Why?

4. How do the Chinese and modern American social structures represent different values?

Customarily the Chinese spoke of their society as composed of four classes: the scholars, the farmers, the artisans, and the merchants. The scholars were given the highest status because they performed what the Chinese regarded as the most important function: the transmission of the ancient heritage and the personification of Chinese virtues. The farmers' standing was second only to the scholars because they were the primary producers, feeding and clothing the nation. The artisans processed what the farmers had produced, and their function was not regarded as so essential as that of the farmers. At the bottom of the social scale were the merchants whom the Chinese regarded as outright exploiters, making profits from what others had produced or processed and contributing nothing themselves. Two other classes were often added to the four described above. One was the soldiers, whose role of burning and killing was very distasteful to the Chinese. Since they destroyed valuable things in society, their standing was inferior to that of merchants. The other class was the so-called "mean people", consisting of domestic slaves, prostitutes, entertainers, and members of lowly professions such as barbers. There was a distinct prejudice against these people even though their numbers were quite small.

A more accurate classification of the Chinese people, some might think, was advanced by Mencius some 2,300 years ago. He asserted that in an ideal society there were two kinds of people: the educated who ruled and the uneducated who were the ruled. Of the four classes mentioned above, all but the scholars would belong in the ruled category. Among them it was often difficult to say who had the highest standing in fact if not in theory. As in most societies, so in China, income often crossed over the established social barriers and became an important determinant of social prestige—but it occupied only an ancillary role not the crucial one. For example, it is true that a great landlord had more prestige than a wealthy merchant, but a shopkeeper was not regarded as inferior to a small, independent farmer, and he was definitely seen as superior to a tenant farmer. Yet the "official" position of the merchant was usually enough to discourage a man of talent from joining their ranks.

While the difference between farmers, artisans and merchants was relatively small in actual life situations, there was no question that scholars towered above them all in prestige and popular esteem. There were several reasons for this. First, because there was no established religion, China did not have an officially recognized priestly class. Yet functions that are traditionally clerical in other societies have to be performed by somebody. The teaching of morals was such a function and in China the Confucian scholars were in the best position to perform this. Secondly, the ultimate goal of almost all scholars was to acquire a position in the government—no higher prestige could be found than that of an imperial minister. And since government officials were in fact selected from the scholars, all scholars shared the prestige that went with government position. A third reason was the difficulty in learning the Chinese written language. Unless he was a born genius, the learner would spend a considerable portion of his life just learning to write in an acceptable style. Most people simply did not have the time to do this, so literacy and learning were limited to a few. Like all commodities, learning commanded a high price when it was difficult to obtain.

Li, Dun J., *The Ageless Chinese*, 3rd edition, © 1979, pages 354–355. Reprinted by permission of Pearson Education, Inc., Upper Saddle River, NJ.

24

China: The Yellow Millet Dream

This brief reading is important because it is indicative of the Chinese system of social values, or what we would call success in life.

Discussion Questions

1. When the poor peasant dreams of "making it" in his society what specifically does he dream?

2. What is the role of the old Daoist in the story?

One evening in A.D.731 a poor peasant and an old Taoist called Liu met together in an inn on the road to Han-tan. In order to forget how hungry they were, they started to chat while the innkeeper prepared a bowl of gruel for their dinner. The peasant spoke of the cares and anxieties of his poverty-stricken life, but when the strange old man offered him a curious porcelain pillow, scarcely had he laid his weary head upon it than he was transported to a wonderful land of dreams, where he possessed a house of his own, was married to a daughter of one of the best families, was rich, looked up to, and respected, and who had passed the civil service examinations with distinction. After filling a number of important posts, he was appointed governor of the capital, and in this capacity, conquered an army of barbarians. As a reward the emperor made him a minister; but a rival faction was successful in its plot to bring about his downfall, and his headlong plunge from the heights of power to the depths of a dungeon nearly ended in his being decapitated. Only at the last minute did he escape execution, and he was then restored to office and given a title to make up for the injustice he had suffered.

From Etienne Balazs, *Chinese Civilization and Bureaucracy*, trans. by H. M. Wright. Copyright 1964, Yale University Press.

His five sons, all high officials, provided him with numerous descendants, and he had come to the point of contemplating retirement, happy to end his days in peace, and looking forward to a final resting place with his ancestors, when he suddenly wakened to find himself once again in the vile inn, where the pot of gruel was still heating on the stove, and the old Taoist was smiling at him and saying, with a wink: "That's the way life passes, quick as a flash."

25

Chinese Technology

Invention/Discovery	Column 1	Column 2
Row cultivation of crops	6C B.C.	2,200
Iron plow	6C B.C.	2,200
Efficient horse collar	3C B.C.	1,000
Recognition of sunspots	4C B.C.	2,000
Accurate map-making	2C A.D.	1,300
Discovery of solar wind	6C A.D.	1,400
Mercator projection	10C A.D.	600
Cast iron	4C B.C.	1,700
Steel	2C B.C.	2,000
Deep drilling for natural gas	1C B.C.	1,900
Belt-drive	1C B.C.	1,400
Water power	1C A.D.	1,200
Suspension bridge	1C A.D.	1,800
Chain-drive	976 A.D.	800
Underwater salvage operations	11C A.D.	800
Lacquer, the first plastic	13C B.C.	3,200
Petroleum & Nat. gas as fuel	4C B.C.	2,300
Paper	2C B.C.	1,400
Wheelbarrow	1C B.C.	1,300
Fishing reel	3C A.D.	1,400
Stirrup	3C A.D.	300
Porcelain	3C A.D.	1,700
Biological pest control	3C A.D.	1,600
Umbrella	4C A.D.	1,200
Matches	577 A.D.	1,000
Chess	6C A.D.	500
Brandy & Whisky	7C A.D.	500
Mechanical clock	725 A.D.	585
Movable type printing	8C A.D.	700
Block printing	1045 A.D.	400
Playing cards	9C A.D.	500
Paper money	9C A.D.	850

Contd...

Adapted from Robert Temple, *The Genius of China*, Simon and Schuster, New York, 1986.

Invention/Discovery	Column 1	Column 2
Spinning wheel	11C A.D.	200
Circulation of the blood	6C B.C.	1,800
Circadian rhythms in human body	2C B.C.	2,150
Endocrinology	2C B.C.	2,100
Vitamin deficiency diseases	3C A.D.	1,600
Diabetes disc. by urinalysis	7C A.D.	1,000
Use of thyroid hormone	7C A.D.	1,250
Immunology (smallpox)	10C A.D.	800
Decimal system	14C B.C.	2,300
Negative numbers	2C B.C.	1,700
Using algebra in geometry	3C A.D.	1,000
Refined value of pi	3C A.D.	1,200
The first compasses	4C B.C.	1,500
Hexagonal structure of snowflakes	2C B.C.	1,800
Seismograph	130 A.D.	1,400
Spontaneous combustion	2C A.D.	1,500
Kite	5C B.C.	2,000
Parachute	2C B.C.	2,000
Hot-air balloons	2C B.C.	1,400
Rudder	1C A.D.	1,100
Paddle-wheel boat	SC A.D.	1,000
Chem, warfare (gas,etc.)	4C B.C.	2,300
Gunpowder	9C A.D.	300
Flame-thrower	10C A.D.	1,000
Multi-stage rockets	14C A.D.	600

Column 1—When China achieved this
Column 2—Number of years before Europe achieved this

26

Chinese Worldview

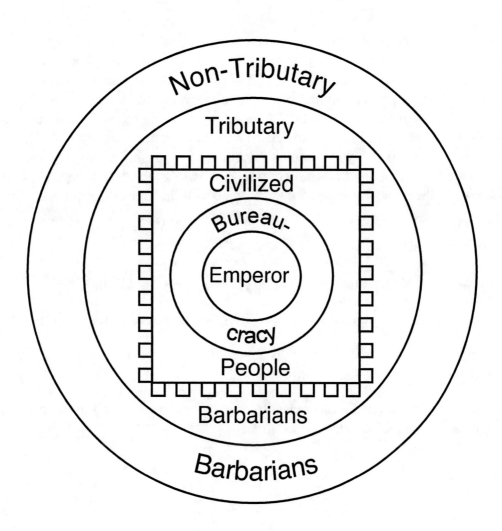

27

China: "Novissima Sinica"

This selection reflects the thinking of the German philosopher and mathematician Wilhelm Leibnitz, who in 1697 published the essay, "Novissima Sinica," or "Latest News of China." From his admiring tone it is clear that China was considered a rich, sophisticated civilization, one that could teach the West a few lessons. At the same time, the Europeans approached the Chinese, and other cultures, from a position of ethnocentrism, that is, with the firm belief that European institutions and beliefs were superior to all others. As you read this selection, look for those Chinese institutions and practices that Leibnitz finds most attractive, as well as the comments that Leibnitz makes about the comparable position of European civilization at the time.

Discussion Questions

1. What does Leibnitz think are the strong points of each civilization?

2. What lessons does Leibnitz think the Europeans could learn from the Chinese?

3. Even though "Novissima Sinica" is about China, what evidence can you cite that reflects Leibnitz' ethnocentrism?

4. What are the reasons Leibnitz cites for his argument that the Chinese should win the "golden apple" of civilization?

I consider it a singular plan of the fates that human cultivation and refinement should today be concentrated, as it were, in the two extremes of our continent, in Europe and in Tschina (as they call it), which adorns the Orient as Europe does the opposite edge of the earth.

Now the Chinese Empire, which challenges Europe in cultivated area, and certainly surpasses her in population, vies with us in many other ways in almost equal combat, so that now they win, now we. But what should I put down first by way of comparison? To go over everything, even though useful, would be lengthy and is not our proper task in this place. In the useful arts and in practical experience with natural objects we are, all things considered, about equal to them, and each people has knowledge which it could with profit communicate to the other. In profundity of knowledge and in the theoretical disciplines we are their superiors. For besides logic and metaphysics, and the knowledge of things incorporeal, which we justly claim as peculiarly our province, we excel by far in the understanding of concepts which are abstracted by the mind from the material, i.e., in things mathematical, as is in truth demonstrated when Chinese astronomy comes into competition with our own. The Chinese are thus seen to be ignorant of that great light of the mind, the art of demonstration, and they remained content with a sort of empirical geometry, which our artisans universally possess. They also yield to us in military science, not so much out of ignorance as by deliberation. For they despise everything which creates or nourishes ferocity in men, and almost in emulations of higher teachings of Christ (and not, as some wrongly suggest, because of anxiety), they are averse to war.

They would be wise indeed if they were alone in the world. But as things are, it comes back to this, that even the good must cultivate the arts of war, so that the evil may not gain power over everything. In these matters, then, we are superior.

But who would have believed that there is on earth a people who, though we are in our view so very advanced in every branch of behavior, still surpass us in comprehending the precepts of civil life? Yet now we find this to be so among the Chinese, as we learn to know them better. And so if we are their equals in the industrial arts, and ahead of them in contemplative sciences, certainly they surpass us (though it is almost shameful to confess this) in practical philosophy, that is, in the precepts of ethics and politics adapted to the present life and use of mortals. Indeed, it is difficult to describe how beautifully all the laws of the Chinese, in contrast to those of other peoples, are directed to the achievement of public tranquility and the establishment of social order, so that men shall be disrupted in their relations as little as possible.

In a vast multitude of men they have virtually accomplished more than the founders of religious orders among us have achieved within their own narrow ranks. So great is obedience toward superiors and reverence toward elders, so religious, almost, is the relation of children toward parents, that for children to contrive anything violent against their parents, even by word, is almost unheard of, and the perpetrator seems to atone for his actions even as we make a parricide pay for his deed. Moreover, there is among equals, or those having little obligation to one another, a marvelous respect, and an established order of duties. To us, not enough accustomed to act by reason and rule, these smack of servitude; yet among them, where these duties are made natural by use, they are observed gladly.

The Reverend Fathers Gerbillon and Bouvet, French Jesuits, along with four others, who are mathematicians from the Academie des Sciences, have been sent to the Orient to teach the monarch, not only the mathematical arts, but also the essence of our philosophy. But if this process should be continued I fear that we may soon become inferior to the Chinese in all branches of knowledge. I do not say this because I grudge them new light; rather I rejoice. But it is desirable that they in turn teach us those things which are especially in our interest: the greatest use of practical philosophy and a more perfect manner of living, to say nothing now of their other arts. Certainly the condition of our affairs, slipping as we are into ever greater corruption, seems to me such that we need missionaries from Chinese who might teach us the use and practice of natural religion, just as we have sent them teachers of revealed theology. And so I believe that if someone expert, not in the beauty of goddesses but in the excellence of peoples, were selected as judge, the golden apple would be awarded to the Chinese, unless we should win by virtue of one great but super human thing, namely, the divine gift of the Christian religion.

28

Japan: Geography and Culture

All societies are influenced by their geographical situation. The point is often made that both China and Japan were to one extent or another "isolated"—China by deserts, mountains and seas; Japan by its island location. The following selection discusses the effect of "isolation" on the evolution of Japanese history.

Discussion Questions

1. What characteristics of Japanese society does the author link to its geographical situation?

2. Are there any differences between Japan and Britain as island nations?

3. What was the relationship between Japan and China in the pre-modern period?

It is never safe to state unequivocally that certain geographic influences have produced certain specific cultural characteristics. One can so easily find other places in the world where similar geographic conditions had no such result . . . One geographic factor, however, stands out as a dominant one in Japan's cultural heritage and an element which distinguished Japan from all the other older civilized lands of the world. This factor is isolation. In pre-modern times, no other important group of people consciously participating in the rich culture of the Eurasiatic land mass lived so far removed from all the other civilized peoples. The straits between Japan and Korea are five times as wide as the Strait of Dover, which have had a significant influence in shaping England's history and the character of her people. The distance between Japan and China, the homeland of her civilization, is even greater. Only in recent centuries have peoples of the civilized world come to live at greater distances from the Eurasiatic land mass and by that time vastly improved techniques of navigation and, now, instantaneous communications have wiped out the factor of isolation.

One obvious influence of isolation on Japan has been the creation of a highly homogeneous race of people there, and what is more important, a very homogeneous culture. The Japanese as a race are primarily a Mongoloid people, as are all the major groups of that part of the world. They differ no more from Koreans and Chinese than Englishmen differ from Frenchmen or Germans....

The Japanese, like all other peoples, are a blend of many diverse elements, but their exact racial composition is, in fact, little known and makes less difference. What is important is that there have been no significant additions of blood to the Japanese race for well over a thousand years. They have had plenty of time to become thoroughly mixed together to form as unified a people as exist anywhere in the world.

Their culture, though repeatedly enriched by foreign borrowings, has also had time to become extremely homogeneous, particularly during the two centuries of Tokugawa isolation (1600-1868). The Japanese culture of the mid-nineteenth century was perhaps more uniform than the culture of any European country of comparable size. Some observers feel that the Japanese have achieved greater cultural uniformity throughout the length and breadth of the land and throughout the vertical stratifications of their society than has ever been achieved in a country of Japan's size, and they compare Japanese cultural homogeneity to that of a primitive tribe....

Another clear influence of geographic isolation on Japan has been the infrequency of close contacts with foreign lands throughout Japanese history and, conversely, the heavy waves of influence from abroad whenever close contacts did exist. Most other parts of the civilized world have been subject throughout history to a continuous stream of foreign influences, so steady and uniform as to have gone virtually unnoticed most of the time. In Japan, however, the very paucity of such influences at most times meant that, whenever close contacts were feasible, there was likely to be heavy, almost frantic borrowing from abroad....

...The alternation of periods of rapid borrowing and comparative isolation has resulted in a clear awareness on the part of the Japanese of the whole process of borrowing.

They have been so acutely conscious of this wholesale learning from abroad during certain periods in the past and have so emphasized this aspect of their history that they have helped create the myth that they are nothing but a race of copiers....

While forced by geographic isolation to develop alone more of their own civilization than have most other peoples, they have been overwhelmed with the concept of borrowing from abroad and have, in compensation, emphasized supposed "native" elements more than other nations have.... It is as if the French were obsessed with the idea that only that part of their culture which was derived from pre-Roman Gaul was native and labeled all else as foreign borrowings. Such an attempt would send the British back to the Druids for their native culture. Naturally, in Japan, it has resulted in a ridiculous emphasis on the primitive and an impossible search in the only hazily known early years of Japanese history for some mysterious source for Japan's later greatness. It has also been the background for a great deal of mystical nonsense about Japan and the Japanese, which has been used to justify a host of absurd political and social doctrines and a particularly virulent brand of nationalistic dogma.

There has been, however, one very good result of Japan's consciousness of foreign borrowing. The Japanese take the process of acculturation for granted and are not afraid or ashamed, when circumstances dictate to borrow whatever they need from abroad. Without the historical example of Japan's heavy borrowing from China a thousand years earlier, it might have been more difficult than it was for the Meiji leaders to conceive the idea of repatterning Japan on Western models and to justify this course of action both to themselves and to their people. Certainly that concept came much more slowly and far more painfully to most of the other peoples of Asia. The Chinese, with their age-old belief that China was the unique civilized land of the world, surrounded by barbarians of varying degrees of inferiority and loyalty to China, found it particularly difficult to accept the idea that anything important could be learned from the West, much less that the Chinese economic and political structure would have to be remade on Western lines. But in Japan it seemed evident that, if the land had been converted into a miniature China in the seventh and eighth centuries, it could be made into an Asiatic England or Germany in the nineteenth. Even today, the concept of another great transformation, dictated this time from abroad, seems less strange and less repugnant to the Japanese than it would to most peoples.

By and large, isolation may have had the curious effect of making the Japanese more ready to accept new things from abroad than were most other peoples—and they certainly have always demonstrated a great enthusiasm for the new—but at the same time isolation has also permitted them to cling more persistently than other nations to the old. The result is Japan's particular form of conservatism, which is the cherishing of the old and outmoded while enthusiastically embracing the new. Perhaps because international friction was less intense in this isolated corner of the globe, and the struggle for cultural survival, therefore, less acute, many of the outmoded aspects of Japanese civilization could continue to exist side by side with the new. The Imperial institution itself is a case in point. The Emperors of Japan by the twelfth century had become incongruous survivals of an earlier age. Almost anywhere else in the world the struggle for national survival would have forced the abandonment of such outgrown forms, but Japanese isolation permitted the coexistence of the old political institutions in theory and the new feudal institutions in practice.... The Japanese are like us in that they are always ready and even eager to adopt the new, but at the same time they are very unlike us in their strong tendency to preserve the old and outmoded.

29

Japan and China

During its early history, Japan was impressed by the achievements of Chinese civilization. While China borrowed relatively little from other cultures, Japan decided, for various reasons, to borrow extensively from China while at the same time trying to maintain the uniqueness of its own values (sometimes called *kokutai*.) This period of borrowing lasted from approximately 538 CE to about 784 CE. One of the highlights of this period was the Seventeen Article Constitution of 604 CE.

Discussion Questions

1. Was Japan trying to become a miniature version of China?

2. In what ways did Japan try to distinguish itself from China?

3. What elements of Chinese civilization were particularly attractive to the Japanese?

The Impact of Chinese Civilization

Japan's cultural borrowing from China began in earnest with the introduction of Buddhism in 552 A.D. (or 538 A.D.) and continued uninterrupted until the end of the Nara period in 784.

If any single term can characterize these two and a half centuries, they may be called a period of "Chinese fixation."[1] When Prince Shotoku wanted to curtail the powers of the great clans and enhance the prestige of the imperial institution, it was to China that he looked for inspiration. When the Taika reforms were initiated, the systems of land tenure and taxation then in force in Tang provided the necessary models. So was the case with the enactment of the Taiho-Yoro codes which set the administrative and criminal codes to be used for generations to come. The Chinese language was employed in early historical writings, along with an attempt to write history in the indigenous tongue which used Chinese characters phonetically. Just as the Chinese people utilized history to create a new self-image, "the holistic ideal, the belief in moral dynamics and a pronounced Sino-centrism,"[2] so did the Japanese people create an image of a "divine land." History was also used to claim legitimacy for the reigning imperial line. In the imperial court, news from China brought by returned students was eagerly received. Men and women consulted the *yin-yang* philosophy, the five elements and the twelve horary signs to look into the future and to find answers to perplexing day-to-day problems. Exchanging poems written in Chinese was considered the highest accomplishment in polite society, and the Chinese poems were also employed to impress upon foreign visitors Japan's cultural advancement at diplomatic receptions. The *Kaijuso*, the first compilation of Chinese poems, completed in 751 and thus ahead of the *Manyoshu*, typified Japan's adulation of China. The first permanent capital of Nara, with its broad-patterned avenues, temples and pagodas, was a replica of the imperial city of Changan. Even in selecting the location of this new capital, the Chinese geomancy was carefully consulted.

However, indigenous elements did not completely submerge when Japan imported Chinese thought and institutions. From the very beginning there was an attempt for adaptation, not mere imitation. This trend was most clearly discernible in the Taiho-Yoro codes. As long as the Chinese institutions provided a means for enhancing the power of the imperial court, they were eagerly adopted. In the case of propagation of Buddhism, the same attitude held true, It was less for spiritual pursuit, and more for political gains that Buddhism was encouraged. This pragmatic approach and the coalescence of indigenous and alien elements were in large measure responsible for the success of Japan's cultural importation.

In their cultural borrowing, the Japanese were selective. They chose only those features of Chinese civilization most advantageous to Japan. For example, Japanese Buddhism was deeply influenced by the Buddhism of northern

---

From *Japan: A Documentary History* by David Lu. M.E. Sharpe, NY, 1997. Reprinted by permission of the author.

[1] compare the term "American fixation," used by Professor E. O. Reischauer in his *Japan, Past and Present* (New York, Knopf, 1964), p. 256.

[2] Arthur F. Wright, "On the Uses of Generalization in the Study of Chinese History," in Louis Gottschalk, ed., *Generalization in the Writing of History* (Chicago: University of Chicago Press, 1963), p. 43.

dynasties, which maintained a strong belief in the ability of Buddhism to protect the state. This was, of course, attractive to Japanese rulers. On the other hand, in literature, a far stronger influence came from southern China, independently of Buddhism in that region.

The relatively long period of time that Japan was subjected to Chinese cultural influence also helped facilitate successful assimilation of this alien civilization. What was once foreign became familiar through a process of education and continuous exposure. Generation after generation of Japanese elite who were educated in Chinese classics shared a certain set of common values with their Chinese counterpart. Meanwhile, the difficulty of sea passage prevented the two groups from becoming homogeneous in their life-styles and world views. The Japanese elite retained their perspectives distinct from the Chinese ones. Yet to the Japanese elite the Chinese values and Japanese perspectives were both part of their heritage. Gradually they created a culture distinctly their own, naturalizing Chinese elements to suit the requirements of the new age in Japan. Then in later years, the culture thus nurtured by the elite would seep downward to become the heritage of the common man.

The Regency of Prince Shotoku

The flowering of civilization and new confidence in the fate of the imperial institution characterized the regency of Prince Shotoku which lasted from 593 to 622. In 604, the Prince promulgated the so-called Seventeen Article Constitution.[3] It was not a basic law in the sense that we understand the term today, but was more of a series of moral precepts and injunctions. In this stylistically correct Chinese writing, the "constitution " quotes freely from Confucian, Legalist, Taoist and Buddhist works. There were unabashed claims for the right of the sovereign (Articles 3 and 12), and attempts to create a "bureaucracy" to replace she domination of the great clans (Articles 7, 8, 11, 13, and 15).

Some of these professed aims remained mere pious wishes, and there is no evidence indicating that the Constitution was ever shown to the great clans whose powers it intended to curtail. However, it could have remained within the imperial household and set the standards which were to be pursued. In this sense, Prince Shotoku paved the way for the eventual success of the Taika reforms. The era of Prince Shotoku coincided with the period when the term Tenno was first used to denote the reigning sovereign. The word ten corresponds to the Chinese tian or heaven, and no to huang or ruler. Thus the term Tenno was endowed with new sacerdotal and political significance. He was not a mere emperor who ruled by the mandate of heaven, but one who was coeval with heaven.

The Seventeen Article Constitution, 604 A.D[4] Summer, 4th month, 3rd day [12th year of Empress Suiko, 604 A.D.]. The Crown Prince personally drafted and promulgated a constitution consisting of seventeen articles, which are as follows:

I. Harmony is to be cherished[5] and opposition for opposition's sake must be avoided as a matter of principle. Men are often influenced by partisan feelings, except a few sagacious ones. Hence there are some who disobey their lords and fathers, or who dispute with their

---

[3] There is a controversy over the authorship of the Constitution, with some evidence pointing to the fact that Prince Shotoku was not its real author. However, the document does reflect the *zeitgeist* which governed the reign of Prince Shotoku, and it can be read in that context.

[4] *Nihon Shoki (Chronicles of Japan)* in *Kokushi Taikei (Major Compilation of National History)*, new and enlarged ed., vol. 1, no. 2 (Tokyo: Yoshikawa Kobunkan, 1967), pp. 142–146.

[5] From the *Analects* of Confucius, I, 12.

neighboring villages. If those above are harmonious and those below are cordial, their discussion will be guided by a spirit of conciliation, and reason shall naturally prevail. There will be nothing that cannot be accomplished.

II. With all our heart, revere the three treasures.[6] The three treasures, consisting of Buddha, the Doctrine, and the Monastic Order, are the final refuge of the four generated beings,[7] and are the supreme objects of worship in all countries. Can any man in any age ever fail to respect these teachings? Few men are utterly devoid of goodness, and men can be taught to follow the teachings. Unless they take refuge in the three treasures, there is no way of rectifying their misdeeds.

III. When an imperial command is given, obey it with reverence. The sovereign is likened to heaven, and his subjects (*yatsuko*) are likened to earth. With heaven providing the cover and earth supporting it, the four seasons proceed in orderly fashion, giving sustenance to all that which is in nature. If earth attempts to overtake the functions of heaven, it destroys everything. Therefore when the sovereign speaks, his subjects must listen; when the superior acts, the inferior must follow his examples. When an imperial command is given, carry it out with diligence. If there is no reverence shown to the imperial command, ruin will automatically result.

IV. The ministers (*machikimitachi*) and functionaries (*tsukasa tsukasa*) must act on the basis of decorum,[8] for the basis of governing the people consists of decorum. If the superiors do not behave with decorum, offenses will ensue. If the ministers behave with decorum, there will be no confusion about ranks. If the people behave with decorum, the nation will be governed well of its own.

V. Cast away your ravenous desire for food and abandon your covetousness for material possessions. If a suit is brought before you, render a clear-cut judgment. … Nowadays, those who are in the position of pronouncing judgment are motivated by making private gains, and as a rule, receive bribes. Thus the plaints of the rich are like a stone flung into water, while those of the poor are like water poured over a stone.[9] Under these circumstances, the poor will be denied recourses to justice, which constitutes a dereliction of duty of the ministers (*yatsuko*).

VI. Punish that which is evil and encourage that which is good. This is an excellent rule from antiquity. Do not conceal the good qualities of others, and always correct that which is evil which comes to your attention. Consider those flatterers and tricksters as constituting a superb weapon for the overthrow of the state, and a sharp sword for the destruction of people. Smooth-tongued adulators love to report to their superiors the errors of their inferiors; and to their inferiors, castigate the errors of their superiors. Men of this type lack loyalty to the sovereign and have no compassion for the people. They

---

[6] *Ratna-traya* in Sanskrit, referring to Buddha, *Dharma*, and *Sangha*. The *sangha* stands for the community of seekers united by their knowledge and right conduct.

[7] Catastro yonayah is Sanskrit. The four processes of being born from eggs, from a womb, moisture-bred, or formed by metamorphosis (e.g., butterflies from caterpillars), hence, all creatures.

[8] The Chinese word li is variously translated decorum, courtesy, proper behavior ceremony, and gentlemanly conduct.

[9] The plaints of the rich meet with no resistance, while those of the poor have no efficacy.

are the ones who can cause great civil disorders.

VII. Every man must be given his clearly delineated responsibility. If a wise man is entrusted with office, the sound of praise arises. If a wicked man holds office, disturbances become frequent.... In all things, great or small, find the right man, and the country will be well governed. On all occasions, in an emergency or otherwise, seek out a wise man, which in itself is an enriching experience. In this manner, the state will be lasting and its sacerdotal functions will be free from danger. Therefore did the sage kings of old seek the man to fill the office, not the office for the sake of the man.

VIII. The ministers and functionaries must attend the court early in the morning and retire late. The business of the state must not be taken lightly. A full day is hardly enough to complete work, and if the attendance is late, emergencies cannot be met. If the officials retire early, the work cannot be completed.

IX. Good faith is the foundation of righteousness, and everything must be guided by good faith. The key to the success of the good and the failure of the bad can also be found in good faith. If the officials observe good faith with one another, everything can be accomplished. If they do not observe good faith, everything is bound to fail.

X. Discard wrath and anger from your heart and from your looks. Do not be offended when others differ with you. Everyone has his own mind, and each mind has its own leanings. Thus what is right with him is wrong with us, and what is right with us is wrong with him. We are not necessarily sages, and he is not necessarily a fool. We are all simply ordinary men, and none of us can set up a rule to determine the right from wrong.... Therefore, instead of giving way to anger as others do, let us fear our own mistakes. Even though we may have a point, let us follow the multitude and act like them.

XI. Observe clearly merit and demerit and assign reward and punishment accordingly. Nowadays, rewards are given in the absence of meritorious work, punishments without corresponding crimes. The ministers, who are in charge of public affairs, must therefore take upon themselves the task of administering a clear-cut system of rewards and punishments.[10]

XII. Provincial authorities (*mikotomochi*)[11]. or local nobles (*kuni no miyatsuko*) are not permitted to levy exactions on the people. A country cannot have two sovereigns, nor the people two masters. The people of the whole country must have the sovereign as their only master. The officials who are given certain functions are all his subjects. Being the subjects of the sovereign, these officials have no more right than others to levy exactions on the people.

XIII. All persons entrusted with office must attend equally to their functions. If absent from work due to illness or being sent on missions, and work for that period is neglected, on their return, they must perform their duties conscientiously by taking into account that which transpired

---

[10] Here is an indication of the influence of the Chinese legalist, Han Fei Zi.

[11] Other renditions for the term *mikotomochi* are *kuni no tsukasa* and *kohishi* (provincial governors). However, the system of provincial governors was not established during the time of Prince Shotoku's regency. Thus, Article XII gives some credence to the theory that Prince Shotoku was not the author of the "Constitution."

before and during their absence. Do not permit lack of knowledge of the intervening period as an excuse to hinder effective performance of public affairs.

XIV. Ministers and functionaries are asked not to be envious of others. If we envy others, they in turn will envy us, and there is no limit to the evil that envy can cause us. We resent others when their intelligence is superior to ours, and we envy those who surpass us in talent. This is the reason why it takes five hundred years before we can meet a wise man, and in a thousand years it is still difficult to find one sage. If we cannot find wise men and sages, how can the country be governed?

XV. The way of a minister is to turn away from private motives and to uphold public good. Private motives breed resentment, and resentful feelings cause a man to act discordantly. If he fails to act in accord with others, he sacrifices public interests for the sake of his private feelings. When resentment arises, it goes counter to the existing order and breaks the law. Therefore it is said in the first article that superiors and inferiors must act in harmony. The purport is the same.

XVI. The people may be employed in forced labor only at seasonable times.[12] This is an excellent rule from antiquity. Employ the people in the winter months when they are at leisure. However, from spring to autumn, when they are engaged in agriculture or sericulture, do not employ them. Without their agricultural endeavor, there is no food, and without their sericulture, there is no clothing.

XVII. Major decisions must not be made by one person alone, but must be deliberated with many. On the other hand, it is not necessary to consult many people on minor questions. If important matters are not discussed fully there may always be fear of committing mistakes. A thorough discussion with many can prevent it and bring about a reasonable solution.

---

[12] From the *Analecats* of Confucius, 1, 5

30

Religions: Comparison of Cultural Perspectives

The most deeply embedded values of even modern societies frequently stem from religious ideas originating thousands of years ago. The following table presents, in comparative form, some of the core views of the three most important cultural traditions which emerged in Eurasia: the Western (Middle Eastern), the Indian and the Chinese (East Asian). Each of the three traditions includes particular religions. For example, the Middle Eastern includes Judaism, Zoroastrianism, Christianity and Islam; the Indian includes Hinduism, Jainism and Buddhism; and the East Asian includes Confucianism, Taoism and Shinto. In this table and the readings that follow, the student should attempt to discover the general ideas which characterize each broad tradition, as well as the distinctions between individual religions within these traditions.

The table below emphasizes mankind's role in the world as expressed through the capacities of will and reason.

Discussion Questions

1. Are any of the three more conducive to what you conceive as "happiness?"

2. Which would most likely be ecologically sound?

3. In which would individualism most likely be important?

4. Would a stress on science or technology be particularly compatible with any of the three?

Comparison of Cultural Perspectives

WESTERN	INDIAN	CHINESE
WILLFULNESS	*WILL-LESSNESS*	*WILLINGNESS*
1. Encourage desire	1. Suppress desire	1. Accept desire
2. Encourage activity	2. Encourage passivity	2. Accept both
3. Idealize progress	3. Idealize eternity	3. Idealize the present
4. Change is pursued	4. Change is illusory	4. Change is natural
5. Idealize productivity	5. Idealize non-attachment	5. Idealize enjoyment of life
6. Ideal of willfulness is God	6. Ideal of will-lessness is Brahman	6. Ideal of willingness is the Tao
7. Change nature	7. Transcend nature	7. Accept nature
8. Ideal person is the producer	8. Ideal person is the yogin	8. Ideal person is the one who follows his own nature
REASON	*INTUITION*	*APPREHENSION*
1. Emphasize distinctions (either a or not-a)	1. Overcome distinctions (neither a nor not-a)	1. Accept distinctions (both a and not-a)
2. Objectivity	2. Subjectivity	2. "Apparent"-cy
3. Ideal person is the specialist	3. Ideal person is the sannyasin	3. Ideal person enjoys life

31

India's Odd, Enduring Patchwork

Discussion Questions

1. What kinds of diversity can be found in India?

2. Can India legitimately be called a "nation"?

3. What binds Indians together as "Indians"?

India's Odd, Enduring Patchwork

A year ago, when India celebrated the 49th anniversary of its independence from British rule, H. D. Deve Gowda, then the Prime Minister, stood at the ramparts of New Delhi's 16th-century Red Fort and delivered the traditional Independence Day address to the nation in Hindi, India's "national language."

"Eight other prime ministers had done exactly the same thing 48 times before, but what was unusual this time was that Mr. Gowda, a southerner from the state of Karnataka, spoke to the country in a language of which he scarcely knew a word. Tradition and politics required a speech in Hindi, so he gave one—the words having been written out for him in his native Kannada script, in which they, of course, made no sense.

Such an episode is almost inconceivable elsewhere, but it represents the best of the oddities that help make India India. Only in India could a country be ruled by a man who does not understand its "national language." Only in India, for that matter, is there a "national language" half the population does not understand. And only in India could this particular solution be found to enable the Prime Minister to address his people.

One of Indian cinema's finest singers, K. J. Yesudas, sang his way to the top of the Hindi music charts with lyrics in that language written in the Malayalam script for him, but to see the same practice elevated to the prime ministerial address on Independence Day was a startling affirmation of Indian pluralism.

We are all minorities in India. A typical Indian stepping off a train, a Hindi-speaking Hindu man from the Gangetic plain state of Uttar Pradesh, might cherish the illusion that he represents the "majority community," to use an expression much favored by the less industrious of our journalists. But he does not. As a Hindu he belongs to the faith adhered to by some 82 percent of the population, but a majority of the country does not speak Hindi, a majority does not hail from Uttar Pradesh, and if he were visiting, say, the state of Kerala, he would discover that a majority there is not even male.

Worse, this archetypal Hindu has only to mingle with the polyglot, polychrome crowds thronging any of India's main railway stations to realize how much of a minority he really is. Even his Hinduism is no guarantee of majorityhood, because his caste automatically places him in a minority as well. If he is a Brahmin, 90 percent of his fellow Indians are not; if he is a Yadav (one of the intermediate castes), 85 percent of Indians are-not, and so on.

Or take language. The Constitution of India recognizes 17 languages today, but in fact there are 35 Indian languages, each spoken by more than a million people—and these are languages with their own scripts, grammatical structures and cultural assumptions, not just dialects (and if we're to count dialects, there are more than 22,000).

No language enjoys majority status in India. Thanks in part to the popularity of Bombay's cinema, Hindi is understood, if not always well spoken, by nearly half the population of India, but it is in no sense the language of the majority. Indeed, its locutions, gender rules and script are unfamiliar to most Indians in the south or northeast.

Ethnicity further complicates the matter. Most of the time, an Indian's name immediately reveals where he is from and what his mother tongue is. When we introduce ourselves we are advertising our origins. Despite some intermarriage among the elites in the cities, Indians still largely remain endogamous, and a Bengali is easily distinguished from a Punjabi.

Such differences among Indians often are stronger than what they may have in common. A Brahmin from Karnataka shares his Hindu faith with a Kurmi from Bihar, but the two diverge completely when it comes to physical appearance, dress, social customs, food, language and political objectives.

At the same time, a Tamil Hindu would feel that he has far more in common with a Tamil Christian or Muslim than with, say, a Jat from Haryana with whom he formally shares the Hindu religion.

So pluralism emerges from the very nature of the country; it is a choice made inevitable by India's geography, reaffirmed by its history and reflected in its ethnography. Indian nationalism is a rare animal indeed. It is not based on language (since we have at least 17 or 35, depending on whether you follow the Constitution or the ethnolinguists).

It is not based on geography, (The "natural" frontiers of India nave been hacked by the partition of 1947.) It is not based on ethnicity. (Indian Bengalis and Punjabis, for instance, have more in common with Bangladeshis and Pakistanis than with other Indians.) And it is not based on religion. (We are home to almost every faith known to mankind, and Hinduism—a religion without a national organization, established church or ecclesiastical hierarchy—exemplifies our diversity more than our common cultural heritage.) Indian nationalism is the nationalism of an idea, the idea of an ever-ever land that is greater than the sum of its contradictions.

This land imposes no narrow conformities on its citizens; you can be many things and one thing. You can be a good Muslim, a good Keralite and a good Indian all at once.

So the idea of India is of one land embracing many. It is the idea that a nation may accommodate differences of caste, creed, color, culture, cuisine, costume and custom, and still be a nation—so long as democracy insures that none of these differences are decisive in determining an Indian's opportunities.

Our founding fathers wrote a constitution that gave passports to their ideals, but violent secessionism has plagued several border states, as some minority groups, like Assam and Punjab, have sought to subtract themselves from the Indian ideal on religious, regional or ethnic grounds.

Some of these troubles continue, but in a land of minorities, no struggle affects all Indians. The power of electoral numbers has been able to lessen caste discrimination. Indeed, last month, for the first time, an "untouchable" was elected as President of India.

For the rest of the world, wary of the endless multiplication of sovereignties, hesitant before the clamor for self-determination echoing in a hundred different dialects, anxious about murderous new fundamentalisms and unconvinced that every sub-nationality is worthy of support, there may be something to be said for the Indian idea.

If the overwhelming majority of a people share the political will for unity, if they wear the dust of a shared history on their foreheads and the mud of an uncertain future on their feet, and if they realize they are better off living in Kozhikode or Kanpur dreaming the same dreams as those in Kohlapur or Kohima, a nation exists, celebrating diversity and freedom. That is the India that has emerged in the last 50 years, and it is well worth celebrating.

32

India: Caste

One of the typical features of traditional societies was their rather rigid and hierarchical social structure. In most of these societies there was relatively little chance to change one's social status; social mobility was not the norm. Frequently the situation of one's birth was considered to be part of a cosmic order, as if one had been assigned a role to play in this life. The attitude one should have toward this role was to be one of acceptance rather than rejection; after all, who wants to reject the cosmic order? (On the more practical level, the fact that these were societies of limited resources and wealth restricted most people's possibilities in life.)

The caste system as it evolved in India may be seen as an extreme variation of this general theme.

Most people view caste as being relatively simple—there are four groups (brahmins, kshatriya, vaishya, and sudra) and one "outgroup", the untouchables. Actually it is much more complex than that since it is really the *jati* (sometimes called sub-caste) that is the most important unit in the system. So the dominant feature of the caste system is its complexity, a complexity which has led to tremendous adaptability over the centuries.

In the following selection, Taya Zinkin illustrates the baffling nature of the caste system and ponders its amazing durability.

Discussion Questions

1. What makes caste so difficult to explain to an outsider?

2. What features of caste make it resistant to change?

3. Why would an Indian see caste as a system of justice rather than injustice?

4. What are the positive aspects of caste for the individual?

It is much easier to say what caste is not than what caste is.

It is not class. In every caste there are educated and uneducated, in most there are rich and poor, well-born and ordinarily born. Most members of the upper classes are in fact from the upper castes, most members of the lowest classes are in fact Untouchables; but the correlation is not necessary, and is diminishing.

It is not colour, though the old pundits sometimes talk as if it was. A Brahmin is no less a Brahmin if he is born jet-black; an Untouchable is no whit less untouchable if she happens to be fair. Most upper-caste people are fairer than most lower-caste people of their region, and fairness is a quality much valued in a bride; but one cannot tell caste from colour. People refuse to take water from Untouchables, not from black men. White men, after all, are Untouchables.

It is not Aryan and non-Aryan, or conqueror and conquered. The Aryans never seem to have penetrated to the East or the South of India; the Brahmins of the South are the highest of high-caste men, but they are not on record as having conquered anybody. Tribal chieftains have become Kshatryas—the second, or warrior, caste—in quite recent times; and most of South India has no Kshatryas at all. Its ruling castes, Mahrattas, Reddis, Nairs, etc., are not even twice-born.

It is not occupation. Many occupations, mostly of artisans, are overwhelmingly identified with particular castes, but the main occupation, agriculture, is open to all, and many castes have priests who are not Brahmins. There have always been soldiers who were not Kshatryas, government servants have always been of various castes. One does not have to be a Bania to be a trader, though many traders are in fact Banias. Sainthood is open even to Untouchables.

It is not even exclusively Hindu or exclusively Indian. Outside India, one finds caste in a more or less rudimentary form in Ceylon, Bali and Pakistan, Untouchables in Japan. Within India, Jews, Christians and Muslims are affected by it in varying degrees. Goans, Catholics for four hundred years, were still twenty years ago looking for brides and bridegrooms of their pre-conversion castes for their children. A Rajput Muslim will not marry his daughter to a non-Rajput Muslim. Some South Indian churches have always made their ex-Untouchables sit apart from their ex-Brahmins. There are Rajput Muslims in Uttar Pradesh who will not let an Untouchable into their house. Even the microscopic Jewish community of Cochin is divided into black, brown and white, and a black Jew is not allowed into the white synagogue.

Nor does the present caste structure bear much relation to the traditional four "Varnas," the Brahmin (priest), the Kshatrya (warrior), the Vaishya (trader), and the Sudra (cultivator or artisan), with the Untouchable outside them all. The Brahmin, it is true, is still here; but who is a Kshatrya, who a Sudra and who a Vaishya is often more than doubtful; the odd castes that were supposed to have arisen from various mixtures of the original four seem mostly not to exist; and even those most unquestioned of Kshatryas, the Rajputs, may well have no connexion with the original Kshatryas, but be the descendants of Scythian invaders or tribal chieftains. Some Untouchability, too, is probably the result not of the original structure of Hindu society, but of the Buddhist horror of taking life.

The average Hindu who observes caste does so because he believes his religion wants him to. Yet caste was never revealed as the Ten Commandments were revealed. The Rigveda, most ancient and sacred of Hindu Hymns, does not talk of the caste system. As Professor Rapson points out, even "the four castes are only definitely mentioned in one of the latest hymns" and it is only in the late Yajur-Veda "that the four great social divisions are hardening into castes and a number of mixed castes are also mentioned." The Mahabharata, India's equivalent of the Iliad, has clear cases where heroes and heroines were able to change their caste because of their deeds or their looks. . . .

Caste may perhaps at the beginning have been very like the eighteenth-century German division of society into princes, nobles, burghers, peasants and serfs between whom no marriage other than morganatic was possible. Even before that, there may have been, in the Mohendjo-Daro civilisation, occupational guilds with separate rituals which may have hardened into caste; and the significance of the Aryans may have been, not their conquest of North West India, but their combination of ritual with the best explanation of the universe the Indian subcontinent had known. The Brahmin held both the magical and the intellectual keys to the mystery of life; naturally his position was unassailable, even in societies like those of South India, where he must have begun as a missionary; one may compare perhaps the position of the Brahmin to that of the Church in medieval Germany.

Whatever the past, in the present caste is a complete system covering every facet of life. "Caste," says K. M. Panikkar, "is a comprehensive system of life, a religion rather than a changing social order, and the rigidity with which its rules are enforced would put to shame even the Great Inquisition."

The simplest definition of caste is Wint's: "A caste is a group of families whose members can marry with each other and can eat in each other's company without believing themselves polluted." To this one must add that each of these groups has its place in a hierarchy. It is above, or below, or equal to, every one of the others; and in theory everybody knows where each group comes.

These groups bear no relation to the original four. There are today hundreds of castes; and even these hundreds are not all. The fundamental unit is indeed not the caste, but the sub-caste, which is the normal unit, for instance, for marriage, and which, as Mayer points out, "while clearly part of a larger unit, has enough properties in common to be a caste-like unit." And of sub-castes there are thousands. It is said that there are over two thousand amongst Brahmins alone (including some Untouchable Brahmin sub-castes like the seventh and eleventh day Brahmins), and Mr. Jagjivan Ram, the Harijan Minister for Railways in the Central Government, once told me that he had counted five hundred and sixty-three Untouchable sub-castes.

It is sub-caste which give Hindu society its character, its typical fragmentation into small groups within which people live and outside which they, and especially the women, keep their contacts to a minimum.

Because Hindu society is thus split into groups, and because it is rural, living in villages each of which is very much a separate unit, it has been a very unchanging society, one much governed by custom and the religious form of custom ritual. Moreover, since the sub-caste is the basic unit, custom and ritual vary from sub-caste to sub-caste....

Diet may differ, marriage and funeral customs may differ, the particular Gods chosen for home worship or the time of worship for general gods may differ. The whole feel and atmosphere of life in one caste is different from that of another; the Brahmin abhors meat and alcohol and violence; the Rajput glories in all three. Even between closely-related sub-castes, one gets this sense of difference. I remember a Deshastha Brahmin girl graduate, who had married a Chitpavan Brahmin graduate, explaining to me how revolutionary a step she had taken for love; how strange she had felt at first in her mother-in-law's house. She and her mother-in-law were both of Maharashtrian Brahmin sub-castes and from the same town; yet, somehow, all their traditions of running a house were different; they even prepared the same vegetables in different ways.

One may put the same point in more anthropological terms. As Professor Dube says, "Hinduism as practised in the village is a religion of prescribed rituals covering all the major crises of life . . . and ritual differs in the practice of different castes." Professor Majumdar puts it rather more widely: "Caste provides codes of conduct and deviations from these are not generally tolerated." And one must always remember that in a society of custom and ritual the terms "codes of conduct" and "prescribed rituals" cover everything, not just how one prays or whether one blasphemes, but how one cooks, when one washes, to whom one talks, even how one dresses. The habits of castes differ from one another in something of the same way that the conventions do; but on a much wider scale.

Caste not only governs how one lives one's life. It also fixes the place in society in which one lives it. Every caste and sub-caste has its ranking. This ranking is fixed neither by wealth nor education nor the ownership of land, but by the taking of water. One takes water from one's equals and one's superiors; one does not take water from one's inferiors unless it is in a brass pot. Water in a clay pot is the main test. But there are others. Food is divided into two categories, pakka khana and kachchha khana. Pakka khana includes such foods as dishes made with clarified butter from flour and sugar, mostly sweetmeats, kachchha khana is cooked in water and/or salt, mostly the staple diet. One takes pakka khana from a wider range of inferiors than kachchha khana, roughly from the same people from whom one takes water in a clay pot. Where the upper castes draw their lines helps to establish the precedence of the lower castes between themselves....

The structure is not quite as rigid as it looks. That the Brahmin is at the top and the Sweeper near the bottom everybody is agreed. In between there can be arguments. A caste can try to go up in the world by changing its custom, trying to imitate the Joneses of caste, or by changing its name and hoping that its origins will be forgotten, or it may claim to be Kshatrya. Many such attempts of course fail; but when a caste is important in a region, or when it increases its education and political power, they may well succeed. The Kayasths of Northern India have now established themselves among the top castes in Bengal, despite the occasional snigger about a Patna High Court decision establishing them as Sudras, but in the U. P. they are still Sudras. And if the Mahrattas wish to call themselves Kshatryas, few in Maharashtra will say them nay. . . .

Untouchability, though the phenomenon by which caste is best known outside India, differs in degree rather than in kind from other caste restrictions. Throughout the caste structure, there are certain relations one does not have with one's inferiors, like marriage, which one does not have with anybody except a member of one's sub-caste, and even within one's sub-caste, one may not be able to marry within a particular section—a member of one's own gotra (gotra includes all these descended from the same ancestor) with Brahmins, or of one's own clan amongst Rajputs. For the Untouchables these restrictions are extended. Not only does one not take water from them, they may not even take water from the same well. Not only does one not marry them, they may not even enter the temple or the house or stroll on the main village streets.

Even their cattle may often not drink from the same pool as a Brahmin's.

Moreover the Untouchables themselves are not all the same. One Untouchable caste may well apply to the Untouchable caste below it much the same restrictions that are applied to it by the Touchable castes above. I was mobbed by Chamars when I persuaded a Dom to draw water from their well—my first contact with Untouchability within Untouchability: A Mang may not draw water from a Mahar well and all over India Chamars will have nothing to do with Sweepers.

Caste is a way of life which divides society into small groups, each of which lives in a rather different way from the rest. Because of these differences, because the groups are so tiny, and because the most important relations of life, above all marriage, take place within them, the groups have great power over their members, and thus great power of survival. To break caste is to cut oneself off from one's group, which means from one's family, from one's friends, and from all those who live exactly as one does oneself, and one cuts oneself off without any hope of being adopted by another group—one is ostracised by everybody in one's own group and will not even be accepted by a lower group. Thus the ostracised Brahmin cannot become a warrior or even an Untouchable since one has to be born within one's caste; only if he finds others from his own caste who have also been ostracised can he once more belong to a group because in a sect a new sub-caste has been created.

Through this great complex of rules, holding it together and giving it meaning, runs the idea of pollution. One does not do that which pollutes. It is the fear of pollution which provides both the sanction for much of what one does and does not do in one's daily life. Still more it is this fear which limits one's contacts outside one's caste. A man is as free with men of other castes as the rules of pollution permit; where pollution begins, contact stops. . . .

Before going into the way in which caste, sub-castes and Untouchability work, it is necessary to remember that the whole system is based upon a combination of the irrevocability of status fixed by birth and rebirth. One is born into a particular station from which there is no escape in this life, for it is the consequence of one's deeds in a past existence. If one performs the duties of one's station conscientiously one may be reborn in a better station, or—supreme bliss—not be reborn at all. Under such circumstances vertical mobility such as we find in the West, where the successful coalminer's son goes to Eton, marries a duke's daughter and ends in the House of Lords, is meaningless. The Hindu equivalent would be the good Sweeper who sweeps humbly, does not mind being treated like a pariah and is reborn a Brahmin.

In caste society, there can be no wedding for Prince Charming and Cinderella, for marriage must be within caste. In India Cinderella's parents would have been as horrified by their love as Prince Charming's; Untouchable parents have been known to kill their daughter for disgracing them by running away with a Rajput prince.

So long as everybody thus accepts his position in life as deserved, the system provides the same stability, security and warmth as there was in Europe when men still thought their station God-given. The sub-caste provides a man with a group to which he belongs utterly, and within which all are kin or potential kin. These are the families into which he must marry, these the connexions on whose support he can count in every crisis. Within the village, moreover, the sub-castes each have their own rank in a known hierarchy. Since there is nothing people dislike as much as uncertainty, there is a great deal to be said for a system by which everybody knows exactly to whom he should pay respect and exactly from whom to expect it. If it had not afforded this satisfaction the caste system would have disintegrated long ago.

In the long turmoil that was Indian history, caste held together the fabric of society: the integrity of the village was built round the framework of caste; the survival of Hinduism under Muslim and Christian onslaughts might well have been impossible without the devotion of peasant and scholar alike to caste-customs and caste-ritual. Caste may not have revelation behind it; but it does have something even more powerful, a network of observances covering every action of daily life, from the direction in which one passes water to the length of the twig with which one cleans one's teeth. A society so governed was a society with an infinity of resistance to outside attacks.

33

Hinduism: The Education of Svetaketu

In the following selection, one of the most famous in the *Upanishads*, Uddalaka, the father, attempts to instruct his son, Svetaketu, about the self (Brahman-atman) and the nature of reality.

Discussion Questions

1. Is the physical world real?

2. What is the "self?" Is it the same thing as the "personality?"

3. What is the relationship between the individual and Brahman?

4. What are the consequences of this view for how the individual sees the world?

❝ Please, sir, tell me more about this Self."

"Be it so. Bring a fruit of that Nyagrodha tree."

"Here it is, sir."

"Break it."

"It is broken, sir."

"What do you see?"

"Some seeds, extremely small, sir."

"Break one of them."

"It is broken, sir."

"What do you see?"

"Nothing, sir."

"The subtle essence you do not see, and in that is the whole of the Nyagrodha tree. Believe, my son, that which is the subtle essence—in that have all things their existence. That is the truth. That is the Self. And that, Svetaketu, THAT ART THOU."

"Please, sir, tell me more about this Self."

"Be it so. Put this salt in water, and come to me tomorrow morning."

From *The Upanishads*, translated by Swami Prabhavananda and Frederick Manchester, the Vedanta Society of Southern California, 1948.

Svetaketu did as he was bidden. The next morning his father asked him to bring the salt which he had put in the water. But he could not, for it had dissolved. Then said Uddalaka:

"Sip the water, and tell me how it tastes."

"It is salty, sir."

"In the same way," continued Uddalaka, "though you do not see Brahman in this body, he is indeed here. That which is the subtle essence—in that have all things their existence. That is the truth. That is the Self. And that, Svetaketu, THAT ART THOU."

34

Hinduism: The Nature of God

In the Judeo-Christian-Muslim religious tradition God is defined as good and the source of all positive traits, evil stems from some other source such as the devil or one's own choices. In the Hindu tradition the picture is quite different as seen in the following selection from the *Bhagavad Gita* where Krishna describes himself as God to Arjuna.

Discussion Questions

1. What is the nature of God as described in this passage?

2. How does this view of God differ from the Judeo-Christian-Muslim image?

I pervade the entire universe in my unmanifested form. All creatures find their existence in me, but I am not limited by them. Behold my divine mystery! These creatures do not really dwell in me, and though I bring them forth and support them, I am not confined within them. They move in me as the winds move in every direction in space.

The foolish do not look beyond physical appearances to see my true nature as the Lord of all creation. The knowledge of such deluded people is empty; their lives are fraught with disaster and evil and their work and hopes are all in vain.

But truly great souls seek my divine nature. They worship me with a one-pointed mind, having realized that I am the eternal source of all. Constantly striving, they make firm their resolve and worship me without wavering. Full of devotion, they sing of my divine glory.

I am the father and mother of this universe, and its grandfather too; I am its entire support. I am the sum of all knowledge, the purifier, the syllable *Om*; I am the sacred scriptures, the Rig, Yajur, and Sama Vedas.

I am the goal of life, the Lord and support of all, the inner witness, the abode of all. I am the only refuge, the one true friend; I am the beginning, the staying, and the end of creation; I am the womb and the eternal seed.

I am heat; I give and withhold the rain. I am immortality and I am death; I am what is and what is not.

Those who worship other gods with faith and devotion also worship me, Arjuna, even if they do not observe the usual forms. I am the object of all worship, its enjoyer and Lord.

I look upon all creatures equally; none are less dear to me and none more dear. But those who worship me with love live in me, and I come to life in them.

Even a sinner becomes holy when he worships me alone with firm resolve. Quickly his soul conforms to dharma and he attains to boundless peace. Never forget this, Arjuna: no one who is devoted to me will ever come to harm.

All those who take refuge in me, whatever their birth, race, sex, or caste, will attain the supreme goal; this realization can be attained even by those whom society scorns. Kings and sages too seek this goal with devotion. Therefore, having been born in this transient and forlorn world, give all your love to me. Fill your mind with me; love me; serve me; worship me always. Seeking me in your heart, you will at last be united with me.

Discrimination, wisdom, understanding, forgiveness, truth, self-control, and peace of mind; pleasure and pain, birth and death, fear and courage, honor and infamy; nonviolence, charity, equanimity, contentment, and perseverance in spiritual disciplines—all the different qualities found in living creatures have their source in me.

I am the beginning, middle, and end of creation. Of all the sciences I am the science of Self-knowledge, and I am logic in those who debate. Among letters I am *A*; among grammatical compounds I am the dvandva. I am infinite time, and the sustainer whose face is seen everywhere.

I am death, which overcomes all, and the source of all beings still to be born. I am the

From *The Bhagavad Gita*, trans. by Eknath Easwaran, pp. 132–136 (passim), 141, 145, 146. Copyright 1985 by the Blue Mountain Center of Meditation. Reprinted by permission of Nilgiri Press, Tomales, CA.

feminine qualities: fame, beauty, perfect speech, memory, intelligence, loyalty, and forgiveness.

I am the gambling of the gambler and the radiance in all that shines. I am effort, I am victory, and I am the goodness of the virtuous.

I am the seed that can be found in every creature, Arjuna; for without me nothing can exist, neither animate nor inanimate.

35

Hinduism: Selfless Service

One of the most famous dialogues in the world's religious literature is the one between Krishna and Arjuna found in the *Bhagavad Gita*, a section of the much longer Indian epic the *Mahabharata*. It is in the *Bhagavad Gita* that the name of Krishna (an avatar of Vishnu) first appears in Hindu theology; some Indian scholars believe he might have been a genuine historical person, a kind of messiah.

Arjuna was a soldier, a member of a clan that has come to strife over their family's throne. In order to secure the throne for his brother, he must fight some of his own relatives and friends. The dialogue takes place just before the battle is to begin, when Arjuna must resolve his inner conflict between doing his duty and following his personal preferences. Essentially the *Bhagavad Gita* is Krishna's advice on how Arjuna should deal with this situation.

Discussion Questions

1. What does Krishna mean by "selfless service?"

2. What are the distinctions between what Krishna calls the ordinary person and the wise man?

3. Is Krishna describing a peculiarly Indian problem?

4. Does karma yoga have any practical application?

Arjuna:

O Krishna, you have said that knowledge is greater than action; why then do you ask me to wage this terrible war? Your advice seems inconsistent. Give me one path to follow to the supreme good.

Sri Krishna:

At the beginning of time I declared two paths for the pure heart: *jnana yoga*, the contemplative path of spiritual wisdom, and *karma yoga*, the active path of selfless service.

He who shirks action does not attain freedom; no one can gain perfection by abstaining from work. Indeed, there is no one who rests for even an instant; every creature is driven to action by his own nature.

Those who abstain from action while allowing the mind to dwell on sensual pleasure cannot be called sincere spiritual aspirants. But they excel who control their senses through the mind, using them for selfless service.

Fulfill all your duties; action is better than inaction. Even to maintain your body, Arjuna, you are obliged to act. Selfish action imprisons the world. Act selflessly, without any thought of personal profit.

At the beginning, mankind and the obligation of selfless service were created together. "Through selfless service, you will always be fruitful and find the fulfillment of your desires": this is the promise of the Creator.

Honor and cherish the devas as they honor and cherish you; through this honor and love

you will attain the supreme good. All human desires are fulfilled by the devas*, who are pleased by selfless service. But anyone who enjoys the things given by the devas without offering selfless acts in return is a thief.

The spiritually minded, who eat in the spirit of service, are freed from all their sins; but the selfish, who prepare food for their own satisfaction, eat sin. Living creatures are nourished by food, and food is nourished by rain; rain itself is the water of life, which comes from selfless worship and service.

Every selfless act, Arjuna, is born from Brahman, the eternal, infinite Godhead. He is present in every act of service. All life turns on this law, O Arjuna. Whoever violates it, indulging his senses for his own pleasure and ignoring the needs of others, has wasted his life. But those who realize the Self are always satisfied. Having found the source of joy and fulfillment, they no longer seek happiness from the external world. They have nothing to gain or lose by any action; neither people nor things can affect their security.

Strive constantly to serve the welfare of the world; by devotion to selfless work one attains the supreme goal of life. Do your work with the welfare of others always in mind. It was by such work that Janaka attained perfection; others, too, have followed this path.

What the outstanding person does, others will try to do. The standards such people create will be followed by the whole world. There is nothing in the three worlds for me to gain, Arjuna, nor is there anything I do not have; I continue to act, but I am not driven by any need of my own. If I ever refrained from continuous

From *The Bhagavad Gita*, Trans. by Eknath Easwaran, pp. 75-79. Copyright 1985 by the Blue Mountain Center of Meditation. Reprinted by permission of Nilgiri Press, Tomales, CA.

* deva - divine being—god

work, everyone would immediately follow my example. If I stopped working I would be the cause of cosmic chaos, and finally of the destruction of this world and these people.

The ignorant work for their own profit Arjuna; the wise work for the welfare of the world, without thought for themselves. By abstaining from work you will confuse the ignorant, who are engrossed in their actions. Perform all work carefully, guided by compassion.

All actions are performed by the gunas* of prakriti**. Deluded by his identification with the ego, a person thinks, "*I* am the doer." But the illumined man or woman understands the domain of the gunas and is not attached. Such people know that the gunas interact with each other; they do not claim to be the doer.

Those who are deluded by the operation of the gunas become attached to the results of their action. Those who understand these truths should not unsettle the ignorant. Performing all actions for my sake, completely absorbed in the Self, and without expectations, fight!—but stay free from the fever of the ego.

Those who live in accordance with these divine laws without complaining, firmly established in faith, are released from karma. Those who violate these laws, criticizing and complaining, are utterly deluded, and are the cause of their own suffering.

Even a wise man acts within the limitations of his own nature. Every creature is subject to prakriti; what is the use of repression? The senses have been conditioned by attraction to the pleasant and aversion to the unpleasant. Do not be ruled by them; they are obstacles in your path.

It is better to strive in one's own dharma than to succeed in the dharma of another. Nothing is ever lost in following one's own dharma, but competition in another's dharma breeds fear and insecurity.

Arjuna:

What is the force that binds us to selfish deeds, O Krishna? What power moves us, even against our will, as if forcing us?

Sri Krishna:

It is selfish desire and anger, arising from the guna of rajas***; these are the appetites and evils which threaten a person in this life.

Just as a fire is covered by smoke and a mirror is obscured by dust, just as the embryo rests deep within the womb, knowledge is hidden by selfish desire—hidden, Arjuna, by this unquenchable fire for self-satisfaction, the inveterate enemy of the wise.

Selfish desire is found in the senses, mind, and intellect, misleading them and burying the understanding in delusion. Fight with all your strength, Arjuna! Controlling your senses, conquer your enemy, the destroyer of knowledge and realization.

The senses are higher than the body, the mind higher than the senses; above the mind is the intellect, and above the intellect is the Atman. Thus, knowing that which is supreme, let the Atman rule the ego. Use your mighty arms to slay the fierce enemy that is selfish desire.

---

* guna – quality

** prakriti – nature

*** rajas – energy, passion

36

Buddhism: Introduction

In the following selection, Walpola Rahula introduces the reader to the general outlines of Buddhism.

Discussion Questions

1. How was the Buddha different from the leaders of other religions?

2. What is the role and position of the individual in Buddhism?

3. Why are freedom and tolerance important?

4. How does Buddhism differ from other religions?

5. Is it important to label religions as one thing or another?

6. Is faith important in Buddhism?

The Buddhist Attitude of Mind

Among the founders of religions the Buddha (if we are permitted to call him the founder of a religion in the popular sense of the term) was the only teacher who did not claim to be other than a human being, pure and simple. Other teachers were either God. or his incarnatlons in different forms or inspired by him. The Buddha was not only a human being; he claimed no inspiration from any god or external power either. He attributed all his realization, attainment and achievements to human endeavour and human intelligence. We can call the Buddha a man par excellence. He was so perfect in his 'human-ness' that he came to be regarded later in popular religion almost as 'super-human'.

Man's position according to Buddhism, is supreme...Man is his own master, and there is no higher being or power that sits in judgment over his destiny.

'One is one's own refuge, who else could be the refuge?' said the Buddha. He admonished his disciples to 'be a refuge to themselves', and never to seek refuge in or help from anybody else. He taught, encouraged and stimulated each person to develop himself and to work out his own emancipation for man has the power to liberate himself from all bondage through his own personal effort and intelligence. The Buddha says: 'You should do your work, for the Tathagatas[1] only teach the way.' If the Buddha is to be called a 'saviour' at all, it is only in the sense that he discovered and showed the Path to liberation, Nirvana. But we must tread the Path ourselves.

It is on this principle of individual responsibility that the Buddha allows freedom to his disciples. In the Mahaparinibbanasutta the Buddha says that he never thought of controlling the Sangha (Order of Monks), nor did he want the Sangha to depend on him. He said that there was no esoteric doctrine in his teaching, nothing hidden in the 'closed-fist of the teacher' or to put it in other words, there never was anything 'up his sleeve'.

The freedom of thought allowed by the Buddha is unheard of elsewhere in the history of religions. This freedom is necessary because, according to the Buddha, man's emancipation depends on his own realization of Truth, and not on the benevolent grace of a god or any external power as a reward for his obedient good behaviour.

According to the Buddha's teaching, doubt is one of the five Hindrances to the clear understanding of Truth and to spiritual progress (or for that matter to any progress). Doubt, however is not a 'sin', because there are no articles of faith in Buddhism. In fact there is no 'sin' Buddhism, as sin is understood in some religions. The root of all evil is ignorance and false views. It is an undeniable fact that as long as there is doubt, perplexity, wavering , no progress is possible. It is also equally undeniable that there must be doubt as long as one does not understand or see clearly. But in order to progress further it is absolutely necessary to get rid of doubt. To get rid of doubt one has to see clearly.

---

[1] Tathagata lit. means 'One who has come to Truth', i.e., 'One who has discovered Truth'. This is the term usually used by the Buddha referring to himself and to the Buddhas in general.

There is no point in saying that one should not doubt or one should believe. Just to say 'I believe' does not mean that you understand and see. When a student works on a mathematical problem, he comes to a stage beyond which he does not know how to proceed, and where he is in doubt and perplexity. As long as he has this doubt, he cannot proceed. If he wants to proceed, he must resolve this doubt. And there are ways of resolving that doubt. Just to say 'I believe', or 'I do not doubt' will certainly not solve the problem. To force oneself to believe and to accept a thing without understanding is political, and not spiritual or intellectual.

Not only the freedom of thought, but also tolerance allowed by the Buddha is astonishing to the student of the history of religions. Once in Nalanda a prominent and wealthy householder named Upali, a well-known lay disciple of Nigantha Nataputta (Jaina Mahavira), was expressly sent by Mahavira. himself to meet the Buddha and defeat him in argument on certain points in the theory of Karma, because the Buddha's views on the subject were different from those of Mahavira.[2] Quite contrary to expectations, Upali, at the end of the discussion, was convinced that the views of the Buddha were right and those of his master were wrong. So he begged the Buddha to accept him as one of his lay disciples. But the Buddha asked him to reconsider it, and not to be in a hurry, for 'considering carefully is good for well-known men like you'. When Upali expressed his desire again, the Buddha requested him to continue to respect and support his old religious teachers as he used to.

In the third century B.C., the great Buddhist Emperor Asoka of India, following this noble example of tolerance and understanding, honoured and supported all other religions in his vast empire. In one of his Edicts carved on rock, the original of which one may read even today, the Emperor declared:

'One should not honour only one's own religion and condemn the religions of others, but one should honour others' religions for this or that reason. So doing, one helps one's own religion to grow and renders service to the religions of others too. In acting otherwise one digs the grave of one's own religion and also does harm to other religions. Whosoever honours his own religion and condemns other religions, does so indeed through devotion to his own religion, thinking "I will glorify my own religion". But on the contrary, in so doing he injures his own religion more gravely. So concord is good: Let all listen, and be willing to listen to the doctrines professed by others'.

We should add here that this spirit of sympathetic understanding should be applied today not only in the matter of religious doctrine, but elsewhere as well.

This spirit of tolerance and understanding has been from the beginning one of the most cherished ideals of Buddhist culture and civilization. That is why there is not a single example of persecution or the shedding of a drop of blood in converting people to Buddhism, or in its propagation during its long history of 2500 years. It spread peacefully all over the continent of Asia, having more than 500 million adherents today. Violence in any form, under any pretext whatsoever, is absolutely against the teaching of the Buddha.

The question has often been asked: Is Buddhism a religion or a philosophy? It does not matter what you call it. Buddhism remains what it is whatever label you may put on it. The label is immaterial. Even the label 'Buddhism' which we give to the teaching of the Buddha is of little importance. The name one gives it is inessential.

---

[2] Mahavira, founder of Jainism, -was a contemporary of the Buddha, and was 'probably a few years older than the Buddha.

What's in a name ? That which we call a rose,
By any other name would smell as sweet.

In the same way Truth needs no label: it is neither Buddhist, Christian, Hindu nor Moslem. It is not the monopoly of anybody. Sectarian labels are a hindrance to the independent understanding of Truth, and they produce harmful prejudices in men's minds.

This is true not only in intellectual and spiritual matters, but also in human relations. When, for instance, we meet a man, we do not look on him as a human being, but we put a label on him, such as English, French, German, American, or Jew, and regard him with all the prejudices associated with that label in our mind. Yet he may be completely free from those attributes which we have put on him.

People are so fond of discriminative labels that they even go to the length of putting them on human qualities and emotions common to all. So they talk of different 'brands' of charity, as for example, of Buddhist charity or Christian charity, and look down upon other 'brands' of charity. But charity cannot be sectarian; it is neither Christian, Buddhist, Hindu nor Moslem. The love of a mother for her child is neither Buddhist nor Christian: it is mother love. Human qualities and emotions like love, charity, compassion, tolerance, patience, friendship, desire, hatred, ill-will, ignorance, conceit, etc., need no sectarian labels; they belong to no particular religions.

To the seeker after Truth it is immaterial from where an idea comes. The source and development of an idea is a matter for the academic. In fact, in order to understand Truth, it is not necessary even to know whether the teaching comes from the Buddha, or from anyone else. What is essential is seeing the thing, understanding it.

Almost all religions are built on faith—rather 'blind' faith it would seem. But in Buddhism emphasis is laid on 'seeing', knowing, understanding and not faith or belief. In Buddhist texts there is a word which is usually *saddha* translated as 'faith' or 'belief. But *saddha* is not 'faith' as such, but rather 'confidence' born out of conviction. In popular Buddhism and also in ordinary usage in the texts the word *saddha*, it must be admitted, has an element of 'faith' in the sense that it signifies devotion to the Buddha, the Dhamma (Teaching) and the Sangha (The Order).

However you put it, faith or belief as understood by most religions has little to do with Buddhism.

The question of belief arises when there is no seeing—seeing in every sense of the word. The moment you see, the question of belief disappears. If I tell you that I have a gem hidden in the folded palm of my hand, the question of belief arises because you do not see it yourself. But if I unclench my fist and show you the gem, then you see it for yourself, and the question of belief does not arise. So the phrase in ancient Buddhist texts reads : 'Realizing, as one sees a gem (or a myrobalan fruit) in the palm'.

It is always a question of knowing and seeing and not that of believing. The teaching of the Buddha is qualified as *ehi-passika*, inviting you to 'come and see', but not to come and believe.

This was more and more appreciated at a time when Brahmanic orthodoxy intolerantly insisted on believing and accepting their tradition and authority as the only Truth without question. Once a group of learned and well-known Brahmins went to see the Buddha and had a long discussion with him. One of the group, a Brahmin youth of 16 years of age, named Kapathika, considered by them all to be an exceptionally brilliant mind, put a question to the Buddha:

'Venerable Gotama, there are the ancient holy scriptures of the Brahmins handed down along the line by unbroken oral tradition of texts. With regard to them, Brahmins come to the absolute conclusion: "This alone is Truth, and everything else is false". Now, what does the Venerable Gotama say about this ?'

The Buddha inquired: 'Among Brahmins is there any one single Brahmin who claims that he personally knows and sees that "This alone is Truth, and everything else is false"?'

The young man was frank, and said: 'No'.

'Then, is there any one single teacher, or a teacher of teachers of Brahmins back to the seventh generation, or even any one of those original authors of those scriptures, who claims that he knows and he sees: "This alone is Truth, and everything else is false" ?'

'No.'

'Then, it is like a line of blind men, each holding on to the preceding one; the first one does not see, the middle one also does not see, the last one also does not see. Thus, it seems to me that the state of the Brahmins is like that of a line of blind men.'

Then the Buddha gave advice of extreme importance to the group of Brahmins: 'It is not proper for a wise man who maintains (lit. protects) truth to come to the conclusion: "This alone is Truth, and everything else is false".'

Asked by the young Brahmin to explain the idea of maintaining or protecting truth, the Buddha said: 'A man has a faith. If he says "This is my faith" cannot proceed to the absolute conclusion: "This alone is Truth, and everything else is false".' In other words, a man may believe what he likes, and he may say 'I believe this'. So far he respects truth. But: because of his belief or faith, he should not say that what he believes is alone the Truth, and everything else is false.

The Buddha says: "To be attached to one thing (to a certain view) and to look down upon other things (views) as inferior— this the wise men call a fetter.'

It is quite clear that the Buddha's teaching is meant to carry man to safety, peace, happiness, tranquillity, the. attainment of Nirvana. The whole doctrine taught by the Buddha leads to this end. He did not say things just to satisfy intellectual curiosity. He was a practical teacher and taught only those things which would bring peace and happiness to man.

37

Buddhism: Irrelevant Issues

The Buddha discouraged wasting one's efforts on issues not related to the understanding of life as it must be lived—issues which do not lead to that perfect enlightenment which alone attains nirvana. The goal is not to be found in an afterlife, but in the here and now; debates and discussions that do not lead to this goal are to be avoided. In the first of the following selections the Buddha reminds a monk what is important and what is not; in the second selection he instructs two Brahmin priests (remember, the Buddha was a Hindu) concerning his views on Brahman-atman (called Brahma in the selection) and man's relation to it.

Discussion Questions

1. What kinds of issues are not relevant according to the Buddha?

2. Does the Buddha accept the Hindu concept of Brahman-atman? How do you explain his attitude?

Questions Which Tend Not to Edification

Thus have I heard.

On a certain occasion the Blessed One was dwelling at Savatthi in Jetavana monastery in Anathapindika's Park. Now it happened to the venerable Malunkyaputta, being in seclusion and plunged in meditation that a consideration presented itself to his mind.

Then the venerable Malunkyaputta arose at eventide from his seclusion, and drew near to where the Blessed One, was; and having drawn near and greeted the Blessed One, he sat down respectfully at one side. And seated respectfully at one side, the venerable Malunkyaputta spoke to the Blessed One as follows:

"Reverend Sir, it happened to me, as I was just now in seclusion and plunged in meditation, that a consideration presented itself to my mind, as follows: `These theories which the Blessed One has left unelucidated, has set aside and rejected,—that the world is eternal, that the world is not eternal, . . . that the saint neither exists nor does not exist after death,—these the Blessed One does not elucidate to me. I will draw near to the Blessed One and inquire of him concerning this matter. If the Blessed One will elucidate them to me, in that case will I lead the religious life under the Blessed One. If the Blessed One will not elucidate them, I will abandon religious training and return to the lower life of a layman.' "

"The religious life, Malunkyaputta, does not depend on the dogma that the world is eternal, nor on the dogma that the world is not eternal. Whether the dogma obtain, Malunkyaputta, that the world is eternal, or that the world is not eternal, there still remains birth, old age, death, sorrow, lamentation, misery, grief, and despair, for the extinction of which in the present life I am prescribing.

"Accordingly, Malunkyaputta, bear always in mind what it is that I have not elucidated, and what it is that I have elucidated. And what, Malunkyaputta, have I not elucidated? I have not elucidated, Malunkyaputta, that the world is eternal; I have not elucidated that the world is not eternal. . . . I have not elucidated that the saint neither exists nor does not exist after death. And why, Malunkyaputta, have I not elucidated this? Because, Malunkyaputta, this profits not, nor has to do with the fundamentals of religion, nor tends to aversion, absence of passion, cessation, quiescence, the supernatural faculties, supreme wisdom, and Nirvana; therefore have I not elucidated it.

"And what, Malunkyaputta, have I elucidated? Misery, Malunkyaputta, have I elucidated; the origin of misery have I elucidated; the cessation of misery have I elucidated; and the path leading to the cessation of misery have I elucidated. And why, Malunkyaputta, have I elucidated this? Because, Malunkyaputta, this does profit, has to do with the fundamentals of religion, and tends to aversion, absence of passion, cessation, quiescence, knowledge, supreme wisdom, and Nirvana; therefore have I elucidated it. Accordingly, Malunkyaputta, bear always in mind what it is that I have not elucidated, and what it is that I have elucidated."

Thus spake the Blessed One; and, delighted, the venerable Malunkyaputta applauded the speech of the Blessed One.

From Henry Clarke Warren, *Buddhism in Translations*, Harvard University Press, 1896.

38

Buddhism: The Story of Kisagotami

To some Buddhism seems to be a very pessimistic religion because it insists on looking at life directly and honestly with all of its faults, ugliness, pain and unsatisfactoriness. In the story of Kisagotami we have a famous example of this aspect of the Buddha's teachings. Compare the Buddha's response to the case of a woman who has lost her son to that of Jesus found in the Gospel according to Luke.

Discussion Questions

1. What method does the Buddha use to instruct Kisagotami about the pain of loss?

2. What lesson does Kisagotami learn?

3. How does the approach of the Buddha differ from that of Jesus?

4. What are the realistic consequences for the parties involved that will stem from these two different approaches?

Kisagotami became in the family way, and when the ten months were completed, gave birth to a son. When the boy was able to walk by himself he died. The young girl, in her love for it, carried the dead child clasped to her bosom, and went about from house to house asking if any one would give her some medicine for it. When the neighbours saw this, they said. "Is the young girl mad that she carries about on her breast the dead body of her son!" But a wise man thinking to himself, "Alas! this Kisagotami does not understand the law of death, I must comfort her," said to her, "My good girl, I cannot myself give medicine for it, but I know of a doctor who can attend to it." The young girl said, "If so, tell me who it is." The wise man continued, "Gautama can give medicine, you must go to him."

Kisagotami went to Gautama, and doing homage to him, said, "Lord and Master, do you know any medicine that will be good for my boy?" Gautama replied, "I know of some." She asked, "What medicine do you require?" He said, "I want a handful of mustard seed." The girl promised to procure it for him, but Gautama continued, "I require some mustard seed taken from a house where no son, husband, parent, or slave has died." The girl said, "Very good," and went to ask for some at the different houses, carrying the dead body of her son astride on her hip. The people said, "Here is some mustard seed, take it." Then she asked, "In my friend's house has there died a son, a husband, a parent, or a slave?" They replied, "Lady, what is this that you say! The living are few, but the dead are many." Then she went to other houses, but one said, "I have lost a son"; another, "I have lost my parents"; another, "I have lost my slave." At last, not being able to find a single house where no one had died, from which to procure the mustard seed, she began to think, "This is a heavy task that I am engaged in. I am not the only one whose son is dead. In the whole of the Savatthi country, everywhere children are dying, parents are dying." Thinking thus, she acquired the law of fear, and putting away her affection for her child she summoned up resolution and left the dead body in a forest; then she went to Gautama and paid him homage. He said to her, "Have you procured the handful of mustard seed?" "I have not," she replied, "the people of the village told me, "The living are few, but the dead are many." Gautama said to her, "You thought that you alone had lost a son; the law of death is that among all living creatures there is no permanence." When Gautama had finished preaching the law, Kisagotami was established in the reward of Sotapatti; and all the assembly who heard the law were also established in the reward of Sotapatti.

Some time afterwards, when Kisagotami was one day engaged in the performance of her religious duties, she observed the lights in the houses now shining, now extinguished, and began to reflect, "My state is like these lamps." Gautama, who was then in the Gandhakuti building, sent his sacred appearance to her, which said to her, just as himself were preaching, "All living beings resemble the flame of these lamps, one moment lighted, the next extinguished; those only who have arrived at Nirvana are at rest." Kisagotami, on hearing this, reached the stage of a Rahanda possessed of intuitive knowledge.

From Buddaghosha's Parables, trans. by Captain T. E. Rogers, Trubner & Co., London 1870.

Jesus and the Widow

Now when he came nigh to the gate of the city, behold there was dead man carried out, the only son of his mother, and she was a widow: and much people of the city was with her.

And when the Lord saw her, he had compassion on her, and said unto her, "Weep not."

And he came and touched the bier: and they that bare him stood still. And he said, "Young man, I pray unto thee, Arise."

And he that was dead sat up, and began to speak. And he delivered him to his mother.

39

Buddhism: The Boddhisattva

Around the time of Christ, there appeared in India a new form of Buddhism. It was founded on the notion that the original form (Theravada, or Hinayana) was too narrow in scope and did not offer enough opportunities for people to achieve nirvana. The key to the new Mahayana Buddhism was the belief that the chief virtue of the Buddha was compassion. Therefore, the Mahayana school developed the figure of the Boddhisattva, who, although qualified to achieve nirvana, nonetheless remained in the worldly sphere to help others attain nirvana. The Mahayanists were convinced many more would now be able to do so. Following is the oath or pledge a Boddhisattva was supposed to have taken to attain this position.

Discussion Questions

1. What are the qualities of the Boddhisattva?

2. Who else in history do you think might have taken a similar oath?

3. How do you think this concept might have contributed to the popularity of Mahayana Buddhism?

A Boddhisattva's Resolution

I take upon myself the burden of all suffering. I am resolved to do so, I will endure it. I do not turn or run away, do not tremble, am not terrified or afraid.

And why? At all costs I must bear the burdens of all beings. All beings I must set free. The whole world of living beings I must rescue, from the terrors of birth, of old age, of sickness, of death and rebirth, of all kinds of moral offence, of all states of woe, of the whole cycle of birth and death, of the jungle of false views, of the loss of wholesome dharmas, of the concommitants of ignorance—from all these terrors I must rescue all beings. My endeavors do not merely aim at my own deliverance. For with the help of the boat of the thought of all knowledge, I must rescue all these beings from the stream of samsara which is so difficult to cross.

And why? Because it is surely better that I alone should be in pain than all these beings should fall into the states of woe. There I must give myself away as a pawn through which the whole world is redeemed from the terrors of the hells, of animal birth, and the world of the god of death.

From Burtt, *The Teachings of Compassionate Buddha.*

40

Judaism: The Torah

A hallmark of religions originating in the Middle East is their concept of a god who has certain expectations of human conduct as seen in a divine law. One of the clearest expositions of this theme of ethical monotheism is to be found in the Torah, the first five books of the Old Testament. All told, there are 613 commandments to be found there; the following selections contain some of them.

Discussion Questions

1. Which of the Ten Commandments would you say were unique to Judaism (or the Judeo-Christian) tradition?

2. What reasons does God give for obeying the various commandments?

From the Book of Exodus

Chapter 20

And God spake all these words, saying,

2. I *am* the Lord thy God, which have brought thee out of the land of Egypt, out of the house of bondage.

3. Thou shalt have no other gods before me.

4. Thou shalt not make unto thee any graven image, or any likeness *of any thing* that *is* in heaven above, or that *is* in the earth beneath, or that *is* in the water under the earth:

5. Thou shalt not bow down thyself to them, nor serve them: for I the Lord thy God *am* a jealous God, visiting the iniquity of the fathers upon the children unto the third and fourth *generation* of them that hate me;

6. And showing mercy unto thousands of them that love me, and keep my commandments.

7. Thou shalt not take the name of the Lord thy God in vain; for the Lord will not hold him guiltless that taketh his name in vain.

8. Remember the sabbath day, to keep it holy.

9. Six days shalt thou labour, and do all thy work:

10. But the seventh day *is* the sabbath of the Lord thy God: *in it* thou shalt not do any work, thou, nor thy son, nor thy daughter, thy manservant, nor thy maidservant, nor thy cattle, nor thy stranger that *is* within thy gates:

11. For *in* six days the Lord made heaven and earth, the sea, and all that in them *is*, and rested the seventh day: wherefore the Lord blessed the sabbath day, and hallowed it.

12. Honour thy father and thy mother: that thy days may be long upon the land which the Lord thy God giveth thee.

13. Thou shalt not kill.

14. Thou shalt not commit adultery.

15. Thou shalt not steal.

16. Thou shalt not bear false witness against thy neighbour.

17. Thou shalt not covet thy neighbour's house, thou shalt not covet thy neighbour's wife, nor his manservant, nor his maidservant, nor his ox, nor his ass, nor any thing that *is* thy neighbour's.

From the Book of Deuteronomy

Chapter 14

Ye *are* the children of the Lord your God: ye shall not cut yourselves, not make any baldness between your eyes for the dead.

2. For thou *art* an holy people unto the Lord thy God, and the Lord hath chosen thee to be a peculiar people unto himself, above all the nations that *are* upon the earth.

3. ¶Thou shalt not eat any abominable thing.

The Torah

4. These *are* beasts which ye shall eat: the ox, the sheep, and the goat,

5. The hart, and the roebuck, and the fallow deer, and the wild goat, and the pygarg, and the wild ox, and the chamois.

6. And every beast that parteth the hoof, and cleaveth the cleft into two claws; *and* cheweth the cud among the beasts, that ye shall eat.

7. Nevertheless these ye shall not eat of them that chew the cud, or of them that divide the cloven hoof; *as* the camel, and the hare, and the coney: for they chew the cud, but divide not the hoof; *therefore* they *are* unclean to you.

8. And the swine, because it divideth the hoof, yet cheweth not the cud, it *is* unclean unto you: ye shall not eat of their flesh, nor touch their dead carcase.

9. ¶These ye shall eat of all that *are* in the waters: all that have fins and scales shall ye eat:

10. And whatsoever hath not fins and scales ye may not eat; it *is* unclean unto you.

11. ¶*Of* all clean birds ye shall eat.

12. But these *are they* of which ye shall not eat: the eagle, and the ossifrage, and the ospray,

13. And the glede, and the kite, and the vulture after his kind,

14. And every raven after his kind,

15. And the owl, and the night hawk, and the cuckow, and the hawk after his kind,

16. The little owl, and the great owl, and the swan,

17. And the pelican, and the gier eagle, and the cormorant,

18. And the stork, and the heron after her kind, and the lapwing, and the bat.

19. And every creeping thing that flieth *is* unclean unto you: they shall not be eaten.

20. *But of* all clean fowls ye may eat.

21. ¶Ye shall not eat *of* any thing that dieth of itself: thou shalt give it unto the stranger that *is* in thy gates, that he may eat it; or thou mayest sell it unto an alien: for thou *art* an holy people unto the Lord thy God. Thou shalt not seethe a kid in his mother's milk.

Chapter 22

9. ¶Thou shalt not sow thy vineyard with divers seeds: lest the fruit of thy seed which thou hast sown, and the fruit of thy vineyard, be defiled.

10. ¶Thou shalt not plow with an ox and an ass together.

11. ¶Thou shalt not wear a garment of divers sorts, *as* of woollen and linen together.

Chapter 23

24. ¶When thou comest into thy neighbour's vineyard, then thou mayest eat grapes thy fill at thine own pleasure; but thou shalt not put *any* in thy vessel.

25. When thou comest into the standing corn of thy neighbour, then thou mayest pluck the ears with thine hand; but thou shalt not move a sickle unto thy neighbour's standing corn.

41

The Course of Western Civilization

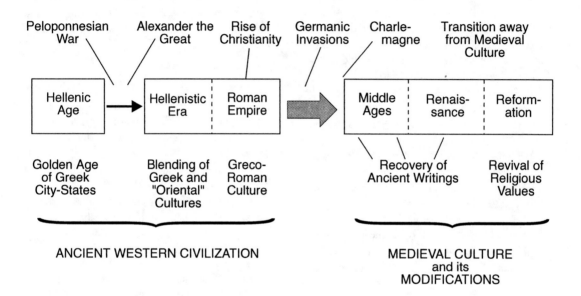

42

Ancient Greece

The event that precipitated the decline of the Greek city-states and the loss of their independence was the Peloponnesian War between Athens and its allies and Sparta and its allies. In some ways it represents the worst-case scenario built into ancient Greece—a general war involving most of the city-states against each other. The basis for this scenario was, as one historian has noted, that the very thing that made Greece great was the same thing that destroyed it. The selection below, from Thucydides' *History of the Peloponnesian War*, is an account of a funeral oration by Pericles, the leading figure in Athens at the time, for soldiers who had died in a battle with Sparta.

Discussion Questions

1. Is Pericles' discussion of democracy an honest portrayal of the realities of Greek political life?

2. Pericles emphasizes the freedom of the citizen as well as the duty of devotion to the city-state. Is there a conflict between the two?

3. During this time Athens had an empire, yet Pericles calls Athens "the school of Hellas (Greece)" and an example to others. Is this consistent?

4. If a contemporary American leader were to deliver a funeral oration for soldiers lost in battle, what similarities and differences would it have with Pericles'?

5. Have you been able to discover what it was that made Greece great and also destroyed it?

The Funeral Oration of Pericles

Most of those who have spoken here before me have commended the lawgiver who added this oration to our other funeral customs; it seemed to them a worthy thing that such an honour should be given at their burial to the dead who have fallen on the field of battle. But I should have preferred that, when men's deeds have been brave, they should be honoured in deed only, and with such an honour as this public funeral, which you are now witnessing. Then the reputation of many would not have been imperilled on the eloquence or want of eloquence of one, and their virtues believed or not as he spoke well or ill. For it is difficult to say neither too little nor too much; and even moderation is apt not to give the impression of truthfulness. The friend of the dead who knows the facts is likely to think that the words of the speaker fall short of his knowledge and of his wishes; another who is not so well informed, when he hears of anything which surpasses his own powers, will be envious and will suspect exaggeration. Mankind are tolerant of the praises of others as long as each hearer thinks that he can do as well or nearly as well himself, but, when the speaker rises above him, jealousy is aroused and he begins to be incredulous. However, since our ancestors have set the seal of their approval upon the practice, I must obey, and to the utmost of my power shall endeavour to satisfy the wishes and beliefs of all who hear me.

I will speak first of our ancestors, for it is right and seemly that now, when we are lamenting the dead, a tribute should be paid to their memory. There has never been a time when they did not inhabit this land, which by their valour they have handed down from generation to generation, and we have received from them a free state. But if they were worthy of praise, still more were our fathers, who added to their inheritance, and after many a struggle transmitted to us their sons this great empire. And we ourselves assembled here today, who are still most of us in the vigour of life, have carried the work of improvement further, and have richly endowed our city with all things, so that she is sufficient for herself both in peace and war. Of the military exploits by which our various possessions were acquired, or of the energy with which we or our fathers drove back the tide of war, Hellenic or Barbarian [non-Greek], I will not speak: for the tale would be long and is familiar to you. But before I praise the dead, I should like to point out by what principles of action we rose to power, and under what institutions and through what manner of life our empire became great. For I conceive that such thoughts are not unsuited to the occasion, and that this numerous assembly of citizens and strangers may profitably listen to them.

Our form of government does not enter into rivalry with the institutions of others. We do not copy our neighbours, but are an example to them. It is true that we are called a democracy, for the administration is in the hands of the many and not of the few. But while the law secures equal justice to all alike in their private disputes, the claim of excellence is also recognised; and when a citizen is in any way distinguished, he is preferred to the public service, not as a matter of privilege, but as the reward of merit. Neither is

From "The History of Thucydides," Book II, translated by Benjamin Jowett, New York, 1909.

poverty a bar, but a man may benefit his country whatever be the obscurity of his condition. There is no exclusiveness in our public life, and in our private intercourse we are not suspicious of one another, nor angry with our neighbour if he does what he likes; we do not put on sour looks at him which, though harmless, are not pleasant. While we are thus unconstrained in our private intercourse, a spirit of reverence pervades our public acts; we are prevented from doing wrong by respect for the authorities and for the laws, having an especial regard to those which are ordained for the protection of the injured as well as to those unwritten laws which bring upon the transgressor of them the reprobation of the general sentiment.

And we have not forgotten to provide for our weary spirits many relaxations from toil; we have regular games and sacrifices throughout the year; our homes are beautiful and elegant; and the delight which we daily feel in all these things helps to banish melancholy. Because of the greatness of our city the fruits of the whole earth flow in upon us; so that we enjoy the goods of other countries as freely as of our own.

Then, again, our military training is in many respects superior to that of our adversaries. Our city is thrown open to the world, and we never expel a foreigner or prevent him from seeing or learning anything of which the secret if revealed to an enemy might profit him. We rely not upon management or trickery, but upon our own hearts and hands. And in the matter of education, whereas they from early youth are always undergoing laborious exercises which are to make them brave, we live at ease, and yet are equally ready to face the perils which they face. And here is the proof. The Lacedaemonians [Spartans] come into Attica not by themselves, but with their whole confederacy following; we go alone into a neighbour's country; and although our opponents are fighting for their homes and we on a foreign soil, we have

seldom any difficulty in overcoming them. Our enemies have never yet felt our united strength; the care of a navy divides our attention, and on land we are obliged to send our own citizens everywhere. But they, if they meet and defeat a part of our army, are as proud as if they had routed us all, and when defeated they pretend to have been vanquished by us all.

If then we prefer to meet danger with a light heart but without laborious training, and with a courage which is gained by habit and not enforced by law, are we not greatly the gainers? Since we do not anticipate the pain, although, when the hour comes, we can be as brave as those who never allow themselves to rest; and thus too our city is equally admirable in peace and in war. For we are lovers of the beautiful, yet simple in our tastes, and we cultivate the mind without loss of manliness. Wealth we employ, not for talk and ostentation, but when there is a real use for it. To avow poverty with us is no disgrace; the true disgrace is in doing nothing to avoid it. An Athenian citizen does not neglect the state because he takes care of his own household; and even those of us who are engaged in business have a very fair idea of politics. We alone regard a man who takes no interest in public affairs, not as a harmless, but as a useless character; and if few of us are originators, we are all sound judges of policy. The great impediment to action is, in our opinion, not discussion, but the want of that knowledge which is gained by discussion preparatory to action. For we have a peculiar power of thinking before we act and of acting too, whereas other men are courageous from ignorance but hesitate upon reflection. And they are surely to be esteemed the bravest spirits who, having the clearest sense both of the pains—and pleasures of life, do not on that account shrink from danger. In doing good, again, we are unlike others; we make our friends by conferring, not by receiving favours. Now he who confers a favour is the firmer friend, because he would fain by kindness keep alive the memory of an obligation; but the recipient is colder in his feelings, because he knows that in requiting another's generosity he will not be winning gratitude but only paying a debt. We alone do good to our neighbours, not upon a calculation of interest, but in the confidence of freedom and in a frank and fearless spirit.

To sum up: I say that Athens is the school of Hellas, and that the individual Athenian in his own person seems to have the power of adapting himself to the most varied forms of action with the utmost versatility and grace. This is no passing and idle word, but truth and fact; and the assertion is verified by the position to which these qualities have raised the state. For in the hour of trial Athens alone among her contemporaries is superior to the report of her. No enemy who comes against her is indignant at the reverses which he sustains at the hands of such a city; no subject complains that his masters are unworthy of him. And we shall assuredly not be without witnesses; there are mighty monuments of our power which will make us the wonder of this and of succeeding ages; we shall not need the praises of Homer or of any other panegyrist whose poetry may please for the moment, although his representation of tile facts will not bear the light of day. For we have compelled every land and every sea to open a path for our valour, and have everywhere planted eternal memorials of our friendship and of our enmity. Such is the city of whose sake these men nobly fought and died; they could not bear the thought that she might be taken from them; and every one of us who survive should gladly toil on her behalf.

I have dwelt upon the greatness of Athens because I want to show you that we are contending for a higher prize than those who enjoy none of these privileges, and to establish by manifest proof the merit of these men whom I am now commemorating. Their loftiest praise has been already spoken. For in magnifying the city I have magnified them, and men like them whose virtues made her glorious. And of how few Hellenes can it be said as of them, that their deeds when weighed in the balance have been found equal to their fame! Methinks that a death such as theirs has been given the true measure of a man's worth; it may be the first revelation of his virtues, but is at any rate their final seal. For even those who come short in other ways may justly plead the valour with which they have fought for their country; they have blotted out the evil with the good, and have benefited the state more by their public services than they have injured her by their private actions. None of these men were enervated by wealth or hesitated to resign for pleasures of life, none of them put off the evil day in the hope, natural to poverty, that a man, though poor, may one day become rich. But, deeming that the punishment of their enemies was sweeter than any of these things, and that they could fall in no nobler cause, they determined at the hazard of their lives to be honourably avenged, and to leave the rest. They resigned to hope their unknown chance of happiness; but in the fact of death they resolved to rely upon themselves alone. And when the moment came they were minded to resist and suffer, rather than to fly and save their lives; they ran away from the word of dishonour, but on the battlefield their feet stood fast, and in an instant, at the height of their fortune, they passed away from the scene, not of their fear, but of their glory.

Such was the end of these men; they were worthy of Athens, and the living need not desire to have a more heroic spirit, although they may pray for a less fatal issue. The value of such a spirit is not to be expressed in words. Any one can discourse to you forever about the advantages of a brave defence, which you know already. But instead of listening to him I would have you day by day fix your eyes upon the greatness of Athens, until you become filled with the love of her; and when you are impressed by the spectacle of her glory, reflect that this empire has been acquired by men who knew their duty and had the courage to do it, who in the hour of conflict had the fear of dishonour always present to them, and who, if ever they failed in an enterprise, would not allow their virtues to be lost to their country, but freely gave their lives to her as the fairest offering which they could present at her feast. The sacrifice which they collectively made was individually repaid to them; for they received again each one of himself a praise which grows not old, and the noblest of all sepulchres—I speak not of that in which their remains are laid, but of that in which their glory survives, and is proclaimed always and on every fitting occasion both in word and deed. For the whole earth is the sepulchre of famous men; not only are they commemorated by columns and inscriptions in their own country, but in foreign lands there dwells also an unwritten memorial of them, graven not on stone but in the hearts of men. Make them your examples, and, esteeming courage to be freedom and freedom to be happiness, do not weigh too nicely the perils of war. The unfortunate who has no hope of a change for the better has less reason to throw away his life than the prosperous who, if he survives, is always liable to a change for the worse, and to whom any accidental fall makes the most serious difference. To a man of spirit, cowardice and disaster coming together are far more bitter than death striking him unperceived at a time when he is full of courage and animated by the general hope.

Wherefore I do not now commiserate the parents of the dead who stand here; I would rather comfort them. You know that your life has been passed amid manifold vicissitudes; and that they may be deemed fortunate who have gained most honour, whether an honourable death like theirs, or an honourable sorrow like

yours, and whose days have been so ordered that the term of their happiness is likewise the term of their life. I know how hard it is to make you feel this, when the good fortune of others will too often remind you of the gladness which once lightened your hearts. And sorrow is felt at the want of those blessings, not which a man never knew, but which were a part of his life before they were taken from him. Some of you are of an age at which they may hope to have other children, and they ought to bear their sorrow better; not only will the children who may hereafter be born make them forget their own lost ones, but the city will be doubly a gainer. She will not be left desolate, and she will be safer. For a man's counsel cannot have equal weight or worth, when he alone has no children to risk in the general danger. To those of you who have passed their prime, I say: Congratulate yourselves that you have been happy during the greater part of your days; remember that your life of sorrow will not last long, and be comforted by the glory of those who are gone. For the love of honour alone is ever young, and not riches, as some say, but honour is the delight of men when they are old and useless.

To you who are the sons and brothers of the departed, I see that the struggle to emulate them will be an arduous one. For all men praise the dead, and, however pre-eminent your virtue may be, hardly will you be thought, I do not say to equal, but even to approach them. The living have their rivals and detractors, but when a man is out of the way, the honour and good-will which he receives is unalloyed. And, if I am to speak of womanly virtues to those of you who will henceforth be widows, let me sum them up in one short admonition: To a woman not to show more weakness than is natural to her sex is a great glory, and not to be talked about for good or for evil among men.

I have paid the required tribute, in obedience to the law, making use of such fitting words as I had. The tribute of deeds has been paid in part; for the dead have been honourably interred, and it remains only that their children should be maintained at the public charge until they are grown up; this is the solid prize with which, as with a garland, Athens crowns her sons living and dead, after a struggle like theirs. For where the rewards of virtue are greatest, there the noblest citizens are enlisted in the service of the state. And now, when you have duly lamented, everyone his own dead, you may depart.

43

Alexander the Great

One of the most influential of the conquerors in the classical era, Alexander of Macedonia, would end the autonomous polis, incorporating Athens and the other city-states of Hellenic Greece into an empire that stretched all the way to India. In the process, Alexander initiated the Hellenistic Era, the blending of Greek culture with Persian, Indian, Egyptian, and Mesopotamian customs and beliefs to create a cosmopolitan ecumene. Though he accomplished much, does he deserve to be considered "great"? This reading introduces some new perspectives on Alexander's life and influence.

Discussion Questions

1. Alexander the Great is listed as 33rd on the list of Hart's Hundred. Does this article support or undercut Alexander's influence in his time and since?

2. What was "Alexander's New Look"?

3. What role did Alexander's father, Philip of Macedon, play in Alexander's success?

4. Of the three characterizations of Alexander that are mentioned in the article—the conqueror, the king, and the globalist—which does the author think is the most accurate assessment?

Alexander's New Look

Young, beautiful, brave, brilliant, charismatic, chivalrous. What's not to like about Alexander the Great? In just 13 years in the fourth century B.C., he built a vast empire that stretched from the Balkans to the Indus River, encompassing, among other lands, what is now Greece, Turkey, Lebanon, Syria, Israel, Egypt, Iran, Iraq, Afghanistan, Pakistan, and parts of India. And if that feat weren't enough, history also has credited him with bringing Greek learning to the "barbarians" in the East —thus transforming the world's cultural and intellectual landscape.

Next week, a new Oliver Stone film about Alexander debuts, starring Colin Farrell as the great man and Angelina Jolie as his infamous mother, Olympias. But historians and archaeologists are also re-examining Alexander, and, unlike Stone, many argue that he may not have been quite so great after all. Prompted in part by fresh archaeological finds, the reappraisal reveals a man both self-indulgent and cruel. Yes, he was a charismatic commander, but he inherited a virtually invincible army from his father, Philip II of Macedonia. And although he has long been celebrated for spreading Greek ideas throughout Asia, new scholarship shows that cultural exchange between East and West had started long before Alexander's reign.

Born in 356 B.C. in Pella, Macedonia, Alexander was only 18 when he distinguished himself as a commander at the bloody Battle of Chaeronea, in which Philip defeated the Greek city-states to the south, bringing them under Macedonian rule. When he became king of Macedonia at age 20 after his father's assassination, he moved swiftly to quell rumors that he and his mother had plotted to kill Philip, executing several nobles—some of whom were potential rivals—as coconspirators. Soon after, the Greek city-state Thebes revolted, and he razed it, killing or enslaving 36,000 citizens. Other rebellious city-states came quickly to heel.

The conqueror. After consolidating his position at home, the fresh-faced monarch turned his attention to the wealthy Persian Empire. His avowed reason for a campaign was "freeing the Greeks" in Asia, notes Oxford University historian Robin Lane Fox, who was a consultant on the new film. He said he wanted to punish the Persians for past offenses during their invasion of Greece a century and a half earlier. But Alexander, in fact, meant to conquer all lands out to the eastern edge of the world, which he mistakenly believed ended somewhere before modern-day Burma and China. In the spring of 334 B.C., he crossed the Dardanelles into Asia with an army of 35,000 men. After the ancient equivalent of a quick photo op in Troy, where the image-savvy king stopped to honor the tomb of his hero Achilles, he swept down the Ionian coast, liberating Greek towns and recruiting additional soldiers.

He trounced an advance Persian force at the Granicus River in what is now Turkey—a victory that opened up much of western Asia Minor to the Macedonians. The next year, he finally met his archrival Darius III, king of Persia, at Issus, also in present-day Turkey; the battle turned into a rout. Darius fled to fight another day, abandoning his wife, mother, and children. Historians have applauded Alexander for treating his opponent's family with respect and courtesy—indeed, Darius's mother was said to have wept years later when she heard of the Macedonian's death. But this gentlemanly behavior is better seen as a claim to the throne than an act of chivalry, argues Jona Lendering, author of the new book Alexander de Grate. "In the ancient Near East," he writes, "a new king took care of the harem and family of his predecessor." Other women in Alexander's path were not so lucky. After Issus, he turned over the wives and children of the Persian soldiers to the Thessalian horsemen as a reward for their gallantry in battle.

The king. Now 23, the triumphant Alexander began referring to himself as ruler of Persia, although he must have known he still had a lot of ground to cover before he could rightfully claim the title. In 322 B.C., the city of Tyre, in what is now Lebanon, fell to his forces after a seven-month siege. The next year Egypt, happy to be free of Darius's yoke, gave Alexander a hero's welcome. At Gaugamela in modern-day Iraq, his forces again crushed those of Darius. Again Darius slipped from his grasp, however. Alexander then occupied Babylon and Persepolis, the capital of the Persian Empire, where he made off with an estimated 3,000 tons of silver and gold.

Even after Darius was killed by one of his own generals, Alexander kept pressing east—into Bactria (Afghanistan), Sogdiana (Uzbekistan and Tajikistan), and finally India, where after weeks of slogging through tropical rains the conqueror's bone-weary soldiers dug their heels into the muck and refused to go farther. Upon his return to Babylon, he fell ill, and 10 days later he died, just six weeks short of his 33rd birthday.

Given the immensity of the empire he built and the sheer number of battles he won, it may seem perverse to argue that Alexander was not the military genius that history has made him

out to be. But revisionists contend that most of those battles were his to lose, given the technical superiority of the army he commanded. No one is questioning his personal courage: Whether battling Greek hoplites or Indians mounted on elephants, he always led the cavalry charge, resplendent in a jewel-encrusted helmet. Still, he would not have amounted to much without his father's genius, argues military historian Victor Davis Hanson in his 2001 book Carnage and Culture: "King Philip [had] crafted a grand new army . . . and organized it differently from anything in past Greek practice." Philip gave the Macedonian phalanx fresh power by lengthening the thrusting spear from 8 to between 16 and 18 feet. He also created a heavily armed cavalry and, for the first time in the history of western warfare, made the coordination of infantry and cavalry a centerpiece of military strategy.

The son's contribution? The impulse to annihilate, says Hanson. Greek soldiers had long been respected for their skill and willingness to fight to the death—indeed, many ancient rulers employed them as mercenaries. But before Alexander, they mostly met on small battlefields where they thrust and stabbed for an hour or so before one side gave up and the killing stopped. Alexander, however, practiced "total pursuit and destruction of the defeated enemy," Hanson argues, "ensur[ing] battle casualties unimaginable just a few decades earlier."

Alexander didn't confine the slaughter to soldiers. Despite historical accounts of his mercy to those who submitted, he butchered hundreds of thousands of civilians. After the siege of Gaza, for instance, Alexander "the Accursed"—as he was known in the East —allowed his troops to rampage through the city, gutting residents at will. Brian Bosworth, a historian at the University of Western Australia, points to his near genocidal campaign against the Mallis in India, in which he systematically razed villages, killing civilians as they fled.

His reputation as a brilliant tactician has also come under fire. After the Battle of Issus, he pursued war booty in Susa and Babylon instead of tracking Darius, giving the king time to rebuild his devastated army, argues University of Missouri historian Ian Worthington. Another costly error, in his view, was the siege of Tyre, To be sure, Alexander needed to control the powerful city. But the Tyrianans had already submitted and only balked at his insistence on sacrificing at their temple during a religious festival. The smart thing for Alexander to do would have been to sacrifice elsewhere and stroll on into the city, says Worthington, but his pride forced him to mount what he probably knew would be a lengthy siege.

The globalist. Historians who embrace the dreamy-eyed notion that he waged war in order to unify East and West have misinterpreted his efforts to win the hearts and minds of the people he conquered, says David Potter, a professor of classical studies at the University of Michigan. Over the years, he adopted elements of Persian royal dress, including a purple-and-white striped tunic. He took a Persian wife and tried to introduce to his court the Oriental custom of prostration before the king. He also appointed local officials as provincial governors, a practice that incensed his officers, who felt that the lucrative posts should not have gone to those who fought for the other side. He persisted, however, because "he recognized that he couldn't control his empire without a buy-in from the conquered," says Potter, not because he envisioned "the peoples of the world singing 'Kumbaya' together on the banks of the Euphrates." Indeed, the whole idea that there was some sort of cultural firewall between East and West before Alexander is wrong headed, argues Walter Burkert in his new book Babylon, Memphis, Persepolis: Eastern Contexts of Greek Culture. The Greeks borrowed heavily from Mesopotamia for their mathematics and

astronomy, for instance. (Indeed, the socalled Pythagorean theorem is found in cuneiform texts about 1,000 years before Pythagoras.) The Greeks learned from eastern craftsmen how to make terra cotta from molds, and facets of their mythology had Oriental roots, including Egyptian funerary lore.

Moreover, Greek culture also had jumped its borders before Alexander's conquest. Thanks to traders and mercenaries, "it was a very cosmopolitan world," says the University of California-Berkeley's Andrew Stewart, who heads up an archaeological dig in Israel of a Phoenician city called Dor, where he and legions of volunteers have uncovered myriad Greek artifacts. As early as the first part of the fifth century B.C., the city's residents were using Greek mixing bowls in their drinking rituals. And by the beginning of the fourth, he says, "anyone with any means at all was eating and drinking off Greek black glaze tableware,"

Still, the Macedonian's conquests obviously left their mark. After Alexander, "there were Greek soldiers crawling all over the Near East," says Stewart. He also founded a host of Greek cities—among them the glittering Alexandria—where the elites of both East and West, including engineers, artisans, and scientists, continued trading ideas and skills. By looting and then spending much of the accumulated wealth of the Persian Empire, he revolutionized local economies, says Tulane University historian Kenneth Harl, who has studied coins unearthed in the ancient town of Gordion. Before Alexander rolled through, the only coins in use had very high value and so were good only for large transactions like settling debts between governments. After him, however, regular people carried coins of low enough value to "buy lunch in the marketplace," he says.

But did Anatolian peasants eating lunch in the marketplace suddenly start spouting Greek poetry? Scholars increasingly think not. Most people's only real contact with Greek culture was "when soldiers came through and grabbed their chickens for food," says Stewart. Nor, increasingly, do scholars think Alexander would have cared. He was, after all, a conqueror and, like others of his ilk, cared passionately about power, not cultural interchange. "We may not like him or approve of him," says Potter, "but there's an integrity to him."

44

The Roman Legacy

In the concluding chapter to his book *The Decline of Rome and the Rise of Medieval Europe*, Solomon Katz attempts to assess the long-term legacy of the Roman Empire for medieval and modern Europe.

Discussion Questions

1. In Katz' opinion did more survive than was lost when the empire disappeared?

2. What were the distinctive strengths of the Roman Empire? Did they survive the fall?

3. What elements of Rome were particularly well preserved during the Middle Ages? Which do we still honor today?

The story of the rise and decline of Rome has stirred the imagination of mankind. In the thousand years of her history Rome, originally a small farming community, had emerged first as master of Italy and finally as ruler of the western world. Her people had consolidated the Empire under the Roman peace and buttressed it for centuries by an efficient system of administration and defense. Latin culture had been modified as a result of exposure to intellectual and artistic crosscurrents from the Graeco-Oriental parts of the Empire, and out of an amalgam of Oriental, Greek, and Roman elements the Romans had created a civilization of high order. The Roman achievement was magnificent; the Roman failure to meet the challenge presented by new experiences and to solve the problems posed by fresh responsibilities was disastrous.

By A.D. 600 peace and unity were shattered and the Roman Empire had disintegrated. In the four centuries from Marcus Aurelius to Justinian the Empire experienced civil war and anarchy, barbarian invasions, and political and economic crises. The Western Empire ceased to exist, and upon its territories the Germanic peoples created their kingdoms. Eastern Roman emperors still ruled from their capital at Constantinople, but over a greatly shrunken empire. The physical decline of Rome was accompanied by a deterioration of her civilization as the ancient structure of thought weakened. The Roman gods, who had been closely identified with Roman civilization and with the state itself, were vanquished by Christianity, whose victory heralded a new epoch.

Confronted by all the profound material and spiritual changes which constitute the phenomenon described as the decline of the Roman Empire, one may well ask not why that empire declined, but rather how it was able to endure for so long. There were weaknesses in the Empire, as we have seen, but there were obviously also enormous reserves of strength. The unity which Rome imposed upon the Mediterranean world and the administrative system and the law which held the Empire together enabled her to resist for a long time the forces of disintegration. These institutions which served Rome so well endured as an important part of the Roman legacy. Roman civilization as a whole was greatly altered, but it survived the crises of the Later Empire and lived on as an integral element of mediaeval and modern civilization. Rome's triumphs and successes were canceled by her failure, but what she accomplished in diverse areas of endeavor was not lost. In the long perspective of history the survival of Roman civilization, the heritage which generation after generation has accepted, is perhaps more significant than the decline of Rome.

Rome's genius was essentially practical, and it was pre-eminently in the domain of administration that the Roman legacy was greatest. The Greeks had failed to achieve political unity and had exhausted their strength in interstate warfare; the Romans, on the contrary, succeeded in building a world-state. By force, diplomacy, and sometimes by chicanery—one may not gloss over the story—the Romans unified the ancient world. For a congeries of antagonistic and mutually warring states Rome substituted the *Pax Romana*, safeguarded by an army, but secured even more by law and by a variety of administrative devices fairly and efficiently applied. The solidly founded political system which Rome extended over her vast empire was the institutional heritage which she bequeathed to later ages.

To the Eastern Roman Empire, which continued Rome's rule over a reduced area, to the barbarian states which took the place of the Western Roman Empire, and to the Christian church, Rome handed on the practices of government. The Eastern Roman emperors who ruled in almost unbroken sequence until the fall of Constantinople in 1453 accepted and maintained Roman principles of statecraft, and the German kings of western Europe likewise found in the Later Roman Empire a model for their absolute rule. They retained many of the features of the Roman administrative system: Roman imperial offices and perhaps municipal institutions, Roman titles and symbols of authority, the Roman system of public finances, Roman coin types, and above all, Roman law. From Rome too during these centuries the church received its basic organization, administration, and law. In the East and the West, church and state accepted the rich institutional heritage of Rome and thus perpetuated the ideals and traditions of the Roman state.

More important than any of these administrative practices was the Roman legacy in the realm of political ideals: common citizenship, political unity, a well-organized state living under law. Whatever the forms of government in their long history, whether monarchy or republic, the Principate of the

Early Empire or the absolute, bureaucratic rule of the Later Empire, the Romans showed a virtual passion for these ideals. Long after the decline of the Empire they endured as Rome's major bequest to the world.

Roman citizenship had been extended to more and more of the inhabitants of the Empire until by the time of the emperor Caracalla (A.D. 212) it was almost universally held by free men. There were divisive forces which sundered East and West and separated the provinces from each other and from Italy itself. Nevertheless, in the great age of the Roman Empire a unified state was created out of peoples of different origins, and within the broad area of imperial unity local diversities of language, religion, customs, and institutions were tolerated. This was the achievement praised in the days of Rome's greatness by the Greek orator Aelius Aristides: "You have made the name of Rome no longer that of a city but of an entire people." It impressed the Christian poet Prudentius and his pagan and Christian contemporaries even in the period when Rome was in manifest decline: "A common law made them equals and bound them by a single name, bringing the conquered into bonds of brotherhood. We live in countries the most diverse like fellow-citizens of the same blood dwelling within the single ramparts of their native city and all united in an ancestral home."*

The ideal of a common citizenship in a unified world was cherished centuries after it had passed out of the realm of practical politics. Although a single Roman Empire was replaced by separate German kingdoms in the West and by an Eastern Roman Empire in Constantinople, men clung tenaciously to their belief in the eternity of the Roman Empire. Long after the living memory of Rome's centralized rule was lost, and when, in fact, the growth of feudalism made such rule impossible, the ideal continued to have an irresistible appeal. The coronation of Charlemagne as Holy Roman Emperor in 800 and of Otto the Great in 962 are concrete manifestations of the persistent conviction that the Roman Empire had never perished and that imperial might had not decayed but had been transferred to other monarchs. However slight may have been the actual strength of the Holy Roman Empire in its history of a thousand years, it was a witness to the evocative power of Rome's name. So, too, the mediaeval ideal of a *Respublica Christiana*, a commonwealth represented by the church, was essentially the Roman tradition of universality modified by Christian thought.

The Roman law, the instrument and the symbol of her unity, was Rome's greatest achievement. The acceptance of this legacy by the Middle Ages gave both church and state a basis for their own systems of law and helped to civilize Europe by spreading widely the principles of equity and humanity which were embodied in the structure of the law. Roman law did not share the fate of the Empire. The barbarian conquerors retained both Roman law and law courts for their Roman subjects, and for their fellow Germans they harmonized Roman law and legal concepts with their own law and customs. In the Eastern Roman Empire, Roman law and legal theory, as crystallized in Justinian's great codification, remained in force for almost a thousand years. In the East and West during the Middle Ages the church erected canon law, its own legal system, upon Roman foundations.

Thus Roman law remained a vital force in the centuries after the decline of the Empire. Then at the end of the eleventh century interest in its principles was rekindled by the study of Justinian's *Corpus Iuris Civilis* at Bologna in

---

* Prudentius, *A Reply to Symmachus*, II, 608–612; tr. by H. J. Thomson, *Prudentius* (Loeb Classical Library, Cambridge, Mass., 1953), II, 55.

Italy, and before long the law became a major subject of study in the universities of Europe. By the sixteenth century Roman law was increasingly applied in the European courts of law, and it served as the basis for the legal systems of the states of continental Europe and their overseas colonies. It still performs its ancient mission of binding together disparate peoples, for a large part of the Western world employs Roman law today. Even where legal systems, such as the common law of the English-speaking peoples, are not Roman in origin, many of their fundamental concepts are derived from Roman law and the very terms used to describe them are of Latin origin. Property, contract, agent, testament, judge, jury, crime: the terms and the legal and juridical concepts which they denominate are Roman.

Through its application Roman law has exercised a continuous influence upon the development of the law of the western world, but the underlying concepts of Roman law have equally influenced jurisprudence, philosophy, and politics ... [F]rom the time of Rome's earliest legal code, the Twelve Tables (c. 443 B.C.), the harshness of the law was steadily modified. Under the impact first of Stoic philosophy and then of Christianity a greater emphasis was placed upon human rights and social justice, and the law became ever more enlightened. When the Roman jurists broadened their understanding of civil law to something like a "law of nations" and eventually to a kind of "natural law," they forged the link which binds Graeco-Roman and modern concepts of the rights and duties of the individual.

It is, however, not only in administration and law that the vitality of the Roman institutional heritage is apparent. The large estates or villas of the Later Empire, which were cultivated by half-free *coloni*, continued into the Middle Ages, and by a fusion of Roman and German elements became the manorial system of that period. Similarly the late Roman system of holding land under the protection of a strong landlord influenced feudal methods of land tenure in mediaeval Europe. Nor did the instruments by which Rome long maintained a flourishing urban life die. Even in the darkest period of the Middle Ages many Roman roads, although neglected, continued to be used. While Roman cities became impoverished and shrank in area and population, the more important ones never disappeared, but survived at least as centers of ecclesiastical administration and for such trade as existed. Today, fifteen hundred years after the end of the Western Empire, the traveler in Europe moves along the routes of ancient Roman roads and visits cities which have had a continuous history from antiquity to the present moment.

To Rome's practical skill as administrator and lawgiver we owe the preservation and dissemination of classical culture, for it was within the frame of institutions which they created that the Romans fashioned their culture by a synthesis of Greek, Oriental, and Roman elements. But for these institutions Roman culture and with it much of Greek culture might not have survived.

Rome's native culture had been changed as a result of her contacts with the Greeks of southern Italy and Sicily and eventually by her acquisition of the Greek East. The culture of her new subjects in the eastern provinces was Greek, and Roman culture itself was soon so thoroughly permeated with Hellenic elements that it may more accurately be described as Graeco-Roman. Roman schools began to offer a system of education which was essentially Greek. Greek literature, philosophy, and rhetoric were eagerly studied at Rome and became acknowledged models for Roman writers. Most of the literary forms employed by Roman authors, much of their imagery and symbolism, their mythology, the very meters of their poetry, were borrowed from the Greeks. Roman artists and architects adapted Greek canons and techniques of art and architecture to their own needs and made them an integral part of the Roman heritage to western civilization. By unifying and by Romanizing the ancient world the Romans enabled their culture, of which the Greek element was so important a part, to spread throughout the Mediterranean basin and western Europe. Strong enough to outlast the collapse of the Empire, Graeco-Roman civilization was preserved by the new states of western Europe, the Eastern Roman Empire, and the church.

To the civilization which they developed the Romans contributed many distinctively Roman elements. Chief among these was the Latin language, which gradually replaced the native tongues of Rome's subjects in the western half of the Empire and which in time the German conquerors adopted as their own language of administration and literature. It was in Latin that the western church Fathers wrote; it was into Latin that St. Jerome translated the Bible; it was in Latin that for centuries poets, historians, and theologians wrote their works. The church in the West used Latin for its ritual and for its official documents, as it does even today. As the language of literature, learning, and law during the Middle Ages, Latin was in effect an international language which recognized no frontiers in the West. In contrast, therefore, to all the centrifugal forces of the period, Latin served as a bond of unity.

For a thousand years after the disintegration of the Empire, Latin survived as the leading, and for much of that time the only, language of literature. For learning and law it was supreme until the seventeenth and eighteenth centuries. Although Latin has been superseded by the modern languages for most scholarly and scientific purposes outside the church, it remains today an important part of the school curriculum wherever the European educational tradition prevails. Thus the key to the treasures of Latin literature has been handed down from generation to generation.

Even when Latin was no longer a regular means of communication, its influence remained strong. It was out of the popular or Vulgar Latin spoken by the common people of the Roman Empire that the Romance languages—Italian, French, Spanish, Portuguese, and Roumanian—gradually came into being during the Middle Ages. Moreover, such non-Latin languages as English contain a high proportion of words derived from Latin; in fact, it has been estimated that from half to two-thirds of the words commonly employed in English are of Latin origin. To Latin the English-speaking peoples owe a large part of their philosophic and scientific vocabulary as well as many of the words by which they denote political, social, and economic institutions. The very scripts used in mediaeval manuscripts were Roman in origin, and the Roman alphabet itself was adopted by the Romance, Celtic, and Germanic languages, several of the Slavic tongues, and by other languages such as Hungarian, Finnish, and Turkish. Clearly the Latin language is one of the greatest and most enduring of Rome's many bequests to western civilization.

For nearly two thousand years men have regarded Latin literature as a very precious part of their inheritance from ancient Rome. Despite their fears that they might be corrupted by them, the church Fathers of the early centuries read and studied Latin authors and by their own example showed how classical literature might be put to Christian uses. Even in the darkest period of the Middle Ages the ancient authors were not forgotten. In the monasteries, the centers of learning at that time, the monks copied and preserved the texts of classical authors, while in the newly established states of western Europe, Germanic kings were often active patrons of Latin letters. Throughout the Middle Ages the literature of ancient Rome remained a fundamental part of the course of study in the schools. When in the later Middle Ages the universities were founded, Latin literature was one of the staples of instruction. Either in its own right or by helping to shape the vernacular literature which eventually superseded it, Latin literature remained a vital force throughout the mediaeval period. With the Renaissance there came not a rebirth but an intensification of interest in a literature which had suffered vicissitudes but whose study had never been abandoned. Latin literature is read today by fewer people than in the past. It is, however, so firmly embedded in the western cultural tradition that it still wields a dominating influence. Scarcely a branch or genre of writing in the modern world can be named which has not to some extent been molded by the work of a Roman author. Cicero helped to fashion the language and thought of the western world, Seneca the philosophy and tragedy, Plautus and Terence the comedy, Virgil and Horace the poetry, Ovid the mythology.

The Roman legacy in architecture and art has been equally rich. Not only was Roman architecture a prime factor in the development of the ecclesiastical architecture of the Middle Ages, but it largely determined the plan of mediaeval secular buildings. The arch, the dome, and the vault—forms of construction which the Romans either developed out of their own creative genius or else made peculiarly their own—have had a continuous life in the East and the West from ancient times to our day. In painting, sculpture and the minor arts, too, Roman standards of craftsmanship and canons of taste have contributed immensely to the establishment of an artistic tradition in western civilization.

However great the Roman institutional and cultural heritage may be, it is overshadowed by one contribution which the Empire, by the very fact of its existence, made to western civilization. It was in the Roman Empire that Christianity came into being and finally won supremacy. The *Pax Romana*, the peace which Rome gave to the ancient world, facilitated the spread of Christianity and made possible the translation into reality of the ideal of a universal religion. When the political unity of the Roman world was destroyed, a new spiritual unity, represented by the church, took its place and served as a binding force for the Middle Ages.

In its triumph the church did not reject the past, but built upon Roman foundations and within the frame furnished by the Roman Empire. From Rome the church inherited its institutions, its organization, its administrative system, and its law. From Rome the church in the West received the Latin language, a potent instrument of unity. Latin literature and learning gave a higher intellectual quality to Christianity, and Roman art furnished the basic forms for Christian art. By accepting and making its own this rich Roman heritage, the church built a bridge between the ancient world and the modern.

Western civilization rests upon Greek, Roman, and Hebrew-Christian foundations. To Rome we owe an incalculable debt for building a great civilization in which was incorporated and preserved the Graeco-Oriental culture which she herself inherited and for providing a setting into which Christianity, her own heir, could come into being. For more than two thousand years the western world has been taught and inspired by Rome. Deeply rooted in western civilization, Roman ideals and practices still bear witness to the magnificent achievement of Eternal Rome.

45

Christianity: The Ranking of Jesus in History

In 1978, Michael Hart, of the Goddard Space Laboratory, published a book titled *The 100: A Ranking of the Most Influential Persons in History*. The title is most revealing: the list he proposed is limited to 100 persons and the emphasis is on the impact each person has had on history, not their greatness as such. The difficulty in proposing such a list is not so much which names to choose as in the ranking of the individuals. Obviously such a list is a personal thing, but Hart has done his best to get beyond his own personal preferences and evaluate how each individual has changed the way people around the world think and act.

The following chapter from the book deals with Jesus, whom Hart ranks Number Three on his list.

Discussion Questions

1. Why does Hart think Jesus should be ranked third on his list? Would you agree with his rationale?

2. How does Hart think Jesus changed history?

3. Since there are more Christians in the world than adherents of any other religion, why doesn't Hart rank Jesus Number One?

Jesus Christ
c. 6 B.C. – c. 30 A.D.

The impact of Jesus on human history is so obvious and so enormous that few people would question his placement near the top of this list. Indeed, the more likely question is why Jesus, who is the inspiration for the most influential religion in history, has not been placed first.

There is no question that Christianity, over the course of time, has had far more adherents than any other religion. However, it is not the relative influence of different religions that is being estimated in this book, but rather the relative influence of individual men. Christianity, unlike Islam, was not founded by a single person but by two people—Jesus and St. Paul—and the principal credit for its development must therefore be apportioned between those two figures.

Jesus formulated the basic ethical ideas of Christianity, as well as its basic spiritual outlook and its main ideas concerning human conduct. Christian theology, however, was shaped principally by the work of St. Paul. Jesus presented a spiritual message; Paul added to that the worship of Christ. Furthermore, St. Paul was the author of a considerable portion of the New Testament, and was the main proselytizing force for Christianity during the first century.

Jesus was still fairly young when he died (unlike Buddha or Muhammad), and he left behind a limited number of disciples. At the time of Jesus' death, his followers simply formed a small Jewish sect. It was due in considerable measure to Paul's writings, and to his tireless proselytizing efforts, that this small sect was transformed into a dynamic and much greater movement, which reached non-Jews as well as Jews, and which eventually grew into one of the great religions of the world.

For these reasons, some people even contend that it is Paul, rather than Jesus, who should really be considered the founder of Christianity. Carried to its logical conclusion, that argument would lead one to place Paul higher on this list than Jesus! However, although it is not clear what Christianity would be like without the influence of St. Paul, it is quite apparent that without Jesus, Christianity would not exist at all.

However, it does not seem reasonable to consider Jesus responsible for all the things which Christian churches or individual Christians later did in his name, particularly since he would obviously disapprove of many of those things. Some of them—for example the religious wars between various Christian sects, and the barbaric massacres and persecutions of the Jews—are in such obvious contradiction to the attitudes and teachings of Jesus that it seems entirely unreasonable to say that Jesus inspired them.

Similarly, even though modern science first arose in the Christian nations of western Europe, it seems inappropriate to think of Jesus as responsible for the rise of science. Certainly, none of the early Christians interpreted the teachings of Jesus as a call for scientific investigation of the physical world. Indeed, the conversion of the Roman world to Christianity was accompanied and followed by a drastic decline in both the general level of technology and the general degree of interest in science.

That science did eventually arise in Europe is indeed an indication that there was something in the European cultural heritage that was favorable to the scientific way of thinking. That something, however, was not the sayings of Jesus, but rather Greek rationalism, as typified by the works of Aristotle and Euclid. It is noteworthy that modern science developed, not during the heyday of church power and of Christian piety, but rather on the heels of the Renaissance, a period during which Europe experienced a renewal of interest in its pre-Christian heritage.

The story of Jesus' life, as it is related in the New Testament, is familiar to most readers and will not be repeated here. However, a few points are worth noting. In the first place, most of the information that we have about Jesus' life is uncertain. We are not even sure what his original name was. Most probably it was the common Jewish name, Yehoshua (Joshua in English). The year of his birth, too, is uncertain, although 6 B.C. is a likely date. Even the year of his death, which must have been well known to his followers, is not definitely known today. Jesus himself left no writings behind, and virtually all our information concerning his life comes from the accounts in the New Testament.

Unfortunately, the Gospels contradict each other on various points. For example, Matthew and Luke give completely different versions of Jesus' last words; both of these versions, incidentally, are direct quotations from the Old Testament.

It was no accident that Jesus was able to quote from the Old Testament; though the progenitor of Christianity, he was himself a devout Jew. It has been frequently pointed out that Jesus was in many ways very similar to the Hebrew prophets of the Old Testament, and was deeply influenced by them. Like the prophets, Jesus had an extraordinarily impressive personality, which made a deep and lasting impression on the people who met him. He was charismatic in the deepest and fullest sense of the word.

However, in sharp contrast to Muhammad, who exercised political as well as religious authority, Jesus had virtually no influence on political developments during his own lifetime, or during the succeeding century. (Both men, of course, have had an enormous indirect influence on long-term political developments.) Jesus made his influence felt entirely as an ethical and spiritual leader.

If it was primarily as an ethical leader that Jesus left his mark, it is surely pertinent to ask to what extent his ethical ideas have influenced the world. One of Jesus' central precepts, certainly, was the Golden Rule. Today, the Golden Rule is accepted by most people, Christians and non-Christians alike, as a reasonable guide to moral conduct. We may not always act in accordance with it, but we usually try to do so. If Jesus had actually originated that almost universally accepted principle, he would surely have been the first man on this list.

In fact, though, the Golden Rule was an accepted precept of Judaism long before Jesus was born. Rabbi Hillel, the leading Jewish rabbi of the first century B.C., explicitly enunciated the Golden Rule and pronounced it the foremost principle of Judaism. Nor was the notion known only to the Western world. The Chinese philosopher Confucius had proposed it in about 500 B.C., and the saying also appears in the *Mahabharata*, an ancient Hindu poem. In fact, the philosophy behind the Golden Rule is accepted by almost every major religious group.

Does this mean that Jesus had no original ethical ideas? Not at all! A highly distinctive viewpoint is presented in Matthew 5:43-44:

Ye have heard that it hath been said, Thou shalt love thy neighbor, and hate thine enemy. But I say unto you, Love your enemies, bless them that curse you, do good to them that hate you, and pray for them which despitefully use you and persecute you.

And a few lines earlier: "…resist not evil: but whosoever shall smite thee on the right cheek, turn to him the other also."

Now, these ideas—which were not a part of the Judaism of Jesus' day, nor of most other religions—are surely among the most remarkable and original ethical ideas ever presented. If they were widely followed, I would have had no hesitation in placing Jesus first in this book.

But the truth is that they are not widely followed. In fact, they are not even generally accepted. Most Christians consider the injunction to "Love your enemy" as—at most— an ideal which might be realized in some perfect world, but one which is *not* a reasonable guide to conduct in the actual world we live in. We do not normally practice it, do not expect others to practice it, and do not teach our children to practice it. Jesus' most distinctive teaching, therefore, remains an intriguing but basically untried suggestion.

46

Christianity: The New Testament

The following bible verses are from The Holy Bible, revised and conformable to the edition of 1611, The World Publishing Company.

Matthew: Chapters 5-7—the Sermon on the Mount

Discussion Questions

1. Would you say that Jesus was in favor of the established order of society? What examples could you cite?

2. Was Jesus a revolutionary, a reformer, or a conservative?

3. Did Jesus support the typical values of a traditional society?

4. Does Jesus seem to follow the teachings and commandments of the Old Testament (or the "old times")?

St. Matthew

Chapter 5

1 And seeing the multitudes, he went up into a mountain: and when he was set, his disciples came unto him:

2 And he opend his mounth, and taught them, saying,

3 Blessed *are* the poor in spirit: for theirs is the kingdom of heaven.

4 Blessed *are* they that mourn: for they shall be comforted.

5 Blessed *are* the meek: for they shall inherit the earth.

6 Blessed *are* they which do hunger and thirst after righteousness: for they shall be filled.

7 Blessed *are* the merciful: for they shall obtain mercy.

8 Blessed *are* the pure in heart: for they shall see God.

9 Blessed *are* the peacemakers: for they shall be called the children of God.

10 Blessed *are* they which are persecuted for righteousness' sake: for theirs is the kingdom of heaven.

11 Blessed are ye, when *men* shall revile you, and persecute *you*, and shall say all manner of evil against you falsely, for my sake.

12 Rejoice, and be exceeding glad: for great *is* your reward in heaven: for so persecuted they the prophets which were before you.

13 Ye are the salt of the earth: but if the salt have lost his savour, wherewith shall it be salted? it is thenceforth good for nothing, but to be cast out, and to be trodden under foot of men.

14 Ye are the light of the world. A city that is set on an hill cannot be hid.

15 Neither do men light a candle, and put it under a bushel, but on a candlestick; and it giveth light unto all that are in the house.

16 Let your light so shine before men, that they may see your good works, and glorify your Father which is in heaven.

17 Think not that I am come to destroy the law, or the prophets: I am not come to destroy, but to fulfil.

18 For verily I say unto you, Till heaven and earth pass, one jot or one tittle shall in no wise pass from the law, till all be fulfilled.

19 Whosoever therefore shall break one of these least commandments, and shall teach men so, he shall be called the least in the kingdom of heaven: but whosoever shall do and teach *them*, the same shall be called great in the kingdom of heaven.

20 For I say unto you, That except your righteousness shall exceed *the righteousness* of the scribes and Phar'- i-sees, ye shall in no case enter into the kingdom of heaven.

21 Ye have heard that it was said by them of old time, Thou shalt not kill; and whosoever shall kill shall be in danger of the judgment:

22 But I say unto you, That whosoever is angry with his brother without a cause shall be in danger of the judgment: and whosoever shall say to his brother, Ra'ca, shall be in danger of the council: but whosoever shall say, Thou fool, shall be in danger of hell fire.

23 Therefore if thou bring thy gift to the altar, and there rememberest that thy brother hath ought against thee;

24 Leave there thy gift before the altar, and go thy way; first be reconciled to thy brother, and then come and offer thy gift.

25 Agree with thine adversary quickly, whiles thou art in the way with him; lest at any time the adversary deliver thee to the judge, and the judge deliver thee to the officer, and thou be cast into prison.

26 Verily I say unto thee, Thou shalt by no means come out thence, till thou hast paid the uttermost farthing.

27 Ye have heard that it was said by them of old time, Thou shalt not commit adultery:

28 But I say unto you, That whosoever looketh on a woman to lust after her hath committed adultery with her already in his heart.

29 And if thy right eye offend thee pluck it out, and cast *it* from thee: for it is profitable for thee that one of thy members should perish, and not *that* thy whole body should be cast into hell.

30 And if thy right hand offend, thee, cut it off, and cast *it* from thee: for it is profitable for thee that one of thy members should perish, and not *that* thy whole body should be cast into hell.

31 It hath been said, Whosoever shall put away his wife, let him give her a writing of divorcement:

32 But I say unto you. That whosoever shall put away his wife, saving for the cause of fornication causeth her to commit adultery: and whosoever shall marry her that is divorced committeth adultery.

33 Again, ye have heard that it hath been said by them of old time, Thou shalt not forswear thyself, but shalt perform unto the Lord thine oaths:

34 But I say unto you, Swear not at all; neither by heaven; for it is God's throne:

35 Nor by the earth; for it is his footstool: neither by Je-ru'sa-lem; for it is the city of the great King.

36 Neither shalt thou swear by thy head, because thou canst not make one hair white or black.

37 But let your communication be, Yea, yea; Nay, nay: for whatsoever is more than these cometh of evil.

38 Ye have heard that it hath been said, An eye for an eye, and a tooth for a tooth:

39 But I say unto you, That ye resist not evil: but whosoever shall smite thee on thy right cheek, turn to him the other also.

40 And if any man will sue thee at the law, and take away *thy* coat, let him have thy cloke also.

41 And whosoever shall compel thee to go a mile, go with him twain.

42 Give to him that asketh thee, and from him that would borrow of thee turn not thou away.

43 Ye have heard that it hath been said, Thou shalt love thy neighbour, and hate thine enemy.

44 But I say unto you, Love your enemies, bless them that curse you, do good to them that hate you, and pray for them which despitefully use you, and persecute you;

45 That ye may be the children of your Father which is in heaven: for he maketh his sun to rise on the evil and on the good, and sendeth rain on the just and on the unjust.

46 For if ye love them which love you, what reward have ye? do not even the publicans the same?

47 And if ye salute your brethren only, what do ye more *than others?* Do not even the publicans so?

48 Be ye therefore perfect, even as your Father which is in heaven is perfect.

Chapter 6

1 TAKE heed that ye do not your alms before men, to be seen of them: otherwise ye have no reward of your Father which is in heaven.

2 Therefore when thou doest *thine* alms, do not sound a trumpet before thee, as the hypocrites do in the synagogues and in the streets, that they may have glory of men. Verily I say unto you, They have their reward.

3 But when thou doest alms, let not thy left hand know what thy right hand doeth:

4 That thine alms may be in secret: and thy Father which seeth in secret himself shall reward thee openly.

5 And when thou prayest, thou shalt not be as the hypocrites *are*: for they love to pray standing in the synagogues and in the corners of the streets, that they may be seen of men. Verily I say unto you, They have their reward.

6 But thou, when thou prayest, enter into thy closet, and when thou hast shut thy door, pray to thy Father which is in secret; and thy Father which seeth in secret shall reward thee openly.

7 But when ye pray, use not vain repetitions, as the heathen *do*: for they think that they shall be heard for their much speaking.

8 Be not ye therefore like unto them: for your Father knoweth what things ye have need of, before ye ask him.

9 After this manner therefore pray ye: Our Father which art in heaven, Hallowed be thy name.

10 Thy kingdom come. Thy will be done in earth, as *it is* in heaven.

11 Give us this day our daily bread.

12 And forgive us our debts, as we forgive our debtors.

13 And lead us not into temptation, but deliver us from evil: For thine is the kingdom, and the power, and the glory, for ever. A-men'.

14 For if ye forgive men their trespasses, your heavenly Father will also forgive you:

15 But if ye forgive not men their trespasses, neither will your Father forgive your trespasses.

16 Moreover when ye fast, be not, as the hypocrites, of a sad countenance: for they disfigure their faces, that they may appear unto men to fast. Verily I say unto you, They have their reward.

17 But thou, when thou fastest, anoint thine head, and wash thy face;

18 That thou appear not unto men. to fast, but unto thy Father which is in secret: and thy Father, which seeth in secret, shall reward thee openly.

19 Lay not up for yourselves treasures upon earth, where moth and rust doth corrupt, and where thieves break through and steal:

20 But lay up for yourselves treasures in heaven, where neither moth nor rust doth corrupt, and where thieves do not break through nor steal:

21 For where your treasure is, there will your heart be also.

22 The light of the body is the eye: if therefore thine eye be single, thy whole body shall be full of light.

23 But if thine eye be evil, thy whole body shall be full of darkness, if therefore the light that is in thee be darkness, how great is that darkness:

24 No man can serve two masters: for either he will hate the one, and love the other; or else he will hold to the one, and despise the other. Ye cannot serve God and mammon.

25 Therefore I say unto you, Take no thought for your life, what ye shall eat, or what ye shall drink; nor yet for your body, what ye shall put on. Is not the life more than meat, and the body than raiment?

26 Behold the fowls of the air: for they sow not, neither do they reap, nor gather into barns; yet your heavenly Father feedeth them. Are ye not much better than they?

27 Which of you by taking thought can add one cubit unto his stature?

28 And why take ye thought for raiment? Consider the lilies of the field, how they grow; they toil not, neither do they spin:

29 And yet I say unto you, That even Sol'o-mon in all his glory was not arrayed like one of these.

30 Wherefore, if God so clothe the grass of the field, which to day is, and to morrow is cast into the oven, *shall he* not much more *clothe* you, O ye of little faith?

31 Therefore take no thought, saying, What shall we eat? or, What shall we drink? or, Wherewithal shall we be clothed?

32 (For after all these things do the Gen'tiles seek:) for your heavenly Father knoweth that ye have need of all these things.

33 But seek ye first the kingdom of God, and his righteousness; and all these things shall be added unto you.

34 Take therefore no thought for the morrow: for the morrow shall take thought for the things of itself. Sufficient unto the day is the evil thereof.

Chapter 7

1   Judge not, that ye be not judged.

2   For with what judgment ye judge, ye shall be judged: and with what measure ye mete, it shall be measured to you again.

3   And why beholdest thou the mote that is in thy brother's eye, but considerest not the beam that is in thine own eye?

4   Or how wilt thou say to thy brother. Let me pull out the mote out of thine eye; and, behold, a beam *is* in thine own eye?

5   Thou hypocrite, first cast out the beam out of thine own eye; and then shalt thou see clearly to cast out the mote out of thy brother's eye.

6   Give not that which is holy unto the dogs, neither cast yc your pearls before swine, lest they trample them under their feet, and turn again and rend you.

7   Ask, and it shall be given you; seek, and yc shall find; knock, and it shall be opened unto you:

8   For every one that asketh receiveth: and he that seekcth findeth; and to him that knocketh it shall be opened.

9   Or what man is there of you, whom if his son ask bread, will he give him a stone?

10 Or if he ask a fish, will he give him a serpent?

11 If ye then, being evil, know how to give good gifts unto your children, how much more shall your Father which is in heaven give good things to them that ask him?

12 Therefore all things whatsoever ye would that men should do to you, do ye even so to them: for this is the law and the prophets.

13 Enter ye in at the strait gate: for wide *is* the gate, and broad *is* the way. that leadeth to destruction, and many there be which go in thereat:

14 Because strait *is* the gate, and narrow *is* the way, which leadeth unto life, and few there be that find it.

15 Beware of false prophets, which come to you in sheep's clothing, but inwardly they are ravening wolves.

16 Ye shall know them by their fruits. Do men gather grapes of thorns, or figs of thistles?

17 Even so every good tree bringeth forth good fruit; but a corrupt tree bringeth forth evil fruit.

18 A good tree cannot bring forth, evil fruit, neither *can* a corrupt tree bring forth good fruit.

19 Every tree that bringeth not forth good fruit is hewn down, and cast into the fire.

20 Wherefore by their fruits ye shall know them.

21 Not every one that saith unto me, Lord. Lord, shall enter into the kingdom of heaven; but he that doeth. the will of my Father which is in heaven.

22 Many will say to me in that day, Lord, Lord, have we not prophesied in thy name? and in thy name have cast out devils? and in thy name done many wonderful works?

Matthew: Chapter 10

Discussion Question

1. Why does Jesus say he has not come to bring peace but a sword?

Chapter 10

1 Think not that I am come to send peace on earth: I came not to send peace, but a sword.

2 For I am come to set a man at variance against his father, and the daughter against her mother, and the daughter in law against her mother in law.

3 And a man's foes *shall be* they of his own household.

4 He that loveth father or mother more than me is not worthy of me: and he that loveth son or daughter more than me is not worthy of me.

5 And he that taketh not his cross, and followeth after me, is not worthy of me.

6 He that findeth his life shall lose it: and he that loseth his life for my sake shall find it.

Matthew: Chapter 16

Discussion Question

1. Does Jesus seem to make Peter the head of the Church?

Chapter 16

1 When Je'sus came into the coasts of Caes-a-rea Phi-lip'pi, he asked his disciples, saying, Whom do men say that I the Son of man am?

2 And they said, Some *say that thou art* John the Bap'tist: some, E-li'as; and others, Jer-e-mi'as, or one of the prophets.

3 He saith unto them, But whom say ye that I am?

4 And Si'mon Pe'ter answered and said, Thou art the Christ, the Son of the living God.

5 And Je'sus answered and said unto him, Blessed art thou, Si'mon Bar-jo'na: for flesh and blood hath not revealed *it* unto thee, but my Father which is in heaven.

6 And I say also unto thee, That thou art Pe'ter, and upon this rock I will build my church; and the gates of hell shall not prevail against it.

7 And I will give unto thee the keys of the kingdom of heaven: and whatsoever thou shalt bind on earth shall be bound in heaven: and whatsoever thou shalt loose on earth shall be loosed in heaven.

Matthew Chapter 19

Discussion Question

1. What does Jesus say is necessary for the individual to enter the kingdom of heaven?

Chapter 19

1 And, behold, one came and said unto him. Good Master, what good thing shall I do, that I may have eternal life?

2 And he said unto him, Why callest thou me good? *there is* none good but one, *that is*, God: but if thou wilt enter into life, keep the commandments.

3 He said unto him, Which? Je'sus said, Thou shalt do no murder, Thou shalt not commit adultery, Thou shalt not steal, Thou shalt not bear false witness,

4 Honour thy father and *thy* mother: and, Thou shalt love thy neighbour as thyself.

5 The young man saith unto him, All these things have I kept from my youth up: what lack I yet?

6 Je'sus said unto him, If thou wilt be perfect, go *and* sell that thou hast, and give to the poor, and thou shalt have treasure in heaven: and come *and* follow me.

7 But when the young man heard that saying, he went away sorrowful: for he had great possessions.

8 Then said Je'sus unto his disciples, Verily I say uhto you. That a rich man shall hardly enter into the kingdom of heaven.

9 And again I say unto you, It is easier for a camel to go through the eye of a needle, than for a rich man to enter into the kingdom of God.

10 When his disciples heard *it*, they were exceedingly amazed, saying, Who then can be saved?

11 But Je'sus beheld *them*, and said unto them, With men this is impossible; but with God all things are possible.

12 Then answered Pe'ter and said unto him, Behold, we have forsaken all, and followed thee; what shall we have therefore?

13 And Je'sus said unto them, Verily I say unto you, That ye which have followed me, in the regeneration when the Son of man shall sit in the throne of his glory, ye also shall sit upon twelve thrones, judging the twelve tribes of Is'ra-el.

14 And every one that hath forsaken houses, or brethren, or sisters, or father, or mother, or wife, or children, or lands, for my name's sake, shall receive an hundredfold, and shall inherit everlasting life.

15 But may *that are* first shall be last; and the last *shall be* first.

St. Paul: Letter to the Romans: Chapter 13

Discussion Question

1. What should be the relationship between the believer and the state?

Romans

Chapter 13

1 Let every, soul be subject unto the higher powers. For there is no power but of God: the powers that be are ordained of God.

2 Whosoever therefore resisteth the power, resisteth the ordinance of God: and they that resist shall receive to themselves damnation.

3 For rulers are not a terror to good works, but to the evil. Wilt thou then not be afraid of the power? do that which is good, and thou shalt have praise of the same:

4 For he is the minister of God to thee for good. But if thou do that which is evil, be afraid; for he beareth not the sword in vain: for he is the minister of God, a revenger to *execute* wrath upon him that doeth evil.

5 Wherefore *ye* must heeds be subject, not only for wrath, but also for conscience sake.

6 For for this cause pay ye tribute also: for they are God's ministers, attending continually upon this very thing.

7 Render therefore to all their dues: tribute to whom tribute *is due*; custom to whom custom; fear to whom fear; honour to whom honour.

8 Owe no man any thing, but to love one another: for he that loveth another hath fulfilled the law.

9 For this, Thou shalt not commit adultery. Thou shalt not kill. Thou shalt not steal, Thou shalt not bear false witness, Thou shalt not covet; and if *there be* any other commandment, it is briefly comprehended in this saying, namely, Thou shalt love thy neighbour as thyself.

10 Love worketh no ill to his neighbour: therefore love is the fulfilling of the law.

St. Paul: First Letter to the Corinthians: Chapter 11

Discussion Question

1. What is to be the relationship between men and women?

Corinthians

Chapter 11

1 Be ye followers of me, even as I also *am* of Christ.

2 Now I praise you, brethren, that ye remember me in all things, and keep the ordinances, as I delivered *them* to you.

3 But I would have you know, that the head of every man is Christ; and the head of the

woman *is* the man; and the head of Christ *is* God.

4 Every man praying or prophesying, having *his* head covered, dishonoureth his head.

5 But every woman that prayeth or prophesieth with *her* head uncovered dishonoureth her head: for that is even all one as if she were shaven.

6 For if the woman be not covered, let her also be shorn: but if it be a shame for a woman to be shorn or shaven, let her be covered.

7 For a man indeed ought not to cover *his* head, forasmuch as he is the image and glory of God: but the woman is the glory of the man.

8 For the man is not of the woman; but the woman of the man.

9 Neither was the man created for the woman; but the woman for the man.

10 For this cause ought the woman to have power on *her* head because of the angels.

11 Nevertheless neither is the man without the woman, neither the woman without the man, in the Lord.

12 For as the woman *is* of the man, even so *is* the man also by the woman; but all things of God.

13 Judge in yourselves: is it comely that a woman pray unto God uncovered?

14 Doth not even nature itself teach you, that, if a man have long hair, it is a shame unto him?

15 But if a woman have long hair, it is a glory to her: for *her* hair is given her for a covering.

St Paul: Letter to the Galatians: Chapter 3

Discussion Question

1. Are Christians required to follow the law (commandments) of the OldTestament? Why or why not?

Galatians

Chapter 3

1 But before faith came, we were kept under the law, shut up unto the faith which should afterwards be revealed.

2 Wherefore the law was our schoolmaster *to bring us* unto Christ, that we might be justified by faith.

3 But after that faith is come, we are no longer under a schoolmaster.

4 For ye are all the children of God by faith in Christ Je'sus.

5 For as many of you as have been baptized into Christ have put on Christ.

6 There is neither Jew nor Greek, there is neither bond nor free, there is neither male nor female: for ye are all one in Christ Je'sus.

7 And if ye *be* Christ's, then are ye A'braham's seed, and heirs according to the promise.

47

Europe: From Crisis to Expansion

In the following selection Fernand Braudel surveys the history of Europe from the decline of the Roman Empire through the early Middle Ages.

Discussion Questions

1. What were the ingredients that made Europe "a coherent whole?"

2. Why is Charlemagne's empire called the "first Europe?"

3. What were the various threats Europe faced and how did the Europeans deal with them?

4. Was feudalism a positive or negative development?

5. How consistent is Braudel's view of Europe with Katz's (#49)?

Europe Takes Shape: Fifth to Thirteenth Centuries

The accompanying maps, showing the major invasions of Europe, make it unnecessary to recount at length the accidents and catastrophes in the course of which the Western end of the European Peninsula gradually became a coherent whole. Europe's geographical area was defined in the course of a series of wars and invasions. It all began with the division of the Roman Empire, confirmed but not caused when it was partitioned on the death of Theodosius in 395 AD.

The Eastern Mediterranean has almost always been populated, endowed with a very old civilization, and engaged in a number of economic pursuits. From the very beginning of the Roman conquest, there was also a Western Mediterranean—a Far West, so to speak, which was primitive if not barbaric. There, by founding cities, Rome partially established a civilization which, if not always exactly Roman, was at least an imitation of the original.

Once the 395 partition had occurred, the *pars Occidentalis* underwent a series of disasters on the three frontiers surrounding it: in the North-East along the Rhine and the Danube; in the South on the Mediterranean; and in the West on the extensive "ocean frontier" from Denmark to Gibraltar, which for a long time had been peaceful and secure. The new threats, and the reaction to them, defined and settled Europe's geographical area.

In the North-East, the double *limes* of the Rhine and the Danube could not resist the pressure of the Barbarians, fleeing from the Huns. In 405, Radagaisus led a Barbarian army into Italy as far as Tuscany. Soon afterwards, on 31 December 406, a horde of Barbarian peoples crossed the frozen Rhine near Mainz and overcame the Gallic provinces.

Once broken through, the door was not closed again until the defeat of the Huns at Chalons-sur-Marne in 451. After that, reconstruction was fairly rapid. Merovingian Gaul re-established the Rhine frontier, and it was soon shifted well to the East: the Carolingians maintained it far beyond the river, imposing their authority over the whole of Germany and pressing as far as "Hungary," then under the Avars. Conversion to Christianity, in which the great St. Boniface played a leading role, consolidated this huge Eastward advance. The West succeeded, in fact, where the caution of Augustus and Tiberius had failed.

From then onwards, Germany protected the Western world against the Asiatic East. It halted the Hungarian cavalry at Merseburg in 933, then crushed it at Augsburg in 955. The Germanic Holy Roman Empire derived its *raison d'etre* from this protective role when in 962 it replaced the Carolingian Empire, which had been founded by Charlemagne on Christmas Day in the year 800.

No longer threatened, the Eastern frontier became a growth point, and was pushed Eastwards with the birth of Christian States in Poland, Hungary and Bohemia, as a result of Germanic colonization in the eleventh to thirteenth centuries. Here, indeed, there was relative peace until the huge Mongol invasion in about 1240, miraculously halted on the edge of Poland and the Adriatic. Its only victim was South-Western Russia.

In the South, a dangerous frontier was created by the first successes of the Muslim conquest—all the more so because of successive

From *A History of Civilizations* by Fernand Bruadel, translated by Richard Mayne. Translation © Richard Mayne, 1993. Reproduced by permission of Penguin Books Ltd.

"defections," by North Africa (hitherto Christian), by Spain and then by Sicily. In the West, the Mediterranean became a "Muslim lake." The first effective reaction against this was the establishment of heavy cavalry, which gave Charles Martel his victory at Poitiers in 732. The result of that victory was the immense but short-lived triumph of the Carolingians, whose influence was felt beyond the Rhine, and as far as Saxony and Hungary.

But Islam was a powerful neighbour, and Christianity had to undertake a difficult and dramatic campaign against it, inventing its own Holy War, the Crusade. Crusading became interminable. The First Crusade—not, obviously, the first war against Islam, but the first that was collective, self-conscious and spectacular—was launched in 1095. The last, which was by no means the end of the struggle, was St. Louis's expedition to Tunisia in 1270.

Although the Egyptian recapture of Acre in 1291 put an end to these great Eastern adventures, the appeal of crusading continued to trouble and excite emotions in the West, leading to unexpected upsurges in the fifteenth and sixteenth centuries. In the seventeenth century, again, there were "the lonely Crusaders," as they were called by Alphonse Dupront, an historian who has traced as far as the nineteenth century this obsessive mystique. It can even be detected as an element in the last days of colonialism.

Recent and very doubtful calculations have estimated that between 1095 and 1291 the Crusades cost the West 4 or 5 million men out of its small population of barely 50 million. No one can say whether these figures are accurate. But in any case the Crusades were a dramatic experience for Europe in the making, and its first real triumph—in at least two respects. The first was its precarious and provisional recapture of the Holy Sepulchre; the second, its definitive reconquest of the rich Mediterranean. The Crusades completed the process whereby the West's Southern borders were fixed; and for a

long time, until the great maritime discoveries in the fifteenth and sixteenth centuries, they were the most important of all.

To the North-West and West, as far South as the Mediterranean, Europe was taken unawares, in the eighth, ninth and tenth centuries, by the Norse invasions—taken unawares and powerless, hence all the more distressed. Except for The Netherlands, Ireland and Italy, Europe was slow to develop seapower of her own. Yet in the long run the invasions proved advantageous.

To say this is not to defend the pitiless Norse pirates. They took a savage toll of Europe. Yet it is hard not to admire admirable exploits: their excursions across the entire breadth of Russia, their discovery of America—no sooner found than lost again because, as Henri Pirenne wrote, "Europe did not yet need it." Economic historians are still more indulgent to the Vikings, arguing that by putting back into circulation the treasures that they pillaged, especially from the Church, they reactivated capital which had been immobilized as precious metal, lying idle since the Western economic recession following the fall of Rome. The Vikings' thefts, it is argued, made them suppliers of money; and it was this money that once more stimulated the economy of the West.

To understand the first European civilization, one has to remember the disasters it suffered, imagine the appalling "Dark Ages" of the ninth and tenth centuries and realize the primary poverty of a continent that had to struggle every day simply to survive. Lacking broad outlets, reduced to a subsistence economy, this impoverished Europe was in Marc Bloch's words "a citadel besieged or rather invaded"; and at that time it could not bear the weight of very large States. They were no sooner formed than they collapsed or crumbled. Charlemagne's Empire, rapidly built, disintegrated not long after the death of the great Emperor in 814. The Germanic Holy Roman Empire fairly soon became a huge dilapidated mansion, and Western Europe split into countless tiny domains. The feudal system (based on the fief or, in Latin, the *feodum*) maintained units that were more theoretical than real within the various kingdoms of the West, some of which were very slowly modernized, like France, while others remained wilfully archaic, like the German Empire.

Yet this troubled world, oppressed from within and attacked from without, was already quite clearly a homogeneous civilization. Despite its diversity, it has to be called, in Lucien Febvre's words, a "feudal civilization," which everywhere tackled the same major problems, in conditions and with solutions that were often alike. This civilization was born of many ethnic and economic strains, with repeated struggles, common beliefs, and above all the same difficulties which it tried to remedy.

Feudalism built Europe. In the eleventh and twelfth centuries, Europe achieved its first youthful vigour under a lively feudal regime—a particular and very original political, social and economic order, based on a civilization that was already at its second or third fermentation.

But how should this multi-coloured civilization be defined?

There could be no feudalism, in Europe or elsewhere, without the previous fragmentation of a larger political entity. In the present case, the entity in question was the huge Carolingian Empire—the first "Europe," its name affirmed as such (*Europa, vel regnum Caroli*), which disappeared soon after the death of its great Emperor, whom a court poet hailed as *"pater Europae,"* the Father of Europe.

Feudalism was the natural consequence of the Empire's fragmentation. In June 1940, when France was falling to the Nazis, a French officer had a dream: he wished that every unit of the army could by some miracle recover for a moment its autonomy, the right to act as it saw fit, without obeying the general orders which

bound it to a High Command that was growing less and less effective and, without wishing to, was dragging everyone into the drift towards defeat. The feudal system was born of a similar reaction—but with the essential difference, among others, that the disaster which prompted it was less rapid than that of June 1940. It took several centuries for feudalism to be formed. Yet its very nature was both defensive and local. The castle on its mount, with the village or villages it protected huddled close to it: this was not an accidental or optional arrangement but a defensive weapon.

Nevertheless, feudalism was something else as well. It was a society based on relations between man and man, a chain of dependencies; it was an economy in which land was not the only but the most frequent recompense for services rendered. The lord received from the king, his suzerain, or from a lord of higher rank than himself, a fief (*feodum*) or lordship. In return, he had to supply a series of services, including assistance in four cases. He had to pay his lord's ransom. He had to pay when his eldest son was dubbed a knight. He had to pay when his eldest daughter was married. He had to pay when his suzerain went on a Crusade. In turn, the lord ceded parts or elements of his own lordship to those subordinate to him, whether minor lords or peasants. To the latter he granted land (we still refer to "tenure" and "tenement"), which the peasant tilled, paying a rent as money (quit-rent), as a portion of the crops (a tithe, or share-cropping), or as labour. The lord in return defended and protected the peasant.

This social pyramid, with its obligations, its rules and its allegiances, mobilizing economic, political and military strength, enabled the West to survive and to safeguard its old Christian and Roman heritage, to which it added the ideas, virtues and ideologies of the seigneurial regime (its own civilization).

Europe by then had forgotten the name of Europe. In practice, it had become a compartmentalized world, where all that mattered was the small region, the narrow, limited mother country.

Certainly, in these early days of Europe's life, there were very great advantages in each region's being able to grow at leisure in its own way, like a plant in the wild. Each was thus able to become a robust and self-aware entity, ready to defend its territory and its independence.

What is interesting is that nevertheless, despite this political compartmentalization, there was a convergence in Europe's civilization and culture. A traveller on a pilgrimage (to St. James of Compostela, for instance) or going about his business, felt as much at home in Lübeck as in Paris, in London as in Bruges, in Cologne as in Burgos, Milan or Venice. Moral, religious and cultural values, and the rules of war, love, life and death were the same everywhere, from one fief to another, whatever their quarrels, their revolts or their conflicts. That is why there was indeed one single Christendom, as Marc Bloch said: there was what might be called a civilization of chivalry, of the minstrel and the troubadour, of courtly love.

The Crusades expressed that unity, because they were mass movements, collective adventures and passions, common to all the innumerable small-scale mother countries.

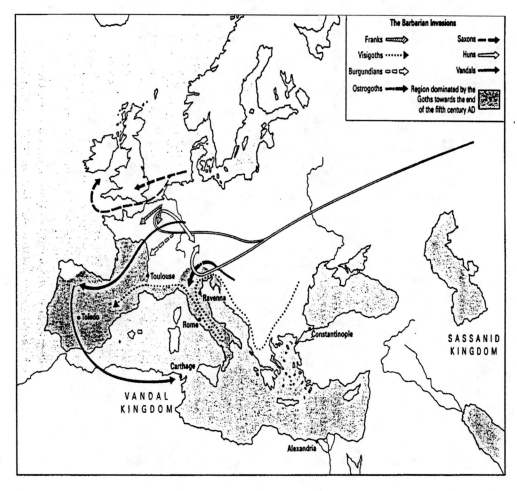

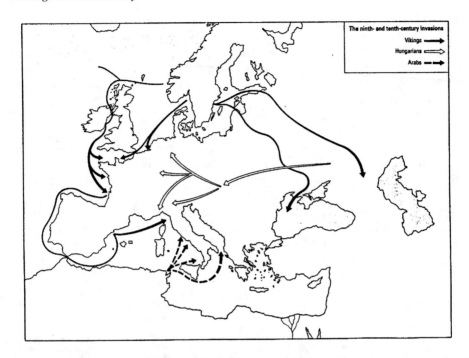

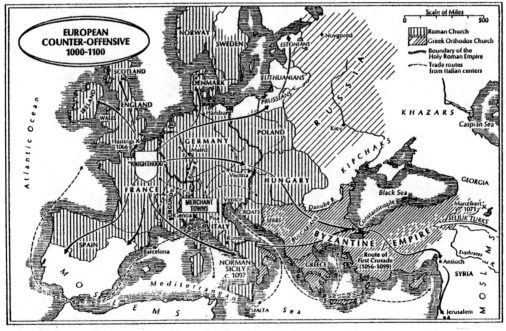

From *A World History*, Third Edition by William H. McNeill. Copyright © 1967, 1971, 1979 by William H. McNeill. Used by permission of Oxford University Press, Inc.

48

The Ranking of Muhammad in History

In his book *The 100*, Hart ranks Muhammad Number One, the most influential person who ever lived (whose name we know and who is dead.)

Discussion Questions

1. What reasons does Hart provide for this ranking? Do you agree with it?

2. Although there are more Christians than Muslims (by 1990 there were an estimated 950 million Muslims to about 1.5 billion Christians), why might the founder of Islam rank higher than the founder of Christianity?

3. Was Muhammad "greater" than Jesus?

Muhammad
570 A.D. – 632 A.D.

My choice of Muhammad to lead the list of the world's most influential persons may surprise some readers and may be questioned by others, but he was the only man in history who was supremely successful on both the religious and secular levels.

Of humble origins, Muhammad founded and promulgated one of the world's great religions, and became an immensely effective political leader. Today, thirteen centuries after his death, his influence is still powerful and pervasive.

The majority of the persons in this book had the advantage of being born and raised in centers of civilization, highly cultured or politically pivotal nations. Muhammad, however, was born in the year 570, in the city of Mecca, in southern Arabia, at that time a backward area of the world, far from the centers of trade, art, and learning. Orphaned at age six, he was reared in modest surroundings. Islamic tradition tells us that he was illiterate. His economic position improved when, at age twenty-five, he married a wealthy widow. Nevertheless, as he approached forty, there was little outward indication that he was a remarkable person.

Most Arabs at that time were pagans, who believed in many gods. There were, however, in Mecca, a small number of Jews and Christians; it was from them no doubt that Muhammad first learned of a single, omnipotent God who ruled the entire universe. When he was forty years old, Muhammad became convinced that this one true God (Allah) was speaking to him, and had chosen him to spread the true faith.

For three years, Muhammad preached only to close friends and associates. Then, about 613, he began preaching in public. As he slowly gained converts, the Meccan authorities came to consider him a dangerous nuisance. In 622, fearing for his safety, Muhammad fled to Medina (a city some 200 miles north of Mecca), where he had been offered a position of considerable political power.

This flight, called the *Hegira*, was the turning point of the Prophet's life. In Mecca, he had had few followers. In Medina, he had many more, and he soon acquired an influence that made him a virtual dictator. During the next few years, while Muhammad's following grew rapidly, a series of battles were fought between Medina and Mecca. This war ended in 630 with Muhammad's triumphant return to Mecca as conqueror. The remaining two and one-half years of his life witnessed the rapid conversion of the Arab tribes to the new religion. When Muhammad died, in 632, he was the effective ruler of all of southern Arabia.

The Bedouin tribesmen of Arabia had a reputation as fierce warriors. But their number was small; and plagued by disunity and internecine warfare, they had been no match for the larger armies of the kingdoms in the settled agricultural areas to the north. However, unified by Muhammad for the first time in history, and

---

From *The 100: A Ranking of the Most Influential Persons in History* by Michael H. Hart. Copyright 1978. Reprinted by permission of Carol Publishing Group.

inspired by their fervent belief in the one true God, these small Arab armies now embarked upon one of the most astonishing series of conquests in human history. To the northeast of Arabia lay the large Neo-Persian Empire of the Sassanids; to the northwest lay the Byzantine, or Eastern Roman Empire, centered in Constantinople. Numerically, the Arabs were no match for their opponents. On the field of battle, though, the inspired Arabs rapidly conquered all of Mesopotamia, Syria, and Palestine. By 642, Egypt had been wrested from the Byzantine Empire, while the Persian armies had been crushed at the key battles of Qadisiya in 637, and Nehavend in 642.

But even these enormous conquests—which were made under the leadership of Muhammad's close friends and immediate successors, Abu Bakr and Umar ibn al-Khattab—did not mark the end of the Arab advance. By 711, the Arab armies had swept completely across North Africa to the Atlantic Ocean. There they turned north and, crossing the Strait of Gibraltar, overwhelmed the Visigothic kingdom in Spain.

For a while, it must have seemed that the Moslems would overwhelm all of Christian Europe. However, in 732, at the famous Battle of Tours, a Moslem army, which had advanced into the center of France, was at last defeated by the Franks. Nevertheless, in a scant century of fighting, these Bedouin tribesmen, inspired by the word of the Prophet, had carved out an empire stretching from the borders of India to the Atlantic Ocean—the largest empire that the world had yet seen. And everywhere that the armies conquered, large-scale conversion to the new faith eventually followed.

Now, not all of these conquests proved permanent. The Persians, though they have remained faithful to the religion of the Prophet, have since regained their independence from the Arabs. And in Spain, more than seven centuries of warfare finally resulted in the Christians reconquering the entire peninsula. However,

Mesopotamia and Egypt, the two cradles of ancient civilization, have remained Arab, as has the entire coast of North Africa. The new religion, of course, continued to spread, in the intervening centuries, far beyond the borders of the original Moslem conquests. Currently, it has tens of millions of adherents in Africa and Central Asia, and even more in Pakistan and northern India, and in Indonesia. In Indonesia, the new faith has been a unifying factor. In the Indian subcontinent, however, the conflict between Moslems and Hindus is still a major obstacle to unity.

How, then, is one to assess the overall impact of Muhammad on human history? Like all religions, Islam exerts an enormous influence upon the lives of its followers. It is for this reason that the founders of the world's great religions all figure prominently in this book. Since there are roughly twice as many Christians as Moslems in the world, it may initially seem strange that Muhammad has been ranked higher than Jesus. There are two principal reasons for that decision. First, Muhammad played a far more important role in the development of Islam than Jesus did in the development of Christianity. Although Jesus was responsible for the main ethical and moral precepts of Christianity (insofar as these differed from Judaism), St. Paul was the main developer of Christian theology, its principal proselytizer, and the author of a large portion of the New Testament.

Muhammad, however, was responsible for both the theology of Islam and its main ethical and moral principles. In addition, he played the key role in proselytizing the new faith, and in establishing the religious practices of Islam. Moreover, he is the author of the Moslem holy scriptures, the Koran, a collection of certain of Muhammad's insights that he believed had been directly revealed to him by Allah. Most of these utterances were copied more or less faithfully during Muhammad's lifetime and were collected together in authoritative form not long after his death. The Koran, therefore, closely represents Muhammad's ideas and teachings and to a considerable extent his exact words. No such detailed compilation of the teachings of Christ has survived. Since the Koran is at least as important to Moslems as the Bible is to Christians, the influence of Muhammad through the medium of the Koran has been enormous. It is probable that the relative influence of Muhammad on Islam has been larger than the combined influence of Jesus Christ and St. Paul on Christianity. On the purely religious level, then, it seems likely that Muhammad has been as influential in human history as Jesus.

Furthermore, Muhammad (unlike Jesus) was a secular as well as a religious leader. In fact, as the driving force behind the Arab conquests, he may well rank as the most influential political leader of all time.

Of many important historical events, one might say that they were inevitable and would have occurred even without the particular political leader who guided them. For example, the South American colonies would probably have won their independence from Spain even if Simón Bolívar had never lived. But this cannot be said of the Arab conquests. Nothing similar had occurred before Muhammad, and there is no reason to believe that the conquests would have been achieved without him. The only comparable conquests in human history are those of the Mongols in the thirteenth century, which were primarily due to the influence of Genghis Khan. These conquests, however, though more extensive than those of the Arabs, did not prove permanent, and today the only areas occupied by the Mongols are those that they held prior to the time of Genghis Khan.

It is far different with the conquests of the Arabs. From Iraq to Morocco, there extends a whole chain of Arab nations united not merely by their faith in Islam, but also by their Arabic language, history, and culture. The centrality of the Koran in the Moslem religion and the fact that it is written in Arabic have probably prevented the Arab language from breaking up into mutually unintelligible dialects, which might otherwise have occurred in the intervening thirteen centuries. Differences and divisions between these Arab states exist, of course, and they are considerable, but the partial disunity should not blind us to the important elements of unity that have continued to exist. For instance, neither Iran nor Indonesia, both oil-producing states and both Islamic in religion, joined in the oil embargo of the winter of 1973-74. It is no coincidence that all of the Arab states, and only the Arab states, participated in the embargo.

We see, then, that the Arab conquests of the seventh century have continued to play an important role in human history, down to the present day. It is this unparalleled combination of secular and religious influence which I feel entitles Muhammad to be considered the most influential single figure in human history.

49

Medieval Europe: Church and State

While many religions accept a distinction of some sort between a specialized religious class and the ordinary person, one of the unique aspects of Christianity was the development of a highly articulated hierarchy among the clergy. The reasons for this were varied, the major factors being the pattern set by the structure of the Roman Empire and the perceived need to define Christian beliefs precisely. The result was a spiritual hierarchy of priests, bishops and popes, the latter of which asserted the authority to pronounce dogma deemed to be orthodox.

But another issue which was also critical in the early church was its relationship to political authorities, specifically the Roman Empire. Jesus had said, "Render unto Caesar the things that are Caesar's and to God the things that are God's;" St. Paul, in his Letter to the Romans, argued that "the powers that be are ordained of God." Just what belonged to Caesar, or any ruler, and what belonged to God?

Pope Gelasius I (492–496) proposed the most influential resolution of the jurisdictional conflicts between church and state in his Theory of the Two Swords. According to this theory, Christian society is governed by two powers, the spiritual (embodied in the church) and the temporal (embodied in the state). But this view should not be confused with the modern notion of the separation of church and state, for to Gelasius there can be no such distinction. Gelasius' spiritual sword reigns over all Christians, rulers and subjects alike. A ruler is primarily responsible for providing a peaceful and orderly atmosphere within which the clergy can carry out their spiritual functions promoting the salvation of souls; and rulers themselves are expected to be good Christians who accept the truth as defined by the church and live in accordance with the sacraments. As a Christian in need of salvation, therefore, a ruler is subject even to a priest. This would permit a priest, bishop or pope to interfere in a way that we today would consider inappropriate or unacceptable. But the opposite could also occur since the church is a worldly institution with temporal assets like land and wealth and procedures such as the election of a pope. In the Middle Ages the state involved itself in both.

One of the most famous conflicts between "church" and "state" in the Middle Ages was the Investiture Controversy of the late 11th century. Since feudalism prevailed in Europe at the time and since it was common for laymen to grant land as a fief to a priest or bishop for ecclesiastical use, laymen "invested" clergy with these estates making the clergy, in effect, vassals of laymen. Pope Gregory VII disputed what amounted to temporal control over churches and issued his famous *Dictatus Papae* (ca. 1090) which was a very strong assertion of papal power for the times.

Assertions such as this continued throughout the rest of the Middle Ages but were often met by opposition from partisans of temporal power. Rulers could and did argue, ala St. Paul, that their power came directly from God, not the church, and that they therefore had their own source of authority.

Discussion Questions

1. How does the *Dictatus Papae* fit in with Gelasius' Theory of the Two Swords?

2. Would the assertions of the *Dictatus Papae* be acceptable today?

Papal Assertions—The *Dictatus Papae*

1. That the Roman church was established by God alone.

2. That the Roman pontiff alone is rightly called universal.

3. That he alone has the power to depose and reinstate bishops.

4. That his legate, even if he be of lower ecclesiastical rank, presides over bishops in council, and has the power to give sentence of deposition against them.

5. That the pope has the power to depose those who are absent [*i.e.,* without giving them a hearing].

6. That, among other things, we ought not to remain in the same house with those whom he has excommunicated.

7. That he alone has the right, according to the necessity of the occasion, to make new laws, to create new bishoprics, to make a monastery of a chapter of canons, and *vice versa*, and either to divide a rich bishopric or to unite several poor ones.

8. That he alone may use the imperial insignia.

9. That all princes shall kiss the foot of the pope alone.

10. That his name alone is to be recited in the churches.

11. That the name applied to him belongs to him alone.

12. That he has the power to depose emperors.

13. That he has the right to transfer bishops from one see to another when it becomes necessary.

14. That he has the right to ordain as a cleric anyone from any part of the church whatsoever.

15. That anyone ordained by him may rule [as bishop] over another church, but cannot serve [as priest] in it, and that such a cleric may not receive a higher rank from any other bishop.

16. That no general synod may be called without his order.

17. That no action of a synod and no book shall be regarded as canonical without his authority.

18. That his decree can be annulled by no one, and that he can annul the decrees of anyone.

19. That he can be judged by no one.

20. That no one shall dare to condemn a person who has appealed to the apostolic seat.

21. That the important cases of any church whatsoever shall be referred to the Roman church [that is, to the pope].

22. That the Roman church has never erred and will never err to all eternity, according to the testimony of the holy scriptures.

23. That the Roman pontiff who has been canonically ordained is made holy by the merits of St. Peter, according to the testimony of St. Ennodius, bishop of Pavia, which is confirmed by many of the holy fathers, as is shown by the decrees of the blessed pope Symmachus.

24. That by his command or permission subjects may accuse their rulers.

25. That he can depose and reinstate bishops without the calling of a synod.

26. That no one can be regarded as catholic who does not agree with the Roman church.

27. That he has the power to absolve subjects from their oath of fidelity to wicked rulers.

Gregory VII, *"Dictatus Papae," A Source Book for Mediaeval History*, ed. Oliver J. Thatcher and Edgar H. MacNeal (New York: Charles Scribner's Sons, 1905), pp. 136–138.

50

Islam: Misconceptions

Despite the many similarities between Judaism, Christianity and Islam, Westerners have often seen the Islamic world as something alien and even hostile, living in a world apart. The next reading deals with some of the most common misperceptions about Islam from the Western perspective.

Discussion Questions

1. What are the misconceptions mentioned in the reading?

2. How does the author refute these misconceptions?

3. How would a Muslim react to these views?

4. Where do misconceptions like this come from?

Islam is a much misunderstood and misrepresented religion. Over the centuries it has been portrayed by many Western writers and speakers as an anti-Jewish and anti-Christian religion, while in fact Islam teaches religious tolerance. In his charter to the city of Medina, Muhammed, the prophet through whom God revealed the truths of Islam, said: "The Jews who attach themselves to our commonwealth shall be protected from all insults and vexations; they shall have an equal right with our own people to our assistance and good offices." He also stated that both Jews and Christians shall be permitted to practice their religion as freely as the Muslims. The Islamic Republic of Pakistan has given concrete expression to this creed of toleration by guaranteeing religious freedom in its Constitution.

Islam recognizes the truth that is contained in the doctrines of Judaism and Christianity and confirms Abraham, Moses, Isaiah, Jesus, and others as true prophets of God who preceded Muhammed. Muhammed was the last and final prophet and therefore is called "the Seal of the Prophets." Islam holds that the Old Testament of the Jews and the New Testament of the Christians were revelations from God, and those who believe in them are called "People of the Book." But these revelations are incomplete, and thus the necessity for the Koran, which embodies the complete and uncorrupted revelation from God. Although Abraham correctly revealed the oneness of God, the Jews who came after him forgot this revelation and took to themselves golden idols. Jesus was chosen by God to reveal this and other truths, but his followers made him a god, thus dehumanizing him and humanizing

God. Jesus, like Muhammed, was a true prophet and a man, not a god.

Western novels and serious historical and religious works have often indicated that the sword was the primary instrument of conversion for Muslims. They allege that it was the practice of the Muslims to give the nonbeliever two choices—conversion or death. There have been incidents when Muslims, caught up in the fury of war or lacking knowledge of the basic tenets of Islam, have used force to convert others to their faith, but the history of many religions is strewn with zealots who have utilized torture and force for this purpose. The followers of Islam have probably sinned less in this regard than the disciples of other religions. Muslims, as a rule, adhere closely to the injunction of the Koran: "If it had been thy Lord's will, they would all have believed,—all who are on earth! Wilt thou then compel mankind, against their will, to believe!" (Surah X, 99) And in the Koran it is also stated: "Let there be no compulsion in religion." (Surah II, 256) And "Unto you be your religion, and unto me mine." (Surah CIX, 6)

A conception of Muslims as addicts of war has also grown up in Western minds. Islam does permit its followers to resist evil, and those who injure others wrongly may be punished to the full extent of the injury. The Muslims also believe in the concept of a jihad, or "holy war," in which those who die become martyrs and go immediately to heaven. But this holy war must be a defensive one or waged to right some wrong. The Koran states: "Defend yourself against your enemies; but attack them not first: for God does not love transgressors." (Surah II, 190) Even when they are engaged in a righteous war, Muhammed required his followers to spare the women and children, sacred objects, and fields of grain and orchards, and to refrain from mutilating the wounded and the dead. Maddened by the passion of war, many forgot the precepts of Muhammed, but these are the basic teachings of Islam on the conduct of war.

Islam has been repeatedly slandered as a degrader of women and a refuge for lascivious men whose libidinous desire may be fully and legitimately satisfied under the protective cloak of religion. Numerous historical romances, past and present, employ this stereotype of Islam to inject sex and spicy incidents into the story. Thus an image of Islam as basically carnal is passed on from generation to generation of Westerners. The only feature of Islam known by many Westerners is that it permits polygamy. Such an image does not present a complete and true picture of Islam's teaching and practice with regard to women. At the time Islam was born in Arabia in the seventh century, women were in a most degraded state. They were at the complete mercy of their husbands and fathers to do with as they liked; they had no inheritance rights; infant daughters were unwanted and frequently killed; and marriage was often conditional and temporary with no recourse for the women should her husband divorce her, as husbands frequently did. Women were looked upon as mere playthings or work animals to be discarded when their usefulness was over. Muhammed did much to mitigate this evil. He prohibited the killing of daughters and demanded that they have the right of inheritance of the family property. His enlightened laws gave to the women of his day and later a status much higher than formerly and prepared the way for the astounding progress that the modern Muslim women are making today toward full equality with men.

Islam views marriage very seriously. A woman must give her full consent before she can be married to any man even if he is a king. Although divorce is permitted in Islam, it is not regarded as a routine solution but as an exceptional one. Before most Muslim marriages, the prospective husband is required to set aside for his future wife a certain sum of money which might be termed a dowry. She may take this dowry at the time of marriage, but it is hers to claim whenever she desires it. Should they be divorced she may take possession of this dowry, if she has not already received it at the time of the marriage or thereafter, and the former husband must support her until she remarries. The Koran states: "For divorced women maintenance should be provided on a reasonable scale. This is a duty for the righteous." (Surah II, 241) Wives are also permitted to initiate divorce proceedings themselves. Islam has elevated the status of women from its previous deplorable depths and given them a certain degree of social, legal, and economic security. But what about polygamy?

The Koran does state: "You may marry two, three, or four wives, but not more." (Surah IV, 3) But Islam lays down a hard condition for those who desire more than one wife, for the Koran also states that if a man cannot deal equitably and justly with more than one wife, he shall marry only one. (Surah IV, 3) This means that a man cannot have more than one wife if he cannot give them all the same material benefits, the same love, the same respect, and the same treatment. Since this is an almost impossible condition for the ordinary man, the true follower of Islam cannot generally practice polygamy. This hard qualification has oriented most Muslims toward monogamy, and today there are relatively few Muslims who have more than one wife.

51

Islam: The Koran

The Muslim holy book is the most tangible symbol of Islam and is considered to be Allah's greatest miracle. Muslims believe it contains the actual words of God himself transmitted to Muhammad through the archangel Gabriel. In that sense it is the "Word of God" in a more literal way than Jews and Christians are accustomed to seeing the Old and New Testaments. It was at first memorized in fragments by Muhammad and then written down shortly after his death by his closest followers. Consisting of 114 surahs, or chapters (it is approximately four-fifths as long as the New Testament), it contains the basic beliefs and practices as well as ethical precepts that Muslims are expected to follow. Literally Islam means "submission," submission of one's own will to the will of God as seen in the Koran. Used as the basic educational as well as religious text, it is the most widely memorized book in the world.

The second selection explains what the Koran (Quran) means to Muslims.

Discussion Questions

1. What are the basic beliefs and practices of Islam? Could you say that Islam is essentially a very simple religion as religions go?
2. What similarities between Islam and Judaism and Christianity can you find in the selection? Are there any differences?
3. From this selection, could you agree that Islam belongs to the same religious tradition that includes Judaism and Christianity?
4. How do you think Muslims would look at the Old and New Testaments?
5. What did you find most surprising in the selection?
6. What parts in the selection could be used to refute the "misconceptions" mentioned in the previous reading?
7. Is the impact of the Quran on the lives of Muslims the same as the impact of the New Testament on Christians or the Old Testament on Jews?
8. How is Islamic law different from any other kind of law?

Selections from the KORAN (QURAN)

The Fatihah
IN THE NAME OF ALLAH
THE COMPASSIONATE
THE MERCIFUL
Praise be to Allah, Lord of the Creation,
The Compassionate, the Merciful,
King of Judgment-day!
You alone we worship, and to You alone
we pray for help.
Guide us to the straight path
The path of those whom You have favored,
Not of those who have incurred Your wrath,
Nor of those who have gone astray. (1:1-7)

Basic Beliefs and Practices

Believers, have faith in Allah and His apostle, in the Book He has revealed to His apostle, and in the Scriptures He formerly revealed. He that denies Allah, His angels, His Scriptures, His apostles, and the Last Day, has strayed far from the truth. (4:136)

Righteousness does not consist in whether you face toward the east or the west. The righteous man is he who believes in Allah and the Last Day, in the angels and the Scriptures and the prophets; who for the love of Allah gives his wealth to his kinsfolk, to the orphans, to the needy, to the wayfarers and to the beggars, and for the redemption of captives; who attends to his prayers and pays the alms-tax; who is true to his promises and steadfast in trial and adversity and in times of war. Such are the true believers; such are the God-fearing. (2:177)

Believers, fasting is decreed for you as it was decreed for those before you; perchance you will guard yourselves against evil. Fast a certain number of days, but if any one of you is ill or on a journey let him fast a similar number of days later on; and for those who can afford it there is a ransom: the feeding of a poor man. He that does good of his own account shall be well rewarded; but to fast is better for you, if you but knew it. (2:183-184)

In the month of Ramadan the Koran was revealed, a book of guidance distinguishing right from wrong. Therefore whoever of you is present in that month let him fast. (2:185)

…Eat and drink until you can tell a white thread from a black one in the light of the coming dawn. Then resume the fast till nightfall and do not approach them (your wives), but stay at your prayers in the mosques. (2:187)

From *The Koran*, translated by N. J. Dawood (Penguin Classics, Fourth revised edition, 1974). Copyright © 1956, 1959, 1966, 1968, 1974 by N. J. Dawood. Reproduced by permission of Penguin Books Ltd.

The Prophets

Such was the argument with which we furnished Abraham against his people. We raise whom We will to an exalted rank. Your Lord is wise and all-knowing. (6:83)

We gave him Isaac and Jacob and guided them as We guided Noah before them. Among his descendants were David and Solomon, Job and Joseph and Moses and Aaron (thus were the righteous rewarded); Zacharias, John, Jesus and Elias (all were upright men); and Ishmael, Elisha, Jonah and Lot. All these we exalted above Our creatures. (6:84)

On those men We bestowed the Scriptures, wisdom and prophethood.

Say: "We believe in Allah and that which is revealed to us; we believe in what was revealed to Abraham, Ishmael, Isaac, Jacob and the tribes; to Moses and Jesus and the other prophets. We make no distinction between any of them, and to Allah we have surrendered ourselves." (2:137)

In the Torah We decreed for them a life for a life, an eye for an eye, a nose for a nose, an ear for an ear, a tooth for a tooth, and a wound for a wound. But if a man charitably forbears from retaliation, his remission shall atone for him. (5:45)

After those prophets We sent forth Jesus, the son of Mary, conforming the Torah already revealed, and gave him the Gospel, in which there is guidance and light, corroborating that which was revealed before it in the Torah, a guide and an admonition to the righteous. (3:46)

And to you (Muhammad) We have revealed the Book with the truth. It confirms the Scriptures which came before it and stands as a guardian over them. (5:48)

And you shall recount in the Book the story of Mary; how she left her people and betook herself to a solitary place in the east.

We sent to her Our spirit in the semblance of a full-grown man. And when she saw him she said: "May the merciful defend me from you! If you fear the Lord, leave me and go your way."

"I am the messenger of your Lord," he replied, "and have come to give you a holy son."

"How shall I bear a child," she answered, "when I am a virgin, untouched by man?"

"Such is the will of your Lord," he replied. "That is no difficult thing for Him. 'He shall be a sign to mankind,' says the Lord, 'and a blessing from Ourself. This is our decree.' "

(After having the child) She made a sign to them (her people), pointing to the child. But they replied, "How can we speak with a babe in the cradle?"

Whereupon he spoke and said: "I am the servant of Allah. He has given me the Gospel and ordained me a prophet. His blessing is upon me wherever I go, and He has commanded me to be steadfast in prayer and to give alms to the poor as long as I shall live. He has exhorted me to honor my mother and has purged me of vanity and wickedness. I was blessed on the day I was born, and blessed shall I be on the day of my death; and may peace be upon me on the day when I shall be raised to-life."

Such was Jesus, the son of Mary. That is the whole truth, which they are unwilling to accept. Allah forbid that He Himself should beget a son! When He decrees a thing He need only say: "Be," and it is. (19:13-36)

People of the Book, do not transgress the bounds of your religion. Speak nothing but the truth about Allah. The Messiah, Jesus the son of Mary, was no more than Allah's apostle and His Word which He cast to Mary: a spirit from Him. So believe in Allah and His apostles and do not say: "Three." Forbear, and it shall be better for you. Allah is but one God. Allah forbid that He should have a son! His is all that the heavens and the earth contain. Allah is the all-sufficient Protector. (4:171)

On the Jews

Children of Israel, remember the favors I have bestowed upon you. Keep your covenant, and I will be true to Mine. Revere Me. Have faith in My revelations, which confirm your Scriptures, and do not be the first to deny them. (2:40)

Children of Israel, remember the blessing I have bestowed on you, and that I have exalted you above the nations. Guard yourselves against the day when every soul will stand alone; when neither intercession nor ransom shall be accepted from it, nor any help be given it. (2:47)

Remember how We delivered you from Pharaoh's people, who had oppressed you cruelly, slaying your sons and sparing your daughters. Surely that was a great trial from your Lord. We parted the sea for you and, taking you to safety, drowned Pharaoh's men before your very eyes. We communed with Moses for forty nights, but in his absence you took up the calf and worshiped it, thus committing evil. Yet after that We pardoned you, so that you might give thanks.

We gave Moses the Scriptures and knowledge of right and wrong, so that you might be rightly guided. (2:48-54)

On the Islamic Brotherhood

If two parties of believers take up arms the one against the other, make peace between them. If either of them commits aggression against the other, fight against the aggressors till they submit to Allah's judgment. When they submit make peace between them in equity and justice; Allah loves those who act in justice.

The believers are a band of brothers. Make peace among your brothers and fear Allah, so that you may be shown mercy.

Believers, let no man mock another man, who may perhaps be better than himself. Let no woman mock another woman, who may perhaps be better than herself. Do not defame one another, nor call one another by nicknames. It is an evil thing to be called by a bad name after embracing the true faith. Those who do not repent are wrongdoers. (49:8-11)

On Riches

Your hearts are taken up with worldly gain from the cradle to the grave.

But you shall know. You shall before long come to know.

Indeed, if you knew the truth with certainty, you would see the fire of Hell: you would see it with your very eyes.

Then, on that day, you shall be questioned about your joys. (102:1-8)

Woe to all back-biting slanderers who amass riches and sedulously hoard them, thinking their treasures will make them immortal!

By no means! They shall be flung to the Destroying Flame. (104:1-7)

Have you thought of him that denies the Last Judgment? It is he who turns away the orphan and does not urge others to feed the poor. Woe to those who pray but are heedless in their prayer; who make a show of piety and give no alms to the destitute. (107:1-7)

On Debt

Believers, have fear of Allah and waive what is still due to you from usury, if your faith be true; or war shall be declared against you by Allah and His apostle. If you repent, you may retain your principal, suffering no loss and causing loss to none.

If your debtor be in straits, grant him a delay until he can discharge his debt; but if you waive the sum as alms it will be better for you, if you but knew it.

Believers, when you contract a debt for a fixed period, put it in writing. Let a scribe write it down for you with fairness; no scribe should refuse to write as Allah has taught him. Therefore let him write; and let the debtor dictate, fearing

Allah his Lord and not diminishing the sum he owes. Call in two male witnesses from among you, but if two men cannot be found, then one man and two women whom you judge fit to act as witnesses; so that if either of them commit an error, the other will remember. Witnesses must not refuse to give evidence if called upon to do so. (2:278-282)

On Inheritance

Allah has thus enjoined you concerning your children:

A male shall inherit twice as much as a female. If there be more than two girls, they shall have two-thirds of the inheritance; but if there be one only, she shall inherit the half. Parents shall inherit a sixth each, if the deceased have a child; but if he leave no children and his parents be his heirs, his mother shall have a third. If he have two brothers, his mother shall have a sixth after payment of his debts and any legacies he may have bequeathed.

You shall inherit the half of your wives' estate if they die childless. If they leave children, a quarter of the estate shall be yours after payment of their debts and any legacies they may have bequeathed.

Your wives shall inherit one quarter of your estate if you die childless. If you leave children, they shall inherit one eighth, after payment of your debts and any legacies you may have bequeathed.

If a man or a woman leave neither children nor parents and have a brother or a sister, they shall each inherit one sixth. If there be more, they shall equally share the third of the estate, after payment of debts and any legacies that may have been bequeathed, without prejudice to the rights of the heirs. That is a commandment from Allah. He is gracious and all-knowing. (4: 11-12)

On Women, Marriage, etc.

Men have authority over women because Allah has made the one superior to the others, and because they spend their wealth to maintain them. Good women are obedient. They guard their unseen parts because Allah has guarded them. (4:34)

Enjoin believing women to turn their eyes away from temptation and to preserve their chastity; to cover their adornments (except those such as are normally displayed); to draw their veils over their bosoms and not to reveal their finery except to their husbands, their fathers, their husbands' fathers, their sons, their step-sons, etc. And let them not stamp their feet in walking so as to reveal their hidden trinkets. (24:31)

The adulterer and the adulteress shall each be given a hundred lashes. Let no pity for them cause you to disobey Allah, if you truly believe in Allah and the Last Day; and let their punishments be witnessed by a number of believers.

The adulterer may marry only an adulteress or an idolatress; and the adulteress may marry only an adulterer or an idolater. True believers are forbidden such marriages.

Those that defame honorable women and cannot produce four witnesses shall be given eighty lashes. No testimony of theirs shall be admissible, for they are great transgressors— except those among them that afterwards repent and mend their ways. Allah is forgiving and merciful.

If a man accuses his wife but has no witnesses except himself, he shall swear four times by Allah that his charge is true, calling down upon himself the curse of Allah if he is lying. But if his wife swears four times by Allah that his charge is false and calls down His curse upon herself if it be true, she shall receive no punishment. (24:2-6)

The Holy Quran

Islam appeared in the form of a book: the Quran. Muslims consider the Quran (sometimes spelled "Koran") to be the Word of God as transmitted by the Angel Gabriel, in the Arabic language, through the Prophet Muhammad. The Muslim view, moreover, is that the Quran supersedes earlier revelations; it is regarded as their summation and completion. It is the final revelation, as Muhammad is regarded as the final prophet—"the Seal of the Prophets."

In a very real sense the Quran is the mentor of millions of Muslims, Arab and non-Arab alike; it shapes their everyday life, anchors them to a unique system of law, and inspires them by its guiding principles. Written in noble language, this Holy Text has done more than move multitudes to tears and ecstasy; it has also, for almost fourteen hundred years, illuminated the lives of Muslims with its eloquent message of uncompromising monotheism, human dignity, righteous living, individual responsibility, and social justice. For countless millions, consequently, it has been the single most important force in guiding their religious, social, and cultural lives. Indeed, the Quran is the cornerstone on which the edifice of Islamic civilization has been built.

The text of the Quran was delivered orally by the Prophet Muhammad to his followers as it was revealed to him. The first verses were revealed to him in or about 610, and the last revelation dates from the last year of his life, 632. His followers at first committed the Quran to memory and then, as instructed by him, to writing. Although the entire contents of the Quran, the placement of its verses, and the arrangement of its chapters date back to the Prophet, as long as he lived he continued to receive revelations. Consequently, the Holy Text could only be collected as a single corpus—"between the two covers"—after the death of Muhammad.

This is exactly what happened. After the battle of al-Yamamah in 633, `Umar ibn al-Khattab, later to become the second caliph, suggested to Abu Bakr, the first caliph, that because of the grievous loss of life in that battle, there was a very real danger of losing the Quran, enshrined as it was in the memories of the faithful and in uncollated fragments. Abu Bakr recognized the danger and entrusted the task of gathering the revelations to Zayd ibn Thabit, who as the chief scribe of the Prophet was the person to whom Muhammad frequently dictated the revelations in his lifetime. With great difficulty, the task was carried out and the first complete manuscript compiled from "bits of parchment, thin white stones—*ostracae*—leafless palm branches, and the memories of men." Later, during the time of 'Uthman, the third caliph, a final, authorized text was prepared and completed in 651, and this has remained the text in use ever since.

The contents of the Quran differ in substance and arrangement from the Old and New Testaments. Instead of presenting a straight historical narrative, as do the Gospels and the historical books of the Old Testament, the Quran treats, in allusive style, spiritual and practical as well as historical matters.

From *Aramco and its World*, edited by Ismail I. Nwwab, Peter C. Speers and Paul F. Hoye, pp. 46–47. Copyright 1980 by Aramco. Reprinted by permission.

The Quran is divided into 114 *surahs*, or chapters, and the surahs are conventionally assigned to two broad categories: those revealed at Mecca and those revealed at Medina. The surahs revealed at Mecca—at the beginning of Muhammad's mission—tend to be short and to stress, in highly moving language, the eternal themes of the unity of God, the necessity of faith, the punishment of those who stray from the right path, and the Last Judgment, when all man's actions and beliefs will be judged. The surahs revealed at Medina are longer, often deal in detail with specific legal, social, or political situations, and sometimes can only be properly understood with a full knowledge of the circumstances in which they were revealed.

All the surahs are divided into *ayahs* or verses and, for purposes of pedagogy and recitation, the Quran as a whole is divided into thirty parts, which in turn are divided into short divisions of nearly equal length, to facilitate study and memorization.

The surahs themselves are of varying length, ranging from the longest, Surah 2, with 282 verses, to the shortest, Surahs 103, 108, and 110, each of which has only three. With some exceptions the surahs are arranged in the Quran in descending order of length, with the longest at the beginning and the shortest at the end. The major exception to this arrangement is the opening surah, "al-Fatihah," which contains seven verses and which serves as an introduction to the entire revelation:

> In the Name of God, the Merciful, the Compassionate.
> Praise be to God, Lord of the Worlds;
> The Merciful, the Compassionate;
> Master of the Day of Judgment;
> Thee only do we worship, and Thee alone we ask for help.
> Guide us in the straight path,
> The path of those whom Thou hast favored; not the path of those who earn Thine anger nor of those who go astray.

Non-Muslims are often struck by the range of styles found in the Quran. Passages of impassioned beauty are no less common than vigorous narratives. The sublime "Verse of the Throne" is perhaps one of the most famous:

> God—There is no god but He,
> The Living, the Everlasting;
> Slumber seizes Him not, neither sleep;
> To Him belongs all that is
> In the heavens and the earth;
> Who is there that can intercede with Him
> Save by His leave?
> He knows what lies before them
> And what is after them,
> Nor do they encompass anything of His knowledge
> Except such as He wills;
> His Throne extends over the heavens and earth;
> The preserving of them wearies Him not;
> He is the Most High, the All-Glorious.

Muslims regard the Quran as untranslatable; the language in which it was revealed—Arabic— is inseparable from its message and Muslims everywhere, no matter what their native tongue, must learn Arabic to read the Sacred Book and to perform their worship. The Quran of course is available in many languages, but these versions are regarded as interpretations rather than translations—partly because the Arabic language, extraordinarily concise and allusive, is impossible to translate in a mechanical, word-for-word way. The inimitability of the Quran has crystallized in the Muslim view of *i'jaz* or "impossibility," which holds that the style of the Quran, being divine, cannot be imitated: any attempt to do so is doomed to failure.

It must also be remembered that the Quran was originally transmitted orally to the faithful and that the Holy Text is not meant to be read only in silence. From the earliest days it has always been recited aloud or, more accurately, chanted. As a result, several traditional means of chanting, or intoning, the Quran were found side by side. These methods carefully preserved the elaborate science of reciting the Quran—with all its intonations and its cadence and punctuation. As the exact pronunciation was important—and learning it took years—special schools were founded to be sure that no error would creep in as the traditional chanting methods were handed down. It is largely owing to the existence of these traditional methods of recitation that the text of the Quran was preserved without error. As the script in which the Quran was first written down indicated only the consonantal skeleton of the words, oral recitation was an essential element in the transmission of the text.

Because the circumstances of each revelation were thought necessary to correct interpretation, the community, early in the history of Islam, concluded that it was imperative to gather as many traditions as possible about the life and actions of the Prophet so that the Quran might be more fully understood. These traditions not only provided the historical context for many of the surahs—thus contributing to their more exact explication—but also contained a wide variety of subsidiary information on the practice, life, and legal rulings of the Prophet and his companions.

This material became the basis for what is called the *sunnah*, or "practice" of the Prophet—the deeds, utterances, and *taqrir* (unspoken approval) of Muhammad. Together with the Quran, the sunnah, as embodied in the canonical collections of traditions, the *hadith*, became the basis for the *shari'ah*, the sacred law of Islam.

Unlike Western legal systems, the shari`ah makes no distinction between religious and civil matters; it is the codification of God's Law, and it concerns itself with every aspect of social, political, economic, and religious life. Islamic law is thus different from any other legal system; it differs from canon law in that it is not administered by a church hierarchy; in Islam there is nothing that corresponds to a "church" in the Christian sense. Instead, there is the *ummah*—the community of the believers—whose cohesion is guaranteed by the sacred law. Every action of the pious Muslim, therefore, is determined by the Quran, by precedents set by the Prophet, and by the practice of the early community of Islam as enshrined in the shari`ah.

No description, however, can fully capture the overwhelming importance of the Quran to Muslims. Objectively, it is the central fact of the Islamic faith, the word of God, the final and complete revelation, the foundation and framework of Islamic law, and the source of Islamic thought, language, and action. It is the essence of Islam. Yet it is, in the deeply personal terms of a Muslim, something more as well. In innumerable, almost indescribable ways, it is also the central fact of Muslim life. To a degree almost incomprehensible in the West it shapes and colors broadly, specifically, and totally the thoughts, emotions, and values of the devout Muslim's life from birth to death.

52

The Islamic Conquests: The Pact of Umar

One of the most important challenges facing the Arabs when they conquered the Middle East was how to relate to the large indigenous populations of non-Arabs and non-Muslims. Since the vast majority of these people were monotheists (Christians, Jews and Zoroastrians), they were not seen as objects for religious conversion by the Arab conquerors. So the question was how to fit these dhimmis (protected persons) into a society ruled by Arab Muslims.

The following selection is an agreement made by the Christian inhabitants of Syria to the Caliph Umar as to their status in the new Arab empire. Though the terms of this "agreement" might not suit modern sensibilities, it should be understood that Syria, like most other areas of the region, had always been governed by one empire or another. The modern ideas of independence and nationalism were never part of the thinking of most people in the region.

Discussion Questions

1. Were the conditions the Christians accepted appropriate for a conquered people?

2. Would the modern concept of "tolerance" be applicable in these conditions?

The Pact of Umar

Abd al-Rahman b. Ghanam[1] related the following: When Umar b. al-Khattab—may Allah be pleased with him—made peace with the Christian inhabitants of Syria, we wrote him the following.

In the name of Allah, the Merciful, the Beneficent.

This letter is addressed to Allah's servant Umar, the Commander of the Faithful, by the Christians of such-and-such city. When you advanced against us, we asked you for a guarantee of protection for our persons, our offspring, our property, and the people of our sect, and we have taken upon ourselves the following obligations toward you, namely:

We shall not build in our cities or in their vicinity any new monasteries, churches, hermitages, or monks' cells. We shall not restore, by night or by day, any of them that have fallen into ruin or which are located in the Muslims' quarters.

We shall keep our gates wide open for passersby and travelers. We shall provide three days' food and lodging to any Muslims who pass our way.

We shall not shelter any spy in our churches or in our homes, nor shall we hide him from the Muslims.

We shall not teach our children the Koran.

We shall not hold public religious ceremonies. We shall not seek to proselytize anyone. We shall not prevent any of our kin from embracing Islam if they so desire.

We shall show deference to the Muslims and shall rise from our seats when they wish to sit down.

We shall not attempt to resemble the Muslims in any way with regard to their dress, as for example, with the qalansuwa[2] the turban[3] sandals, or parting the hair (in the Arab fashion). We shall not speak as they do, nor shall we adopt their kunyas.[4]

We shall not ride on saddles.

We shall not wear swords or bear weapons of any kind, or ever carry them with us.

We shall not engrave our signets in Arabic.

We shall not sell wines.

We shall clip the forelocks of our head.

We shall always adorn ourselves in our traditional fashion. We shall bind the zunnar[5] around our waists.

We shall not display our crosses or our books anywhere in the Muslims' thoroughfares or in their marketplaces. We shall only beat our clappers in our churches very quietly. We shall not raise our voices when reciting the service in our churches, nor when in the presence of Muslims. Neither shall we raise our voices in our funeral processions.

We shall not display lights in any of the Muslim thoroughfares or in their marketplaces.

The Pact of Umar, translated from al_Turtushi, 1872.

[1] He died in 697

[2] The qalansuwa was a conical cap.

[3] The turban came to be considered the "crown of Arabs" and the "badge of Islam"

[4] Arabic byname, formed with abu (father of, or possessor of).

[5] A kind of belt

We shall not come near them with our funeral processions.

We shall not take any of the slaves that have been allotted to the Muslims.

We shall not build our homes higher than theirs.

(When I brought the letter to Umar—may Allah be pleased with him—he added the clause "We shall not strike any Muslim.")

We accept these conditions for ourselves and for the members of our sect, in return for which we are to be given a guarantee of security.

Should we violate in any way these conditions which we have accepted and for which we stand security, then there shall be no covenant of protection for us, and we shall be liable to the penalties for rebelliousness and sedition.

Then Umar—may Allah be pleased with him—wrote: "Sign what they have requested, but add two clauses that will also be binding upon them; namely, they shall not buy anyone who has been taken prisoner by the Muslims, and that anyone who deliberately strikes a Muslim 'will forfeit the protection of this pact."

53

A City That Echoes Eternity

"Nothing less than the future relationship of the Islamic, Christian, and Jewish worlds are at stake" in settling the political issue of Jerusalem today. So states historian Bernard Wasserstein, in his 2001 article, "The Politics of Holiness in Jerusalem." He argues that the city's historical role has "waxed and waned" according to social, cultural, and, above all, political developments. What the sacred city means to the three monotheistic religions originating in the region is the focus of this reading.

Discussion Questions

1. We have examined the notions of "sacred geography" in other religions. How and why did Jerusalem become identified with all three of the monotheistic religions of Judaism, Christiany, and Islam? Can you compare Jerusalem with religious sites in India, China, the Americas, Africa?

2. What does the article author mean when he states that, ". . Jerusalem exists more vividly, more powerfully, more *dangerously* within the longitude and latitude of the religious imagination"?

3. Why isn't Jerusalem "just another city on a hill?"

4. What is the connection of each of the monotheistic religions to Jerusalem, and do you think that one claim is more valid than any other?

A City That Echoes Eternity

One man, Jesus warned, cannot serve two masters. Yet Jerusalem is sacred stone and soil to Jew and Christian and Muslim alike. A place on the map like any other city, Jerusalem exists more vividly, more powerfully, more dangerously within the longitude and latitude of the religious imagination. In that fertile region of the mind, what has already occurred in time past—the building of Solomon's temple, the crucifixion of Christ, the ascension of the Prophet Muhammad—is also promise of what is to come, "when time shall be no more." Among all the cities of the earth, only Jerusalem is seen as the locus of redemption and final judgment. For that reason alone, it inspires the fanatic. It is a burden no merely civil administration should ever have to bear. But short of that eschatological moment, Jerusalem seems to be always searching for respite from political tension, that it might live up to the meaning of its name: City of Peace.

To know what Jerusalem means to the three great monotheisms is to realize that politics alone can bring only a provisional kind of peace. Jews have the oldest identification with the city—and the Bible, which mentions Jerusalem 667 times, for their witness. In the background is God's promise of land and progeny to Abraham, His obedient servant. In the Book of Exodus, that promise takes the specific form of Canaan—the Holy Land—for the wandering tribes of Israel. King David made Jerusalem his capital and there, some 30 centuries ago, Solomon built the first temple. The exile of the Jews to Babylon only made the yearning for Jerusalem more intense. "If I forget you, O Jerusalem," wrote the Psalmist, "let my right hand wither." A second temple was built by King Herod, only to be destroyed in A.D. 70 by the Romans. What remains of the Western wall is now Judaism's holiest shrine. Jerusalem, wrote Abraham Joshua Heschel right after the Israeli occupation of the city in 1967, is "a city of witness, an echo of eternity." It is also a city of waiting, the place where the messiah, when he comes, will rebuild the temple. To die in Jerusalem, pious Jews believe, is to be assured of atonement.

For Christians, the messiah has already come and atonement has been accomplished in the person of Jesus. Jerusalem is where he suffered, died and rose again in glory— and where he will return to judge the living and the dead. It is also the city where the Last Supper was celebrated and where, at Pentecost, the church itself was born. As a place of Christian pilgrimage, Jerusalem has no equal. Medieval maps place it at the center of the universe (as did Dante), and paintings show medieval Jerusalem descending as the heavenly city to come. Today pilgrims can touch the rock where Jesus was crucified and, under the same church roof, the tomb where he was buried. The cross is gone, but in the Christian iconography, it continues to be the axis mundi connecting earth with heaven in the sacred drama of redemption.

For Muslims, Jerusalem is the third holiest. place, after Mecca and Medina. To Muhammad, it was the city of the holy prophets who had preceded him. And so, before Mecca became the center of the Islamic universe, Muhammad directed all Muslims to bow for prayer toward

Jerusalem. According to later interpretations of a passage in the Qur'an, Muhammad himself made a mystical "night flight" to Jerusalem aided by the angel Gabriel. From there, on the very rock where Abraham had offered his son as a sacrifice (now the shrine of the Dome of the Rock, atop the Temple Mount), Muhammad ascended a ladder to the throne of Allah. This ascension confirmed the continuity between Muhammad and all previous prophets and messengers of God, including Jesus, in a lineage going back to Adam. It also established a divine connection between Mecca and Jerusalem.

Thus, for billions of believers who may never see it, Jerusalem remains a city central to their sacred geography. This is why the future of the city is not just another Middle Eastern conflict between Arabs and Jews. From a purely secular perspective, of course, the shrines dear to Jews, Christians and Muslims are precious tourist attractions, and as such important sources of revenue. But Jerusalem is not some kind of Disneyland of the spirit. Both Israel and the Palestinians have real roots in the Holy Land, and both want to claim Jerusalem as their capital. The United Nations, supported by the Vatican, would have the city internationalized and under its jurisdiction. The issue, however, is not merely one of geopolitics. There will be no enduring solution to the question of Jerusalem that does not respect the attachments to the city formed by each faith. Whoever controls Jerusalem will always be constrained by the meaning the city has acquired over three millenniums of wars, conquest and prophetic utterance. Blessed or cursed, Jerusalem is built with the bricks of the religious imagination. Were this not so, Jerusalem would be what it has never been just another city on a hill.

54

Southernization

In modern history we are familiar with a global process called "Westernization" through which Western ideas, technologies and institutions have spread throughout the world and altered the course of nearly all societies. This was achieved both through force (in the form of imperialism and colonialism) and imitation. A similar process called *"Southernization"* has been identified by Professor Lynda Shaffer[*] of Tufts University as having played a parallel role during the pre-modern era. The focal and originating points of Southernization were India and Southeast Asia, both in the southern part of the northern hemisphere (see map). Indian innovations included cotton and sugar manufacturing, mathematics and even Buddhism; Southeast Asia contributed the opening of new maritime trade routes, the production and marketing of spices and a more drought-resistant rice.

The earliest agents of Southernization were Indian and Malay merchants and their clients in Africa, the Middle East and China. All societies touched by them were transformed in one way or another by these innovations and products. By the 8th century, the Arabs, who had taken control of much of the Afro-Eurasian Intercommunicating Zone, became the major agents of Southernization and were responsible for transmitting southern products throughout their domain and beyond. The result was what Professor Shaffer calls "a rich south and a poor north." The modern reversal of that situation is at least partly due to the fact that the north (what we call western Europe today) became "Southernized"—i.e., gained contact with the Afro-Eurasian Intercommunicating Zone in such places as Spain and Sicily from the 11th century on. Inheriting the technological, scientific and economic innovations of this zone stimulated the Europeans to grow and expand to the point that they created a new intercommunicating zone in the Atlantic Ocean basin which in many ways became the starting point for the modern process of Westernization and the creation of "a rich north and a poor south."

---

[*] In *Journal of World History*, Volume 5, Number 1, Spring 1994.

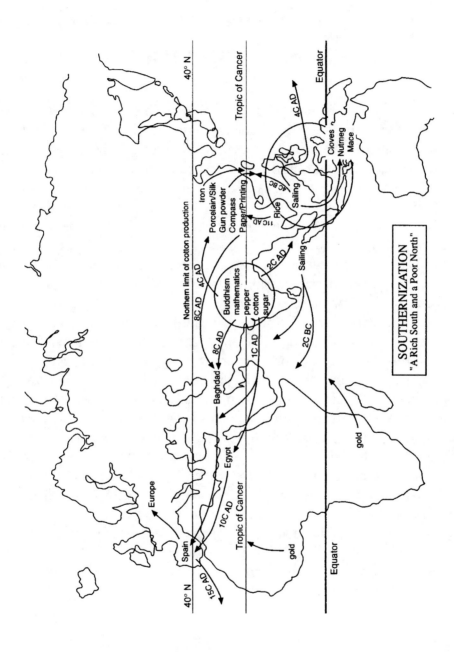

SOUTHERNIZATION
"A Rich South and a Poor North"

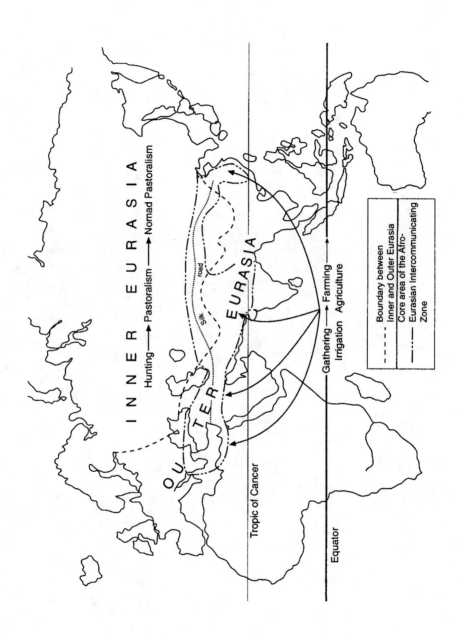

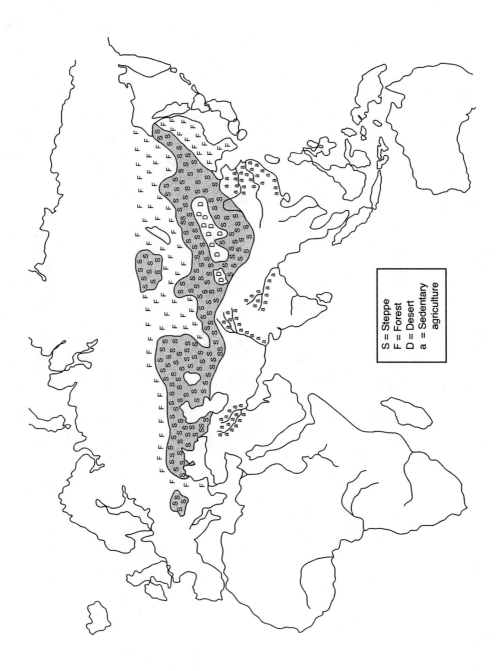

55

The Muslim Synthesis: Science

Compared to the Germanic invasions of the Roman Empire in the west in the fifth and sixth centuries, which contributed to the decline of educational standards, the invasions of the Persian and Byzantine Empires by the Arabs resulted in the blossoming of almost all aspects of culture. Despite the fact that their level of cultural development may not have been much higher than the Germanic peoples, Islam brought to the Arabs both unity and an interest in learning. Muhammad is reputed to have said, "Seek learning, though it be in China," "The search for knowledge is obligatory to every Muslim," and "The ink of scholars is worth more than the blood of martyrs." As the Arabs invaded the Persian and Byzantine Empires, they eventually absorbed and built upon what they learned from the various cultures they ruled and had contact with. The new Arab Empire, which stretched from Spain to India, acted as perhaps the greatest cultural catalyst in history until after 1500.

Among many other contributions, the Islamic world had an especially important impact on the sciences. The two selections that follow explain the nature of the Islamic achievement and the special situation of Spain as a multicultural society which proved particularly creative. Spain was also the most important point of contact between Christian Europe and the Intercommunicating Zone and allowed the Europeans to acquire for the first time an extensive knowledge of the ancient Greek achievements in philosophy and science along with very valuable Muslim commentaries. This contact is to large extent responsible for the acceleration of European cultural evolution which led ultimately to the renaissances of the twelfth and fifteenth centuries and European exploration and expansion.

Discussion Questions

1. What were the differences between the attitudes of the Umayyad and Abbasid caliphates toward the cultures they had come to rule?
2. What is the relationship of modern science to the achievements of the Muslim world?
3. What were the most important Muslim contributions in the sciences?

The Islamic Legacy

The Arabs were the inheritors of the scientific tradition of late antiquity. They preserved it, elaborated it, and, finally, passed it on to Europe.

The story of how this came about is far from simple, and much research needs to be done before its details are completely understood, but the broad outlines are clear.

When Egypt, Palestine, Syria, Iraq, Asia Minor and Persia fell to Islamic forces in the seventh century they included a heterogeneous population. Although the cultivated classes of the former provinces of the Byzantine Empire spoke Greek, the people spoke a number of other languages—Coptic in Egypt and various Aramaic dialects in Syria and Iraq. These populations were for the most part Christian. In Persia, the majority language was Pahlavi—an earlier form of the language spoken there today—and the state religion was Zoroastrianism, with substantial Christian minorities and a few centers of Buddhism.

Throughout this immense area, there were two main scientific traditions. The first, and by far the most important, was that of Greece. The second was that of India, strongest in Persia because of the geographical proximity of the two countries.

At a surprisingly early date, the Arab ruling dynasty of the Umayyads, with its capital at Damascus, evinced an interest in Greek science. The little Umayyad audience hall and bath of Qasr'Amra, built in the Syrian desert around A.D. 711—only 79 years after the death of the Prophet Muhammad—contains, on the inside of the dome, a painted representation of the zodiac made on a stereographic projection, perhaps showing a familiarity with the methods of Ptolemy. The same room contains paintings of personifications of History, Poetry and Philosophy; each figure is labeled in Greek.

The interest of the Umayyads in Greek science attested by the paintings at Qasr' Amra is confirmed by early Muslim historians, who record the experiments in alchemy made by Khalid ibn al-Yazid, a grandson of the first Umayyad caliph Mu'awiya.

Astronomy and alchemy were thus the first sciences to preoccupy the Muslims. It is noteworthy that they were also typical of the interests of the Greek scholars of late antiquity, particularly of those in Alexandria. In fact, it was to be this tradition, with its emphasis on mathematics, physics, astronomy and medicine, that was to be most fruitfully elaborated by Muslim scientists.

Although the great library of Alexandria, repository of the learning of the classical world, no longer existed at the time of the Arab conquests, the works of many of the Greek scholars who studied there now exist only in Arabic translation. How did this come about? How did the Arabs, who had little or no *direct* contact with Greek science, and in any case were unfamiliar with the Greek language, gain their very detailed knowledge of it?

The answer to this question lies in the continued presence of a Greek-speaking (or reading) educated class among the subject populations of the Muslim empire. When the Umayyad dynasty—the language of whose administration, until A.D. 699, was Greek—was

From *Science: The Islamic Legacy*, by Paul Lunde, Aramco World, May–June 1982, vol. 33, no. 3. Copyright by Aramco Services Co., Houston. Reprinted with permission.

supplanted by that of the Abbasids in A.D. 750, the center of the empire shifted eastward. A new capital, Baghdad, was built in Iraq on the banks of the Tigris. Here, not far from the old Persian capital of Ctesiphon, the character of the empire changed.

Although the Umayyads had made use of non-Arab, Greek-speaking civil servants, they had remained firmly Arab in their tastes and philosophy of rule, and had made little effort to attract the subject population to the religion of Islam. Now, all this was changed; the Abbasids from the beginning conceived of an Islamic polity based on religious affiliation rather than national origin. Baghdad became an international city, where Persians, Indians, Greeks, Sogdians—from beyond the Oxus—Armenians, Turks, Jews and Arabs lived side by side. This inevitably led to a mingling of varied intellectual traditions; at the same time, the language of the court—and increasingly of the people—was Arabic.

The Arabic-speaking intelligentsia of Baghdad were of course aware, through their contacts with Greek-speaking Muslims and Christians, of the great achievements of classical scientists. The university of Gondeshapur, the great intellectual center of Sassanid Persia, was not far from Baghdad. When the Council of Ephesus in 431 excommunicated Nestorius, his followers sought refuge in Persia, where the Sassanid Shahs welcomed them. The Nestorians brought with them a knowledge of two sciences which were, with their help, later to be cultivated by the Muslims—medicine and astronomy.

Another Christian sect, the Monophysites, fleeing Byzantine persecution 20 years later, also settled in Persia, as well as in Syria, where they founded schools at Edessa, Nisibis, Antioch and Beirut, where law and rhetoric were particularly studied. These two disciplines were also later to become fruitful areas of Muslim scholarship.

There was, therefore, no complete rupture between the late classical and the Muslim world,

as far as the scientific tradition was concerned. A Greek-speaking physician like Alexander of Tralles, who was active at about the time the Prophet Muhammad was born—around A.D. 570—wrote a standard medical textbook which was later translated into Arabic and eventually from Arabic into Latin, and had considerable influence on medieval European medical practice. One of the most striking confirmations of this continuity is the fact that the Alexandrian Academy survived, albeit in shadowy form, into Islamic times, when it was moved to Antioch, where enrollment fell until only one professor and two students were left. One of these students in turn taught one of the foremost Abbasid translators, while the other taught a student who in turn instructed one of the greatest Arab philosophers, al-Farabi.

The Indian scientific tradition mingled with that of Greece at Gondeshapur and other centers of Christian learning in Persia. The Indians were particularly concerned with mathematics, astrology and the scientific study of grammar. About the year 600—during the lifetime of the Prophet Muhammad—Indian mathematicians developed the symbol zero and the system of place notation. This invention, first mentioned in the Islamic cultural area in a Syriac text written in A.D. 662, when the Umayyad caliph Mu'awiya was ruling in Damascus, revolutionized the study of mathematics and made possible the great achievements of Muslim mathematicians.

It was during the early Abbasid period, however, that the tentative beginnings made under the Umayyads blossomed into a true scientific renaissance. Several of the early Abbasid caliphs made a systematic effort to translate Greek and Indian scientific texts into Arabic.

This effort began during the reign of the second Abbasid caliph, al-Mansur, who founded Baghdad and ruled from A. D. 754 to 775. Al-Mansur sent embassies to the Byzantine emperor to ask for Greek mathematical texts—in particular for the *Elements* of Euclid; the famous al-Ma'mun, later did the same. Ibn Khaldun, writing in North Africa in the 14th century, but making use of a wide variety of earlier sources, describes the remarkable efforts made by these caliphs to enrich the intellectual life of the Muslim community:

> When the Byzantine emperors conquered Syria, the scientific works of the Greeks were still in existence. Then God brought Islam, and the Muslims won their remarkable victories, conquering the Byzantines as well as all other nations. At first, the Muslims were simple, and did not cultivate learning, but as time went on, and the Muslim dynasty flourished, the Muslims developed an urban culture which surpassed that of any other nation.

> They began to wish to study the various branches of philosophy, of whose existence they knew from their contact with bishops and priests among their Christian subjects. In any case, man has always had a penchant for intellectual speculation. The Caliph al-Mansur therefore sent an embassy to the Byzantine emperor, asking him to send him translations of books on mathematics. The emperor sent him Euclid's *Elements* and some works on physics.

> Muslim scholars studied these books, and their desire to obtain others was whetted. When al-Ma'mun, who had some scientific knowledge, assumed the caliphate, he wished to do something to further the progress of science. For that purpose, he sent ambassadors and translators to the Byzantine empire, in order to search out works on the Greek sciences and have them translated into Arabic. As a result of these efforts, a great deal of material was gathered and preserved.

Other Muslim historians record the arrival of an Indian scientist named Manka at the Abbasid court in A.D. 770, and he seems to have had a considerable influence on the mathematicians and astrologers of Baghdad, although we know little of the precise nature of this influence.

Under al-Ma'mun, a more systematic effort was made to translate Greek scientific texts into Arabic. He founded an institute for the purpose, called the *Bait al-Hikma*, The House of Wisdom, and staffed it with salaried Christian and Muslim scholars. The work of translation was complex. Christian translators first rendered the Greek texts into Syriac, the language with which they were most familiar. These preliminary versions were then put into Arabic, with Muslim Arabic-speakers correcting them for style.

Muslim scientists were much influenced by the Greek notion that the science of mathematics was the key to all other sciences. Aristotle, whom the Arabs called "The Foremost Teacher," had inscribed above the door of his house: "Let no one enter who does not have a knowledge of mathematics." This could equally well serve as a motto for the House of Wisdom. We have seen that one of the first Greek books brought to Baghdad from Constantinople was a copy of Euclid's *Elements*. This was translated into Arabic a number of times, as were several of the Greek commentaries upon it, in particular that of the inventor and mathematician, Hero of Alexandria, whose experiments with automata in the third century B.C. were to be so strangely echoed by Muslim scientists. As late as the 13th-century, Nasir al-Din al-Tusi wrote a detailed commentary on the *Elements*, which was among the first Arabic texts to be printed in the original in 16th-century Italy.

Many other Greek mathematical works found their way into Arabic through the efforts of the scholars at the House of Wisdom and their successors. Euclid, Apollonius of Perga, Nichomachus of Gerasa—the magnificent classical ruin presently called Jerash, in Jordan—Menelaus, Archimedes and Theodosius of Tripoli were all translated at an early date, as were works by astronomers like Ptolemy, Autolycus, Dorotheus, Aristarchus, Hipparchus, Theon of Alexandria, Aratus and Geminus of Rhodes. A number of these works were later translated into Latin and Hebrew and thus became known to medieval Europe.

The exact sciences—mathematics, astronomy and optics—perhaps occupied pride of place for Muslim scholars, but the natural sciences, particularly medicine and its ancillary disciplines, were also assiduously cultivated. Again, the first phase was translation of Greek medical writings—particularly those by or attributed to Galen and Hippocrates—into Arabic. There then followed a period of original research by Muslim scientists, often leading to major revisions of the received tradition, and finally a period of codification in which the results of previous research were incorporated into convenient handbooks. Botany, particularly in so far as it was related to *materia medica*, received its first impetus from an illuminated copy of Dioscorides sent by the Byzantine emperor to the Abbasid court; this fundamental classical work was quickly rendered into Arabic, and many corrections and new plant identifications were added to it, particularly by scholars in North Africa and Muslim Spain. It was in Spain too that the first scientific works on agronomy were composed, works that are a prime source for our knowledge of medieval agricultural techniques in the Muslim world— techniques that were passed to Europe and greatly increased productivity.

Aristotle's work *Generation of Animals* was early translated into Arabic, and was made use of by al-Jahiz in his amusing *Book of Animals*, which includes a great deal of linguistic, literary and historical information in addition to passages of accurate, if amusing, scientific observation. Various handbooks of veterinary medicine were also composed, although these have so far received little attention from scholars.

Very few works of Greek science failed to find their way into Arabic during the Abbasid period. For one of the few times in human history, a culture with its own language, religion and customs embarked upon the extraordinary task of translating an alien intellectual tradition into its own language and fitting it into its own conceptual framework. In the process, old errors were corrected, and the experimental method, the basis of all scientific progress, was clearly enunciated. For one of the great achievements of medieval Muslim scientists was their willingness to correct the texts they transmitted. Just as they recomputed the circumference of the earth, and corrected the geographical information in Ptolemy on the basis of their own observations, so they dared question even Aristotle.

The works of Muslim scientists reached medieval Europe through Latin and Hebrew translations, for the most part made in Spain and somewhat later in Sicily. As early as the 10th century, astronomical works were being translated into Latin in Catalonia, and perhaps elsewhere in Spain. Later, during the 12th and 13th centuries, the works of Avicenna (Ibn Sina), Averroes (Ibn Rushd), Avempace (Ibn Bajja) and a host of others were translated into Latin and in the 13th century, at the court of Alfonso the Wise, into Spanish. At the very time that Baghdad fell to the Mongols, in 1258, and the Abbasid caliphate came to an end, scribes in Europe were preserving the Muslim scientific tradition. This is why, just as many Greek texts now survive only in Arabic dress, many Arabic scientific works only survive in Latin.

It is upon this tenuous and almost miraculous line of transmission that the scientific achievements of the modern world are based: the work of scholars of many different religious and linguistic backgrounds carefully transmitting, correcting and adding to a tradition that stretches back to Aristotle and beyond, each bound to his predecessor by a shared devotion to truth.

Science in Al-Andalus

The medieval Christians of Spain had a legend that Roderick, the last King of the Visigoths, was responsible for unleashing the Arab invasion of the Iberian Peninsula because, in defiance of his plighted word, he unlocked the gates of an enchanted palace he had sworn not to tamper with.

As far as the West was concerned, the Arab invasion *did* unlock an enchanted palace. Following the collapse of the Roman Empire, Vandals, Huns and Visigoths had pillaged and burned their way through the Iberian Peninsula, establishing ephemeral kingdoms which lasted only as long as loot poured in, and were then destroyed in their turn. Then, without warning, in the year 711, came the Arabs—to settle, fall in love with the land and create the first civilization Europe had known since the Roman legions had given up the unequal fight against the barbarian hordes.

Spain first prospered under the rule of the Umayyads, who established a dynasty there after they had lost the caliphate in the east to the Abbasids. At first, the culture of the Umayyad court at Cordoba was wholly derivative. Fashions, both in literature and dress, were imitative of those current in the Abbasids' newly founded capital of Baghdad. Scholars from the more sophisticated lands to the east were always assured of a warm reception at the court of Cordoba, where their colleagues would listen avidly for news of what was being discussed in the capital, what people were wearing, what songs were being sung, and—above all—what books were being read.

For Islamic culture was pre-eminently a culture of the book. The introduction of paper from China in 751 gave an impetus to learning and an excitement for ideas which the world had never before known. Books became more available than they had been even in Rome, and incomparably cheaper than they were in the Latin West, where they continued to be written on expensive parchment. In the 12th century, a man sold 120 acres of land in order to buy a single Book of Hours. In the ninth century, the library of the monastery of St. Gall was the largest in Europe. It boasted 36 volumes. At the same time, that of Cordoba contained 500,000. The cultural lag between East and West in the Middle Ages can be attributed partly to the fact that the Arabs had paper, while the Latin West did not.

It took much more than paper to create an intellectual and scientific culture like that of Islamic Spain, of course. Islam, with its tolerance and encouragement of both secular and religious learning, created the necessary climate for the exchange of ideas. The court of Cordoba, like that of Baghdad, was open to Muslims, Jews and Christians alike, and one prominent bishop complained that young Christian men were devoting themselves to the study of Arabic, rather than to Latin—a reflection of the fact that Arabic, in a surprisingly short time, had become the international language of science, as English has today.

Islamic culture in Spain began to flourish in earnest during the reign of 'Abd al-Rahman II of Cordoba—as Arabic spread increasingly among his non-Muslim subjects, especially in the cities, and led to a great flowering of intellectual activity of all kinds.

In a courtly society, the tastes and predilections of the ruler set the tone for society at large, and 'Abd al-Rahman II, passionately interested in both the religious and the secular sciences, was determined to show the world that his court was in no way inferior to the court of the Caliphs at Baghdad. To this end, therefore, he actively recruited scholars by offering handsome inducements to overcome their initial reluctance to live in what many from the lands in the East considered the provinces. As a result, many scholars, poets, philosophers, historians and musicians migrated to al-Andalus, and established the basis of the intellectual tradition and educational system which made Spain so outstanding for the next 400 years.

Another result was that an infrastructure of libraries—both public and private—mosques, hospitals, and research institutions rapidly grew up and famous scholars in the East, hearing of these amenities, flocked to the West. They in turn attracted students of their own; in the Islamic world it was not at all unusual for a student to travel thousands of miles to study at the feet of a famous professor.

One of the earliest of these scholars was 'Abbas ibn Firnas, who died in the year A.D. 888 and who, had he lived in the Florence of the Medici, would have been a "Renaissance Man." He came to Cordoba to teach music, then a branch of mathematical theory, but—not a man to limit himself to a single field of study—soon became interested in the mechanics of flight. He constructed a pair of wings, made out of feathers in a wooden frame, and attempted to fly—anticipating Leonardo da Vinci by some 600 years.

Luckily, 'Abbas survived, and, undiscouraged, turned his mind to the construction of a planetarium in which the planets actually revolved—it would be extremely interesting to know the details of the gearing mechanism. It also simulated such celestial phenomena as thunder and lightning and was, of course, a wild

success. Next 'Abbas turned to the mathematical problems involved in the regularity of the facets of certain crystals and evolved a formula for manufacturing artificial crystals.

It must be remembered that a knowledge of the achievements of men like 'Abbas has come to us purely by chance. It has been estimated that today there are 250,000 Arabic manuscripts in Western and Eastern libraries, including private collections. Yet in the 10th century, private libraries existed which contained as many as 500,000 books. Literally millions of books must have perished, and with them the achievements of a great many scholars and scientists, whose books, had they survived, might have changed the course of history. As it is, even now, only a tiny proportion of existing Arabic scientific texts have been studied, and it will take years to form a more exact idea of the contributions of Muslim scientists to the history of ideas.

One of the fields most assiduously cultivated in Spain was natural science. Although Andalusian scholars did not make contributions as fundamental as those made by their colleagues in the East, those that they did make had more effect on the later development of science and technology, for it was through Spain and the scholars of al-Andalus that these ideas reached the West.

No school of translators comparable to the House of Wisdom of al-Ma'mun existed in Spain, and Andalusian scholars seem not to have interested themselves in the natural sciences until the translations of the House of Wisdom reached them.

Interest in mathematics, astronomy, and medicine was always lively, because of their obvious utility—mathematics for commercial purposes, computation of the rather complicated Islamic laws of inheritance, and as a basis for measuring distances. Astronomy was useful for determining the times of prayer and adjusting the calendar, and the study of medicine needed no apology. The introduction of the new

Aristotelian ideas, however, even in Arab dress, aroused a certain amount of suspicion in the conservative West, and it was some time before public opinion would accept that Aristotelian logic did not conflict with the Revelation.

Part of the suspicion with which certain of the ideas emanating from the scholars of the Abbasid court were viewed was due to an inadequate distinction between sciences and pseudo-sciences. This was a distinction which the Muslims made at a much earlier date than Western scholars, who, even during the Renaissance, tended to confound astronomy with astrology, chemistry with alchemy. Ibn Hazm, a leading Andalusian scholar of the 11th century and staunchly conservative, was very outspoken on this point. People who advocated the efficacy of talismans, magic, alchemy, and astrology he calls shameless liars. This rational approach did much to make Islam preeminent in the natural sciences.

The study of mathematics and astronomy went hand in hand. Al-Khwarizmi's famous book entitled *The Calculation of Integration and Equation* reached al-Andalus at an early date, and became the foundation of much later speculation. In it, Al-Khwarizmi dealt with equations, algebraic multiplication and division, measurement of surfaces, and other questions. Al-Khwarizmi was the first to introduce the use of what he called "Indian" and what we call "Arabic" numerals. The exact method of the transmission of these numerals—and the place-value idea which they embodied—is not known, but the symbols used to represent the numbers had slightly different forms in Eastern and Western Islam, and the forms of our numerals are derived from those used in al-Andalus. The work of al-Khwarizmi, which now only survives in a 12th century Latin translation made in Spain, together with a translation of Euclid's *Elements,* became the two foundations of subsequent mathematical developments in al-Andalus.

The first original mathematician and astronomer of al-Andalus was the 10th century's Maslama al-Majriti. He had been preceded by competent scientists—men like Ibn Abi 'Ubaida of Valencia, who in the ninth century was a leading astronomer—and the *emigré* from Baghdad, Ibn Taimiyyah, who was both a well-known physician and an astronomer, but al-Majriti was in a class by himself. He wrote a number of works on mathematics and astronomy, studied and elaborated the Arabic translation of Ptolemy's *Almagest* and enlarged and corrected the astronomical tables of al-Khwarizmi himself. He compiled conversion tables, in which the dates of the Persian calendar were related to *Hijra* dates, so that for the first time the events of Persia's past could be dated with precision.

Al-Zarqali, known to the Latin West as Arzachel, was another leading mathematician and astronomer who flourished in Cordoba in the 11th century. He combined theoretical knowledge with technical skill, and excelled at the construction of precision instruments for astronomical use. He built a waterclock capable of determining the hours of the day and night and indicating the days of the lunar month. He contributed to the compilation of the famous *Toledan Tables,* a highly accurate compilation of astronomical data. His *Book of Tables,* written in the form of an almanac (almanac is an Arabic word meaning climate, originally indicating the stations of the moon) contains tables which allow one to find on what day the Coptic, Roman, lunar and Persian months begin; others give the position of the various planets at any given time; and still others allow prediction of solar and lunar eclipses. He also compiled valuable tables of latitude and longitude; many of his works were translated, both into Spanish and into Latin.

Still another luminary was al-Bitruji (the Latin scholars of the middle ages called him Alpetragius), who developed a new theory of stellar movement and wrote *the Book of Form* in which it is detailed.

The influence of these astronomical works was immense. Today, for example, the very appellations of the constellations still bear the names given them by Muslim astronomers— Acrab (from *'aqrab*, "scorpion"), Altair (from *al-ta'ir*, "the flyer"), Deneb (from *dhanb*, "tail"), Pherkard (from *farqad*, "calf")—and words such as zenith, nadir and azimuth, all still in use today, recall the works of the Muslim scholars of al-Andalus.

But the Muslim science *par excellence* was the study of medicine. Interest in medicine goes back to the very earliest times. The Prophet himself stated there was a remedy for every illness and was aware that some diseases were contagious.

The great contribution of the Arabs was to put the study of medicine on a scientific footing, and eliminate superstition and harmful folk-practices. Medicine was considered a highly technical calling, and one which required long study and training. Elaborate codes were formulated to regulate the professional conduct of doctors. It was not enough to have a mastery of one's subject in order to practice medicine. Certain moral qualities were mandatory. Ibn Hazm said that a doctor should be kind, understanding, friendly, good, able to endure insults and adverse criticism; he must keep his hair short, and his fingernails as well; he must wear clean, white clothes, and behave with dignity.

Before doctors could practice, they had to pass an examination, and if they passed they had to take the Hippocratic oath, which, if neglected, could lead to dismissal.

Hospitals were similarly organized. The large one built in Cordoba was provided with running water and baths, had different sections for the treatment of various diseases, each section of which was headed by a specialist. Hospitals were required to be open 24 hours a day to handle emergency cases, and could not turn any patient away.

Muslim physicians made many important additions to the body of medical knowledge which they inherited from the Greeks. Ibn al-Nafis, for example, discovered the lesser circulation of the blood hundreds of years before Harvey and ideas of quarantine sprang from an empirical notion of contagion.

Another example is Ibn Juljul who was born in Cordoba in 943, became a leading physician by the age of 24 (he began his studies of medicine at the age of 14) and compiled a commentary on the *De Materia Medica* of Dioscorides, and a special treatise on drugs found in al-Andalus. In his *Categories of Physicians,* composed at the request of one of the Umayyad princes, he also presents a history of the medical profession from the time of Aesculapius to his own day.

During the 10th century, al-Andalus produced a large number of excellent physicians. Several went to Baghdad, where they studied Greek medical works under the famous translators Thabit Ibn Qurra and Thabit ibn Sinan. On their return, they were lodged in the government complex at Madinat al-Zahra. One of these men, Ahmad ibn Harran, was placed in charge of a dispensary which provided free medical care and food to poor patients.

Ibn Shuhaid, also known as a popular doctor, wrote a fundamental work on the use of drugs. He—like many of his contemporaries—recommended drugs only if the patient did not respond to diet, and said that if they must be used, simple drugs should be employed in all cases but the most serious.

Al-Zahrawi, who died in 1013, was the most famous surgeon of the Middle Ages. He was court physician of al-Hakam II, and his great work, the *Tasrif,* was translated into Latin by Gerard of Cremona and became a leading medical text in European universities in the later middle ages. The section on surgery contains a number of illustrations of surgical instruments of elegant, functional design and great precision. It describes lithotrites, amputations, ophthalmic and dental surgery, the treatment of wounds and fractures.

Ibn Zuhr, known as Avenzoar who died in 1162, was born in Seville and earned a great reputation throughout North Africa and Spain. He described abscesses and mediastinal tumors for the first time, and made original experiments in therapeutics. One of his works, the *Taysir,* was translated into Latin in 1280 and became a standard work.

An outgrowth of the interest in medicine was the study of botany. The most famous Andalusian botanist was Ibn Baitar, who wrote a famous book called *Collection of Simple Drugs and Food.* It is an alphabetically arranged compendium of medicinal plants of all sorts, most of which were native to Spain and North Africa, which he spent a lifetime gathering. Where possible, he gives the Berber, Arabic, and sometimes Romance names of the plant, so that for linguists his work is of special interest. In each article, he gives information about the preparation of the drug and its administration, purpose and dosage.

The last of the great Andalusian physicians was Ibn al-Khatib, who was also a noted historian, poet, and statesman. Among his other works, he wrote an important work on the theory of contagion: "The fact of infection becomes clear to the investigator who notices how he who establishes contact with the afflicted gets the disease, whereas he who is not in contact remains safe, and how transmitting is effected through garments, vessels, and earrings."

Ibn al-Khatib was the last representative of the Andalusian medical tradition. Soon after his death, the energies of the Muslims of al-Andalus were wholly absorbed in the long costly struggle against the Christian *reconquista.*

Another field that interested the scholars of al-Andalus was the study of geography and many of the finest Muslim works in this field were produced there. Economic and political considerations played some part in the development of the study of geography, but it was above all their all-consuming curiosity about the world and its inhabitants that motivated the scholars who devoted themselves to the description of the earth and its inhabitants. The first steps had been taken in the east, when "Books of Routes," as they were called, were compiled for the use of the postmasters of the early `Abbasid Caliphs. Soon, reports on far away lands, their commercial products and major physical features were compiled for the information of the Caliph and his ministers. Advances in astronomy and mathematics made the plotting of this information on maps feasible, and soon cartography had become an important discipline in its own right.

Al-Khwarizmi, who did so much to advance the science of mathematics, was also one of the earliest scientific descriptive geographers. Basing his work on information made available through the Arabic translation of Ptolemy, al-Khwarizmi wrote a book called *The Form of the Earth*, which included maps of the heavens and of the earth. In al-Andalus, this work was carried forward by Ibn Muhammad al-Razi—Rhazes—who died in 936, and who wrote a basic geography of al-Andalus for administrative purposes. Muhammad ibn Yusuf al-Warraq, a contemporary of al-Razi, wrote a similar work describing the topography of North Africa. The wide-ranging commercial relations of al-Andalus allowed the collection, from returning merchants, of a great deal of detailed information about regions as far north as the Baltic. Ibrahim ibn Ya'qub, for example, who travelled widely in Europe and the Balkans in the late ninth century—he must have been a brave man indeed—left itineraries of his travels.

Two men who wrote in the 11th century collected much of the information assembled by their predecessors, and put it into convenient form. One of them, al-Bakri, is particularly interesting. Born in Saltes in 1014, al-Bakri was the son of the governor of the province of Huelva and Saltes. Al-Bakri himself was an important minister at the court in Seville, and undertook several diplomatic missions. An accomplished scholar, as well as *littérateur*, he wrote works on history, botany and geography as well as poetry and literary essays. One of his two important geographical works is devoted to the geography of the Arabian Peninsula with particular attention to the elucidation of its place names. It is arranged alphabetically, and lists the names of villages, towns, wadis, and monuments which he culled from the *hadith* and histories. His other major work has not survived in its entirety, but it was an encyclopedic treatment of the entire world.

Al-Bakri arranged his material by country—preceding each entry by a short historical introduction—and describes the people, customs, climate, geographical features and the major cities—with anecdotes about them. He says of the inhabitants of Galicia, for example: "they are treacherous, dirty, and bathe once or twice a year, even then with cold water; they never wash their clothes until they are worn out because they claim that the dirt accumulated as the result of their sweat softens their body."

Perhaps the most famous geographer of the time was al-Idrisi, "the Strabo of the Arabs." Born in 1100 and educated in Cordoba, al-Idrisi travelled widely, visiting Spain, North Africa, and Anatolia, until he eventually settled in Sicily, where he was employed by the Norman King, Roger II, to write a systematic geography of the world, which is still extant, and is usually known as *The Book of Roger.*In it, al-Idrisi describes the world systematically, following the Greek division of it into seven "climes" each divided into 10 sections. Each of the climes is mapped—and the maps are highly accurate for the time in which they were compiled. He gives the distances between major cities, describes the

customs, people, products, and climate of the entire known world. He even records the voyage of a Moroccan navigator who was blown off course in the Atlantic, sailed for 30 days, and returned to tell of a fertile land inhabited by naked savages. America?

The information contained in *The Book of Roger* was engraved on a silver planisphere, which was one of the wonders of the age.

Al-Andalus also produced the authors of two of the most interesting travel books ever written. Both exist in good English translation. The first is by Ibn Jubair, secretary to the Governor of Granada who, in 1183, made the Hajj, and wrote a book about his journey, called simply *Travels*. The book is in the form of a diary, and gives a detailed account of the eastern Mediterranean world at the height of the Crusades. It is written in clear elegant style, and is filled with the perceptive intelligent comments of a tolerant—and often witty—man.

The most famous of all the Andalusian travellers was Ibn Battuta—the greatest tourist of his age—and perhaps of any. He went to North Africa, Syria, Makkah, Medina and Iraq. He went to Yemen, sailed down the Nile, the Red Sea, Asia Minor, and the Black Sea. He went to the Crimea and to Constantinople. He went to Afghanistan, India and China. He died in Granada at the age of 73.

It is impossible to do justice to all the scholars of al-Andalus who devoted themselves to the study of history and linguistic sciences. Both were the prime "social sciences" cultivated by the Arabs, and both were brought to a high level of art in al-Andalus. For example, Ibn al-Khatib, whose theory of contagious diseases we have touched on already, was the author of the finest history of Granada that has come down to us.

Ibn al-Khatib was born in 1313, near Granada, and followed the traditional educational curriculum of his time—he studied grammar, poetry, natural sciences, and Islamic law, as well, of course, as the Koran. His father, an important official, was killed by the Christians in 1340. The ruler of Granada invited his son to occupy the post of secretary in the Department of Correspondence. He soon became the confidant of the ruler, and gained a position of great power.

Despite his busy political career, Ibn al-Khatib found time to write more than 50 books on travel, medicines, poetry, music, history, politics and theology.

The achievements of Ibn al-Khatib were rivalled only by those of his near contemporary, Ibn Khaldun, the first historian to seek to develop and explicate the general laws which govern the rise and decline of civilizations. His huge, seven volume history is entitled *The Book of Examples and Collections from Early and Later Information Concerning the Days of Arabs, Non-Arabs and Berbers.* The first volume, entitled *Introduction* gives a profound and detailed analysis of Islamic Society and indeed, of human society in general, for he constantly refers to other cultures for comparative purposes. He gives a sophisticated analysis of how human society evolved from nomadism to urban centers, and how and why these urban centers decay, and finally succumb to less developed invaders. Many of the profoundly disturbing questions raised by Ibn Khaldun have still not received the attention they should from all thinking men. Certainly, anyone interested in the problems of the rise and fall of civilizations, the decay of cities, the complex relationship between technologically advanced societies and traditional ones should read Ibn Khaldun's *Introduction to History.*

Another great area of Andalusian intellectual activity was philosophy but it impossible to do more than glance at this difficult and specialized study. From the ninth century, Andalusian scholars, like those in Baghdad, had to deal with the theological problems posed by the introduction of Greek philosophy into a context of Islam. How could reason be reconciled with Revelation? This was the central question.

Ibn Hazm was one of the first to deal with this problem. He supported certain Aristotelian concepts with enthusiasm and rejected others. For example he wrote a large and detailed commentary on Aristotle's *Posterior Analects,* that abstruse work on logic. Interestingly, Ibn Hazm appears to have had no trouble relating logic to Islam—in fact, he gives illustrative examples of how it can be used in solving legal problems drawn from the *Shari'ah.* Nothing illustrates the ability of Islam to assimilate foreign ideas and acclimatize them better than Ibn Hazm's words in the introduction to his work: "Let it be known that he who reads this book of ours will find that the usefulness of this kind of work is not limited to one single discipline but includes the Koran, *hadith,* and legal decisions concerning what is permissible and what is not, and what is obligatory and what is lawful."

Ibn Hazm considered logic a useful tool, and philosophy to be in harmony, or at least not in conflict, with Revelation. He has been described as "one of the giants of the intellectual history of Islam," but it is difficult to form a considered judgment of a man who wrote more than 400 books, most of which have perished or still remain in manuscript.

Ibn Bajjah, whom western scholastic theologians called Avempace, was another great Andalusian philosopher. But it was Averroes—Ibn Rushd—who earned the greatest reputation. He was an ardent Aristotelian, and his works had a lasting effect, in their Latin translation, on the development of European philosophy.

Islamic technological innovations also played their part in the legacy of al-Andalus to medieval Europe. Paper has been mentioned, but there were others of great importance—the windmill, new techniques of working metal, making ceramics, building, weaving and agriculture. The people of al-Andalus had a passion for gardens, combining their love of beauty with their interest in medicinal plants. Two important treatises on agriculture—one of which was partially translated into Romance in the Middle Ages, were written in al-Andalus. Ibn al-`Awwam, the author of one of these treatises, lists 584 species of plants and gives precise instructions regarding their cultivation and use. He writes, for example, of how to graft trees, make hybrids, stop blights and insect pests and how to make floral essences and perfumes.

This area of technological achievement has not yet been examined in detail, but it had as profound an influence on medieval European material culture as the Muslim commentators on Aristotle had on medieval European intellectuals. For these were the arts of civilization, the arts that make life a pleasure rather than a burden, and without which philosophical speculation is arid and exercise.

Some English Words Derived from Arabic

Admiral	Check	Nadir
Alchemy	Chess	Orange
Alcohol	Coffee	Rice
Alcove	Cotton	Risk
Alfalfa	Cupola	Rocket
Algebra	Cipher	Saccharin
Algorithm	Drug	Sapphire
Alkali	Elixer	Satin
Almanac	Fanfare	Shellac
Amalgam	Gallant	Sherbert
Antimony	Gazette	Shrub
Apricot	Ginger	Sofa
Arsenal	Giraffe	Spinach
Artichoke	Guitar	Sugar
Atlas	Jar	Syrup
Balcony	Lilac	Talc
Banana	Lemon	Tariff
Bismuth	Magazine	Teak
Blouse	Mattress	Zenith
Cable	Mocha	Zero
Caliber	Monsoon	Zircon
Camelot	Musket	
Candy	Muslin	

From W. Montgomery Watt, *The Influence of Islam on Europe*, Edinburgh University Press, Edinburgh, 1972.

56

The Missing Conqueror: Genghis Khan and the Making of the Modern World

This reading explores the life and achievements of the Mongol Genghis Khan (Chinggis Khan) as well as providing insight into the culture of the steppe nomads in the 12th and 13th centuries. The Mongols, under Genghis Khan's leadership, would create the largest empire of all time, yet their image, along with his, has been largely absent from history or subject to great distortion. Contemporaries of the Mongols would write of them with fear and loathing, as they awaited the "scourge" of their powerful military. Diplomats and heads of state would write of them with disdain, highlighting instances of barbarity. Even to this day, a true depiction of Genghis Khan and the Mongols continues to elude us, and stereotypes of their leader and behavior abound.

Discussion Questions

1. What does the "Spirit Banner" mentioned in the reading symbolize about the life and beliefs of the Mongols and Genghis Khan? Is it similar to any other artifact that we've studied?

2. Genghis Khan's early life was filled with adversity. What particular character traits are mentioned that made him the leader that he became? Can you compare him with any other conqueror?

3. If, as the reading states, "The Mongols made no technological breakthroughs, founded no new religions, wrote few books or dramas," how do you account for their huge success in creating a "new world order"?

4. What does the reading tell you about the military strategies of the Mongols? About their culture and values?

5. What are some of the key achievements of the Mongols under the Khan's leadership?

6. After this reading, how would you characterize the Mongols and Genghis Khan? Does he deserve to be ranked higher on Hart's list of the 100 most influential people in history?

7. Of the regions conquered by the Mongols, which fared best? Worst?

The Missing Conqueror

In 1937, The Soul of Genghis Khan disappeared from the Buddhist monastery in central Mongolia along the River of the Moon below the black Shankh Mountains where the faithful lamas had protected and venerated it for centuries. During the 1930s, Stalin's henchmen executed some thirty thousand Mongols in a series of campaigns against their culture and religion. The troops ravaged one monastery after another, shot the monks, assaulted the nuns, broke the religious objects, looted the libraries, burned the scriptures, and demolished the temples. Reportedly, someone secretly rescued the embodiment of Genghis Khan's soul from the Shankh Monastery and whisked it away for safekeeping to the capital in Ulaanbaatar, where it ultimately disappeared.

Through the centuries on the rolling, grassy steppes of inner Asia, a warrior-herder carried a Spirit Banner, called a *sulde*, constructed by tying strands of hair from his best stallions to the shaft of a spear, just below its blade. Whenever he erected his camp, the warrior planted the Spirit Banner outside the entrance to proclaim his identity and to stand as his perpetual guardian. The Spirit Banner always remained in the open air beneath the Eternal Blue Sky that the Mongols worshiped. As the strands of hair blew and tossed in the nearly constant breeze of the steppe, they captured the power of the wind, the sky, and the sun, and the banner channeled this power from nature to the warrior. The wind in the horsehair inspired the warrior's dreams and encouraged him to pursue his own destiny. The streaming and twisting of the horsehair in the wind beckoned the owner ever onward, luring him away from this spot to seek another, to find better pasture, to explore new opportunities and adventures, to create his own fate in his life: in this world. The union between the man and his Spirit Banner grew so intertwined that when he died, the warrior's spirit was said to reside forever in those tufts of horsehair. While the warrior lived, the horsehair banner carried his destiny; in death, it became his soul. The physical body was quickly abandoned to nature, but the soul lived on forever in those tufts of horsehair to inspire future generations.

Genghis Khan had one banner made from white horses to use in peacetime and one made from black horses for guidance in war. The whiteone disappeared early in history, but the black one survived as the repository of his soul. In the centuries after his death, the Mongol people continued to honor the banner where his soul resided. In the sixteenth century, one of his descendants, the lama Zanabazar, built the monastery with a special mission to fly and protect his banner. Through storms and blizzards, invasions and civil wars, more than a thousand monks of the Yellow Hat sect of Tibetan Buddhism guarded the great banner, but they proved no match for the totalitarian politics of the twentieth century. The monks were killed, and the Spirit Banner disappeared.

Fate did not hand Genghis Khan his destiny; he made it for himself; It seemed highly unlikely that he would ever have enough horses to create a Spirit Banner, much less that he might follow it across the world. The boy who became Genghis Khan grew up in a world of excessive tribal

---

violence, including murder, kidnapping, and enslavement. As the son in an outcast family left to die on the steppes, he probably encountered no more than a few hundred people in his entire childhood, and he received no formal education. From this harsh setting, he learned, in dreadful detail, the full range of human emotion: desire, ambition, and cruelty. While still a child he killed his older half brother, was captured and enslaved by a rival clan, and managed to escape from his captors.

Under such horrific conditions, the boy showed an instinct for survival and self-preservation, but he showed little promise of the achievements he would one day make. As a child, he feared dogs and he cried easily. His younger brother was stronger than he was and a better archer and wrestler; his half brother bossed him around and picked on him. Yet from these degraded circumstances of hunger, humiliation, kidnapping, and slavery, he began the long climb to power. Before reaching puberty, he had already formed the two most important relationships of his life. He swore eternal friendship and allegiance to a slightly older boy who became the closest friend of his youth but turned into the most dedicated enemy of his adulthood, and he found the girl whom he would love forever and whom he made the mother of emperors. The dual capacity for friendship and enmity forged in Genghis Khan's youth endured throughout his life and became the defining trait of his character. The tormenting questions of love and paternity that arose beneath a shared blanket or in the flickering firelight of the family hearth became projected onto the larger stage of world history. His personal goals, desires, and fears engulfed the world.

Year by year, he gradually defeated everyone more powerful than he was, until he had conquered every tribe on the Mongolian steppe. At the age of fifty, when most great conquerors had already put their fighting days behind them, Genghis Khan's Spirit Banner beckoned him out of his remote homeland to confront the armies of the civilized people who had harassed and enslaved the nomadic tribes for centuries. In the remaining years of life, he followed that Spirit Banner to repeated victory across the Gobi and the Yellow River into the kingdoms of China, through the central Asian lands of the Turks and the Persians, and across the mountains of Afghanistan to the Indus River.

In conquest after conquest, the Mongol army transformed warfare into an intercontinental affair fought on multiple fronts stretching across thousands of miles. Genghis Khan's innovative fighting techniques made the heavily armored knights of medieval Europe obsolete, replacing them with disciplined cavalry moving in coordinated units. Rather than relying on defensive fortifications, he made brilliant use of speed and surprise on the battlefield, as well as perfecting siege warfare to such a degree that he ended the era of walled cities. Genghis Khan taught his people not only to fight across incredible distances but to sustain their campaign over years, decades, and, eventually, more than three generations of constant fighting.

In twenty-five years, the Mongol army subjugated more lands and people than the Romans had conquered in four hundred years. Genghis Khan, together with his sons and grandsons, conquered the most densely populated civilizations of the thirteenth century. Whether measured by the total number of people defeated, the sum of the countries annexed, or by the total area occupied, Genghis Khan conquered more than twice as much as any other man in history. The hooves of the Mongol warriors' horses splashed in the waters of every river and lake from the Pacific Ocean to the Mediterranean Sea. At its zenith, the empire covered between 11 and 12 million contiguous square miles, an area about the size of the African continent and considerably larger than North America, including the United States, Canada, Mexico, Central America, and the islands of the Caribbean combined. It stretched from the snowy tundra of Siberia to the hot plains of India, from the rice paddies of Vietnam to the wheat fields of Hungary, and from Korea to the Balkans. The majority of people today live in countries conquered by the Mongols; on the modern map, Genghis Kahn's conquests include thirty countries with well over 3 billion people. The most astonishing aspect of this achievement is that the entire Mongol tribe under him numbered around a million, smaller than the workforce of some modern corporations. From this million, he recruited his army, which was comprised of no more than one hundred thousand warriors—a group that could comfortably fit into the larger sports stadiums of the modern era.

In American terms, the accomplishment of Genghis Khan might be understood if the United States, instead of being created by a group of educated merchants or wealthy planters, had been founded by one of its illiterate slaves, who, by the sheer force of personality, charisma, and determination, liberated America from foreign rule, united the people, created an alphabet, wrote the constitution, established universal religious freedom, invented a new system of warfare, marched an army from Canada to Brazil, and opened roads of commerce in a free-trade zone that stretched across the continents. On every level and from any perspective, the scale and scope of Genghis Khan's accomplishments challenge the limits of imagination and tax the resources of scholarly explanation.

As Genghis Khan's cavalry charged across the thirteenth century, he redrew the boundaries of the world. His architecture was not in stone but in nations. Unsatisfied with the vast number of little kingdoms, Genghis Khan consolidated smaller countries into larger ones. In eastern Europe, the Mongols united a dozen Slavic principalities and cities into one large Russian state. In eastern Asia, over a span of three generations, they created the country of China by weaving together the remnants of the Sung dynasty in the south with the lands of the Jurched in Manchuria, Tibet in the west, the Tangut Kingdom adjacent to the Gobi, and the Uighur lands of eastern Turkistan. As the Mongols expanded their rule, they created countries such as Korea and India that have survived to modern times in approximately the same borders fashioned by their Mongol conquerors.

Genghis Khan's empire connected and amalgamated the many civilizations around him into a new world order. At the time of his birth in 1162, the Old World consisted of a series of regional civilizations each of which could claim virtually no knowledge of any civilization beyond its closest neighbor. No one in China had heard of Europe, and no one in Europe had heard of China, and, so far as is known, no person had made the journey from one to the other. By the time of his death in 1227, he had connected them with diplomatic and commercial contacts that still remain unbroken.

As he smashed the feudal system of aristocratic privilege and birth, he built a new and unique system based on individual merit, loyalty, and achievement. He took the disjointed and languorous trading towns along the Silk Route and organized them into history's largest free-trade zone. He lowered taxes for everyone, and abolished them altogether for doctors, teachers, priests, and educational institutions. He established a regular census and created the first international postal system. His was not an empire that hoarded wealth and treasure; instead, he widely distributed the goods acquired in combat so that they could make their way back into commercial circulation. He created an international law and recognized the ultimate supreme law of the Eternal Blue Sky over all people. At a time when most rulers considered themselves to be above the law, Genghis Khan insisted on laws holding rulers as equally accountable as the lowest herder. He granted religious freedom within his realms, though he demanded total loyalty from conquered subjects of all religions. He insisted on the rule of law and abolished torture, but he mounted major campaigns to seek out and kill raiding bandits and terrorist assassins. He refused to hold hostages and, instead, instituted the novel practice of granting diplomatic immunity for all ambassadors and envoys, including those from hostile nations with whom he was at war.

Genghis Khan left his empire with such a firm foundation that it continued growing for another 150 years. Then, in the centuries that followed its collapse, his descendants continued to rule a variety of smaller empires and large countries, from Russia, Turkey, and India to China and Persia. They held an eclectic assortment of titles, including khan, emperor, sultan, king, shah, emir, and the Dalai Lama. Vestiges of his empire remained under the rule of his descendants for seven centuries. As the Moghuls, some of them reigned in India until 1857, when the British drove out Emperor Bahadur Shah II and chopped off the heads of two of his sons and his grandson. Genghis Khan's last ruling descendant, Alim Khan, emir of Bukhara, remained in power in Uzbekistan until deposed in 1920 by the rising tide of Soviet revolution.

History has condemned most conquerors to miserable, untimely deaths. At age thirty-three, Alexander the Great died under mysterious circumstances in Babylon, while his followers killed off his family and carved up his lands. Julius Caesar's fellow aristocrats and former allies stabbed him to death in the chamber of the Roman Senate. After enduring the destruction and reversal of all his conquests, a lonely and embittered Napoleon faced death as a solitary prisoner on one of the most remote and inaccessible islands on the planet. The nearly seventy-year-old Genghis Khan, however, passed away in his camp bed, surrounded by a loving family, faithful friends, and loyal soldiers ready to risk their life at his command. In the summer of 1227, during a campaign against the Tangut nation along the upper reaches of the Yellow River, Genghis Khan died—or, in the words of the Mongols, who havean abhorrence of mentioning death or illness, he "ascended into heaven." In the years after his death, the sustained secrecy about the cause of death invited speculation, and later inspired legends that with the veneer of time often appeared as historic fact. Piano di Carpini, the first European envoy to the Mongols, wrote that Genghis Khan died when he was struck by lightning. Marco Polo, who traveled extensively in the Mongol Empire during the reign of Genghis Khan's grandson Khubilai, reported that Genghis Khan succumbed from an arrow wound to the knee. Some claimed that unknown enemies had poisoned him. Another account asserted that he had been killed by a magic spell of the Tangut king against whom he was fighting. One of the stories circulated by his detractors asserted that the captured Tangut queen inserted a contraption into her vagina so that when Genghis Khan had sex with her, it tore off his sex organs and he died in hideous pain.

Contrary to the many stories about his demise, his death in a nomad's *ger*, essentially similar to the one in which he had been born, illustrated how successful he had been in preserving the traditional way of life of his people; yet, ironically, in the process of preserving their lifestyle, he had transformed human society. Genghis Khan's soldiers escorted the body of their fallen khan back to his homeland in Mongolia for secret burial. After his death, his followers buried him anonymously in the soil of his homeland without a mausoleum, a temple, a pyramid, or so much as a small tombstone to mark the place where he lay. According to Mongol belief, the body of the dead should be left in peace and did not need a monument because the soul was no longer there; it lived on in the Spirit Banner. At burial, Genghis Khan disappeared silently back into the vast landscape of Mongolia from whence he came. The Final destination remained unknown, but in the absence of reliable information, people freely invented their own history, with many dramatic flourishes to the story. An often repeated account maintains that the soldiers in his funeral cortege killed every person and animal encountered on the forty-day journey, and that after the secret burial, eight hundred horsemen trampled repeatedly over the area to obscure the location of the grave. Then, according to these imaginative accounts, the horsemen were, in turn, killed by yet another set of soldiers so that they could not report the location of the site; and then, in turn, those soldiers were slain by yet another set of warriors.

After the secret burial in his homeland, soldiers sealed off the entire area for several hundred square miles. Noone could enter except members of Genghis Khan's family and a tribe of specially trained warriors who were stationed there to kill every intruder. For nearly eight hundred years, this area the *Ikh Khorig*, the Great Taboo, deep in the heart of Asia— remained closed. All the secrets of Genghis Khan's empire seemed to have been locked up inside his mysterious homeland. Long after the Mongol Empire collapsed, and other foreign armies invaded parts of Mongolia, the Mongols prevented anyone from entering the sacred precinct of their ancestor. Despite the eventual conversion of the Mongols to Buddhism, his successors nevertheless refused to allow priests to build a shrine, a monastery, or a memorial to mark his burial.

In the twentieth century, to assure that the area of Genghis Khan's birth and burial did not become a rallying point for nationalists, the Soviet rulers kept it securely guarded. Instead of calling it the Great Taboo or using one of the historic names that might hint at a connection to Genghis Khan, the Soviets called it by the bureaucratic designation of Highly Restricted Area. Administratively, they separated it from the surrounding province and placed it under the direct supervision of the central government that, in turn, was tightly controlled from Moscow. The Soviets further sealed it off by surrounding 1 million hectares of the Highly Restricted Area with an equally large Restricted Area. To prevent travel within the area, the government built neither roads nor bridges during the Communist era. The Soviets maintained a highly fortified MiG air base, and quite probably a storehouse of nuclear weapons, between the Restricted Area and the Mongolian capital of Ulaanbaatar. A large Soviet tank base blocked the entrance into the forbidden zone, and the Russian military used the area for artillery practice and tank maneuvers.

The Mongols made no technological breakthroughs, founded no new religions, wrote few books or dramas, and gave the world no new crops or methods of agriculture. Their own craftsmen could not weave cloth, cast metal, make pottery, or even bake bread. They manufactured neither porcelain nor pottery, painted no pictures, and built no buildings. Yet, as their army conquered culture after culture, they collected and passed all of these skills from one civilization to the next.

The only permanent structures Genghis Khan erected were bridges. Although he spurned the building of castles, forts, cities, or walls, as he moved across the landscape, he probably built more bridges than any ruler in history. He spanned hundreds of streams and rivers in order to make the movement of his armies and goods quicker. The Mongols deliberately opened the world to a new commerce not only in goods, but also in ideas and knowledge. The Mongols brought German miners to China and Chinese doctors to Persia. The transfers ranged from the monumental to the trivial. They spread the use of carpets everywhere they went and transplanted lemons and carrots from Persia to China, as well as noodles, playing cards, and tea from China to the West. They brought a metalworker from Paris to build a fountain on the dry steppes of Mongolia, recruited an English nobleman to serve as interpreter in their army, and took the practice of Chinese fingerprinting to Persia. They financed the building of Christian churches in China, Buddhist temples and stupas in Persia, and Muslim Koranic schools in Russia. The Mongols swept across the globe as conquerors, but also as civilization's unrivaled cultural carriers.

The Mongols who inherited Genghis Khan's empire exercised a determined drive to move products and commodities around and to combine them in ways that produced entirely novel products and unprecedented invention. When their highly skilled engineers from China, Persia, and Europe combined Chinese gunpowder with Muslim flamethrowers and applied European bell-casting technology, they produced the cannon, an entirely new order of technological innovation, from which sprang the vast modern arsenal of weapons from pistols to missiles. While each item had some significance, the larger impact came in the way the Mongols selected and combined technologies to create unusual hybrids.

The Mongols displayed a devoutly and persistently internationalist zeal in their political, economic, and intellectual endeavors. They sought not merely to conquer the world but to institute a global order based on free trade, a single international law, and a universal alphabet with which to write all languages. Genghis Khan's grandson, Khubilai Khan, introduced a paper currency intended for use everywhere and attempted to create primary schools for universal basic education of all children in order to make everyone literate. The Mongols refined and combined calendars to create a ten thousand year calendar more accurate than any previous one, and they sponsored the most extensive maps ever assembled. The Mongols encouraged merchants to set out by land to reach their empire, and they sent out explorers across land and sea as far as Africa to expand their commercial and diplomatic reach.

In nearly every country touched by the Mongols, the initial destruction and shock of conquest by an unknown and barbaric tribe yielded quickly to in unprecedented rise in cultural communication, expanded tirade, and improved civilization. In Europe, the Mongols slaughtered the aristocratic knighthood of the continent, but, disappointed with the general poverty of one area compared with the Chinese and Muslim countries, turned away and did not bother to conquer the cities, loot the countries, or incorporate them to the expanding empire. In the end, Europe suffered the least yet acquired the advantages of contact through merchants such as the Polo family of Venice and envoys exchanged between the Mongol khans and the popes and kings of Europe. The new technology, knowledge, and commercial wealth created the Renaissance in which Europe rediscovered some of its prior culture, but more importantly, absorbed the technology for printing, firearms, the compass, and the abacus from the East. As English scientist Roger Bacon observed in the thirteenth century, the Mongols succeeded not merely from martial superiority; rather, "they have succeeded by means of science." Although the Mongols "are eager for war," they have advanced so far because they "devote their leisure to the principles of philosophy."

Seemingly every aspect of European life—technology, warfare, clothing, commerce, food, art, literature, and music—changed during the Renaissance as a result of the Mongol influence. In addition to new forms of fighting, new machines, and new foods, even the most mundane aspects of daily life changed as the Europeans switched to Mongol fabrics, wearing pants and jackets instead of tunics and robes, played their musical instruments with the steppe bow rather than plucking them with the fingers, and painted their pictures in a new style.

The Europeans even picked up the Mongol exclamation *hurray* as an enthusiastic cry of bravado and mutual encouragement.

With so many accomplishments by the Mongols, it hardly seems surprising that Geoffrey Chaucer, the first author in the English language, devoted the longest story in *The Canterbury Tales* to the Asian conqueror Genghis Khan of the Mongols. He wrote in undisguised awe of him and his accomplishments. Yet, in fact, we are surprised that the learned men of the Renaissance could make such comments about the Mongols, whom the rest of the world now view as the quintessential, bloodthirsty barbarians. The portrait of the Mongols left by Chaucer or Bacon bears little resemblance to the images we know from later books or films that portray Genghis Khan and his army as savage hordes lusting after gold, women, and blood.

Despite the many images and pictures of Genghis Khan made in subsequent years, we have no portrait of him made within his lifetime. Unlike any other conqueror in history, Genghis Khan never allowed anyone to paint his portrait, sculpt his image, or engrave his name or likeness on a coin, and the only descriptions of him from contemporaries are more intriguing than informative. In the words of a modern Mongolian song about Genghis Khan, "we imagined your appearance but our minds were blank."

Without portraits of Genghis Khan or any Mongol record, the world was left to imagine him as it wished. No one dared to paint his image until half a century after his death, and then each culture projected its particular image of him. The Chinese portrayed him as an avuncular elderly man with a wispy beard and empty eyes who looked more like a distracted Chinese sage than a tierce Mongol warrior. A Persian miniaturist portrayed him as a Turkish sultan seated on a throne. The Europeans pictured him as the quintessential barbarian with a fierce visage and fixed cruel eyes, ugly in every detail.

Mongol secrecy bequeathed a daunting task to future historians who wished to write about Genghis Khan and his empire. Biographers and historians had so little on which to base an account. They knew the chronology of cities conquered and armies defeated; yet little reliable information existed regarding his origin, his character, his motivation, or his personal life. Through the centuries, unsubstantiated rumors maintained that soon after his death, information on all these aspects of Genghis Khan's life had been written in a secret document by someone close to him. Chinese and Persian scholars referred to the existence of the mysterious document, and some scholars claimed to have seen it during the apex of the Mongol Empire. Nearly a century after Genghis Khan's death, the Persian historian Rashid al-Din described the writings as an "authentic chronicle" written "in the Mongolian idiom and letters." But he warned that it was guarded in the treasury, where "it was hidden and concealed from outsiders." He stressed that "no one who might have understood and penetrated" the Mongol text "was given the opportunity." Following the collapse of Mongol rule, most traces of [he secret document seemed to have disappeared, and in time, many of the best scholars came to believe that such a text never existed, that it was merely one more of the many myths about Genghis Khan.

Just as the imaginative painters of various countries portrayed him differently, the scholars did likewise. From Korea to Armenia, they composed all manner of myths and fanciful stories about Genghis Khan's life. In the absence of reliable information, they projected their own fears and phobias onto these accounts. With the passage of centuries, scholars weighed the atrocities and aggression committed by men such as Alexander, Caesar, Charlemagne, or Napoleon against their accomplishments or their special mission in history. For Genghis Khan and the Mongols, however, their achievements lay forgotten, while their alleged crimes and brutality became magnified. Genghis Khan became the stereotype of the barbarian, the bloody savage, the ruthless conqueror who enjoyed destruction for its own sake. Genghis Khan, his Mongol horde, and to a large extent the Asian people in general became unidimensional caricatures, the symbol of all that lay beyond the civilized pale.

By the time of the Enlightenment, at the end of the eighteenth century, this menacing image appeared in Voltaire's *The Orphan of China*, a play about Genghis Khan's conquest of China: "He is called the king of kings, the fiery Genghis Khan, who lays the fertile fields of Asia waste." In contrast to Chaucer's praise for Genghis Khan, Voltaire described him as "this destructive tyrant... who proudly... treads on the necks of kings," but "is yet no more than a wild Scythian soldier bred to arms and practiced in the trade of blood" (Act I, scene I). Voltaire portrayed Genghis Khan as a man resentful of the superior virtues of the civilization around him and motivated by the basic barbarian desire to ravish civilized women and destroy what he could not understand.

The tribe of Genghis Khan acquired a variety of names—*Tartar, Tatar, Mughal, Moghul, Moal*, and *Mongol*—but the name always carried an odious curse. When nineteenth-century scientists wanted to show the inferiority of the Asian and American Indian populations, they classified them as Mongoloid. When doctors wanted to account for why mothers of the superior white race could give birth to retarded children, the children's facial characteristics made "obvious" that one of the child's ancestors had been raped by a Mongol warrior. Such blighted children were not white at all but members of the Mongoloid race. When the richest capitalists flaunted their wealth and showed antidemocratic or antiegalitarian values, they were derided as *moguls*, the Persian name for Mongols.

In due course, the Mongols became scapegoats for other nations' failures and shortcomings. When Russia could not keep up with the technology of the West or the military power of imperial Japan, it was because of the terrible Tatar Yoke put on her by Genghis Khan. When Persia fell behind its neighbors, it was because the Mongols had destroyed its irrigation system. When China lagged behind Japan and Europe, the cause was the cruel exploitation and repression by its Mongol and Manchu overlords. When India could not resist British colonization, it was because of the rapacious greed of Moghul rule. In the twentieth century, Arab politicians even assured their followers that Muslims would have invented the atomic bomb before the Americans if only the Mongols had not burned the Arabs' magnificent libraries and leveled their cities. When American bombs and missiles drove the Taliban from power in Afghanistan in 2002, the Taliban soldiers equated the American invasion with that of the Mongols, and therefore, in angry revenge, massacred thousands of Hazara, the descendants of the Mongol army who had lived in Afghanistan for eight centuries. During the following year, in one of his final addresses to the Iraqi people, dictator Saddam Hussein made similar charges against the Mongols as the Americans moved to invade his country and remove him from power.

Amidst SO much political rhetoric, pseudoscience, and scholarly imagination, the truth of Genghis Khan remained buried, seemingly lost to posterity. His homeland and the area where he rose to power remained closed to the outside world by the Communists of the twentieth century, who kept it as tightly sealed as the warriors had done during the prior centuries. The original Mongolian documents, the so-called *Secret History of the Mongols*, were not only secret but had disappeared, faded into the depths of history even more mysteriously than Genghis Khan's tomb.

57

Africa: The Myth and the Fact

Our images of Africa have tended to come from television, where anthropological studies have portrayed the diverse lifestyles of indigenous peoples, or from Hollywood, where Africa is seen as exotic, dangerous, the land of fantasy. While these images are by no means entirely false, when used to define an entire continent and its peoples, they fall into the category of myth. A myth is a belief which may have the ring of truth, but contains exaggerations of fact, created to reinforce certain cultural values of a society at a given time. As this reading suggests, the European explorers, merchants and missionaries in the 17th century developed a set of myths as much to define themselves and their purposes as to explain Africa and the Africans. The function of the myths that were created was, above all, to underscore the ethnocentrism of Europeans. That the myths identified by Bohannan and Curtin still persist, is testimony to not only the power of myth, but also to the influence of those myths on historical research as well as present day reporting on Africa. In this reading the authors attempt to separate myth from fact so as to allow us to view African history as Africans lived it, and not as Europeans and Americans have created it.

Discussion Questions

1. What myths of Africa do the authors identify, and what facts are used to refute them?

2. Where did Europeans get the information that led them to create the myths mentioned by the authors?

3. What do these myths tell us about Europeans and Americans, both past and present?

4. What possible interests might be served by creating and perpetuating such myths?

Africa has, for generations now, been viewed through a web of myth so pervasive and so glib that understanding it becomes a twofold task: the task of clarifying the myth and the separate task of examining whatever reality has been hidden behind it. Only as it is stated and told can the myth be stripped away. Only if the myth is stripped away can the reality of Africa emerge.

Africa splashed into the consciousness of the rest of the world in July of 1960 with the eruption of the newly independent Congo, all but forgotten since the days of the slave trade. In the century between 1860 and 1960 Africa had been the province of Africans, and of a few missionaries, colonial government officials, and scholars. Occasionally the isolation was pierced by travelers: yet men like André Gide, when they broke the dark barrier, admitted that they saw problems and moral questions of which they had sooner remain ignorant. For the rest, there was Dr. Schweitzer and there were the maunderings of moralistic and naïvely romantic journalists to stand between Martin Johnson's *Lion* and today's New York *Times*. All of them, for one reason or another, had an interest in preserving the myths.

Africa was the "Dark Continent," but the darkness had much more to do with the European and American visitors to it, and workers in it, than it had to do with Africans. It was in the interests of officials to say, in their reports to their governments and indeed in their letters home, that Africa was peaceful and was progressing along predetermined lines. It was in the interests of missionaries, in emphasizing their undoubted victories, to exaggerate the depravity of the base line from which their ministrations had brought their converts. It was, on the other hand, in the interest of physical and biological scientists either to disregard Africans or to treat them as specimens. It was in the interests of many anthropologists who were studying alien cultures to look only at Africa's bright side....

Since the middle 1960s, however, the attention of the American public has been less directly riveted on Africa—the African news is reported along with that from other parts of the world, while public attention has turned to Vietnam, the conflict between China and Russia, and periodic snipings across the Suez. Africa has attained a place in world affairs, but is not (as we write) one of the focal points in world affairs.

However, our information is still scattered and disorganized. Nobody has, as yet, found a way to bring together systematically what is known to scholars, what the missionaries have learned, and what business and industrial representatives know.

Although it is of limited sort, missionaries have amassed a tremendous knowledge about Africa that should be utilized. Missionaries speak the languages of the peoples they missionize. They tend to stay in these places from three to twenty-five years (with breaks, of course, because one cannot stay away from one's own culture for too long without its becoming diluted). However, lack of utilization of missionaries by scholars is only part of the problem. Missionaries, with all of their knowledge, have garnered it for specific purposes. We do not questions these purposes, but only state that they are not the purposes of statesmanship or scholarship.

Businessmen who have been in and out of Africa also know an amazing amount about it—people in the copper companies, trading companies, and more recently the banks, oil companies, and the flour mills. Their knowledge is about very different subjects from that of the missionaries or the scientists, but they do have a tremendous fund of untapped information. There is little opportunity for businessmen, missionaries, and scholars to forgather and talk.

Because informed people were rare, and because those who did exist did not pool their knowledge, American and other Westerners became aware and conscious of Africa with all the myths intact. Although some of those myths have been dispersed, they have been replaced by others.

Some of the oldest and most pervasive myths are the simplest: the myth of the lions in the jungles. Lions do not live in jungles in the first place. Only about 5 percent of the African continent can be called jungle in any case. What few lions there are live in the grasslands. But darkness goes with jungles and wild beasts, and the lions in the jungles persist as a symbol for the unrecognized fear that Americans have of Africa.

The myth that Africa is the Dark Continent is, actually, a subject-object confusion. Europe was certainly isolated—as isolated as Africa has ever been. During the Middle Ages, Africans and Arabs and Indians had an active trade across the Indian Ocean and across the Sahara—even across the Mediterranean. Morocco leather was made south of the Sahara—it was bought from the Moroccans by Europeans, who did not ask further where it came from. In the twelfth and thirteenth centuries the whole subcontinent of Africa south of the Sahara was flooded with cowrie shells, which became a currency—and they came from the Maldive Islands, via Venice and the Arabs. Africa was in touch with the rest of the world while most of Europe slept. Africa was even in touch with the fringes of Europe.

There are portraits of Africans on Greek vases; there are portrait busts of Negroes in Roman art. Europe must recognize the fact that it was *Europe* that woke up only in the fifteenth century. Although Africa too was isolated from the major civilizations of the world, it was Europe's isolation that created Europe's emerging problems.

The next myth—and it is one that will be met everywhere—is that Africa was "savage." The myth began in the seventeenth and eighteenth centuries when savages became a philosophical necessity for the emergence of Europe. Savages, both depraved and noble, explained historical as well as psychic problems—but the ideas concerning savages were buttressed with few facts. Savages were next to "missing links," mythical creatures of a cosmographic theory known as the "chain of being" outliving the theory that spawned them. Savages were clean, and unriddled by the problems of industrialization and vast (and vastly painful) social change. Savages, on the other hand, could not speak, knew not fire, and were at the mercy of the destructive forces of brute nature. Such savages were what we all might have been, except for the grace of God. It must also be admitted that missionaries, probably more than any other single group, kept the myth of savagery alive. The more "savage" a place, the greater the missionaries' mundane as well as supermundane rewards. Their undeniable fortitude and the hardships they bore were translated into the imagery of "savagery" by congregations and mission societies at home, even if they did not themselves write them so (and many were level-headed observers who did not). They knew better, as their papers show: yet the image they cast before them was that of heroes doing battle with cannibalism, lust, and depravity—the forces of "darkness."

Today, we can admit the facts on which such a myth was based, at the same time that we can be objective about them. African culture shares more of its traits, its history, and its social organizations with Europe than Asia shares with Europe and certainly more than the North American Indians and the Australian aborigines share with Europe. Economically, Africa and Europe are a single sphere. Methods of production of food in Africa are pretty much the same as they were in Europe a few centuries, and in some instances a few millennia, ago. Market organization was the same. The religions are variations on the same basic themes. Family organization reflects pretty much the same values, although Africans tend to be polygynous and Europeans tend to be monogamous. But the values are quite the same. Such could not be said of the Chinese or the Aztecs.

Moreover, there were in 1960 literally thousands of Africans who were trained and ready to take over the administration of their countries: not as many as they themselves desired, but in most of British and French Africa—particularly those without European settlers—there were enough to start with. Along with their traditionalism, there was a very broad streak of modernism in all Africans. Unlike some peoples of the Pacific and the Americas, Africans have shown comparatively little resistance to change and so-called modernization. This again may stem largely from the fundamental similarity of African and European (including American) cultures. They share anciently a great common pool of culture, and although the African manifestations of it are different from those of Europeans, the differences are superficial when measured against the gulfs that separate either from Australian aborigines, Malays, or even the Japanese. Perhaps even more important, they share Europe's diseases and so were not decimated on contact.

But there are other myths to be exploded: one is the more generalized myth, in America, about race. Africans are "supposed" to be Negroes—but lots of Africans are not. There are Caucasians and there are Bushmen.

The whole subject of race has been torn asunder and "exposed" by modern genetics, yet the very term has encapsulated connotations from false scientific claims and ethical judgments of centuries. The word "race" means, to geneticists, an interbreeding population with distinct and heritable characteristics. The difficulty comes in properly delimiting the relevant characteristics. For a century and more, race and language were confused—race and culture are still being confused. Language is often a characteristic of an interbreeding population, but it is not a biotic characteristic, and therefore has nothing to do with "race." The same is true of culture. In the guise of differential intelligence (whatever that may eventually come to mean) and therefore "cultural potential," the old problem is still with us, and is still given a false biological base. Like witchcraft to the Age of Reformation, the concept of race seems to be the non sequitur by which the modern world explains forces that it does not understand. Race as a social problem is still with us—and it is the social problem that must be dealt with.

The racial myth leads us to another: that is the myth among American Negroes about what Africa is and what its nature is. American Negroes came to this country, as we are all constantly aware, as slaves. The first Negro arrived in the New World in 1494. Negroes provided as much of the heritage of the American continent as any other modern immigrant group. They have been here longer than most. American Negroes, toward the end of the nineteenth century, when they were being more systematically closed out from the dominant culture than they had ever been before, turned back to Africa in search of security.

There have been two reactions to the black search for Africa. The earliest was a bourgeois denial of any kind of association with Africa. The striving black middle class tended to look at Africa with the myths of the dominant culture, and to deny any association. The second reaction was an embrace of Africa by black groups in search of a cultural base on which to build a black ethnicity in America that could demand respect equal to the ethnic background of any other group. Pan-Africanism started as a movement among American Negroes; they were its driving force from the late nineteenth century until the end of World War II. After the war, many became grossly disappointed, because African aims were nationalistic and their own were equalitarian. However, after 1960 none could any longer deny Africa, even culturally.

There are sometimes difficulties between Africans and American Blacks, similar to those between the British and American Whites—they expect to be very much alike and are shocked to discover that it is not so. Africans are sometimes brutally cruel to American Blacks, calling them slaves. The situation is reversed and American Blacks sometimes say—jokingly, perhaps—that to marry an African is to ask for trouble. The cultures are a little too far apart in the everyday matters.

Yet today no black American dares to deny Africa or his African heritage. To do so would be to deny the blackness of his skin and to deny, that is, to be a traitor to, the great force that French-speaking Africans call *negritude* and that burns vibrantly in the black revolution in the United States. Educated and upper middle-class American Negroes are caught between Black Muslims or Black Panthers and Africans—wishing to deny both, but able to deny neither.

American Blacks are as American as American Swedes, and their African heritage has made great contributions to American culture: from attitudes toward child care to southern cooking. Africanism came into America the way that Polishisms came into it. People came in, and people always react to new situations according to the dictates of their old fundamental experience. If that experience was African or Swedish, this is "the way they do things." People bring up their children basically as they themselves were brought up. When one starts being a nursemaid or a mother or a father or an uncle, only a narrow part of the whole arc of culture is in Dr. Spock's book. The rest is learned in the social relationships in which one is involved when young. Therefore, all basic values and ways of behavior tend to persist, even as they may be reinterpreted, or even superficially rejected.

But the Africanisms in American culture share another characteristic with analogous "isms" from Poland or Britain or Italy—they are no longer the province merely of the people who brought them. The Polish mode of seasoning sausage is the mode of all Americans today; the British mode of making laws is that of all of us; Italian modes of cookery and clothing tastes, love of the sun, and the masculine ideal affect us all. Africanisms are to be found in the culture of all of us. They do not cluster—or at least they did not until conscious efforts were made in the 1960s by large numbers of people—in a "black culture."

Most white American groups have gone through a period—a so-called "second generation"—when they denied the culture of their immigrant ancestors. Only in the fourth—sometime the third—generation did the children or grandchildren of Poles and Italians and Swedes become interested in returning at least to some of the superficial aspects of their "parent" cultures. Because of the specific social conditions for American Blacks, their "second-generations syndrome" was unduly prolonged—indeed, to several centuries. Today in the 1970s, however, the descendants of African immigrants are turning to the culture of Africa in a search very like that of the descendants of the European immigrants—to find their own roots. This has been—and remains—the American pattern of keeping the country safe for cultural differentness. "The Melting Pot" is a second-generation idea; we are now well "Beyond the Melting Pot."

Black Americans have been denying old myths of Africa—and building new ones. Indeed, the Negro American myth of Africa is one of the most dominant—and one of the most false, precisely because Negroes too were subject to the dominant myths about Africa. For many a Negro American, the myth that he has not contributed to American culture is compounded with—and confounded by—that other myth that Africans were "savages." The Negroes' problem was that cultural forces were at play making it necessary for them to subscribe to the myths about Africa at the same time that psychic forces of *amour-propre* forced them to dissociate from Africa. They had either to dissociate and give the lie to the first myth or turn their African background into a Golden Age. The contradiction was blatant, and often destructive.

Today that phase has passed. Black Americans have turned to African clothes, to soul food (much of which did indeed originated in African cookery), and to a kind of warmth and far-flung brotherhood that they half-imagine, half-discover in African culture. The new myths are of very great importance—but they are not always what a pedantic scholar could consider "accurate."...

One last point must be made clearly—although it is easier to do so today than it was a few years ago. The West does not so much have an African problem as Africa has a European problem. South Africa is enough a European country to appear to have a native problem, but the "natives" think of it as a European problem. East Africans have a European problem. So do the Katangese. It was only half in jest that Kwame Nkrumah suggested building a monument in Accra to the Anopheles mosquito, the carrier of the malaria that made Europeans reject West Africa as "unsuitable for colonization."

In the fifteenth and sixteenth centuries, the European nations began an expansion that is only now being reversed. This expansion against the rest of the world was intrinsic to Euro-American culture, an integral part of its growth. Europeans combined classical and Judaeo-Christian ideas to provide the basis of an emergent morality.

Christianity has always been an expanding, proselytizing religion. With the beginnings of the Industrial Revolution, the need for raw materials and for markets thrust European cultures outward in all directions. The rest of the peoples of the world were hit from outside. With the settling of the Europeans in American and Australia and South Africa, the people who were already there either collapsed as the Australian aborigines did or fought against hopeless odds until they had been turned into dependent remnant tribes as the American Indians did in the face of white power. But Africans adapted and adopted.

After Europe expanded and collided with all these people, the new society needed clerks and catechists and laborers in order to carry on business and achieve its purposes. Europeans started teaching people to use shovels and pencils, to figure and to read. When a man learns to read, the door has been opened—Malcolm X makes this point vividly and dramatically in his *Autobiography*.

Once people see culture that, in a colonial situation, they are by definition not allowed to have, they become a deprived people. They are perfectly capable of practicing that culture, but are not allowed to participate in it. Africans, when they were living a pre-colonial life, were not deprived people. Lives of tremendous dignity and valued rewards can be lived away from the trappings of Western civilization. But once the consciousness of those trappings seeps into awareness, a new day has arrived, a new struggle must ensue, and new myths must be forged....

58

Africa's Storied Past

The noted anthropologist, Eric Wolf, used the term "people without a history" to describe those societies that had been, for one reason on another, largely ignored by the scholarly community. This reading seeks to correct earlier writings that traditional African peoples had a long and complex past that mirrored developments in other parts of the world.

Discussion Questions

1. How do people's stories "get lost?" What does this reading add to the RGH readings on the myths of Africa, and Africa's role in world history?

2. What are some of the key developments in Africa's early history that have "confounded" our impressions of Africa? How are these discoveries changing our view of traditional Africa?

3. What have been the most effective methods used by archaeologists and others in recapturing Africa's history?

4. Does the example of Africa as a "lost civilization" compare with others that we have studied?

Africa's Storied Past

For too long, scholars preoccupied with finding archaeological firsts dismissed Africa as a cultural backwater unworthy of serious study. Advances such as food production, urbanism, technology, and state formation were presumed to have happened first in Europe or the Near East, then been sown by outsiders on fertile African soil. "Africa had already lapsed into provincialism during the Late Pleistocene," wrote the British archaeologist Grahame Clark in 1961. "From this time, much of the continent remained a kind of cultural museum, without contributing to the main course of human progress." The slow growth of African archaeology was largely a product of "dark continent" stereotypes, images that still live in the "see the forbidden and nightmarish landscape and live to describe it" genre of travelogues and bleak futurologies of African anarchy at the millennium's end. Ignoring robust economies, explosive democracy, and vibrant pluralism of most African countries, these visions cling to Conrad's familiar *Heart of Darkness*, the story of a European's metaphorical voyage up the Congo River into the abyss of time:

> We penetrated deeper and deeper into the heart of darkness; We were wanderers on a Prehistoric Earth.... We could not understand because we were too far and could not remember because we were traveling in the Night of First Ages; Of those Ages that are gone, leaving hardly a sign and no memories.

Here is the barbarous fringe of history's privileged lands, the Nile, Mesopotamia, and Europe. Lurking along the banks are peoples without history, perversely impervious to enlightenment from without.

With a few notable exceptions, the archaeology of Africa is less than 50 years old, but what a half-century it has been! Pottery thousands of years older than that of the Near East and Europe, true steel two and a half millennia before its nineteenth-century European "invention," urban civilizations without despots and wars—all are confounding, our old images of Africa. But these are more than just African insights; they are fundamental revelations about how humans have interacted with each other and their environment and how societies have changed in the past. With these examples before them, researchers working in other parts of the globe can never again look at their data in the same way.

Precocious Herders

Today all of the world's pastoralists depend to some degree on settled farmers; in Kenya, for example, Maasai herders get grain from Kikuyu farmers. That no modern pastoralists live entirely independent of farmers, however, has led to the theory that agriculture must always have preceded herding. During the last 20 years, evidence has emerged that in Africa full-time herding appeared millennia before farming.

At Bir Kiseiba and Nabta Playa in Egypt's Western Desert, Fred Wendorf of Southern Methodist University has shown that foragers were managing herds of wild cattle as early as 7500 B.C. Barbara Barich of the University of Rome has obtained similar dates for the management of Barbary sheep in the Tadrart Acacus region of Libra. Nabta Playa, in particular, has created a stir because of the discovery of astronomically aligned megalithic arrangements dating from some 6,500 ago. Beneath some of these megaliths and in nearby tumuli are ceremonial cattle burials and even a large rock intentionally shaped to resemble a cow. Clearly the systematic management of wild herds had evolved by this date into true domestication. Once it developed, herding spread rapidly across the Sahara, reaching the Atlantic as early as the mid-sixth millennium B.C.

In the 1940s, botanists declared Africa to be the home of several major cereals—sorghum, millet, and African rice—and an entire suite of roots and tubers. Nonetheless, it was thought that the idea of domestication was imported from the Near East during the Egyptian late predynastic period, then dated to the turn of the third millennium B.C. Beginning in the late 1980s, Wendorf's excavations at Nabta Playa found evidence of experiments with sorghum and millet 9,000 years ago; about the same time, a French team led by Nicole Petit-Maire was finding grinding stones and storage pits for processing wild grains about 4500 B.C. at Foum el-Alba in Mali. Independent of agricultural developments in the Near East, these early experiments took their own course, apparently in response to a highly unpredictable climate: millet was domesticated by 900 B.C. in the Tichitt region of Mauritania, excavated by a French team since the 1960s, and sorghum by 250 B.C. at Jenne-jeno in Mali—more than six millennia after the first herding at Nabta Playa.

Settling Down

Even before the people of Tichitt domesticated millet, they seem to have become settled. The region has hundreds of sites: stone-built settlements stretching in a 250-mile arc against the base and on top of a U-shaped cliff, and scatters of stone tools on the floodplain of an adjacent lake. Between 2000 and 900 B.C., people there ate wild grain from the lake shore and kept cattle, sheep, and goats. Debate rages about whether any of these early settlements, some of which cover more than 200 acres, were truly urban. But it has all the hallmarks of sedentarism (living year-round in the same place) without agriculture, which is quite at odds with the traditional model of the emergence of villages, derived from the Near Eastern Neolithic, as a consequence of cereal farming.

This kind of sedentarism went hand in hand with the distinctive nature of economies in parts of the southern Sahara. Some communities collected mainly wild plants; others specialized in fishing, gathering shellfish, or hunting aquatic animals like hippos, manatees, and crocodiles. These communities were interspersed in such a way that they could trade among themselves and capitalize on each other's skills—the same kinds of connections between communities that would contribute to the development of true towns in Africa.

In the late 1980s, Malian archaeologist Téréba Togola and Kevin MacDonald of the University of London studied similar webs of interaction in the Méma region of Mali. In the second millennium B.C., communities of fishers, herders, and perhaps gatherers came together, at least seasonally, resulting in clusters of settlements observed in the archaeological record. In the early first millennium A.D., these clusters became permanent and attracted metalworkers, long-distance travelers carrying exotic items, and others with specialized skills and knowledge. Some remained small and undistinguished, while others grew to as many as 33 linked communities; the largest individual settlements covered more than 200 acres. This urban pattern finds its greatest expression on the Middle Niger floodplain, at sites such as Jenne-jeno, which covers 84 acres and was part of an interlocked congerie of 69 separate sites, totaling 483 acres spread over 20 square miles.

This African urban pattern is far removed from our standard image of the preindustrial town, with its concentrated population cowering behind a city wall, its hinterland depopulated because of regional instability. It is comparable to the extensive webs of specialist hamlets that make up Bronze Age cities in China, where archaeologists are having a hard time finding early cities in the traditional mold. (The African data may hold a lesson about how to refocus their search.) That cities emerged independently in sub-Saharan Africa also counters our expectation of 50 years ago that they must have been a late derivative of the Islamic towns of North Africa.

Cities Without Kings

In Africa and just about everywhere else, archaeologists long assumed that monuments, palatial architecture, and conspicuously wealthy burials reflected some degree of stratified, state organization. Only the powerful, so the thesis went, only those with a degree of despotic control over the lives of others and with a court or bureaucracy to organize their labor, could undertake such displays. In some cases, such as Great Zimbabwe, the archaeological evidence supports this argument (see *Archaeology*, May/June 1998, pp. 44–49). A number of African cases, however, call this model into question. Throughout the 1,600-year history of Jenne-jeno there are no elite burials, no monumental buildings, and no palaces. Precious artifacts, like decorated ceramics and copper ornaments, are found in houses of all sizes.

From southeastern Nigeria we have the curious case of Igbo Ukwu, excavated beginning in 1959 by Thurstan Shaw of the University of Ibadan. Here, at the end of the first millennium A.D., an individual was buried amid a wealth of exquisite bronze and ivory objects, more than 100,000 imported glass and carnelian beads, and symbol-rich regalia. Yet this site is in the middle of a region that historically has resisted centralization and where there is no evidence of earlier coercive states. Today decision-making is in the hands of a number of religious brotherhoods, or secret societies, each of which is in charge of a particular aspect of community life or relations between communities. Anyone can join these societies and decisions are made communally. Most archaeologists accept Shaw's argument that the Igbo Ukwu individual was a leading member of one of these societies rather than a despotic king.

Senegal boasts thousands of earthen and stone-covered tumuli, some of which are 50 or more feet tall and arranged in groups ranging from a dozen to hundreds. Overlapping them is a zone of thousands of carved megaliths. At M'Baké, in the middle of the country, there are about 150 tumuli. Yet all archaeology, all oral tradition, and all historical documentation available for the early centuries of the present millennium deny the presence of organized states. Like southeastern Nigeria, parts of Senegal have early traditions of political organization in which authority is shared among craft, kin, and other special-interest groups encompassing a broad cross-section of society.

These and other African cases are increasingly cited in debates between scholars who see hierarchy in all monuments and complex societies and others (growing in number) who argue for heterarchy (the horizontal organization of society with internal checks to prevent monopolization of authority) as an equally viable alternative structure. There can be reasons to build monumentally, not just to glorify an elite, and many ways to organize these efforts, not all of which require coercion.

The Bantu Expansion

Archaeologist have a love-hate relationship with migrations. You can't deny that they happened in the past, yet they are the devil to document and often harder still to assign causes to. Fifty years ago, the model prehistoric migration was the rapid spread throughout Europe of Indo-European-speakers: all later ones, such as the peopling of the New World or the colonization of Polynesia, were thought to have followed the same lightning course.

Earlier in this century, when linguists realized the close affinities of Bantu languages spoken across much of central, eastern, and southern Africa, they began scouring linguistic maps looking for a Bantu homeland. At first, they were divided into two camps: Joseph Greenberg of Stanford University held that the homeland had been along what is now the Cameroon-Nigeria border, while Malcolm Guthrie argued for a more southern homeland somewhere near the Congo-Angola border. Whichever side you took, the presumption—following the Indo-European model—was that the spread of Bantu-speakers was rapid and quite recent, no earlier than the first millennium A.D. Trying to explain how Bantu-speakers spread so quickly across such a large area, archaeologists on Guthrie's side turned to technology, in this case iron, source of axes to tame the forest and hoes to till the heavy alluvial soil—key advantages over indigenous hunter-gatherers. Along with new tools went a more sedentary life-style, and different Bantu subpopulations were identified with various prehistoric ceramic traditions. All of these changes were supposed to have been quite abrupt.

By the early 1990s, linguistic and archaeological consensus had solidified in favor of the more northern origin. An important site in this area is the rock-shelter of Shum Laka, Cameroon, excavated by Pierre de Maret of the Free University of Brussels between the early 1980s and 1995. But de Maret found that Shum Laka lacked the expected abrupt change from the Late Stone Age (supposedly pre-Bantu) to the Iron Age (early Bantu). Stone remained in use even after iron was introduced between 400 B.C. and A.D. 200; so-called proto-Bantu ceramics appear even before the iron. At the very least, we can say that the Bantu expansion was far earlier and more gradual than the traditional model would have it. These findings also challenge old historical models in which advancement happens abruptly and in stages—art in the European Upper Palaeolithic, agriculture in the Neolithic, metalworking in the Bronze Age.

The Miracle of Iron

This is not to underestimate the importance of iron. In the 1970s, iron furnaces dating from the eighth century B.C. were found at Taruga in Nigeria; others possibly as early as 1300 B.C. are known from the Termit area of Niger, but the dates are controversial. There was an explosion of different types of smelting and smithing furnaces quite unlike anything elsewhere in the world, suggesting that people were perhaps experimenting with ways of producing different grades of iron in different furnaces. This innovative burst culminated in the invention of true steel by the middle of the first millennium B.C. at sites in the Buhaya region of Tanzania, and independently in West Africa, where we see it by 250 B.C. at Jenne-jeno in Mali.

Going beyond the technology, the African data have stimulated a reassessment of the role of smiths in society and the social context of the spread of metal use. Iron was not accepted along a migrating, monolithic front. In some places, such as eastern and southern Africa, the metal moves 2,000 miles in two centuries. In others, even in pockets of West Africa very close to early iron-production centers, some people appear to have used only stone tools well into the first millennium A.D. Nonprecious metals including iron and copper became status symbols with a value surpassing gold, ironworking took on an occult significance, and royal investitures included ritual ironworking.

Responses to Outside Contact

The frontier of African prehistory and history provides many examples of new states and kinds of government arising to take advantage of opportunities and react to massive disruptions as Africa came in contact with the expanding Arab world, India, and finally Europe. The wealth of Great Zimbabwe derived in part from commerce with the wider, non-African world, in this case the Indian Ocean gold trade. Some of the most interesting research of the past few years concerns the archaeological record of European contact. In the 1960s, historical archaeologists concentrated on finding sites like the slave forts of Ghana known from European historical accounts, determining their building histories, and sometimes reconstructing them. More recently interest has shifted to what Africans and Europeans were doing at these sites, how they were interacting, and the impact of this interaction on African societies. We can now appreciate that the African response to contact was anything but passive. Slave forts and colonial cities had adjacent African trading settlements, and new states arose thanks to the economic realities of the times or new technologies like firearms or steamships. The

kingdom of Benin, for example, flourished in Nigeria thanks in part to trade with Europeans, who exchanged gold for slaves, ivory, and red pepper.

The Future

The first generation of African archaeologists, those trained in the late 1950s and early 1960s, just before or just upon independence, was largely absorbed into the new national bureaucracies. They rarely had the time or the funding to go into the field. That is changing. Despite severe financial crises, several African nations have a well-trained second generation—Africans trained in Africa to do African archaeology. Many see as their primary challenge sparking local interest in archaeology. The benefits will be many—new information volunteered for cultural heritage inventories, locals to monitor the preservation of sites and historical monuments, and surveillance of sites that might otherwise be looted. At the national level, the challenge for these archaeologists is to cajole their governments into adequately funding field research, museums, and research institutions; to ensure the passage of cultural property protection laws; and to find ways to make archaeology relevant to the concerns of all citizens. If they succeed, not only will they have won a victory for Africa, but they have set an example for the rest of the world.

59

Africa in World History

African history has often been considered in isolation, its institutions and ideas often disregarded when comparisons are made with other cultures. Or, if treated in a comparative historical way, its developments have often been defined as "backward," or as "problems," presumably resolved or modified by contact with the West. This reading places Africa within the mainstream of comparative history by focusing on the values, technology, and key historical influences such as the nomad-sedentary conflict and the coming of Islam that Africa shared with other civilizations. In doing so, the authors challenge the racist and ethnocentric views that permeate much of African history, while at the same time providing reasons for the apparent "lag" in African development after approximately 1000 A.D., when compared with Europe.

Discussion Questions

1. What reasons do the authors present for the alleged "lag" in African development after about 1100 AD? Does this mean that Africa was "backward?"

2. What are the criteria used by the authors to evaluate African civilizations in relationship to other cultures? Do you think those criteria are valid?

3. In an earlier reading, one historian stated that the most important factor in any civilization's development is its "accessibility" to a variety of ideas and cultures. How would that statement relate to the information on Africa presented in this reading?

4. In what ways do the authors place Africa within the framework of world history? Just how isolated and exceptional was Africa in the premodern period?

The position of sub-Saharan Africa compared to other world civilizations is one of the most sensitive historical problems of the present day. The fact that Africans were brought to the New World as slaves and the fact that African societies were conquered by the Europeans and dominated by them for half a century seemed at one time to imply some degree of African inferiority to Western culture. In an era when racism and ethnocentric history were accepted (consciously or unconsciously), African cultural and intellectual inferiority were unquestioned assumptions. These attitudes were spelled out in elaborate theoretical works, and they permeated the whole fabric of historical and anthropological "knowledge." As modern Africa emerges from the colonial era, and Afro-Americans demand an equal share in their own society, historians of all races and nationalities must seek to readjust their view of Africa and its place in world history.

The racism and cultural arrogance of the old view are now discredited in respectable intellectual circles, even though some of the interpretations that grew out of them are still in the textbooks. Some stubborn facts also remain: in recent history, Africa *did* appear to lag behind European civilization; Africans *were* brought to the New World as slaves; and Africa *was* conquered by the Europeans at the end of the last century. Given the extensive racism that still exists in the popular culture of Europe and America, these facts are still sometimes used to support the old and discredited view of Africa. At the same time, African and Afro-American historians are tempted to overreact with exaggerated claims that great civilizations existed in the African past. The problem is to assess the true nature and meaning of any "lag" in African development, and any such assessment is doubly difficult because it carries strong political and emotional implications that stretch out in every direction.

Culture and Value Judgments

One basic problem is that of making rational judgments about the comparative quality of different human cultures. Scholars once talked in terms of "high" cultures and "low" cultures, but these judgments were based on Western values. Many aspects of culture cannot be judged rationally outside the context of a particular culture or style. Western music critics may agree in believing that one eighteenth-century string quartet sounds better than another one does, but the judgment is made within the framework of a particular style and by men who share present-day musical culture. (And even within this framework, the only "proof" of the superiority of one composition over the other is the consensus of trained judges.) Once the framework of common style and common culture is left behind, judgment is still more difficult. A particular piece of African music may sound "better" or "worse" than a particular Western composition, but there is no way of convincing someone else of the "fact" by rational argument. Even though a symphony orchestra may have more players and a more complex score than an African ensemble has, this is merely a matter of technology without any necessary bearing on the beauty of the sound produced. Similar considerations apply to the whole range of possible aesthetic judgments.

In other matters, such as ethics and morality, many cultures share certain ideas about right and wrong. Needless killing of human beings is generally considered to be wrong, but the key word is "needless." A few African societies used to practice human sacrifice, because they believed it was necessary to the well-being of society as a whole. In the West, criminals are executed for the same reason. Even if the ethical standard is universal, the interpretation is often culture-bound.

A few aspects of culture, however, may be subject to rational judgment. Technology is one of these. A technique is a *means* of doing something, and its value can be measured by its effectiveness in serving the desired end. An iron ax is demonstrably better than a stone ax—though some cultures may still prefer stone axes for ethical or aesthetic reasons. A phonetic alphabet is demonstrably more efficient than a system of ideographs, but aesthetic considerations make Chinese ideographs endure. In technology, then—and perhaps in that field alone—it is possible to make estimates of the degree of advancement of particular cultures at particular times, keeping in mind that such judgments apply only to technology and not to the whole culture.

Comparative Technological Progress

Taking only technology into account, it is clear that Africa of the nineteenth century—the period of its major confrontation with the West—was the weaker of the two societies. In the longer run of history, however, it is equally clear that northwestern Europe has not always been ahead. In the first millennium before Christ, the western Sudan and northwestern Europe were nearly on a par. Both had taken over iron and agriculture from the Middle East; neither had yet moved on to evolve an urban civilization. The differences that stood out in the nineteenth and twentieth centuries

were therefore the product of historical change over the past twenty-five hundred years or so. During those centuries, Europe developed the most efficient technology in the world, while Africa changed more slowly. It was a dual process requiring a dual explanation—partly in African history and partly in European. In fact, the explanation has to be sought in a broader view of world history, since the rise of barbarian Europe to world dominance was a process that involved the whole of the Afro-Eurasian land mass.

From this perspective, it is clear that neither Europeans nor Africans invented civilization. The combination of metallurgy, writing, agriculture, and cities first developed in only a few places, thousands of miles apart—lower Egypt and the eastern Mediterranean, the Indus Valley, Mesopotamia, and the north Chinese river valleys. In each case the technological base was similar, but early development lead them down divergent paths. By about 1000 B.C., all of these small foci of technological progress were in indirect communication with one another; an invention or discovery in any one of them could be borrowed sooner or later by the others. As communication improved, the range of mutual borrowing and the rate of technological progress increased.

In the millennium before Christ, each of these foci of civilization began to expand. The east Mediterranean center spread westward, taking in the whole of the Mediterranean basin and parts of Europe north of the Alps. By the time of Christ, the Roman Empire had organized the culture area politically. Indian Ocean trade and land routes across central Asia to China gave a new intensity to its contacts with the other centers. These culture areas had also expanded, each in its own neighborhood. By this period, the Afro-Eurasian land mass was divided into two distinct technological zones. One was the region of intercommunication and relatively developed technology. The second was more isolated, a zone of fringe communication with the major centers, where development was often held up by difficult environments.

Both sub-Saharan Africa and northwestern Europe were part of this underdeveloped world of the pre-Christian era, but the Alps created a small barrier compared to the Sahara. As Roman civilization spread through Roman conquest, part of northwestern Europe joined the intercommunicating zone, at least for a few centuries. The fall of the Western Roman Empire in the fifth century ended northwestern Europe's full membership in the "civilized world"; but Byzantium and the Islamic world south of the Mediterranean remained in the core zone, and northwest Europe was close enough to be able to pull itself back over the horizon of literacy, city life, and direct communication with the outside world. Between the tenth century and the thirteenth, Europe rebuilt its civilization through the mediation of Byzantium and Islamic civilization and reentered the intercommunicating zone. Overland trade linked the Baltic and North seas to the Mediterranean, and seaborne traders ventured regularly into the Atlantic. The sudan, on the other hand, remained cut off behind the barrier of the Sahara.

But the Sahara was not an impenetrable barrier; traders could cross it with difficulty. Iron and agriculture were continually spreading toward the southern tip of the continent. A series of states came into existence along the frontier between savanna and desert. Some of these predated the Iron Age itself. The kingdom of Kush had been in existence since the end of the second millennium B.C. Others came much later. In about the first century A.D., settlers from Arabia founded the kingdom of Axum in the Ethiopian highlands, which later conquered part of southern Arabia as well. In about A.D. 350, Axum invaded the Nilotic Sudan to the west and destroyed the city of Meroe. With that, the kingdom of Kush disappeared from history,

but sedentary civilization continued on the upper Nile. Kush was succeeded by a group of Nubian states, contemporaries of the Roman Empire. Before the year A.D. 600, both the Nubian states and Axum responded to their contacts with Rome; both were converted to the Monophysite variety of Christianity by missionaries from Roman Egypt.

Meanwhile, other states had made their appearance farther west. Takrur or Futa Toro came into existence along the middle valley of the Senegal River. Between the Senegal and the Niger bend, the Soninke state of Ghana was also founded before A.D. 600. Still another center of state formation was found in the basin of Lake Chad in the Central Sudan, and we can assume that still other states probably existed, even though we lack direct evidence.

Unlike Axum and Kush, where contact with the north was easier by way of the Nile or the Red Sea, state formation in the central and western sudan owed comparatively little to its fragile communication with the Roman world. In the western sudan political organization had long taken the form of more or less self-sufficient villages, politically independent of one another. In many parts of West Africa, this pattern lasted until the end of the nineteenth century. In the absence of dangerous enemies or extensive trade, these small units were probably considered preferable to the economic drain of tribute payments to a distant capital. But the growth of trade, the need to protect the trade routes and organize markets made a larger political unit necessary. The earliest states all appeared on the desert-savanna frontier, where differences in ecology favored exchange—salt from the desert and animals from the steppe against millet from the savanna. It is possible, in fact, that local trade of this kind had led to state formation long before extensive trade across the Sahara made the existence of those states known to the Mediterranean world.

Nomads and Sedentaries

Still another reason why people living on the savanna side of the desert-savanna fringe needed a large political unit was the danger of their location. In the steppe to the north, too dry for farming, were the nomadic pastoralists—Berber, Tuareg, and others. The very fact that they had to move in search of pasture gave them a military advantage. They could concentrate their forces for raids against their richer sedentary neighbors. If the sedentary peoples failed to organize large populations and large territories for mutual defense, they might become tribute paying dependents of the nomads. The result, for later times in the full light of historical knowledge, was the seesaw of nomadic-sedentary conflict. Well-organized sedentary states not only could protect their desert frontier; they were also able to reach out and control the desert trade routes themselves. Less well-organized peoples living on the fringes and in the oases of the Sahara became tributaries.

This ancient opposition between nomadic and sedentary peoples was not peculiar to the Sahara and its fringes. It was a regular and constant part of human experience in similar environments over very long period of time—from the emergence of pastoral nomads to the Industrial Revolution. The recurrency of similar patterns of events is sometimes called a "style of history." A "style" of this kind falls short of the necessity required of a scientific "law," but it is a useful concept. Even though all the variables cannot be taken into account, the degree of observed regularity is great enough to permit generalization; and generalizations about "styles" of history is a convenient analytical device for understanding how human societies change through time.

This particular style of nomadic-sedentary relations was common to much of the Afro-Eurasian land mass. The Sahara is simply the western end of a wide belt of arid and semi-arid lands stretching eastward from the Atlantic coast in Mauritania, across Africa, across the Red Sea to Arabia, on beyond the Persian Gulf into central Asia, finally across the Gobi Desert and along the northwest frontier of China to reach the Pacific at the Sea of Okhotsk. From the beginning of recorded history, a pattern of nomadic raids into sedentary territory is apparent from the Great Wall frontier of China to the steppe frontier of eastern Europe, from the northeast frontier of India to the northern and southern frontiers of the Sahara.

Historical recognition of the nomadic-sedentary conflict is almost as ancient as the conflict itself. In the book of Genesis, it was the mythic origin of violence and murder within the human family. "Abel was a keeper of sheep, and Cain a tiller of the ground." The Lord preferred Abel's offering to that of Cain, and his ecological preference led to murder. Much later, in fourteenth-century Tunisia, Ibn Khaldun, one of the founders of analytical history, used the nomad-sedentary conflict as the theme of his greatest work, the *Muqaddimah*, which analyzed the rise and fall of Islamic dynasties. Still more recently, Owen Lattimore's investigations of ecological tensions along the northwest frontier of China have added still more to our knowledge of historical patterns along the frontier between the desert and the sown.

In Lattimore's terms, the struggle between nomads and sedentary farmers was a struggle for land that was marginal to either form of occupation. Nomads were not content with land that could be used *only* for grazing. In Lattimore's aphorism, "The pure nomad is a poor nomad." The nomadic ecology could be far more productive if it could be linked to better land, which sedentary farmers could have used equally—or if it could be linked to the agricultural wealth of desert oases easily dominated by nomadic military power. Nomads therefore could be expected to use their advantage in mobility in order to seize control of the oases and the marginal lands.

These same marginal lands and oases were equally important to the sedentary society. Its strength, countering the mobility of the nomads, was its wealth based on the higher yields of sedentary agriculture and greater density of population. But this wealth also had to be organized for frontier defense. Farmers were tied down to their fields, immovable capital, and stores of grain. If these were to be defended, the nomads had to be stopped before they could concentrate for a raid. This in turn required elaborate preparations, which could go as far as building a permanent military line like the Great Wall of China.

At the very least, the marginal lands had to be brought under control. The desert oases were also important as strongholds for sedentary control over the steppe. The key was political organization. When a sedentary state was strong and united, it could mobilize its wealth for frontier defense. If organization broke down, it was open to nomadic attack. The oases and marginal lands often went first; larger raids could then penetrate into the heart of sedentary territory.

The nature and outcome of these raids depended on nomadic leadership and intentions. When they were led by men who were fully integrated into the nomadic culture, the raids were destructive and little more. Their aim was simply to seize the accumulated wealth of the sedentary society or to exact tribute, and they rarely led to a permanent military occupation that might tap the sedentary sources of wealth on a long-term basis. From time to time, however, nomadic leaders were able to seize control of the sedentary state and set themselves up as a new dynasty. To do this required a special kind of leadership that was culturally marginal—men who knew enough of nomadic life to gain a nomadic following, yet who also understood the structure and norms of the sedentary state.

They could then try to seize control of the state, not destroy it. As leaders of this kind assimilated the sedentary way of life, they might carry some of their original following with them as subordinate officials. Those who failed to make the adjustment drifted back into the desert. The new dynasty would then find itself in the same position as its predecessors, confronted by a nomad threat. If it could profit by its newness to make a clean sweep of administrative inefficiency, it would again seize the marginal lands and drive the nomads back into the least favorable environment to await a new weakening of the frontier, a chance to seize the marginal lands, and the opportunity to begin the process all over again under new leadership.

Needless to say, a simplistic model of this kind is not intended to be interpreted as an accurate description of specific events, much less a "law of history." But it can serve as a useful description of a style of history over a very long span of centuries—until the Industrial Revolution finally gave sedentary powers the ability to dominate the desert once and for all.

The Rise of Islam

The rise of Islam in nearby Arabia was immensely important for the future of Africa, and the new religious message was spread in circumstances that took on the historical style of nomadic-sedentary conflict. By A.D. 600, the Western Roman Empire had fallen to barbarian infiltration and invasion. The Eastern or Byzantine portion was still strong in the Balkan peninsula and Anatolia, and it still controlled Egypt and Syria. At this period it was also changing internally, becoming less universal and Roman in character and more narrowly Greek. These changes affected the loyalty of the Egyptian and Syrian provinces, which followed the Monophysite version of Christianity in opposition to the established Orthodox Church of Constantinople. Byzantine rule came to look more and more like a form of foreign domination combined with religious persecution. Byzantium's neighbor to the east was the Sassanian Empire in Persia and Mesopotamia. It too was weakened by religious controversy, and both empires had been weakened by a long series of Byzantine-Sassanian wars.

In the Arabian Desert to the south of these sedentary empires lived bedouin nomads, divided among themselves and worshiping many different local gods, although both Jewish and Christian influences were also present. Along the Red Sea coast, however, a number of trading towns like Mecca and Medina were in closer touch with the currents of sedentary civilization to the north. Here then was a setting in which culturally marginal men from the trading towns had enough contact with the nomads to establish their leadership, and also understood sedentary civilization well enough to lead a dynasty-founding invasion of the decrepit empires that controlled the Fertile Crescent from Egypt to Mesopotamia. Nomadic unity came from the ideological base of a new religion. Muhammad, a young merchant from Mecca, began to preach the new message early in the seventh century, drawing on Christian and Jewish roots but also incorporating some of the cultural traditions of Arabia itself. By the time of Muhammad's death in A.D. 632, his followers controlled the key cities of Mecca and Medina and much of Arabia. By 635, they had united the desert nomads into a mobile force capable of moving north. By 651, they had conquered the whole of the Sassanian Empire and the Byzantine provinces of Syria and Egypt.

Thus, in hardly more than a decade and a half, culturally marginal leaders from the Arabian cities had set themselves up as a new dynasty controlling parts of the former Roman and Sassanian empires. They moved the capital of Damascus and soon lost control of most of Arabia. They took the Arabic language with them, but the Islamic civilization that emerged owed far more to Persian and Roman traditions than it did to Arabian. The new dynasty took over Byzantine administrative forms along with some of the Byzantine administrators. The real base for its later conquests eastward into central Asia and westward to Spain was the Fertile Crescent, not Arabia.

Conquest was followed by conversion, but it was more than mere conversion to a new religion. The political unity of the caliphate lasted only a short time, but the religious unity of the Islamic world made for a new region of intercommunication. Islamic civilization became heir to the cultural and technological heritage of the zone stretching from the Atlantic to the frontiers of India and China. With Arabic as the universal language of religion, the Islamic world was in a position to act as mediator and transmitting agent, even between culture areas that had not been conquered or converted to Islam. Greek philosophy, for example, was taught to northwestern Europe through Muslim transmitters, and the "Arabic" system of numbers was diffused from India to Muslim Spain and then to the rest of Europe.

Islam in Africa

From the eighth century to the eighteenth, Islamic civilization was to be Africa's chief contact with the intercommunicating zone. Nevertheless, Islam was slow to move into sub-Saharan Africa, as though the very success of the Muslim drive to the north had removed the temptation to move in other directions. The Christian kingdoms of the upper Nile and the Ethiopian highlands were left alone for several centuries. As a result, they found themselves more isolated than they had been in Roman times—cut off from easy contact with their co-religionists in Egypt by the fact of Muslim rule there.

Much the same was true of the Indian Ocean network of maritime trade. Roman ships had traded as far south as present-day Tanzania, and Sassanian Persia had later dominated the western basin of the Indian Ocean, keeping up communication between the African coast and the civilizations to the north. But the rise of Islam and the Muslim conquest of Persia drew Persia into a new orbit of trade and communication within the Islamic world itself. It was not until the twelfth and thirteenth centuries that Muslim states participated actively in Indian Ocean commerce. Here too the first consequence of Islam was to increase African isolation.

Nor was contact between North Africa and the sudanic states intensified at first by the rise of Islam. Muslim conquest drove rapidly across North Africa to Spain in the first Islamic century, but the nomadic peoples of the Sahara were hardly touched by that conquest. Nomads, from the Beja of the Red Sea coast to the Berbers of the western Sahara, looked on the sedentary civilization as nomads have usually done—that is, as fair game. The "Arabs" who now ruled North Africa found themselves in charge of a sedentary civilization with a frontier to defend. Aside from defensive operations, they left the desert people alone. Most of them became Muslim by voluntary conversion, but rarely before the tenth century and often much later.

Thus, the rise of Islam created a new zone of very intense intercommunication, stretching from Spain to Persia and beyond, but sub-Saharan Africa was not included. At least until the year 1000 or so, black Africa was in much the same position as northwestern Europe during the Dark Ages—on the fringes, having some commercial contact with the Islamic world, but, through religious difference as well as physical barriers, beyond the frontier of "civilization." But Europe's return to the inner zone was comparatively easy. Northwestern Europe still retained some of the culture and technology of the Roman Empire, and Islamic civilization was

also an heir of Rome. Christendom and Islam also faced one another across military frontiers in northern Spain, Italy, and the Mediterranean islands. For sub-Saharan Africa, however, the barrier of the desert remained. Contact between the sedentary peoples on either side of the desert was possible only through the mediation of desert nomads, whom no sedentary state could easily control. But gradually the barriers began to crumble. From the eleventh century onward, Islam began to penetrate south of the desert, bringing knowledge of the alphabet, literacy for some, and at least a distant and tenuous contact with the dominant civilization of the time.

Like earlier influences from the outside, Islam came to sub-Saharan Africa through several different channels. In the far west, the Sanhaja Berbers of the Sahara were converted to Islam shortly before A.D. 1000. Commercial contacts and missionary work then carried the religion to the Senegal Valley, just south of the desert. In about 1030, the rulers of Takrur became the first sub-Saharan dynasty to embrace Islam. Other states in the western sudan, however, resisted religious change. Ghana, which reached its greatest power in the ninth and tenth centuries, appears to have kept its traditional religion in spite of its commercial contact with the north.

A second route of Islamic penetration was southward from Libya through Fezzan to Lake Chad. Roman penetration of the desert had followed this direction, and the Fezzani had long dominated the Sahara trade. Their conversion to Islam in the ninth century was a step toward the conversion of Kanem, the most important black state in the Lake Chad basin. The first Kanembu ruler to accept Islam came to power in 1085, though religious conversion of the general population undoubtedly took place only gradually in the centuries that followed.

Conversion came less peacefully to the Nile Valley. In the early centuries after the rise of Islam, commercial contacts across the Red Sea and movement of people from Arabia to Africa brought some degree of Islamic influence, but the Christian Nubian kingdoms still held out—along the desert reaches of the river where the Nile provides irrigation water, as well as in the savanna country farther south. In the 1280s and 1290s, however, attacks from Muslim Egypt destroyed Christian Nubia along the Nile. Even though the savanna kingdom of 'Alwa lived on, there was no longer a sedentary state capable of controlling the desert. Partly as a result, Arabs began to move into Africa in greater numbers than ever before. During the fourteenth and fifteenth centuries this migration became so large that the Nilotic sudan was permanently Arabized in language and many aspects of culture, though the Arab immigrants also mixed with Africans to create a present-day population that is only partly of Arab descent. This Arab penetration of the sudan resembles other nomadic attacks on a sedentary state, but in this case the marginal leadership was missing. Rather than seizing or re-creating a new state, these Arab invasions destroyed Christian Nubia without putting anything in its place. About 1500 a Muslim sedentary state, the Funj sultanate, did emerge in the savanna country of the upper Nile, but it was founded by black Africans, not by Arab nomads.

In Ethiopia and the horn of Africa, Islam also entered into competition with existing Christian states. Commercial and cultural contact between Ethiopia and Yemen had always been close, and Islam spread first to the port towns on the African side of the Gulf of Aden. By A.D. 1000, peaceful conversion was already well advanced in the eastern highlands of Ethiopia, while Christianity was spreading in the meanwhile in the western highlands. By about 1300, the Muslim sultanate of Ifat emerged as a military competitor of Christian Abyssinia for the control of Ethiopia, but this time the Christian state won. By 1415, most of the Muslims had been driven out or forcibly converted to Christianity.

Outside influence came to East Africa by sea, and not merely from the Muslim world. Traders came from India, Indonesia, and even China, but commercial ties with Persia and Arabia became dominant from the thirteenth century onward, and the port towns of East Africa began to enter the intercommunicating zone. Mogadishu in present-day Somalia was the principal center for the northern coast. Farther south, Kilwa came to dominate the trade that flowed from the Rhodesian gold fields to the coast at Sofala. Here and elsewhere along the coast, stone-built towns whose remains can be seen today are evidence of African membership in the greater world of Islam. But Islam was engrafted to an African cultural base. Arabic was used for writing and religion, but a Bantu language ancestral to modern Swahili was the language of ordinary speech.

By 1450 or so, on the eve of maritime contact with the Europeans, Islam had penetrated at many points on the fringes of sub-Saharan Africa, but Africa as a whole was still isolated from the main currents of change. In spite of eight centuries in the shadow of Islamic civilization, constraints to communication with the outside world remained impressive. In the Nilotic sudan, for example, Islam came through Arab infiltration and invasion—really another case of nomadic attack on a fragile sedentary state. The region became Muslim, but its communication with the Mediterranean world were no more regular or effective than they had been during Roman times.

The obvious prosperity of the East African port towns is also deceptive. They were African towns, but they looked toward the Indian Ocean. The trade with the interior appears to have been carried by people from the interior, and the immediate hinterland was sparsely populated. Wide belts were infested with tsetse fly, or were semi-arid. It was not, perhaps, such a formidable barrier as the Sahara, but it was barrier enough.

One sign of isolation is the geographical knowledge available in the Muslim world. The Arab geographers were avid for any scrap of information they could come by. From the eleventh century to the fourteenth, they were able to give a fair account of the geography and culture of the western sudan, but they knew almost nothing about the interior of East Africa.

Any assessment of African and world development over the period from about A.D. 600 to about 1500 must be one of sharp contrasts. The sweep of Islamic civilization, stretching by the end of this period from Morocco to Malaya, had brought an intensity of intercommunication never reached before in Afro-Eurasian history. One result of this change was the rapid development of northwestern Europe, largely through its ability to borrow and assimilate the technology that was available anywhere—from Greek science to Chinese printing and gunpowder, from Indian positional numbers to Muslim ship's rigging and algebra. But Africa was still largely isolated, and its technological lag behind the intercommunicating world was greater than ever—not because Africa was unchanging, but because the rest of the world was changing more rapidly than ever before. African achievements up until this point had been considerable, in art, music, jurisprudence, and material technology, but they were necessarily based mainly on what Africans could invent for themselves.

60

The Americas:
The Indigenous Population

By the time Europeans reached the Americas in force, they were populated by tens of millions of people who had achieved various levels of cultural development. In that respect, the western hemisphere was no different from the eastern.

Discussion Questions

1. In what respect might the "discovery" of the "New World" really be considered an encounter between two "Old" Worlds?

2. How early did human beings populate the Americas?

3. How did the various Europeans look at this "New World"?

Indians as Diverse as Their "Discoverers"

It is only an accident of history, rooted in ignorance, that the first inhabitants of the Western Hemisphere are lumped together as "Indians."

Although the earliest Americans were all descended from Asiatic stock, their cultures were as diverse as the peoples of Europe: the roving, big-game hunters of the North American plains and the city builders of Central America were as different as, say, the Vandals and the Romans.

Scholars have identified 400 distinct languages and many more dialects in the Americas. In North America alone, there were probably 240 different tribes when the Europeans arrived.

"I think if an Aztec and an Incan were to meet, they would view each other as complete foreigners, but not as aliens from another world," said Elizabeth Boone, director of Pre-Columbian Studies at Dumbarton Oaks. "They shared some fundamental concepts, some central ideas, but they all developed in different ways at different times."

"Every segment of every river valley had its own unique development and history," said Bruce Smith of the Smithsonian Institution.

No one is certain when people first crossed into Alaska from Asia to settle the New World. The traditional story holds that the earliest Americans crossed a land or ice bridge from Asia during an ice age, perhaps 20,000 years ago or possibly even earlier.

Aboriginal Americans appear to have spread thoughout North and South America very quickly. Over the millenia, Boone said, the new arrivals adapted and learned to exploit the varying environments, producing distinct cultures as a result.

Smith refers to the process as "environmental possiblism." "Think of it as the New World presenting a lot of environmental challenges and then solving those environmental puzzles in myriad ways," he said.

There were, no doubt, peoples who led miserable, hardscrabble lives. Some retained a tradition of hunting and gathering. Many developed rich societies based on agriculture. Most were governed by clan leaders and chiefdoms, some hereditary and some elective.

A few developed large, powerful states, with stratified societies and priests, potters and poets, a central bureaucracy capable of constructing large urban centers, municipal water works and monumental architecture designed to last for millenia. And they appear to have done it without use of the wheel or without beasts of burden more brawny than dogs and llamas.

When the Spanish arrived at Tenochtitlan, the capital of the Aztec world, it supported a population of 150,000 people. It was probably the largest city the Europeans had ever seen. Seville, the jumping-off point for Spanish conquistadors, harbored no more than 70,000 in the 16th century.

Moreover, the various cultures were not developing in lock step. One culture waxed as another waned. As the elaborate and sophisticated Maya world broke apart in 900 AD, for example, the temple-mound builders were flourishing in what would be the eastern United States.

Scholars have long been engaged in a vigorous debate over the earliest arrival date of the Asian migrants. All agree that the Indians were here by 11,500 years ago, the date associated with long, sharp flint spear tips unearthed in Clovis, N.M.

Some accept estimates, based on radiocarbon dates, that people were at Wilson Butte Cave in Idaho 14,000 years ago and at the Meadowcroft Rockshelter near Pittsburgh around 16,000 years ago.

Some other researchers believe the date could be much earlier. Based on excavations of medicinal plants that appear to have been chewed by humans at Monte Verde in Chile, Tom Dillehay of the University of Kentucky argues that people were there 30,000 years ago.

The earliest Americans are famed for hunting the megafauna of the New World, the giant ground sloths, camels, tapirs, horses, elk, mastodon and mammoth of around 10,000 years ago. But as George Stuart of the National Geographic Society put it, a Paleoindian may have killed a mastodon once, and then spent the rest of his life bragging about it.

A feminist critique of early American history holds that these people should be thought of as "gatherer-hunters" because gathering—typically women's work—is well known to supply more food than hunting.

In addition to their differences, the pre-Columbian peoples of North and South America shared technologies and beliefs. Boone mentions ballgames, dogs and agriculture built around maize, which was domesticated in Mexico before spreading north and south. Moreover, scholars find that many of the pre-Columbian peoples' myths and beliefs appear to have common threads.

"All of the Americas share fundamental aspects of world view. Concepts of underworld, certain ways of thinking of man and nature that are very different from Judeo-Christian ideas, where humans own nature," Boone said. "All the pre-Columbian people thought of themselves as a part of—and at the mercy of—natural forces. And their job was not so much to appease the forces of nature, but harmonize and work within confines."

"Despite all the differences, more and more I see a sameness," said Stuart, whose speciality is middle America. "They had this concept of the sacred landscape. They regarded themselves as very much a part of Earth. A lot of the mythology, about caves and hollow mountains and the underworld, show up again and again."

The European invaders who found this old world and called it new, who turned it upside down and eventually destroyed much of it, varied widely in their approaches to the cultures they found.

The English, French and Dutch came to North America. The Spanish and Portuguese went to South and Central America and Mexico, and all of them went to the Caribbean, where the indigenous, people were quickly wiped out and soon replaced by African slaves.

Although the English first came to the New World seeking riches, they soon became settlers. The English used America as a place to dump their extra sons (who lost to the rule of primogeniture), their foppish gentry, their debtors, religious outcasts and felons. The men came with families. They seldom intermarried with the local peoples. What they wanted was land, for the development of agricultural colonies. They did not conquer so much as push the Indians west.

"The French were not interested in dumping population," said Dean Snow of the State University of New York at Albany. "They were a trading operation, not colonists. They were more willing to marry into Indian communities. They sent men over. Fur traders, not families."

The Spanish also were more interested in exploitation, in political and military conquest. They pursued a feudal system known as *encomienda*, in which military men were given land and the indigenous people were viewed as serfs.

"The Spanish looked to Latin America as a warehouse," Boone said. "They never felt as if they were a part of Latin America. They viewed the New World as a natural resource, like gold." Nevertheless, because the Spanish brought fewer families to the new world, there was more intermingling with native populations in Latin America, where the veneer of European culture often leaves more signs of indigenous culture uncovered than in North America.

But wherever Indians encountered the European invaders, they suffered. Under both the British and the Spanish, few indigenous cultures, except the most isolated, escaped without profound and often disastrous transformation.

61

The Maya

The following selection was written in response to the movie *Apocalypto* which was famous for its portrayal of Mayan society as full of violence and drenched in blood. Professor David Friedel attempts to correct the record and paint a more complex and realistic picture of the Maya based on the latest archaeological evidence.

Discussion Questions

1. How and why has the portrayal of the Maya changed over time?

2. What did the Maya have in common with other civilizations and even with the modern world?

The Maya

King Kan B'ahlam of Palenque in Chiapas, Mexico, commissioned three beautiful temples in the late seventh century A.D. Inside each is a smaller one, just big enough to house a large relief framed by long inscriptions. Written in verse, the inscriptions recount the births of the kingdoms three patron gods and show that they were the beloved of the king; nurtured as a mother suckles a baby; and given new homes, revived, and healed after a terrible desecration at the hands of enemies almost a century earlier. The story weaves the history of the kingdom and Kan B'ahlam into the fabric of the cosmos.

For much of the twentieth century, the American public heard from scholarly professionals such as J. Eric Thompson about how the Classic Maya (A.D. 250-900) were peaceful theocrats overwhelmed by brutal Toltec invaders who established militaristic and materialistic states in the Terminal Classic and Early Post classic periods (A.D. 750-1100). Archaeologists, including Thompson, who wrote popular, accessible books about Maya archaeology, called the last years of the Postclassic, just preceding the Spanish conquest, the Decadent period (A.D, 1350-1500) because of the inferior quality of the art and architecture of the time, Thompson's notion of the Classic Maya as generally peaceful was belied by the amazing and colorful battle painted on a wall discovered at Bonampak in Chiapas in the late 1940s, but his view was influential among both archaeologists and the public. Popular magazines featured articles on the contemporary Maya of Yucatán and Guatemala and juxtaposed them with the towering pyramids of Chichén Itzá or Tikal, and gorgeous jade, shell, and ceramic artifacts. Throughout the 1950s and 1960s, popular images of the Maya in the United States and Mexico emphasized art and architecture, but also featured pictures of beautiful virgins being thrown into the Sacred Well of Chichén Itzá or draped over sacrificial altars by muscular priests. The latter still grace, in living color, the advertising calendars pinned up in garages throughout Yucatán. Meanwhile, scholars in the field continued working to determine, for example, whether the Classic Maya lived in cities or in villages scattered around ceremonial centers presided over by the priestly elite envisioned by Thompson.

Surveys at the Classic sites of Tikal in Guatemala and Dzibilchaltun in Yucatán during the 1950s and 1960s made a strong case for Maya cities. Excavations revealed remarkable buildings adorned with complex decoration in stone and painted plaster. At Tikal, tunneling excavations uncovered magnificent royal tombs stocked with beautiful ceramics, jade adornments, and other artifacts. These discoveries supported a view of Classic Maya society different from Thompson's, one structured into tiers of elites, professionals, and commoners ruled by powerful kings. Courtiers, craftsmen, warriors, and merchants—the usual professions of urban life—have been documented archaeologically and pictorially in the Classic Maya record.

Were Classic Maya cities the dens of iniquity.... Extensive research has not revealed the slums depicted on the outskirts of the film's

From *Archaeology* Magazine, March/April 2007 by David Freidel. Copyright © 2007 by Archaeological Institute of America. Reprinted by permission.

city; most people lived in simple wood-and-thatch homes resembling the rural ones the Maya have used since the Spanish conquest. Moreover, some researchers, such as Mayanists Arlen and Diane Chase, who have worked at the Classic city site of Caracol in Belize since the 1980s, have found substantive evidence for a prosperous urban middle class alongside royalty and commoners.

Were city dwellers bloodthirsty predators....? Simply put, they were not. With the deciphering of Maya glyphic texts and continued field research since the 1970s, the classic Maya have emerged as more recognizably worldly. For them, warfare was a staple of statecraft—sadly a hallmark trait of virtually all civilizations. Their religious practices and social organization are also coming into focus. While the great bulk of Maya literature was on bark paper and is now lost, what we have in stone provides a wonderful glimpse of the aesthetics, intellectual life, and historical consciousness of Maya nobility....

The Maya lived in and revered their rainforest environment, but they had thoroughly transformed it with 2,000 years of fanning. In 1972 and 73, I conducted surveys on the island of Cozumel, where the Spanish under Cortés made landfall in 1519. While the Spanish describe woods on the island, virtually the entire landscape was defined by stone walls dividing habitation and fanning plots. Evidently this strategy allocated land for slash-and- burn agriculture in small plots that could recover during fallow periods. All along the coast of the Yucatán Peninsula, the Spanish encountered people living in towns. To be sure, in the sixteenth century large regions of the interior southern lowlands had reverted to mature rainforest and were sparsely inhabited. But even there the Maya had towns. The rural villagers who lived in the Petén and other interior areas were farmers planting a wide variety of crops.

Ordinary Maya were peasant maize farmers and craftspeople from 1000 B.C. This fact is not incidental; Maya religion in the Preclassic and Classic periods exalted the maize god and tied royal power to him.

Ideas about social and political failure from the ninth-century crisis in the southern lowlands—the Classic Maya "collapse"—with the posited "decadence" of the period of the Spanish arrival five centuries later. These periods may have some links, bur they are as distinct as the periods of the Magna Carta and the U.S. Constitution. The "decadence" of the Late Post classic period is an aesthetic attribution by mid-twentieth-century scholars who observed that the quality and scale of public architecture had diminished compared with buildings raised several centuries earlier. My teachers, Jeremy Sabloff of the University of Pennsylvania Museum and William Rathje of Stanford University, argued that the Late Postclassic Maya were reallocating resources away from public architecture and into trade, commerce, and comfortable residences. The elite may have had less access to the wealth of the people, this theory goes, but the societies were more equal. Whether that was the case is a matter of ongoing inquiry, but the term "decadent" is no longer used to describe that period by Maya archaeologists.

Were the later, "decadent" Maya more materialistic and secular than the Classic Maya? The later Maya have emerged, through ethnohistorical and archaeological investigation, as cosmopolitan and pious peoples who sustained long traditions of city life, literacy, and commerce. Some modern Maya towns in these areas have been continuously occupied since centuries before the Spanish conquest. Even in the southern lowlands, kingdoms rose again after the ninth-century decline and persisted into the seventeenth century. While the ancient Maya had their shortcomings, including the organized violence typical of civilized people, they were remarkable in the achievements.

As to the ninth-century "collapse," the nature of that social change is more contested by experts than ever before, while the Maya fought many protracted wars during the Classic period, the victims of combat, capture, and sacrifice that we know of—based on artistic representations of the rituals from sites such as Tikal, Yaxchilan, and Piedras Negras, and in glyphic texts from sites such as Dos Pilas, Uaxactun, Yaxuna, and El Perú-Waká among others—were members of the elite and even royals, not ordinary city dwellers or peasants. This is not to say that ordinary people did not fight, suffer, and die in conflict, but that they were not of interest to the elite. Moreover, mass sacrifice can only be inferred in a few exceptional cases, as in the walls of carved skulls of the Terminal Classic period at northern lowland sites such as Chichén Itzá ....purely savage killing fields are alien to the Maya world. The Maya practice of public execution of important military and political enemies is akin to practices unfortunately common in Western history. The lesson I draw from the ninth-century collapse is that Maya leaders, like their modern counterparts, were capable of taking societies in catastrophic directions through arrogant ambition blind perseverance, and stilted political imagination. Direct predation and slaughter of ordinary people is a reality in some times and places, but it is a slander when attributed to the ancient Maya.

How modern people depict the ancient Maya matters because we use the past to reflect on the present and the future. Jared Diamond, drawing principally on the work of Maya archaeologist David Webster, features the case of the Classic Maya in Collapse, his latest contemplation on human history. But the dark lessons of antiquity are not the only ones. In the twentieth century, the Maya have emerged in public consciousness as master mathematicians who invented place notation and the concept of zero, brilliant astronomers whose calendars were as accurate as any in the Old World, and revered architects— Frank Lloyd Wright is reputed to have declared Puuc-style architecture in the northern lowlands the best in the Western Hemisphere. We newcomers to the Americas, with our shallow roots in this old place, could hold up the Maya with pride to our contemporaries elsewhere and their millennia-old dues and institutions. Our continent is rich in ancient accomplishment, too, and our admiration has been earned through clear-minded appraisal of the material record, and increasingly the historical one. The Classic Maya wrote history, scripture, and poetry that contain knowledge of the human condition and spirit, as well as wisdom that compares favorably with that of ancient Egypt, Mesopotamia, and other hearths of civilization. Finally, the accuracy of modern depictions of ancient Maya matters deeply and personally to those of us who care about the millions of people who speak a Mayan language and the societies that they call home in Mexico, Central America, and the United States.

62

China and Europe

This excerpt from Jacques Gernet's *A History of Chinese Civilization* describes the comparative backwardness of Europe relative to China and the debt of Europe to China for many of the ingredients of its own cultural revival and development.

Discussion Questions

1. To what does Gernet attribute the growth of Europe?

2. What did Europe owe to China?

After a general survey of eleventh to thirteenth-century China, one is left with the impression of an amazing economic and intellectual upsurge. Marco Polo's surprise at the end of the thirteenth century was not simulated. The time lag between East Asia and the Christian West is striking, and we have only to compare the Chinese world with the Christian world of this period in each domain—volume of trade, level of technology, political organization, scientific knowledge, arts and letters—to be convinced of Europe's very considerable "backwardness." The two great civilizations of the eleventh to thirteenth centuries were incontestably those of China and Islam.

There is nothing surprising about this Western backwardness: the Italian cities which took on a new life at the end of the Middle Ages were at the terminus of the great commercial routes of Asia. Situated at the end of the Eurasian continent, Europe was at a distance from the great currents of civilization and the great trade routes. But its situation also explains its immunity, at any rate in its western areas, from the most serious invasions; it was making progress at the very time when the Mongol occupation, from Mesopotamia to the Bay of Bengal, was leading to the decline of the Islamic world. It profited from the new waves of trade and borrowings set in motion by the creation of a vast Mongol empire extending from Korea to the Danube. What we have acquired the habit of regarding—according to a history of the world that is in fact no more than a history of the West—as the beginning of modern times was only the repercussion of the upsurge of the urban, mercantile civilizations whose realm extended, before the Mongol invasion, from the Mediterranean to the Sea of China. The West

gathered up part of this legacy and received from it the leaven which was to make possible its own development. The transmission was favoured by the crusades of the twelfth and thirteenth centuries and by the expansion of the Mongol empire in the thirteenth and fourteenth centuries. The mere enumeration of East Asia's contributions to medieval Europe at this time— indirect borrowings or inventions suggested by Chinese techniques—is sufficient to indicate their importance: paper, compass, and stern-post rudder at the end of the twelfth century, the application of the water-mill to looms, the counterweight trap, which was to revolutionize warfare before the development of firearms, then the wheelbarrow at the beginning of the thirteenth century, explosives at the end of the same century, the spinning-wheel about 1300, wood-block printing, which was to give rise, as in China, to printing with movable type, and cast iron (end of the fourteenth century). There we have, together with innovations of lesser importance, all the great inventions which were to make possible the advent of modern times in the West.

The upsurge of the West, which was only to emerge from its relative isolation thanks to its maritime expansion, occurred at a time when the two great civilizations of Asia were threatened. China, much weakened in the fourteenth century by the Mongol exploitation and by a long period of rebellions and wars, had to make a tremendous effort to restore its agrarian economy and to find its equilibrium again. The social redistribution and the new autocratic tendencies of the political authority were hardly favourable during most of the Ming period (1368–1644) to rapid development in the Chinese world.

From *A History of Chinese Civilization* by Jacques Gernet, translated by J. R. Foster. Reprinted with the permission of Cambridge University Press.

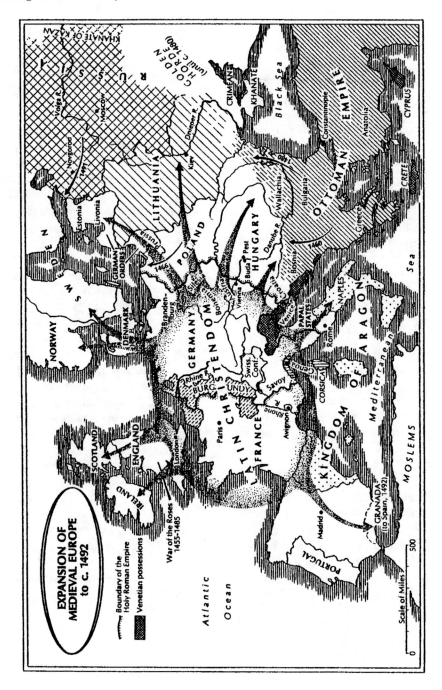

63

Europe: The Black Death

One of the most familiar aspects of the emergence of a global economy is the transference of organisms of all sorts all over the world. An early example of this was the Black Death which first struck Europe in late 1347, but which had already hit China in 1331. This pandemic is usually attributed to the opening of trade routes in Inner Eurasia by the creation of the Mongol Empire. The Black Death was actually a cluster of diseases (Bubonic, pneumonic and septicaemic) transmitted by fleas who lived on rats. Europeans are thought to have acquired the disease at a port on the Crimea in southern Russia which was a terminus of trade routes coming from the East. It spread with alarming rapidity covering virtually all of Europe within two years and killing an estimated twenty-five to forty percent of the population.

The following selection from Giovanni Boccaccio's *Decameron* describes the nature and effects of the plague as it struck Florence in 1348.

Discussion Questions

1. To what does Boccaccio attribute the plague?

2. How did people attempt to avoid contracting the disease?

3. What were the social consequences of the plague?

The Black Death

I say, then, that it was the year of the bountiful Incarnation of the Son of God, 1348. The mortal pestilence then arrived in the excellent city of Florence, which surpasses every other Italian city in nobility. Whether through the operations of the heavenly bodies, or sent upon us mortals through our wicked deeds by the just wrath of God for our correction, the plague had begun some years before in Eastern countries. It carried off uncounted numbers of inhabitants, and kept moving without cease from place to place. It spread in piteous fashion towards the West. No wisdom or human foresight worked against it. The city had been cleaned of much filth by officials delegated to the task. Sick persons were forbidden entrance, and many laws were passed for the safeguarding of health. Devout persons made to God not just modest supplications and not just once, but many, both in ordered processions and in other ways. Almost at the beginning of the spring of that year, the plague horribly began to reveal, in astounding fashion, its painful effects.

It did not work as it had in the East, where anyone who bled from the nose had a manifest sign of inevitable death. But in its early stages both men, and women too, acquired certain swellings, either in the groin or under the armpits. Some of these swellings reached the size of a common apple, and others were as big as an egg, some more and some less. The common people called them plague-boils. From these two parts of the body, the deadly swellings began in a short time to appear and to reach indifferently every part of the body. Then, the appearance of the disease began to change into black or livid blotches, which showed up in many on the arms or thighs and in every other part of the body. On some they were large and few, on others small and numerous. And just as the swellings had been at first and still were an infallible indication of approaching death, so also were these blotches to whomever they touched. In the cure of these illnesses, neither the advice of a doctor nor the power of any medicine appeared to help and to do any good. Perhaps the nature of the malady did not allow it; perhaps the ignorance of the physicians (of whom, besides those trained, the number had grown very large both of women and of men who were completely without medical instruction) did not know whence it arose, and consequently did not take required action against it. Not only did very few recover, but almost everyone died within the third day from the appearance of these symptoms, some sooner and some later, and most without any fever or other complication. This plague was of greater virulence, because by contact with those sick from it, it infected the healthy, not otherwise than fire does, when it is brought very close to dry or oily material.

The evil was still greater than this. Not only conversation and contact with the sick carried the illness to the healthy and was cause of their common death. But even to handle the clothing or other things touched or used by the sick seem to carry with it that same disease for those who came into contact with them. You will be amazed to hear what I now must tell you. If the eyes of many, including my own, had not seen it, I would hardly dare to believe it, much less

Source: Seven Cultural Traditions by J. F. Watts (NY, Simon & Schuster, 1994).

to write it, even if I had heard it from a person worthy of faith. I say that the character of the pestilence we describe was of such virulence in spreading from one person to another, that not only did it go from man to man, but many times it also apparently did the following, which is even more remarkable. If an animal outside the human species contacted the belongings of a man sick or dead of this illness, it not only caught the disease, but within a brief time was killed by it. My own eyes, as I said a little while ago, saw one day (and other times besides) this occurrence. The rags of a poor man dead from this disease had been thrown in a public street. Two pigs came to them and they, in their accustomed manner, first rooted among them with their snouts, and then seized them with their teeth and tossed them about with their jaws. A short hour later, after some staggering, as if the poison was taking effect, both of them fell dead to earth upon the rags which they had unhappily dragged.

Such events and many others similar to them or even worse conjured up in those who remained healthy diverse fears and imaginings. Almost all were inclined to a very cruel purpose, that is, to shun and to flee the sick and their belongings. By so behaving, each believed that he would gain safety for himself. Some persons, advised that a moderate manner of living, and the avoidance of all excesses, greatly strengthened resistance to this danger. Seeking out companions, such persons lived apart from other men. They closed and locked themselves in those houses where no sick person was found. To live better, they consumed in modest quantities the most delicate foods and the best wines, and avoided all sexual activity. They did not let themselves speak to anyone, nor did they wish to hear any news from the outside, concerning the dead or the sick. They lived amid music and those pleasures which they were able to obtain.

Others were of a contrary opinion. They affirmed that heavy drinking and enjoyment, making the rounds with singing and good cheer, the satisfaction of the appetite with everything one could, and the laughing and joking which derived from this, were the most effective medicine for this great evil. As they recommended, so they put into practice, according to their ability. Night and day, they went now to that tavern and now to another, drinking without moderation or measure. They did even more in the houses of others; they had only to discern there things which were to their liking or pleasure. This they could easily do, since everyone, as if he was destined to live no more, had abandoned all care of his possessions and of himself. Thus, most houses had become open to all, and strangers used them as they happened upon them, as their proper owner might have done. With this inhuman intent, they continuously avoided the sick with all their power.

In this great affliction and misery of our city, the revered authority of both divine and human laws was left to fall and decay by those who administered and executed them. They too, just as other men, were all either dead or sick or so destitute of their families, that they were unable to fulfill any office. As a result everyone could do just as he pleased.

Many others held a middle course between the two mentioned above. Not restraining themselves in their diet as much as the first group, not letting themselves go in drinking and other excesses as the second, they satisfied their appetites sufficiently. They did not go into seclusion but went about carrying flowers, fragrant herbs and various spices which they often held to their noses, believing it good to comfort the brain with such odors since the air was heavy with the stench of dead bodies, illness and pungent medicines. Others had harsher but perhaps safer ideas. They said that against plagues no medicine was better than or even equal to simple flight. Moved by this reasoning and giving heed to nothing but themselves, many men and women abandoned their own city, their houses and homes, their relatives and belongings in search of their own country places or those of others. Just as if the wrath of God, in order to punish the iniquity of men with the plague, could not pursue them, but would only oppress those within city walls! They were apparently convinced that no one should remain in the city, and that its last hour had struck.

Although these people of various opinions did not all die, neither did they all live. In fact many in each group and in every place became ill, but having given example to those who were still well, they in turn were abandoned and left to perish.

We have said enough of these facts: that one townsman shuns another; that almost no one cares for his neighbor; that relatives rarely or never exchange visits, and never do they get too close. The calamity had instilled such terror in the hearts of men and women that brother abandoned brother, uncle nephew, brother sister, and often wives left their husbands. Even more extraordinary, unbelievable even, fathers and mothers shunned their children, neither visiting them nor helping them, as though they were not their very own.

Consequently, for the enormous number of men and women who became ill, there was no aid except the charity of friends, who were few indeed, or the avarice of servants attracted by huge and exorbitant stipends. Even so, there weren't many servants, and those few men and women were of unrefined capabilities, doing little more than to hand the sick the articles they required and to mark their death. Serving in such a capacity, many perished along with their earnings. From this abandonment of the sick by neighbors, relatives and friends and from the scarcity of servants arose an almost

unheard-of custom. Once she became ill, no woman, however attractive, lovely or well-born, minded having as her servant a man, young or old. To him without any shame she exhibited any part of her body as sickness required, as if to another woman. This explains why those who were cured were less modest than formerly. A further consequence is that many died for want of help who might still be living. The fact that the ill could not avail themselves of services as well as the virulence of the plague account for the multitude who died in the city by day and by night. It was dreadful to hear tell of it, and likewise to see it. Out of necessity, therefore, there were born among the survivors customs contrary to the old ways of the townspeople.

It used to be the custom, as it is today, for the female relatives and neighbors of the dead man to gather together with those closest to him in order to mourn. Outside the house of the dead man his friends, neighbors and many others would assemble. Then, according to the status of the deceased, a priest would come with the funeral pomp of candles and chants, while the dead man was borne on the shoulders of his peers to the church chosen before death. As the ferocity of the plague increased, such customs ceased either totally or in part, and new ones took their place. Instead of dying amidst a crowd of women, many left this life without a single witness. Indeed, few were conceded the mournful wails and bitter tears of loved ones. Instead, quips and merrymaking were common, and even normally compassionate women had learned well such habits for the sake of their health. Few bodies had more than ten or twelve neighbors to accompany them to church, and even those were not upright citizens, but a species of vulture sprung from the lowly who called themselves "grave-diggers," and sold their services. They shouldered the bier and with hurried steps went not to the church designated by the deceased, but more often than not to the nearest church. Ahead were four or six clerics with little light or sometimes none, who with the help of the gravediggers placed the dead in the nearest open grave without straining themselves with too long or solemn a service.

Much more wretched was the condition of the poor people and even perhaps of the middle class in large part. Because of hope or poverty, these people were confined to their houses. Thus keeping to their quarters, thousands fell ill daily and died without aid or help of any kind, almost without exception. Many perished on the public streets by day or by night, and many more ended their days at home, where the stench of their rotting bodies first notified their neighbors of their death. With these and others dying all about, the city was full of corpses. Now a general procedure was followed more out of fear of contagion than because of charity felt for the dead. Alone or with the help of whatever porters they could find, they dragged the corpses from their houses and piled them in front so, particularly in the morning, anyone abroad could see countless bodies. It was not an isolated bier which carried two or three together. This happened not just once, but many biers could be counted which held in fact a wife and husband, two or three brothers, or father and son. Countless times, it happened that two priests going forth with a cross to bury someone were joined by three or four biers carried behind by bearers, so that whereas the priests thought they had one corpse to bury, they found themselves with six, eight or even more. Nor were these dead honored with tears, candles or mourners. It had come to such a pass that men who died were shown no more concern than dead goats today.

All of this clearly demonstrated that although the natural cause of events with its small and occasional stings had failed to impress the wise to bear such trials with patience, the very magnitude of evils now had forced even the simple people to become indifferent to them.

Every hour of every day there was such a rush to carry the huge number of corpses that there was not enough blessed burial ground, especially with the usual custom of giving each body its own place. So when the ground was filled, they made huge trenches in every churchyard, in which they stacked hundreds of bodies in layers like goods stowed in the hold of a ship, covering them with a bit of earth until the bodies reached the very top.

And so I won't go on searching out every detail of our city's miseries, but while such hard times prevailed, the surrounding countryside spared nothing. There, in the scattered villages (not to speak of the castles which were like miniature cities) and across the fields, the wretched and impoverished peasants and their families died without any medical aid or help from servants, not like men but like beasts, on the roads, on their farms and about the houses by day and by night. For this reason, just like the townspeople, they became lax in their ways and neglected their chores as if they expected death that very day. They became positively ingenious, not in producing future yields of crops and beasts, but in ways of consuming what they already possessed. Thus, the oxen, the asses, sheep, goats, pigs and fowl and even the dogs so faithful to man, were driven from the houses, and roamed about the field where the abandoned wheat grew uncut and unharvested. Almost as if they were rational, many animals having eaten well by day returned filled at night to their houses without any shepherding.

To leave the countryside and to return to the city, what more can be said? Such was heaven's cruelty (and perhaps also man's) that between March and the following July, the raging plague and the absence of help given the sick by the fearful healthy ones tore from this life more than one hundred thousand human beings within the walls of Florence. Who would have thought before this deadly calamity that the city had held so many inhabitants? Oh, how many great palaces, how many lovely houses, how many noble mansions once filled with families of lords and ladies remained empty even to the lowliest servant! Alas! How many memorable families, how many ample heritages, how many famous fortunes remained without a lawful heir!

What number of brave men, beautiful ladies, lively youths, whom not only others, but Galen, Hippocrates, and Aesculapius themselves would have pronounced in the best of health, breakfasted in the morning with their relatives, companions and friends, only to dine that very night with their ancestors in the other world!

64

Formerly Known as Prince

The Renaissance, which began in 15th-century Italy as a literary and artistic movement, led to an appreciation of the writings of the ancient Greeks and Romans, a more secular and humanistic outlook on life, and a healthy skepticism about political power. Niccolo Machiavelli, the dominant political theorist in all of Europe, would suffer insult; his leading work, "The Prince," was not even published during his lifetime, yet his ideas continue to find an audience in contemporary America, from politicians to rappers and Wall Street tycoons.

Discussion Questions

1. Why does the author suggest that Machiavelli's ideas are enjoying a resurgence of popularity, even finding an audience in rap lyrics?

2. What are Machiavelli's key ideas on the nature of political power?

3. What advice did he give to his Prince, and is it sage advice for leaders today?

4. What does the author mean by "the Machiavellian Moment"?

5. Considering the excerpts from "The Prince," along with this reading, does Machiavelli deserve to be listed as one of the most influential people that have ever lived (79th on Hart's Hundred)?

Formerly Known as Prince

Riding the subway home late one night this summer, I looked up from my newspaper and noticed a man in a fedora and a dark pinstriped suit—it was dirty and frayed, but recently pressed. He was lost in a slender, well-worn paperback adorned with a familiar etching. It was Niccolò Machiavelli, peering out from the cover of his most famous work, "The Prince."

Anyone who has ever taken Government 101 would recognize this portrait: the black frock with the thin red collar; the smooth, peach-colored skin; the closely cropped brown hair descending into a dramatic widow's peak above the forehead; and finally, that mouth, curling up into what looks like a smirk.

Until recently, this diminutive Italian philosopher (1469-1527) had little to smile about. Underappreciated during his lifetime, Machiavelli never got to see "The Prince" in print. When the book was posthumously published, a prominent English bishop claimed that it had been inspired by the Devil. Our founding fathers demonized the book as well, wrinkling their puritanical noses at its instructions for good governing. For much of the 20th century, American politicians invoked his name to impugn a rival's character. But those were different times: the Machiavellian Moment is now upon us.

Simply type his name into Amazon.com and you'll discover a whole trove of Machiavelliana. There's Harriet Rabin's book "The Princess: Machiavelli for Women," written for a new generation of feminists—"Why fight like Machiavelli," Rubin asks, "when we can light like Machiavella?"—and Machiavelli for precocious kids. "A Child's Machiavelli: A Primer on Power" (alas, "The Little Prince" was taken) certainly looks like a children's book, with its cuddly illustrations of Peter Rabbit, but Claudia Hart's text doesn't quite conform: "Either be really nice to people or kill 'em," the author writes, and adds, "A gun is man's best friend." *Put that .22 away until you've finished your homework, young man!*

In the field of politics, there's Michael A. Ledeen's "Machiavelli on Modern Leadership," a conservative rehabilitation of Machiavelli arguing that is hard-headed realism is exactly what America needs now. On the other end of the ideological spectrum is "The New Prince: Machiavelli Updated for the Twenty-first Century," which claims that Machiavelli would have counseled today's politicians to simply follow the polls. The cover of "The New Prince" describes its author as Machiavelli's "modern equivalent"—yes, it's Clinton's erstwhile consigliere, Dick Morris.

Then there's Machiavelli as self-help guru for hapless middle managers: "What Would Machiavelli Do? The Ends-Justify the Meanness," described to me by its author, Stanley Bing, as "a how-to book for people who are insufficiently unkind." This fall will yield yet another book, a biography by a professor of politics at Princeton, Maurizio Viroli. Viroli assumes a radically different task: to humanize his subject. His Machiavelli is the ultimate patriot, a man whose principal concern was the freedom of his beloved Florence.

From *New York Times Book Review*, September 3, 2000 by Jonathan Mahler. Copyright © by New York Times Company. Reprinted by permission.

The Machiavelli industry hasn't simply domesticated the late philosopher, it has democratized him too He's become an icon for the oppressed. The rapper Tupac Shakur recorded a CD under the name "Makaveli" and Mike Tyson studied Machiavelli while in prison.

So what is it, exactly, about 21st-century America that seems to be calling us back to Renaissance Italy? The theories that Machiavelli gave voice to in "The Prince" began germinating during his years as Florence's defense secretary. At the time, Florence was in a precarious place, caught in the middle of regional warfare between the papai states, Spain. Venice, France and the Holy Roman Empire. As the Florentine republic's chief emissary, Machiavelli spent his days galloping from one far-flung palace to the next attempting (usually in vain) to negotiate agreements that would keep his homeland, which at the time had no organized militia, independent.

It was, in short, a difficult time to be a prince. Today's commanders in chief can relate. After all what's the value of military supremacy when a few casualties will turn public opinion against you? The modern president faces meddlesome news media, an aggressively partisan Congress and a public that is hostile to regulation—a problem Machiavelli cleverly anticipated when he declared that there are two kinds of people: those who want to rule, and those who don't want to be ruled (Consider its modern-day echo: the era of big government is over.)

Machiavelli also understood the value of spin. A prince, he wrote, must not actually be religious but he must be able to simulate religious belief. What's more, Machiavelli knew that commanding a majority requires a certain, well, flexibility. A prince, he wrote, 'needs to have a spirit disposed to change as the winds. of fortune and variations of things command him." Behold the birth of triangulation.

The Machiavellian Moment is by no means confined to the realm of politics. "The Prince" is a how-to book for leaders, and these days you're not likely to find our nation's most dynamic leaders in Washington. Business has replaced politics as the best means of acquiring and maintaining power, which is, at bottom, a prince's main concern. In this context, it seems fitting that "The Prince" was, in effect an unsolicited job application. Machiavelli addressed the book to Lorenzo de' Medici in hopes of currying" favor with the ruling family and gaining a government position, any position — even, as he put it at the time, "rolling along a stone." (As it turned out, Lorenzo promptly set the book aside and never returned to it; he was more interested in two large dogs that had been presented to him on the same day.)

Machiavelli wrote that to rule is to rule alone *uno solo* — an ideal maxim, it would seem, for the new economy, where a 20-year-old millionaire is born every day. The new economy rewards entrepreneurs,. not company men; Loyalty is for suckers Machiavelli also knew that perception is more important than reality—"men judge more by then eyes than their hands"— another cherished truism on Wall Street today.

Of course, things change quickly, As sure as "Machiavellian" once meant evil, "dot-corn" may soon enter our lexicon as a synonym for fraud. And thanks in no small part to Bill Gates's recent run-in with the government, a rather un-Machiavellian motto seems to be gaining currency in the marketplace, one first uttered by none other than Abraham Lincoln: "Malice toward none."

So does this mean that the Machiavellian Moment has almost passed, that Niccolo's famous smile may soon turn into a frown?

Not necessarily. Machiavelli's most relevant legacy to us may be a good deal more timeless, more universal, than our recent fixation on his maxims would suggest. Interestingly, perhaps his most enduring insights into the human condition are to be found not in his political writings but in his personal letters, where he reflects on a life characterized not by Machiavellian triumphs but by guileless defeats. It's a life that invites neither hatred nor envy, but sympathy.

In 1513, the year Machiavelli started writing "Of Principalities," the booklet that would become known as "The Prince;" he was living in forced retirement in his farmhouse in the Italian countryside. Wrongly accused of having participated in a plot to overthrow the Medicis, Machiavelli had been imprisoned, tortured and beaten nearly to death before finally being released. Freedom provided little solace to poor Machiavelli. Once among Florence's great men, he had been disgraced and discarded, shut out of the affairs of state and the bustling intellectual life of Florence that had been so dear to him.

Machiavelli described his days on the farm and his method of recapturing—if just for a moment—the nobility of his life as it had been in a letter to a friend. His secret? Some great books and an active imagination. "When evening comes, I return home and enter my study; on the threshold, I take off my work-day clothes, covered with mud and dirt, and put on the garments of court and palace," Machiavelli wrote. "Fitted out appropriately, I step inside the venerable courts of the ancients, where, solicitously received by them, I nourish myself on that food that alone is mine and for which I was born; where I am unashamed to converse with them and to question them about the motives for their actions, and they, out of their human kindness, answer me."

Living during the Renaissance, Machiavelli was surrounded by the best and the brightest, which must have only exacerbated his feelings of frustration. Yet he managed to keep everything in perspective. Toward the end of his life, he signed a letter "Niccolò Machiavelli, Historian, Comic Author and Tragic Author." The thing is, Niccolò Machiavelli never wrote any tragedies. Like the rest of us, he was just trying to preserve his dignity in a world that was taking him for granted—while never losing his sense of humor about his many failures. Maybe this is the true Machiavelli of the moment.

65

The Italian Renaissance: Machiavelli

Niccolo Machiavelli (1469–1527) is perhaps the most famous political theorist in the history of European civilization. This fame, or infamy some might say, derives from his brief essay *The Prince* in which he discusses how a ruler can hold onto power. His approach was in sharp contrast to other such advisories to rulers such as the near contemporary *The Education of a Christian Prince* by Desiderius Erasmus, the most widely respected intellectual of his day. In opposition to the typical prince's manual, which emphasized what it meant to be a good Christian, Machiavelli recommends that a prince should not be constrained by either morality or immorality but use whatever means best achieves the end of gaining or holding power—the true and proper role of a prince. He thereby secularizes political thought and on top of that had the work put into print which was quite shocking at the time.

Discussion Questions

1. What does it mean to be a prince?

2. What does Machiavelli think ought to be the personal qualities of a prince?

3. What place should morality and religion play in the policies of a prince?

4. Is Machiavelli simply describing what all princes (and politicians) actually do? Or is *The Prince* a work of satire?

Chapter XV. Of the Means by Which Men, and Especially Princes, Win Applause, or Incur Censure

It remains now to be seen in what manner a prince should conduct himself towards his subjects and his allies; and knowing that this matter has already been treated by many others, I apprehend that my writing upon it also may be deemed presumptuous, especially as in the discussion of the same I shall differ from the rules laid down by others. But as my aim is to write something that may be useful to him for whom it is intended, it seems to me proper to pursue the real truth of the matter, rather than to indulge in mere speculation on the same; for many have imagined republics and principalities such as have never been known to exist in reality. For the manner in which men live is so different from the way in which they ought to live, that he who leaves the common course for that which he ought to follow will find that it leads him to ruin rather than to safety. For a man who, in all respects, will carry out only his professions of good, will be apt to be ruined amongst so many who are evil. A prince therefore who desires to maintain himself must learn to be not always good, but to be so or not as necessity may require. Leaving aside then the imaginary things concerning princes, and confining ourselves only to the realities, I say that all men when they are spoken of, and more especially princes, from being in a more conspicuous position, are noted for some quality that brings them either praise or censure. Thus one is deemed liberal, another miserly (*misero*) to use a Tuscan expression (for avaricious is he who by rapine desires to gain, and miserly

we call him who abstains too much from the enjoyment of his own). One man is esteemed generous, another rapacious; one cruel, another merciful; one faithless, and another faithful; one effeminate and pusillanimous, another ferocious and brave; one affable, another haughty; one lascivious, another chaste; one sincere, the other cunning; one facile, another inflexible; one grave, another frivolous; one religious, another sceptical; and so on.

I am well aware that it would be most praiseworthy for a prince to possess all of the above-named qualities that are esteemed good; but as he cannot have them all, nor entirely observe them, because of his human nature which does not permit it, he should at least be prudent enough to know how to avoid the infamy of those vices that would rob him of his state; and if possible also to guard against such as are likely to endanger it. But if that be not possible, then he may with less hesitation follow his natural inclinations. Nor need he care about incurring censure for such vices, without which the preservation of his state may be difficult. For, all things considered, it will be found that some things that seem like virtue will lead you to ruin if you follow them; whilst others, that apparently are vices, will, if followed, result in your safety and well-being.

Chapter XVI. Of Liberality and Parsimoniousness

To begin with the first of the above-named qualities, I say that it is well for a prince to be deemed liberal; and yet liberality, indulged in so that you will no longer be feared, will prove injurious. For liberality worthily exercised, as it

From *Historical, Political and Diplomatic Writings of Niccolo Machiavelli*, C.E. Detmold, editor and translator, J.R. Osgood & Co., Boston, 1882, Volume II, pp. 48–52, 73–74.

should be, will not be recognized, and may bring upon you the reproach of the very opposite. For if you desire the reputation of being liberal, you must not stop at any degree of sumptuousness; so that a prince will in this way generally consume his entire substance, and may in the end, if he wishes to keep up his reputation for liberality, be obliged to subject his people to extraordinary burdens, and resort to taxation, and employ all sorts of measures that will enable him to procure money. This will soon make him odious with his people; and when he becomes poor, he will be contemned by everybody; so that having by his prodigality injured many and benefited few, he will be the first to suffer every inconvenience, and be exposed to every danger. And when he becomes conscious of this and attempts to retrench, he will at once expose himself to the imputation of being a miser.

A prince then, being unable without injury to himself to practise the virtue of liberality in such manner that it may be generally recognized, should not, when he becomes aware of this and is prudent, mind incurring the charge of parsimoniousness. For after a while, when it is seen that by his prudence and economy he makes his revenues suffice him, and that he is able to provide for his defence in case of war, and engage in enterprises without burdening his people, he will be considered liberal enough by all those from whom he takes nothing, and these are the many; whilst only those to whom he does not give, and which are the few, will look upon him as parsimonious.

In our own times we have not seen any great things accomplished except by those who were regarded as parsimonious; all others have been ruined. Pope Julius II., having been helped by his reputation of liberality to attain the Pontificate, did not afterwards care to keep up that reputation to enable him to engage in war against the king of France; and he carried on ever so many wars without levying any extraordinary taxes. For his long-continued economy enabled him to supply the extraordinary expenses of his wars.

If the present king of Spain had sought the reputation of being liberal, he would not have been able to engage in so many enterprises, nor could he have carried them to a successful issue. A prince, then, who would avoid robbing his own subjects, and be able to defend himself, and who would avoid becoming poor and abject or rapacious, should not mind incurring the reputation of being parsimonious; for that is one of those vices that will enable him to maintain his state. And should it be alleged that Julius Caesar attained the Empire by means of his liberality, and that many others by the same reputation have achieved the highest rank, then I reply, that you are either already a prince, or are in the way of becoming one; in the first case liberality would be injurious to you, but in the second it certainly is necessary to be reputed liberal. Now Caesar was aiming to attain the Empire of Rome; but having achieved it, had he lived and not moderated his expenditures, he would assuredly have ruined the Empire by his prodigality.

And were any one to assert that there have been many princes who have achieved great things with their armies, and who were accounted most liberal, I answer that a prince either spends his own substance and that of his subjects, or that of others. Of the first two he should be very sparing, but in spending that of others he ought not to omit any act of liberality. The prince who in person leads his armies into foreign countries, and supports them by plunder, pillage, and exactions, and thus dispenses the substance of others, should do so with the greatest liberality, as otherwise his soldiers would not follow him. For that which belongs neither to him nor to his own subjects, a prince may spend most lavishly, as was done by Cyrus, Caesar, and Alexander. The spending of other people's substance will not diminish, but rather increase, his reputation; it is only the spending of his own that is injurious to a prince.

And there is nothing that consumes itself so quickly as liberality; for the very act of using it causes it to lose the faculty of being used, and will either impoverish and make you contemned, or it will make you rapacious and odious. And of all the things against which a prince should guard most carefully is the incurring the hatred and contempt of his subjects. Now, liberality will bring upon you either the one or the other; there is therefore more wisdom in submitting to be called parsimonious, which may bring you blame without hatred, than, by aiming to be called liberal, to incur unavoidably the reputation of rapacity, which will bring upon you infamy as well as hatred.

Chapter XVII. Of Cruelty and Clemency, and Whether It Is Better to Be Loved Than Feared

Coming down now to the other aforementioned qualities, I say that every prince ought to desire the reputation of being merciful, and not cruel; at the same time, he should be careful not to misuse that mercy. Cesar Borgia was reputed cruel, yet by his cruelty he reunited the Romagna to his states, and restored that province to order, peace, and loyalty; and if we carefully examine his course, we shall find it to have been really much more merciful than the course of the people of Florence, who, to escape the reputation of cruelty, allowed Pistoja to be destroyed. A prince, therefore, should not mind the ill repute of cruelty, when he can thereby keep his subjects united and loyal; for a few displays of severity will really be more merciful than to allow, by an excess of clemency, disorders to occur, which are apt to result in rapine and murder; for these injure a whole community, whilst the executions ordered by the prince fall only upon a few individuals. And, above all others, the new prince will find

it almost impossible to avoid the reputation of cruelty, because new states are generally exposed to many dangers. It was on this account that Virgil made Dido to excuse the severity of her government, because it was still new, saying,—

> … "My cruel fate,
> And doubts attending an unsettled state,
> Force me to guard my coasts from foreign foes."
>
> —Dryden

A prince, however, should be slow to believe and to act; nor should he be too easily alarmed by his own fears, and should proceed moderately and with prudence and humanity, so that an excess of confidence may not make him incautious, nor too much mistrust make him intolerant. This, then, gives rise to the question "whether it be better to be beloved than feared," or "to be feared than beloved." It will naturally be answered that it would be desirable to be both the one and the other; but as it is difficult to be both at the same time, it is much more safe to be feared than to be loved, when you have to choose between the two. For it may be said of men in general that they are ungrateful and fickle, dissemblers, avoiders of danger, and greedy of gain. So long as you shower benefits upon them, they are all yours; they offer you their blood, their substance, their lives, and their children, provided the necessity for it is far off; but when it is near at hand, then they revolt. And the prince who relies upon their words, without having otherwise provided for his security, is ruined; for friendships that are won by rewards, and not by greatness and nobility of soul, although deserved, yet are not real, and cannot be depended upon in time of adversity.

Besides, men have less hesitation in offending one who makes himself beloved than one who makes himself feared; for love holds by a bond of obligation which, as mankind is bad, is broken on every occasion whenever it is for the interest of the obliged party to break it. But fear holds by the apprehension of punishment, which never leaves men. A prince, however, should make himself feared in such a manner that, if he has not won the affections of his people, he shall at least not incur their hatred; for the being feared, and not hated, can go very well together, if the prince abstains from taking the substance of his subjects, and leaves them their women. And if you should be obliged to inflict capital punishment upon any one, then be sure to do so only when there is manifest cause and proper justification for it; and, above all things, abstain from taking people's property, for men will sooner forget the death of their fathers than the loss of their patrimony. Besides, there will never be any lack of reasons for taking people's property; and a prince who once begins to live by rapine will ever find excuses for seizing other people's property. On the other hand, reasons for taking life are not so easily found, and are more readily exhausted. But when a prince is at the head of his army, with a multitude of soldiers under his command, then it is above all things necessary for him to disregard the reputation of cruelty; for without such severity an army cannot be kept together, nor disposed for any successful feat of arms....

Chapter XVIII. In What Manner Princes Should Keep Their Faith

It must be evident to every one that it is more praiseworthy for a prince always to maintain good faith, and practise integrity rather than craft and deceit. And yet the experience of our own times has shown that those princes have achieved great things who made small account of good faith, and who understood by cunning to circumvent the intelligence of others; and that in the end they got the better of those whose actions were dictated by loyalty and good faith. You must know, therefore, that there are two ways of carrying on a contest; the one by law,

and the other by force. The first is practised by men, and the other by animals; and as the first is often insufficient, it becomes necessary to resort to the second.

A prince then should know how to employ the nature of man, and that of the beasts as well. This was figuratively taught by ancient writers, who relate how Achilles and many other princes were given to Chiron the centaur to be nurtured, and how they were trained under his tutorship; which fable means nothing else than that their preceptor combined the qualities of the man and the beast; and that a prince, to succeed, will have to employ both the one and the other nature, as the one without the other cannot produce lasting results.

It being necessary then for a prince to know well how to employ the nature of the beasts, he should be able to assume both that of the fox and that of the lion; for whilst the latter cannot escape the traps laid for him, the former cannot defend himself against the wolves. A prince should be a fox, to know the traps and snares; and a lion, to be able to frighten the wolves; for those who simply hold to the nature of the lion do not understand their business.

A sagacious prince then cannot and should not fulfil his pledges when their observance is contrary to his interest, and when the causes that induced him to pledge his faith no longer exist. If men were all good, then indeed this precept would be bad; but as men are naturally bad, and will not observe their faith towards you, you must, in the same way, not observe yours to them; and no prince ever yet lacked legitimate reasons with which to color his want of good faith. Innumerable modern examples could be given of this; and it could easily be shown how many treaties of peace, and how many engagements, have been made null and void by the faithlessness of princes; and he who has best known how to play the fox has ever been the most successful.

But it is necessary that the prince should know how to color this nature well, and how to be a great hypocrite and dissembler. For men are so simple, and yield so much to immediate necessity, that the deceiver will never lack dupes. I will mention one of the most recent examples. Alexander VI. never did nor ever thought of anything but to deceive, and always found a reason for doing so. No one ever had greater skill in asseverating, or who affirmed his pledges with greater oaths and observed them less, than Pope Alexander; and yet he was always successful in his deceits, because he knew the weakness of men in that particular.

It is not necessary, however, for a prince to possess all the above-mentioned qualities; but it is essential that he should at least seem to have them. I will even venture to say, that to have and to practise them constantly is pernicious, but to seem to have them is useful. For instance, a prince should seem to be merciful, faithful, humane, religious, and upright, and should even be so in reality; but he should have his mind so trained that, when occasion requires it, he may know how to change to the opposite. And it must be understood that a prince, and especially one who has but recently acquired his state, cannot perform all those things which cause men to be esteemed as good; he being often obliged, for the sake of maintaining his state, to act contrary to humanity, charity, and religion. And therefore is it necessary that he should have a versatile mind, capable of changing readily, according as the winds and changes of fortune bid him; and, as has been said above, not to swerve from the good if possible, but to know how to resort to evil if necessity demands it.

A prince then should be very careful never to allow anything to escape his lips that does not abound in the above-named five qualities, so that to see and to hear him he may seem all charity, integrity, and humanity, all uprightness, and all piety. And more than all else is it necessary for a prince to seem to possess the last

quality; for mankind in general judge more by what they see and hear than by what they feel, every one being capable of the former, and but few of the latter. Everybody sees what you seem to be, but few really feel what you are; and these few dare not oppose the opinion of the many, who are protected by the majesty of the state; for the actions of all men, and especially those of princes, are judged by the result, where there is no other judge to whom to appeal.

A prince then should look mainly to the successful maintenance of his state. The means which he employs for this will always be accounted honorable, and will be praised by everybody; for the common people are always taken by appearances and by results, and it is the vulgar mass that constitutes the world. But a very few have rank and station, whilst the many have nothing to sustain them. A certain prince of our time, whom it is well not to name, never preached anything but peace and good faith; but if he had always observed either the one or the other, it would in most instances have cost him his reputation or his state.

Chapter XXI. How Princes Should Conduct Themselves to Acquire a Reputation

Nothing makes a prince so much esteemed as the undertaking of great enterprises and the setting a noble example in his own person. We have a striking instance of this in Ferdinand of Aragon, the present king of Spain. He may be called, as it were, a new prince; for, from being king of a feeble state, he has, by his fame and glory, become the first sovereign of Christendom; and if we examine his actions we shall find them all most grand, and some of them extraordinary. In the beginning of his reign he attacked Granada, and it was this undertaking that was the very foundation of his greatness. At first he carried on this war leisurely and without fear of opposition; for he kept the nobles of Castile occupied with this enterprise, and, their minds being thus engaged by war, they gave no attention to the innovations introduced by the king, who thereby acquired a reputation and an influence over the nobles without their being aware of it. The money of the Church and of the people enabled him to support his armies, and by that long war he succeeded in giving a stable foundation to his military establishment, which afterwards brought him so much honor. Besides this, to be able to engage in still greater enterprises, he always availed himself of religion as a pretext, and committed a pious cruelty in spoliating and driving the Moors out of his kingdom, which certainly was a most admirable and extraordinary example. Under the same cloak of religion he attacked Africa, and made a descent upon Italy, and finally assailed France. And thus he was always planning great enterprises, which kept the minds of his subjects in a state of suspense and admiration, and occupied with their results. And these different enterprises followed so quickly one upon the other, that he never gave men a chance deliberately to make any attempt against himself....

A prince should also show himself a lover of virtue, and should honor all who excel in any one of the arts, and should encourage his citizens quietly to pursue their vocations, whether of commerce, agriculture, or any other human industry; so that the one may not abstain from embellishing his possessions for fear of their being taken from him, nor the other from opening new sources of commerce for fear of taxes. But the prince should provide rewards for those who are willing to do these things, and for all who strive to enlarge his city or state. And besides this, he should at suitable periods amuse his people with festivities and spectacles. And as cities are generally divided into guilds and classes, he should keep account of these bodies, and occasionally be present at their assemblies, and should set an example of his affability and magnificence; preserving, however, always the majesty of his dignity, which should never be wanting any occasion or under any circumstances.

66

Cortes and the Aztecs

It would take almost two years, from 1519 to 1521, for the Spanish conquistadors, under the command of Hernando Cortes, to defeat the Aztecs, forcing the surrender of their capital, Tenochtitlan. While there were numerous Spanish accounts of the last days of the Aztec Empire, there survived a few indigenous accounts, and these have been compiled into a landmark book, *Broken Spears*. Though the Spanish burned many Aztec writings, or codices, missionaries like Bernardino de Sahagun (cited in the reading) took pains to preserve them along with songs and narratives of life before and after the Conquest. In this passage, the Aztec king, Motecuhzoma, attempts to understand the arrival of the Spanish within the context of his world.

Discussion Questions

1. What did Motecuhzoma assume about Cortes and his men when he learned of their arrival? Why did he send them gifts? What role did religion play?

2. From the list of gifts sent to Cortes, what can you conclude about the standard of living of the Aztecs?

3. How did Cortes respond?

4. What was Motecuhzoma's mood and reaction to the messengers' accounts of their encounter with Cortes?

5. Why is it helpful to have indigenous accounts of historical events?

The Messengers' Journeys

The native documents—principally those by Sahagun's informants—describe the various journeys made by Motecuhzoma's messengers to the Gulf coasts where the strangers had appeared. The texts describing the instructions that Motecuhzoma gave to his envoys are presented first. These show clearly how the Nahuas attempted to explain the coming of the Spaniards by a projection of earlier ideas: they assumed that the new arrivals were Quetzalcoatl and other deities.

Then the documents relate how the messengers reached the coast and were received by the Spaniards, to whom they brought gifts from Motecuhzoma. The descriptions of the gifts offered to Cortes, and of his successful attempt to frighten the messengers by firing an arquebus in front of them, are especially interesting.

The third part of this chapter deals with the messengers' return to Tenochtitlan and the information they brought back to Motecuhzoma about the Spaniards, their firearms, the animals they rode (a species of huge "deer," but without horns), their mastiff dogs and so on.

All the texts in this chapter are from the *Codex Florentine*.

Motecuhzoma Instructs His Messengers

Motecuhzoma then gave orders to Pinotl of Cuetlaxtlan and to other officials. He said to them: "Give out this order: a watch is to be kept along all the shores at Nauhtla, Tuztlan, Mictlancuauhtla, wherever the strangers appear." The officials left at once and gave orders for the watch to be kept.

Motecuhzoma now called his chiefs together: Tlilpotonque, the serpent woman,[1] Cuappiatzin, the chief of the house of arrows,[2] Quetzalazatazin, the keeper of the chalk[3], and Hecateupatiltzin, the chief of the refugees from the south. He told them the news that had been brought to him and showed them the objects he had ordered made. He said: "We all admire these blue turquoises, and they must be guarded well. The whole treasure must be guarded well. If anything is lost, your houses will be destroyed and your children killed, even those who are still in the womb."

The year 13-Rabbit now approached its end. And when it was about to end, they were seen again. The report of their coming was brought to Motecuhzoma, who immediately sent out messengers. It was as if he thought the new arrival was our prince Quetzalcoatl.

This is what he felt in his heart: *He has appeared! He has come back! He will come here, to the place of his throne and canopy, for that is what he promised when he departed!*

Motecuhzoma sent five messengers to greet the strangers and to bring them gifts. They were led by the priest in charge of the sanctuary of

From The Broken Spears by Miguel Leon-Portilla. Copyright © 1962, 1990 by Miguel Leon-Portilla, expanded and updated edition © 1991 by Miguel Leon-Portilla. Reprinted by permission of Beacon Press, Boston.

[1] 'The king's chief counselor was traditionally given this title, which was the name of an earth goddess with masculine as well as feminine attributes. This word coatl, "serpent," also means "twin."

[2] The suffix -tzin indicates high rank or influence.

[3] 'Official in charge of the colors with which the priests painted their bodies before performing certain rituals.

Yohualichan. The second was from Tepoztlan; the third, from Tizatlan; the fourth, from Huehuetlan; and the fifth, from Mictlan the Great.[4] He said to them: "Come forward, my Jaguar Knights, come forward. It is said that our lord has returned to this land. Go to meet him. Go to hear him. Listen well to what he tells you; listen and remember."

The Gift Sent to the New Arrivals

Motecuhzoma also said to the messengers; "Here is what you are to bring our lord. This is the treasure of Quetzalcoatl." This treasure was the god's finery: a serpent mask inlaid with turquoise, a decoration for the breast made of quetzal[5] feathers, a collar woven in the petatillo style[6] with a gold disk in the center, and a shield decorated with gold and mother-of-pearl and bordered with quetzal feathers with a pendant of the same feathers.

There was also a mirror like those which the ritual dancers wore on their buttocks. The reverse of this mirror was turquoise mosaic: it was encrusted and adorned with turquoises. And there was a spear-thrower inlaid with turquoise, a bracelet of chalchihuites[7] hung with little gold bells and a pair of sandals as black as obsidian.

Motechzoma also gave them the finery of Tezcatlipoca.[8] This finery was: a helmet in the shape of a cone, yellow with gold and set with many stars, a number of earrings adorned with little gold bells, a fringed and painted vest with feathers as delicate as foam and a blue cloak known as "the ringing bell," which reached to the ears and was fastened with a knot.

There was also a collar of fine shells to cover the breast. This collar was adorned with the finest snail shells, which seemed to escape from the edges. And there was a mirror to be hung in back, a set of little gold bells and a pair of white sandals.

Then Motecuhzoma gave them the finery of Tlaloc.[9] This finery was: a headdress made of quetzal feathers, as green as if it were growing, with an ornament of gold and mother-of-pearl, earrings in the form of serpents, made of *chalchihuites*, a vest adorned with *chalchihuites* and a collar also of *chalchihuites*, woven in the petatillo style, with a disk of gold.

There was also a serpent wand inlaid with turquoise, a mirror to be hung in back, with little bells, and a cloak bordered with red rings.

Then Motecuhzoma gave them the finery of Quetzalcoatl. This finery was: a diadem made of jaguar skin and pheasant feathers and adorned with a large green stone, round turquoise earrings with curved pendants of shell and gold, a collar of *chalchihuites* in the petatillo style with a disk of gold in the center, a cloak with red borders, and little gold bells for the feet.

There was also a golden shield, pierced in the middle, with quetzal feathers around the rim and a pendant of the same feathers, the crooked staff of Ehecatl[10] with a cluster of white stones at the crook, and his sandals of fine soft rubber.

These were the many kinds of adornments that were known as "divine adornments." They were placed in the possession of the messengers to be taken as gifts of welcome along with many other objects, such as a golden snail shell and a golden diadem. All these objects were

---

[4] Mitia, in the Oaxaca region.

[5] A tropical bird of Central America.

[6] Like a petate (rush mat), but with a finer weave.

[7] 'Green stones: jade and jadeite.

[8] Chief god of the pantheon, with solar attributes.

[9] God of the rain.

[10] God of the wind, a frequent guise of Quetzalcoatl.

packed into great baskets; they were loaded into panniers for the long journey.

Then Motecuhzoma gave the messengers his final orders. He said to them: "Go now, without delay. Do reverence to our lord the god. Say to him: 'Your deputy, Motecuhzoma, has sent us to you. Here are the presents with which he welcomes you home to Mexico.'"

The Messengers Contact the Spaniards

When they arrived at the shore of the sea, they were taken in canoes to Xicalanco. They placed the baskets in the same canoes in which they rode, in order to keep them under their personal vigilance. From Xicalanco they followed the coast until they sighted the ships of the strangers.

When they came up to the ships, the strangers asked them: "Who are you? Where are you from?"

"We have come from the City of Mexico.[11]

The strangers said: "You may have come from there, or you may not have. Perhaps you are only inventing it. Perhaps you are mocking us." But their hearts were convinced; they were satisfied in their hearts. They lowered a hook from the bow of the ship, and then a ladder and the messengers came aboard.

One by one they did reverence to Cortes by touching the ground before him with their lips. They said to him: "If the god will deign to hear us, your deputy Motecuhzoma has sent us to render you homage. He has the City of Mexico in his care. He says: 'The god is weary.'"

Then they arrayed the Captain in the finery they had brought him as presents. With great care they fastened the turquoise mask in place, the mask of the god with its crossband of quetzal feathers. A golden earring hung down on either side of this mask. They dressed him in the decorated vest and the collar woven in the petatillo style-the collar of *chalchihuites*, with a disk of gold in the center.

Next they fastened the mirror to his hips, dressed him in the cloak known as "the ringing bell" and adorned his feet with the greaves used by the Huastecas[12] which were set with chalchihuites and hung with little gold bells. In his hand they placed the shield with its fringe and pendant of quetzal feathers, its ornaments of gold and mother-of-pearl. Finally they set before him the pair of black sandals. As for the other objects of divine finery, they only laid them out for him to see.

The Captain asked them: "And is this all? Is this your gift of welcome? Is this how you greet people?"

They replied: "This is all, our lord. This is what we have brought you."

Cortes Frightens the Messengers

Then the Captain gave orders, and the messengers were chained by the feet and by the neck. When this had been done, the great cannon was fired off. The messengers lost their senses and fainted away. They fell down side by side and lay where they had fallen. But the Spaniards quickly revived them: they lifted them up, gave them wine to drink and then offered them food.

The Captain said to them: "I have heard that the Mexicans are very great warriors, very brave and terrible. If a Mexican is fighting alone, he

---

[11] The Spaniards and the messengers could communicate because Cortes had brought with him La Malinche and Jeronirno de Aguilar. La Malinche was a native of the Gulf coast who spoke both Nahuatl and Mayan. She joined the Spaniards (who called her Dona Marina) of her own free will and served them faithfully as interpreter throughout the Conquest. Aguilar was a Spaniard who had been shipwrecked in Yucatan in 1511 during a voyage from Darien to Hispaniola. By the time Cortes ransomed him from the natives eight years later, he spoke Mayan fluently. La Malinche translated the Nahuatl of the messengers into Mayan for Aguilar, who then translated it into Spanish for the conquistadors.

[12] Indians of eastern Mexico.

knows how to retreat, turn back, rush forward and conquer, even if his opponents are ten or even twenty. But my heart is not convinced. I want to see it for myself. I want to find out if you are truly that strong and brave."

Then he gave them swords, spears and leather shields. He said: "It will take place very early, at daybreak. We are going to fight each other in pairs, and in this way we will learn the truth. We will see who falls to the ground!"

They said to the Captain: "Our lord, we were not sent here for this by your deputy Motecuhzoma! We have come on an exclusive mission, to offer you rest and repose and to bring you presents. What the lord desires is not within our warrant. If we were to do this, it might anger Motecuhzoma, and he would surely put us to death,"

The Captain replied: "No, it must take place. I want to see for myself, because even in Castile they say you are famous as brave warriors. Therefore, eat an early meal. I will eat too. Good cheer!"

With these words he sent them away from the ship. They were scarcely into their canoes when they began to paddle furiously. Some of them even paddled with their hands, so fierce was the anxiety burning in their souls. They said to each other: "My captains, paddle with all your might! Faster, faster! Nothing must happen to us here! Nothing must happen…!"

They arrived in great haste at Xicalanco, took a hurried meal there, and then pressed on until they came to Tecpantlayacac. From there they rushed ahead and arrived in Cuetlaxtlan. As on the previous journey, they stopped there to rest. When they were about to depart, the village official said to them: "Rest for at least a day! At least catch your breath!"

They said: "No, we must keep on! We must report to our king, Motecuhzoma, We will tell him what we have seen, and it is a terrifying thing. Nothing like it has ever been seen before!" Then they left in great haste and continued to the City of Mexico. They entered the city at night, in the middle of the night.

Motecuhzoma Awaits Word from the Messengers

While the messengers were away, Motecuhzoma could neither sleep nor eat, and no one could speak with him. He thought that everything he did was in vain, and he sighed almost every moment. He was lost in despair, in the deepest gloom and sorrow. Nothing could comfort him, nothing could calm him, nothing could give him any pleasure.

He said: "What will happen to us? Who will outlive it? Ah, in other times I was contented, but now I have death in my heart! My heart burns and suffers, as if it were drowned in spices …! But will our lord come here?"

Then he gave orders to the watchmen, to the men who guarded the palace: "Tell me, even if I am sleeping: 'The messengers have come back from the sea.'" But when they went to tell hint, he immediately said: "They are not to report to me here. I will receive them in the House of the Serpent. Tell them to go there." And he gave this order: "Two captives are to be painted with chalk."

The messengers went to the House of the Serpent, and Motecuhzoma arrived. The two captives were then sacrificed before his eyes: their breasts were torn open, and the messengers were sprinkled with their blood. This was done because the messengers had completed a difficult mission: they had seen the gods, their eyes had looked on their faces. They had even conversed with the gods!

The Messengers' Report

When the sacrifice was finished, the messengers reported to the king. They told him how they had made the journey, and what they had seen, and what food the strangers ate.

Motecuhzoma was astonished and terrified by their report, and the description of the strangers' food astonished him above all else.

He was also terrified to learn how the cannon roared, how its noise resounded, how it caused one to faint and grow deaf. The messengers told him: "A thing like a ball of stone comes out of its entrails: it comes out shooting sparks and raining fire. The smoke that comes out with it has a pestilent odor, like that of rotten mud. This odor penetrates even to the brain and causes the greatest discomfort. If the cannon is aimed against a mountain, the mountain splits and cracks open. If it is aimed against a tree, it shatters the tree into splinters. This is a most unnatural sight, as if the tree had exploded from within."

The messengers also said: "Their trappings and arms are all made of iron. They dress in iron and wear iron casques on their heads. Their swords are iron; their bows are iron; their shields are iron; their spears are iron. Their deer carry them on their backs wherever they wish to go. These deer, our lord, are as tall as the roof of a house.

"The strangers' bodies are completely covered, so that only their faces can be seen. Their skin is white, as if it were made of lime. They have yellow hair, though some of them have black. Their beards are long and yellow, and their moustaches are also yellow. Their hair is curly, with very fine strands.

"As for their food, it is like human food. It is large and white, and not heavy. It is something like straw, but with the taste of a cornstalk, of the pith of a cornstalk. It is a little sweet, as if it were flavored with honey; it tastes of honey, it is sweet-tasting food.

"Their dogs are enormous, with flat ears and long, dangling tongues. The color of their eyes is a burning yellow; their eyes flash fire and shoot off sparks. Their bellies are hollow, their flanks long and narrow. They are tireless and very powerful. They bound here and there, panting, with their tongues hanging out. And they are spotted like an ocelot."

When Motecuhzoma heard this report, he was filled with terror. It was as if his heart had fainted, as if it had shriveled. It was as if he were conquered by despair.

67

Columbus and the Amerindians

The encounter between the Europeans and the inhabitants of the Americas after 1492 is one of the most fascinating and perhaps lamentable cultural clashes in history. In effect, virtually the entire high culture of the Amerindian civilizations was destroyed in an instant and the indigenous population was rapidly reduced by about 90%. The Europeans who migrated to the Americas have been the heirs to the void created by the initial encounter and the moral questions it raises. In the following selection, Howard Zinn describes the arrival of Columbus in the West Indies and its implications for both the Europeans and the Arawak people.

Discussion Questions

1. What were Columbus and his men looking for when they arrived in the Americas? What did they find?

2. Rank the importance of God, Gold and Glory as motivating factors for the Europeans.

3. What characteristics most differentiated the Europeans from the Arawaks?

4. How does Zinn's portrayal of Columbus differ from the popular image?

5. Was it necessary to destroy the Amerindians and their cultures in order to bring "progress" to the Americas?

Columbus, the Indians, and Human Progress

Arawak men and women, naked, tawny, and full of wonder, emerged from their villages onto the island's beaches and swam out to get a closer look at the strange big boat. When Columbus and his sailors came ashore, carrying swords, speaking oddly, the Arawaks ran to greet them, brought them food, water, gifts. He later wrote of this in his log:

> They…brought us parrots and balls of cotton and spears and many other things, which they exchanged for the glass beads and hawks' bells. They willingly traded everything they owned. …They were well-built, with good bodies and handsome features…. They do not bear arms, and do not know them. for I showed them a sword, they took it by the edge and cut themselves out of ignorance. They have no iron. Their spears are made of cane…. They would make fine servants…. With fifty men we could subjugate them all and make them do whatever we want.

These Arawaks of the Bahama Islands were much like Indians on the mainland, who were remarkable (European observers were to say again and again) for their hospitality, their belief in sharing. These traits did not stand out in the Europe of the Renaissance, dominated as it was by the religion of popes, the government of kings, the frenzy for money that marked Western civilization and its first messenger to the Americas, Christopher Columbus.

Columbus wrote:

> As soon as I arrived in the Indies, on the first Island which I found, I took some of the natives by force in order that they might learn and might give me information of whatever there is in these parts.

The information that Columbus wanted most was: Where is the gold? He had persuaded the king and queen of Spain to finance an expedition to the lands, the wealth, he expected would be on the other side of the Atlantic—the Indies and Asia, gold and spices. For, like other informed people of his time, he knew the world was round and he could sail west in order to get to the Far East.

Spain was recently unified, one of the new modern nation-states, like France, England, and Portugal. Its population, mostly poor peasants, worked for the nobility, who were 2 percent of the population and owned 95 percent of the land. Spain had tied itself to the Catholic Church, expelled all the Jews, driven out the Moors. Like other states of the modern world, Spain sought gold, which was becoming the new mark of wealth, more useful than land because it could buy anything.

There was gold in Asia, it was thought, and certainly silks and spices, for Marco Polo and others had brought back marvelous things from their overland expeditions centuries before. Now that the Turks had conquered Constantinople and the eastern Mediterranean, and controlled the land routes to Asia, a sea route was needed. Portuguese sailors were working their way around the southern tip of Africa. Spain decided to gamble on a long sail across an unknown ocean.

In return for bringing back gold and spices, they promised Columbus 10 percent of the

---

profits, governorship over new-found lands, and the fame that would go with a new title: Admiral of the Ocean Sea. He was a merchant's clerk from the Italian city of Genoa, part-time weaver (the son of a skilled weaver), and expert sailor. He set out with three sailing ships, the largest of which was the *Santa Maria*, perhaps 100 feet long, and thirty-nine crew members.

Columbus would never have made it to Asia, which was thousands of miles farther away than he had calculated, imagining a smaller world. He would have been doomed by that great expanse of sea. But he was lucky. One-fourth of the way there he came upon an unknown, uncharted land that lay between Europe and Asia—the Americas. It was early October 1492, and thirty-three days since he and his crew had left the Canary Islands, off the Atlantic coast of Africa. Now they saw branches and sticks floating in the water. They saw flocks of birds. These were signs of land. Then, on October 12, a sailor called Rodrigo saw the early morning moon shining on white sands, and cried out. It was an island in the Bahamas, the Caribbean sea. The first man to sight land was supposed to get a yearly pension of 10,000 maravedis for life, but Rodrigo never got it. Columbus claimed he had seen a light the evening before. He got the reward.

So, approaching land, they were met by the Arawak Indians, who swam out to greet them. The Arawaks lived in village communes, had a developed agriculture of corn, yams, cassava. They could spin and weave, but they had no horses or work animals. They had no iron, but they wore tiny gold ornaments in their ears.

This was to have enormous consequences: it led Columbus to take some of them aboard ship as prisoners because he insisted that they guide him to the source of the gold. He then sailed to what is now Cuba, then to Hispaniola (the island which today consists of Haiti and the Dominican Republic). There, bits of visible gold in the rivers, and a gold mask presented to Columbus by a local Indian chief, led to wild visions of gold fields.

On Hispaniola, out of timbers from the *Santa Maria*, which had run aground, Columbus built a fort, the first European military base in the Western Hemisphere. He called it Navidad (Christmas) and left thirty-nine crew members there, with instructions to find and store the gold. He took more Indian prisoners and put them aboard his two remaining ships. At one part of the island he got into a fight with Indians who refused to trade as many bows and arrows as he and his men wanted. Two were run through with swords and bled to death. Then the *Nina* and the *Pinta* set sail for the Azores and Spain. When the weather turned cold, the Indian prisoners began to die.

Columbus's report to the Court in Madrid was extravagant. He insisted he had reached Asia (it was Cuba) and an island off the coast of China (Hispaniola). His descriptions were part fact, part fiction:

> Hispaniola is a miracle. Mountains and hills, plains and pastures, are both fertile and beautiful...the harbors are unbelievably good and there are many wide rivers of which the majority contain gold.... There are many spices. and great mines of gold and other metals....

The Indians, Columbus reported, "are so naive and so free with their possessions that no one who has not witnessed them would believe it. When you ask for something they have, they never say no. To the contrary, they offer to share with anyone...." He concluded his report by asking for a little help from their Majesties, and in return he would bring them from his next voyage "as much gold as they need...and as many slaves as they ask." He was full of religious talk: "Thus the eternal God, our Lord, gives victory to those who follow His way over apparent impossibilities."

Because of Columbus's exaggerated report and promises, his second expedition was given seventeen ships and more than twelve hundred men. The aim was clear: slaves and gold. They went from island to island in the Caribbean, taking Indians as captives. But as word spread of the Europeans' intent they found more and more empty villages. On Haiti, they found that the sailors left behind at Fort Navidad had been killed in a battle with the Indians, after they had roamed the island in gangs looking for gold, taking women and children as slaves for sex and labor.

Now, from his base on Haiti, Columbus sent expedition after expedition into the interior. They found no gold fields, but had to fill up the ships returning to Spain with some kind of dividend. In the year 1495, they went on a great slave raid, rounded up fifteen hundred Arawak men, women, and children, put them in pens guarded by Spaniards and dogs, then picked the five hundred best specimens to load onto ships. Of those five hundred, two hundred died en route. The rest arrived alive in Spain and were put up for sale by the archdeacon of the town, who reported that, although the slaves were "naked as the day they were born," they showed "no more embarrassment than animals." Columbus later wrote: "Let us in the name of the Holy Trinity go on sending all the slaves that can be sold."

But too many of the slaves died in captivity. And so Columbus, desperate to pay back dividends to those who had invested, had to make good his promise to fill the ships with gold. In the province of Cicao on Haiti, where he and his men imagined huge gold fields to exist, they ordered all persons fourteen years or older to collect a certain quantity of gold every three months. When they brought it, they were given copper tokens to hang around their necks. Indians found without a copper token had their hands cut off and bled to death.

The Indians had been given an impossible task. The only gold around was bits of dust garnered from the streams. So they fled, were hunted down with dogs, and were killed.

Trying to put together an army of resistance, the Arawaks faced Spaniards who had armor, muskets, swords, horses. When the Spaniards took prisoners they hanged them or burned them to death. Among the Arawaks, mass suicides began, with cassava poison. Infants were killed to save them from the Spaniards. In two years, through murder, mutilation, or suicide, half of the 250,000 Indians on Haiti were dead.

When it became clear that there was no gold left, the Indians were taken as slave labor on huge estates, known later as *encomiendas*. They were worked at a ferocious pace, and died by the thousands. By the year 1515, there were perhaps fifty thousand Indians left. By 1550, there were five hundred. A report of the year 1650 shows none of the original Arawaks or their descendants left on the island.

The chief source—and, on many matters the only source—of information about what happened on the islands after Columbus came is Bartolomé de las Casas, who, as a young priest, participated in the conquest of Cuba. For a time he owned a plantation on which Indian slaves worked, but he gave that up and became a vehement critic of Spanish cruelty. Las Casas transcribed Columbus's journal and, in his fifties, began a multi-volume *History of the Indies*. In it, he describes the Indians. They are agile, he says, and can swim long distances, especially the women. They are not completely peaceful, because they do battle from time to time with other tribes, but their casualties seem small, and they fight when they are individually moved to do so because of some grievance, not on the orders of captains or kings.

Women in Indian society were treated so well as to startle the Spaniards. Las Casas describes sex relations:

> Marriage laws are non-existent: men and women alike choose their mates and leave

them as they please, without offense, jealousy or anger. They multiply in great abundance; pregnant women work to the last minute and give birth almost painlessly; up the next day, they bathe in the river and are as clean and healthy as before giving birth. If they tire of their men, they give themselves abortions with herbs that force stillbirths, covering their shameful parts with leaves or cotton cloth; although on the whole, Indian men and women look upon total nakedness with as much casualness as we look upon a man's head or at his hands.

The Indians, Las Casas says, have no religion, at least no temples. They live in

large communal bell-shaped buildings, housing up to 600 people at one time...made of very strong wood and roofed with palm leaves.... They prize bird feathers of various colors, beads made of fishbones, and green and white stones with which they adorn their cars and lips, but they put no value on gold and other precious things. They lack all manner of commerce, neither buying nor selling, and rely exclusively on their natural environment for maintenance. They are extremely generous with their possessions and by the same token covet the possessions of their friends and expect the same degree of liberality....

In Book Two of his *History of the Indies*, Las Casas (who at first urged replacing Indians by black slaves, thinking they were stronger and would survive, but later relented when he saw the effects on blacks) tells about the treatment of the Indians by the Spaniards. It is a unique account and deserves to be quoted at length:

Endless testimonies...prove the mild and pacific temperament of the natives...But our word was to exasperate, ravage, kill, mangle and destroy; small wonder, then, if they tried to kill one of us now and then.... The admiral, it is true, was blind as those who came after him and he was so anxious to please the King that he committed irreparable crimes against the Indians....

Las Casas tells how the Spaniards "grew more conceited every day" and after a while refused to walk any distance. They "rode the backs of Indians if they were in a hurry, or were carried on hammocks by Indians running in relays." "In this case they also had Indians carry large leaves to shade them from the sun and others to fan them with goose wings."

Total control led to total cruelty. The Spaniards "thought nothing of knifing Indians by tens and twenties and of cutting slices off them to test the sharpness of their blades." Las Casas tells how "two of these so-called Christians met two Indian boys one day, each carrying a parrot; they took the parrots and for fun beheaded the boys."

The Indians' attempts to defend themselves failed. And when they ran off into the hills they were found and killed. So, Las Casas reports, "they suffered and died in the mines and other labors in desperate silence, knowing not a soul in the world to whom they could turn for help." He describes their work in the mines:

...mountains are stripped from top to bottom to top a thousand times; they dig, split rocks, move stones, and carry dirt on their backs to wash it in the rivers, while those who wash gold stay in the water all the time with their backs bent so constantly it breaks them; and when water invades the mines, the most arduous task of all is to dry the mines by scooping up pansful of water and throwing it up outside....

After each six or eight months' work in the mines, which was the time required of each crew to dig enough gold for melting, up to a third of the men died.

While the men were sent many miles away to the mines, the wives remained to work the soil, forced into the excruciating job of digging and making thousands of hills for cassava plants.

Thus husbands and wives were together only once every eight or ten months and when they met they were so exhausted and depressed on both sides . . . they ceased to procreate. As for the newly born, they died early because their mothers, overworked and famished, had no milk to nurse them, and for this reason, while I was in Cuba, 7000 children died in three months. Some mothers even drowned their babies from sheer desperation.... In this way, husbands died in the mines, wives died at work, and children died from lack of milk...and in a short time this land which was so great, so powerful and fertile...was depopulated.... My eyes have seen these acts so foreign to human nature, and now I tremble as I write....

When he arrived on Hispaniola in 1508, Las Casas says, "there were 60,000 people living on this island, including the Indians; so that from 1494 to 1508, over three million people had perished from war, slavery, and the mines. Who in future generations will believe this? I myself writing it as a knowledgeable eyewitness can hardly believe it...."

Thus began the history, five hundred years ago, of the European invasion of the Indian settlements in the Americas. That beginning, when you read Las Casas—even if his figures are exaggerations (were there 3 million Indians to begin with, as he says, or 250,000, as modern historians calculate?)—is conquest, slavery, death. When we read the history books given to children in the United States, it all starts with heroic adventure—there is no bloodshed—and Columbus Day is a celebration.

Past the elementary and high schools, there are only occasional hints of something else. Samuel Eliot Morison, the Harvard historian, was the most distinguished writer on Columbus, the author of a multi-volume biography, and was himself a sailor who retraced Columbus's route across the Atlantic. In his popular book *Christopher Columbus, Mariner*, written in 1954, he tells about the enslavement and the killing: "The cruel policy initiated by Columbus and pursued by his successors resulted in complete genocide."

That is on one page, buried halfway into the telling of a grand romance. In the book's last paragraph, Morison sums up his view of Columbus:

He had his faults and his defects, but they were largely the defects of the qualities that made him great—his indomitable will, his superb faith in God and in his own mission as the Christ-bearer to lands beyond the seas, his stubborn persistence despite neglect, poverty and discouragement. But there was no flaw, no dark side to the most outstanding and essential of all his qualities—his seamanship.

One can lie outright about the past. Or one can omit facts which might lead to unacceptable conclusions. Morison does neither. He refuses to lie about Columbus. He does not omit the story of mass murder; indeed he describes it with the harshest word one can use: genocide.

But he does something else—he mentions the truth quickly and goes on to other things more important to him. Outright lying or quiet omission takes the risk of discovery which, when made, might arouse the reader to rebel against the writer. To state the facts, however, and then to bury them in a mass of other information is to say to the reader with a certain infectious calm: yes, mass murder took place, but it's not that important—it should weigh very little in our final judgments; it should affect very little what we do in the world.

It is not that the historian can avoid emphasis of some facts and not of others. This is as natural to him as to the mapmaker, who, in order to produce a usable drawing for practical purposes, must first flatten and distort the shape of the earth, then choose out of the bewildering mass of geographic information those things needed for the purpose of this or that particular map.

My argument cannot be against selection, simplification, emphasis, which are inevitable for both cartographers and historians. But the mapmaker's distortion is a technical necessity for a common purpose shared by all people who need maps. The historian's distortion is more than technical, it is ideological; it is released into a world of contending interests, where any chosen emphasis supports (whether the historian means to or not) some kind of interest, whether economic or political or racial or national or sexual.

Furthermore, this ideological interest is not openly expressed in the way a mapmaker's technical interest is obvious ("This is a Mercator projection for long-range navigation—for short-range, you'd better use a different projection"). No, it is presented as if all readers of history had a common interest which historians serve to the best of their ability. This is not intentional deception; the historian has been trained in a society in which education and knowledge are put forward as technical problems of excellence and not as tools for contending social classes, races, nations.

To emphasize the heroism of Columbus and his successors as navigators and discoverers, and to deemphasize their genocide, is not a technical necessity but an ideological choice. It serves—unwittingly—to justify what was done.

My point is not that we must, in telling history, accuse, judge, condemn Columbus *in absentia*. It is too late for that; it would be a useless scholarly exercise in morality. But the easy acceptance of atrocities as a deplorable but necessary price to pay for progress (Hiroshima and Vietnam, to save Western civilization; Kronstadt and Hungary, to save socialism; nuclear proliferation, to save us all)—that is still with us. One reason these atrocities are still with us is that we have learned to bury them in a mass of other facts, as radioactive wastes are buried in containers in the earth. We have learned to give them exactly the same proportion of attention that teachers and writers often give them in the most respectable of classrooms and textbooks. This learned sense of moral proportion, coming

from the apparent objectivity of the scholar, is accepted more easily than when it comes from politicians at press conferences. It is therefore more deadly.

The treatment of heroes (Columbus) and their victims (the Arawaks)—is only one aspect of a certain approach to history, in which the past is told from the point of view of governments, conquerors, diplomats, leaders. It is as if they, like Columbus, deserve universal acceptance, as if they—the Founding Fathers, Jackson, Lincoln, Wilson, Roosevelt, Kennedy, the leading members of Congress, the famous Justices of the Supreme Court—represent the nation as a whole. The pretense is that there really is such a thing as "the United States," subject to occasional conflicts and quarrels, but fundamentally a community of people with common interests. It is as if there really is a "national interest" represented in the Constitution, in territorial expansion, in the laws passed by Congress, the decisions of the courts, the development of capitalism, the culture of education and the mass media.

"History is the memory of states," wrote Henry Kissinger in his first book, *A World Restored*, in which he proceeded to tell the history of nineteenth-century Europe from the viewpoint of the leaders of Austria and England, ignoring the millions who suffered from those statesmen's policies. From his standpoint, the "peace" that Europe had before the French Revolution was "restored" by the diplomacy of a few national leaders. But for factory workers in England, farmers in France, colored people in Asia and Africa, women and children everywhere except in the upper classes, it was a world of conquest, violence, hunger, exploitation—a world not restored but disintegrated.

My viewpoint, in telling the history of the United States, is different: that we must not accept the memory of states as our own. Nations are not communities and never have been. The history of any country, presented as the history of a family, conceals fierce conflicts of interest (sometimes exploding, most often repressed) between conquerors and conquered, masters and slaves, capitalists and workers, dominators and dominated in race and sex. And in such a world of conflict, a world of victims and executioners. It is the job of thinking people, as Albert Camus suggested, not be on the side of the executioners.

Thus, in that inevitable taking of sides which comes from selection and emphasis in history, I prefer to try to tell the story of the discovery of America from the viewpoint of the Arawaks, of the Constitution from the standpoint of the slaves, of Andrew Jackson as seen by the Cherokees, of the Civil War as seen by the New York Irish, of the Mexican was as seen by the deserting soldiers of Scott's army, of the rise of industrialism as seen by the young women in the Lowell textile mills, of the Spanish-American war as seen by pacifists, the New Deal as seen by blacks in Harlem, the postwar American empire as seen by peons in Latin America. And so on, to the limited extent that any one person, however he or she strains, can "see" history from the standpoint of others.

My point is not to grieve for the victims and denounce the executioners. Those tears, that anger, cast into the past, deplete our moral energy for the present. And the lines are not always clear. In the long run, the oppressor is also a victim. In the short run (and so far, human history has consisted only of short runs), the victims, themselves desperate and tainted with the culture that oppresses them, turn on other victims.

Still, understanding the complexities, this book will be skeptical of governments and their attempts, through politics and culture, to ensnare ordinary people in a giant web of nationhood pretending to a common interest. I will try not to overlook the cruelties that victims inflict on one another as they are jammed together in the boxcars of the system. I don't want to romanticize them. But I do remember (in rough paraphrase) a statement I once read: "The cry of the poor is not always just, but if you don't listen to it, you will never know what justice is."

I don't want to invent victories for people's movements. But to think that history-writing must aim simply to recapitulate the failures that dominate the past is to make historians collaborators in an endless cycle of defeat. If history is to be creative, to anticipate a possible future without denying the past, it should, I believe, emphasize new possibilities by disclosing those hidden episodes of the past when, even if in brief flashes, people showed their ability to resist, to join together, occasionally to win. I am supposing, or perhaps only hoping, that our future may be found in the past's fugitive moments of compassion rather than in its solid centuries of warfare.

68

The Americas:
The Columbian Exchange

The voyages of Columbus and the conquests of Cortes and Pizarro led to the establishment of a Spanish Empire in the Americas that would transform those societies and the world forever. The following selections highlight the impact of the interaction between the Old World and the New World, the legacy of which is still being debated. The article on the Black Legend, sometimes referred to as "the first modern propaganda campaign," discusses not only the origins of the Legend, but also the nature of the society that would be called Spanish America. Another group of articles deal with the migrations of disease, food, animals and plants, that historian Alfred Crosby has called the "Columbian Exchange." The final selections introduce the economic, social and human ramifications of this era of exploration by focusing on the triangular trade that followed the "Sugar Revolution," and the origins and human costs of the African slave trade.

Discussion Questions

1. Who was the author of the Black Legend and why was it written? Does the article basically substantiate or refute the charges?

2. What were the short-term and long-term consequences of the Columbian Exchange? What evidence can you cite to support the author's contention that the results of this exchange were revolutionary?

3. Why was the sugar trade in the 17th and 18th centuries so lucrative? Who benefitted the most from the trade, and in what ways?

4. What evidence does the author present to support his contention that "without slavery the New World would not have been developed?" What were the immediate and long-term consequences of slavery for the Americas, for Africa and for the world?

The Black Legend: Were the Spaniards *That* Cruel?

For the Spanish, the Columbus Quincentennial stirs an ambivalent nostalgia, blending pride and pain. Spain's shining memories of its Golden Age, when the nation stood at the summit of world power, have been tarnished by critics who call the 1492 arrival of the Spanish in the New World "an invasion" fueled by greed and leading to "genocide." In their words, Spaniards hear echoes of age-old malevolence: a body of anti-Spanish prejudices they know as *la leyenda negra*, the Black Legend, that tarred the Spanish as incomparably savage and avaricious. It created a national image that Spain is still trying to dispel.

The Black Legend was born in the 16th century, when Spain controlled the greatest empire the West had ever known, stretching from Holland to Austria to Italy, and westward across the Atlantic to the Americas. The Spanish were prosperous, powerful and smug. And almost everyone else in Europe hated them.

Fearful and envious of Spain but poorer and militarily inferior, rival European nations resorted to a paper war, the first modern propaganda campaign. Throughout the century and beyond it, pamphleteers from London to Frankfurt made malice toward the Spanish a byword of patriotism. Their tracts depicted the Spanish as a people inherently barbaric, corrupt and intolerant; lovers of cruelty and bloodshed. "Tyranny," one 1597 French screed began, "is as proper and natural to a Spaniard as laughter is to a man." Others warned that if Europeans had been outraged by the Inquisition, or by Spain's expulsion of the Jews in 1492 (two centuries, it

should be noted, after they were expelled from England), these were kindnesses compared to what Spain did in the Americas. William of Orange, the Dutch nobleman who led the Protestants of Holland in revolt against Spanish authority, railed in 1580 that Spain "committed such horrible excesses that all the barbarities, cruelties and tyrannies ever perpetrated before are only games in comparison to what happened to the poor Indians."

Were the Spanish that bad? Well, there's no reason to print up *I Love The Conquest* bumper stickers. As with most legends, la leyenda negra has some basis in fact. Like many invaders, the Spanish committed horrifying atrocities. But savagery was not the norm for the Spanish, or even commonplace. To understand their conduct in the Americas, one must look at the world as the Spanish did in the 15th century. By their standards, they acted with moderation. When the English and French arrived in the Americas, they systematically drove the natives from their land. The Spanish accepted the Indians into their society—however rudely—and sought to provide a philosophical and moral foundation for their actions in the New World.

If that isn't the history presented in many American schoolbooks, novels and films, it is perhaps because the attitudes of most North Americans are a cultural legacy from the same people—English, German, Dutch, French—who fought Spain for 300 years. Varnished and repeated through those centuries, the Black Legend continues to distort our vision of the past, as well as the present, in repugnant stereotypes of Hispanics in both hemispheres, from the vicious *cholo* to the "lazy wetback." Politics and religion, those two tinderbox subjects, gave the Black Legend its momentum and its staying power. Rivals like France—where even today Spain is sometimes dismissed with the jeer "Africa begins at the Pyreness"—resented Spanish domination and coveted its empire. Religion added a more visceral animus. Charles V began his reign as King of Spain in 1517, the same year that Martin Luther launched the Protestant Reformation. He was also Holy Roman Emperor, the anointed protector of Christianity, and saw it as his duty to purge the heresy from the Continent. Leading the bloody Counter-Reformation, Spain fought in Germany in the 1540s, began an 80-year war with Holland in 1568 and sent the disastrous Armada against England in 1588. Protestants saw Spain as the agent of the Devil; its extermination was an article of faith. Opening Parliament in 1656, Oliver Cromwell called Spain the "enemy abroad, who is head of the Papal interest, the head of that anti-Christian interest, that is so described in Scripture . . . and upon this account you have a quarrel with the Spaniard. And truly he hath an interest in your bowels."

Ironically, it was Spain's sense of religious mission, and the broad freedom of speech it permitted in its colonies, that helped foster the Black Legend. From Ferdinand onward, Spanish monarchs encouraged candid reports, favorable or unfavorable, on conditions in the Americas. One of the most tireless critics of Spanish rule was a Dominican bishop, Bartolomé de Las Casas, who worked for 50 years to improve the treatment of the Indians. A skilled politician, in 1552 he published a passionate tract called "A Brief Account of the Destruction of the Indies." In graphic and sometimes exaggerated detail, he recounted Spanish cruelties to the Indians, describing, in one instance, how Spaniards hanged natives in groups of 13, "thus honoring our Redeemer and the twelve apostles," then lit fires beneath them.

Spain's enemies ate it up. In the next 100 years, 42 editions of Las Casas's "Brief Account" appeared in Germany, France, Holland and England, some illustrated with lurid engravings by the Dutch artist Theodore DeBry, who had never crossed the Atlantic. One English edition was subtitled "A Faithful Narrative of the Horrid and Unexampled Massacres, Butcheries, and all Manner of Cruelties that Hell and Malice could invent, committed by the Popish Spanish." A U.S. edition of Las Casas was even published in 1898, to bolster support for the Spanish-American War.

Yet, as historian William Maltby points out, "the most powerful indictment of Spain's cruelty and avarice is at the same time a monument to its humanitarianism and sense of justice." Las Casas, other Spanish clergy and their sympathizers were not lonely do-gooders. They embodied a Spanish moral impulse that led the royal court to conduct a soul-searching ethical inquiry into the Spanish Conquest throughout the 16th century. "Spain was constantly debating with itself. `Am I right, am I wrong? What is it I'm doing with these peoples?' " notes Mexican writer Carlos Fuentes in his television documentary "The Buried Mirror: Reflections on Spain and the New World."

From the beginning of their conquest, the Spanish recognized the need to mediate between the conflicting demands of Christianity and profit. Bernal Díaz, a soldier in the army of Cortés who later wrote a history of the conquest of Mexico, explained the motives of the conquistadors: "We came here to serve God, and also to get rich." It is easy to view the former as a rationale for the latter. But the 16th-century Spanish lived in an age of devotion, when every aspect of life was examined through the lens of religious faith. Spaniards believed they offered the Indians a gift worth any earthly pain: eternal life in heaven.

God had ordained a social hierarchy, most Renaissance Spaniards thought. They accepted

Aristotle's concept of "natural slavery"—that large masses of humanity are simply born to serve. The papacy sanctioned slavery and was a large slaveholder. But where the Indians fit in the ranks of mankind baffled the Spanish.

Early on, Isabella of Castile established the policy that Indians who accepted Christianity were free crown subjects. (Those who didn't could be sold into slavery.) But like other subjects, they were expected to pay royal tribute, which could be extracted in the form of labor. With so few colonists, Indian labor was a necessity, but one which, Isabella's counselors reasoned, could teach the natives useful habits of industry. The Spanish devised the *encomienda*, a labor system intended as a sort of trusteeship. A deserving Spaniard was given Indians to use for mining gold or silver or growing cash crops. In return, he would feed the Indians, provide for their instruction in the faith and defend them.

That was the theory. In practice the encomienda varied with the agenda of each Spaniard. Most conquistadors were ex-soldiers, merchants, craftsmen, ex-convicts—"nobodies who wanted to become somebodies," as historian L. B. Simpson put it. Those who wanted to get rich quick and return to Spain drove the Indians hard. Others saw the New World as a permanent home and the Indians as future clients who should be treated well. The encomienda was always, if sometimes only marginally, better than outright slavery. "The people remained in a community even if they were exploited," explains Yale historian David Brion Davis. "They had a certain cultural integrity; their family structure and customs weren't, for the most part, interfered with."

Out of Christian duty, and to keep a close rein on its New World colonies, the Spanish throne consistently ordained that the natives be treated with humane respect. In 1512, Ferdinand's Laws of Burgos provided, among other things, that "no Indian shall be whipped or beaten or called 'dog' or any other name, unless it is

his proper name." These and later laws were often ignored or watered down, but under them many Spaniards were punished for mistreating Indians.

Spanish monarchs were also willing to experiment with new systems of government and labor. Las Casas was given a chance to convert an area of Guatemala without the interference of soldiers and met with mixed success. There were four separate, failed experiments on Caribbean islands to see if, given the tools, Indians could live alone like civilized people—that is, like Spaniards. In 1530, Vasco de Quiroga, a Mexican bishop, established a cooperative society in Michoacán, with communal property and what we would call social-welfare benefits.

If these experiments treated the natives as naive children, that is perhaps no more offensive than today's tendency to believe the Indians were helpless before the Spanish. In fact, they were quite resourceful, argues historian Steve Stern: "Indigenous peoples shaped everyday life and social structures much more than our stereotyped imagery would have it." Cortés could not have conquered Mexico without the aid of tribes dominated by the Aztecs. For their help, these natives happily accepted titles, coats of arms and encomiendas from the Spanish crown. The encomienda itself was molded by tributary labor practices long established among the Indians. In many regions, Indians dictated to Spaniards the form and amount of payment to be given. A group of Peruvian Indian chiefs hired a lawyer and sailed to Spain in the 1560s to make a case before Philip II for curtailing the encomienda. In the best political tradition, they even offered him a bribe. "Indians entered into the Spanish legal system to use it for their own purposes," says Stern. "And to some effect." Always a legalistic people, the Spanish created General Indian Courts where the natives aired their grievances. As historian Philip Wayne Powell wrote, "Spaniards did not try to impose upon America something hypocritically foreign or inferior to what they lived with at home." Spain's rulers taxed the New World colonists less heavily than their European subjects. In America, the Spanish built schools—23 universities in the New World—that graduated white, mestizo and Indian alike, along with some blacks. They established hospitals to provide the Indians with medical care, such as it was in the era of barber-surgeons and leeches.

If only for economic reasons, the Spanish cared deeply for the welfare of the natives. "Genocide," in fact, may be the unfairest of all the accusations leveled at Spain—if the term is used in its proper sense, to describe the intentional, systematic eradication of a race. Millions of Indians died after the arrival of the Spanish. But a host of pestilences brought from Europe wiped out the vast majority, not war or abuse. The whole of Spain's treatment of the Indians seems almost beneficent compared with the way other colonial powers dealt with natives. "The Spanish made a place for the Indians—as part of the lowest order, but at least they had a place," says Woodrow Borah of the University of California, Berkeley. "North Americans in many cases simply exterminated the Indians." The Spanish mingled with the Indians, at times with the encouragement of the crown. "The Spanish were conquered in turn by those they conquered," says Mexican poet Homero Aridjis. The marriage of blood and cultures created *la raza*—the new mestizo people who compose most of today's Latin Americans. North America, where the natives were excluded, driven off their land and eventually hunted down, remained white. The United States elected several presidents—Andrew Jackson, William Henry Harrison, Zachary Taylor—who first made a name for themselves as Indian fighters. It is a piece of our heritage that may help explain the potency of U.S. racism.

Today, Spain has invested $20 billion worldwide in Columbus Quincentennial projects, still hoping to escape the distortions of the Black Legend. But if the 16th-century Spanish can be granted motives beyond profit, they appear no worse—and often far better—than the nations who castigated them for their sins. Spain committed terrible deeds while bringing "the light of Christianity" to the New World. But history offers no shortage of acts of cruelty performed in the service of religious, social, political and economic ideals. Susan Milbrath, a Florida museum curator whose recent Quincentennial exhibit was greeted with pickets, asks why people concentrate on the morality of Columbus and the Spanish: "The big question to me is, are *human beings good?*" The Black Legend casts a shadow on us all.

The Great Disease Migration

Only weeks before the great conquistador Hernán Cortés seized control of Tenochtitlán (Mexico City) in 1521, his forces were on the verge of defeat. The Aztecs had repeatedly repelled the invaders and were preparing a final offensive. But the attack never came, and the beleaguered Spaniards got an unlikely chance to regroup. On Aug. 21 they stormed the city, only to find that some greater force had already pillaged it. "I solemnly swear that all the houses and stockades in the lake were full of heads and corpses," Cortés's chronicler Bernal Díaz wrote of the scene. "It was the same in the streets and courts...We could not walk without treading on the bodies and heads of dead Indians. I have read about the destruction of Jerusalem, but I do not think the mortality was greater there than here in Mexico...Indeed, the stench was so bad that no one could endure it...and even Cortés was ill from the odors which assailed his nostrils."

The same scent followed the Spaniards throughout the Americas. Many experts now believe that the New World was home to 40 million to 50 million people before Columbus arrived and that most of them died within decades. In Mexico alone, the native population fell from roughly 30 million in 1519 to 3 million in 1568. There was similar devastation throughout the Caribbean islands, Central America and Peru. The eminent Yale historian David Brion Davis says this was "the greatest genocide in the history of man." Yet it's increasingly clear that most of the carnage had nothing to do with European barbarism. The worst of the suffering was caused not by swords or guns but by germs.

Contrary to popular belief, viruses, bacteria and other invisible parasites aren't designed to cause harm; they fare best in the struggle to survive and reproduce when they don't destroy their hosts. But when a new germ invades a previously unexposed population, it often causes devastating epidemics, killing all but the most resistant individuals. Gradually, as natural selection weeds out the most susceptible hosts and the deadliest strains of the parasite, a sort of mutual tolerance emerges. The survivors repopulate, and a killer plague becomes routine childhood illness. As University of Chicago historian William McNeill observes in his book "Plagues and Peoples," "The more diseased a community, the less destructive its epidemics become."

By the time Columbus set sail, the people of the Old World held the distinction of being thoroughly diseased. By domesticating pigs, horses, sheep and cattle, they had infected themselves with a wide array of pathogens. And through centuries of war, exploration and city-building, they had kept those agents in constant circulation. Virtually any European who crossed the Atlantic during the 16th century had battled such illnesses as smallpox and measles during childhood and emerged fully immune.

By contrast, the people of the Americas had spent thousands of years in biological isolation. Their own distant ancestors had migrated from the Old World, crossing the Bering Strait from Siberia into Alaska (page 14). But they traveled in bands of several hundred at most. The microbes that cause measles, smallpox and other "crowd type" diseases require pools of several million people to sustain themselves. By the time Columbus arrived, groups like the Aztecs and Maya of Central America and Peru's Incas had built cities large enough to sustain major epidemics. Archeological evidence suggests they suffered from syphilis, tuberculosis, a few intestinal parasites and some types of influenza (probably those carried by waterfowl). Yet they remained untouched by diseases that had raged for centuries in the Old World. When the newcomers arrived carrying mumps, measles, whooping cough, smallpox, cholera, gonorrhea and yellow fever, the Indians were immunologically defenseless.

The disaster began almost as soon as Columbus arrived, fueled mainly by smallpox and measles. Smallpox—the disease that so ravaged Tenochtitlán on the eve of Cortés's final siege—was a particularly efficient killer. Alfred Crosby, author of "The Columbian Exchange," likens its effect on American history to "that of the Black Death on the history of the Old World." Smallpox made its American debut in 1519, when it struck the Caribbean island of Santo Domingo, killing up to half of the indigenous population. From there outbreaks spread across the Antilles islands, onto the Mexican mainland, through the Isthmus of Panama and into South America. The Spaniards were moving in the same direction, but their diseases often outpaced them. "Such is the communicability of smallpox and the other eruptive fevers," Crosby notes, "that any Indian who received news of the Spaniards could also have easily received the infection."

By the time the conquistadors reached Peru in the 1520s, smallpox was already decimating the local Incan civilization and undermining its political structure. The empire's beloved ruler, Huayna Cápaj, had died. So had most of his family, including the son he had designated as his heir. The ensuing succession struggle had split the empire into two factions that were easily conquered by Francisco Pizarro and his troops. "Had the land not been divided," one Spanish soldier recalled, "we would not have been able to enter or win."

Smallpox was just one of many afflictions parading through defenseless communities, leaving people too weak and demoralized to harvest food or tend their young. Some native populations died out altogether; others continued to wither for 100 to 150 years after surviving particularly harsh epidemics. The experience wrought irrevocable changes in the way people lived.

Persuaded that their ancestral gods had abandoned them, some Indians became more susceptible to the Christianity of their conquerors. Others united to form intertribal healing societies and Pan-Indian sects. Marriage patterns changed, too. In North America most pre-Columbian Indians lived in communities of several hundred relatives. Tradition required that they marry outside their own clans and observe other restrictions. As populations died off and appropriate marriage partners became scarce, such customs became unsustainable. People

had two choices, says University of Washington anthropologist Tsianina Lomawaima. They could "break the rules or become extinct." Occasionally, whole new tribes arose as the survivors of dying groups banded together. The epidemics even fueled the African slave trade. "The fact that Africans shared immunities with Europeans meant that they made better slaves," says anthropologist Charles Merbs of Arizona State University. "That, in part, determined their fate."

The great germ migration was largely a one-way affair; syphilis is the only disease suspected of traveling from the Americas to the Old World aboard Spanish ships. But that does not diminish the epochal consequences of the exchange. Columbus's voyage forever changed the world's epidemiological landscape. "Biologically," says Crosby, "this was the most spectacular thing that has ever happened to humans."

That isn't to say it was unique. Changes in human activity are still creating rich new opportunities for disease-causing organisms. The story of AIDS—an affliction that has emerged on a large scale only during the past decade and that now threatens the stability and survival of entire nations—is a case in point. No one knows exactly where or how the AIDS virus (HIV) was born. Many experts suspect it originated in central Africa, decades or even centuries ago, when a related virus crossed from monkeys into people and adapted itself to human cells.

Like venereal syphilis, AIDS presumably haunted isolated communities for hundreds of years before going global. And just as sailing ships brought syphilis out of isolation during the 16th century, jet planes and worldwide social changes have unleashed AIDS in the 20th. War, commercial trucking and growth of cities helped propel HIV through equatorial Africa during the 1960s. And when the virus reached the developed world during the 1970s, everything from changing sexual mores to the rise of new medical technologies (such as blood transfusion) helped it take root and thrive.

AIDS won't be the last pandemic to afflict humankind. As the Columbian Exchange makes clear, social changes that spawn one epidemic tend to spawn others as well. Researchers have documented outbreaks of more than a dozen previously unknown diseases since the 1960s. Like smallpox or syphilis or AIDS, most seem to result from old bugs exploiting new opportunities. "What's happening today is just what we've been doing for thousands of years," Crosby says. "Bit by bit by bit, we're getting more homogenized. In the Middle Ages the population got big enough and technologically sophisticated enough to send out a boat and bring back the Black Death. Columbus brought together two worlds that were a huge distance apart. People were living side by side, then elbow to elbow. Soon we'll be living cheek to jowl. Everybody's diseases will be everybody else's diseases."

The Great Food Migration

Imagine, if you will, a time when English food was actually worse than it is today.

Imagine Italian cuisine without tomatoes, or Mexican food that was literally grub—insect larvae, as well as eggs. Columbus, sailing West in search of Eastern spices and gold, brought about cultural revolutions that reached virtually every nation in the world. The changes in the global menu don't simply mean better eating— the new foods altered the fates of nations and strengthened a growing sense of national identity. "The French, Italian, and Spanish food `traditions' we now think of as primeval all sprang up relatively recently," writes Raymond Sokolov in his new book "Why We Eat What We Eat," "and would be unrecognizable without the American foods sent across the water, mostly in Spanish boats."

Europe was certainly ready for a change. The lower and merchant classes had put up with a dull menu for years. Peasants commonly ate dark bread made with rye and wheat; cabbage soup and cheeses (or cheese curds) filled out a typical meal. Wealthier families ate much of the same things, but they enjoyed more variety in flavors, thanks to the obsession with Asian spices that first set Columbus on his way. Spices also had a practical purpose for the pre-refrigerator era: they blanketed the smell and flavor of decay.

At the upper end of the social scale, meals approached the orgiastic. A noble meal might include whole roasted peacocks with skin and feathers reattached after cooking—or even four and twenty blackbirds baked in a pie. "Presentation was enormously important," says Bridget Henisch, a food historian at State College in Pennsylvania. Feasts, she explains, "went with the whole medieval enjoyment of heraldry and drama, the music and trumpets announcing the arrival of the main dish." The thing they were hungriest for was novelty—and Columbus provided it.

Each new cargo transformed the European menu. The Americas may not have produced traditional spices and condiments such as clove, ginger, cardamom and almonds, but they produced potatoes, corn and other colorful crops that excited the 16th century palate. Peanuts and vanilla, as well as by green beans, pineapple and turkey all broadened the horizons of European chefs. Some of the exotic new crops had humble beginnings; before the tomato made its way into the cuisines of Spain, Italy and other European societies, it was a weed in the Aztec maize fields.

The Aztecs came to cultivate tomatoes in astonishing varieties. Food historian Sophie Coe found a description of markets in the writings of a 16th-century Aztec chronicler. (In reading the following passage, it is best to imagine it being narrated by John Cleese.) "The tomato seller sells large tomatoes, small tomatoes, leaf tomatoes, thin tomatoes, sweet tomatoes, nipple-shaped tomatoes, serpent tomatoes. He also sells coyote tomatoes, sand tomatoes, those which are yellow, very yellow, quite yellow, red, very red, quite ruddy, ruddy, bright red, reddish, rosy dawn colored." Not all the tomatoes were easy on the palate, the Aztec noted: "The bad tomato seller sells spoiled tomatoes, bruised tomatoes, those which cause diarrhea; the sour, the very sour. Also he sells the green, the hard ones, those which scratch one's throat, which disturb—trouble one; which make one's saliva smack, make one's saliva flow; the harsh ones, those which burn the throat."

The first tomatoes to reach Europe were probably yellow, since the Italian word for it is *pomodòro* "golden apple." While the tomato took root in every European culture, it truly conquered Italy, where the warm climate proved ideal for the source of rich red sauces. Still, Europeans were slow to accept it. Like many exotic foods—including the far less assertive potato (page 236)—it was first thought to be either a poison or an aphrodisiac.

While Europe was coming to grips with the tomato, the Americas were being invaded by new foods as well. Before Columbus, many native cultures were relatively meatless. In the 16th century, writes food historian Reay Tannahill, Mexicans began their day "with a bowl of maize porridge, sweetened with honey or spiced with red pepper. The main meal of the day was at the hottest time, in the early afternoon. Then there would be tortillas to eat, a dish of beans—which were grown in Mexico in great variety—and a sauce made from tomatoes or peppers." For a change of pace some dishes contained grubs, insect eggs and pond scum.

With Columbus came an explosion of new foods. To provide familiar table fare for Spanish colonists, the crown sent over crops and animals from home. Before Columbus, Peru's meat specialty had been the guinea pig; after the explorer's visits, Mexico and Peru suddenly had beef and pork, as well as milk and cheeses. Chickens, sheep and goats also provided new meats that quickly became staples. Columbus brought vegetable seeds, wheat, chickpeas and sugar cane to the Caribbean in his later voyages.

The novel foods not only broadened menus; some of them transformed whole cultures. The advent of crops like potatoes and corn, which could produce far more nutrition per acre than the grains that came before, allowed for population growth. Some even claim potatoes, through their influence, made the industrial rise of Germany possible—and, by extension, the first world war.

The spicy peppers of the capsicum genus have not had quite the public-relations triumph of the potato, but as their partisans know they have their own way of making an impression. Columbus, having failed to find the Indian spices he sought, brought back the capsicum peppers he found. The peppers flourished in southern climes and took hold in dishes like Italy's *arrabbiàta* (angry) sauce. Eventually the capsicum peppers of the New World even made their way into the cuisine of India, where spices were much favored, and into the Sichuan and Hunan provinces of China, too. Food writer Sokolov cites scholars who suggest that Portuguese traders carried the Columbian Exchange into those two nations. Portuguese traders in the Middle East could have passed peppers along to the Turks, whose Ottoman Empire stretched all the way to the Balkans. Few Northern European peoples were interested in peppers, which were hard to grow in their climate. But the Magyars of present-day Hungary took to them lustily and gave them a name derived from their own word for pepper: paprika. Today, Hungarian paprikas run the gamut from sweet to fiery hot—and form a link in a chain that stretches all the way back to Mexico.

As the foods spread around the world and ingredients became shared, you might have expected to see a common "international cuisine"—a kin of culinary Esperanto—result. Mercifully, things didn't turn out that way. People took the same ingredients and did different things with them: beef, corn and chilies might become a taco in Mexico, a stir-fry in China or a spicy meatball beside a dish of Italian polenta. The food dispersion coincided with a period of evolving nationalism. Says food historian Tannahill: "The cuisines of individual countries began to take on consciously individual characteristics."

And so food came to be one the pillars of national identity. (If you doubt this, try walking into a French restaurant asking for pizza.) Once foods caught on, they quickly came traditions, and the fact that they were relatively recent arrivals was forgotten. One of the highest expressions of French culinary pride, for example, lies in artistic desserts often rich with chocolate. Chocolate, of course, came from tropical cacao plants in the New World. It didn't catch on with the French until the mid-17th century. Even then the French saw chocolate only as a drink until the early 1800s, when it first came into mass production in block form.

Africa was also a major player in the food exchange. Thanks to Columbus, it got such crops as maize, sweet potatoes, manioc and green beans, which opened up new agricultural possibilities to a continent that had previously been confined to a relatively narrow spectrum of foodstuffs. Then those foods made their way back to the New World in the misery of the slave ships. African culinary habits—from frying to the use of such ingredients as okra—have been nearly as profound an influence on the American table as African music has been on American entertainment. "When you see a hush puppy," says Sokolov, "it's not just a dish for good old boys: it's something they picked up from the African migration to this country."

The revolution is still going on, one bite at a time. It's easy to spot in the menus of chic new restaurants, where regional American cooking has turned menus into road maps. New foods are constantly coming into the markets to tempt the jaded palate. The latest pepper to make its faddish way into specialty stores is the scorching *habanero*, a Latin favorite also known in Anglophone countries as Scotch Bonnet for its distinctive shape. Even McDonald's, the definition of mainstream American food, boasts Mexican and other *picante* items ranging from *fajitas* to spicy chicken wings. (If you care to enjoy the thrill of culinary subversion firsthand, the new McDonald's Cajun hot sauce tastes awfully good on its Egg McMuffin.)

In some places, the revolution is more obvious than in others. Recently Sokolov took a stroll through the great savory melting pot that is Jackson Heights in Queens, New York. Having traveled the world to track the results of the Columbian food migration, he seems nearly giddy with the gastronomic kaleidoscope that Queens presents. The neighborhood, he exults, "is the epitome of how this country works: immigrants come to America looking for a better life, but bringing the best of their old culture with them—happily, that always includes the food."

He stops in at an Indian grocery for a bag of crispy spiced chickpeas, then ducks into an Uruguayan restaurant—there are several in the neighborhood, along with eateries featuring the cuisines of Colombia and Brazil. The Uruguayan meal includes roasted sweetbreads and a black blood sausage pungent with cinnamon, polished off with a Colombian red wine and snackings of the chickpeas between helpings of the meat. "Who would imagine we could get a rather complete Uruguayan meal in New York City?" Sokolov asks, marvelling at the forces of immigration that put not one but two such restaurants on one block. Down the street, a Colombian bakery does a brisk business in heavy pastries and cakes. In the front window sits a massively multitiered wedding cake—and Ninja Turtle toys.

Maybe it's the wine, but such sights and flavors bring on the thought that we really are what we eat. The global table turns out to be a vast potluck, with everyone tasting and sharing everyone else's dishes. Through the language of our foods, we come to know one another better. he boy's name was Olaudah, and he was born in 1745 in the kingdom of Benin, in what is now part of Nigeria. He was the youngest child of an *embrenche*, or chieftain, of the Ibo people, and he was his mother's pride and joy. Sometime in 1756, when he was 11 years old, Olaudah was kidnapped by rival tribesmen and sold to European slavers. He never forgot the terror of that moment, and his account of his delivery to the white man is a rare and indisputably authentic description of the slave trade as seen by Africans:

Potato - How It Shaped the World

It was the start of a beautiful friendship. Juan de Castellanos, a conquistador charting the wilds of Colombia, came upon a deserted Indian village in whose houses he found "maize, beans, and truffles." In fact, the "truffles" were potatoes which, the explorer noted, were "good of flavor, a gift very acceptable to Indians and a dainty dish even for Spaniards." This union-potatoes and Europeans-would change the course of world history as much as any gold or silver pilfered from the Incan Empire.

The true daintiness of the potato would not be discovered until a later age. At the outset, Europeans treated it as a food for the masses. Potatoes were loaded aboard Spanish treasure ships as a cheap food for sailors bringing home the booty of the New world. They reached England and Germany courtesy of Sir Francis Drake, who apparently picked up a batch during a stop in Colombia in 1556,where he was seeking to stake out part of the New World for Elizabeth I.

It wasn't so much the potato's taste that appealed to the European elite; they imagined it was an aphrodisiac. "Let the sky rain potatoes!" cried Shakespeare's Falstaff in a moment of passion. Europe's peasants were more cautious: before they came to subsist on the potato, they mistrusted it, even thought it might be poisonous. In 1619 potatoes were banned in Burgundy because "too frequent use of them caused the leprosy." Even starving Prussians refused to touch them when, in 1774, Frederick the Great sent a wagonload of potatoes to Kolberg to relieve famine.

Over time, however, necessity and familiarity dulled the peasantry's bias. "One and a half acres, planted with potatoes, would provide enough food, with the addition of a bit of milk, to keep a family hearty for a year," wrote Alfred Crosby in "The Colombian Exchange." In Ireland, the potato was not ruined when battle raged over the ground in which it grew, and it could remain safely hidden in the earth throughout the winter, even when a peasant's home and stores were raided or set afire by English soldiers. Because potatoes are ideally suited to northern climates, Catherine the Great launched a pro-potato campaign as a antidote to famine in 18th-century Russian. Vodka soon followed, and the potato thus became indelibly fixed in the Russian diet. (The instant popularity of vodka should be no surprise; one of the Russian drinks it replaced was fermented grapes with a hunk of meat thrown in for flavor.)

But it was in Ireland that the potato made its greatest mark. "It was not exceptional for an Irishman to consume 10 pounds of potatoes a day and very little else," wrote Crosby. On this diet, the Irish population nearly tripled between 1754 and 1846. But depending on the potato was precarious; when the potato blight hit Europe in 1845 the consequences were devastating. In Ireland, as food historian Reay Tannahill describes it, "the potato famine meant more than food scarcity. It meant no seed potatoes from which to grown next year's crop. It meant that the pig or cow which would normally have been sold to pay the rent had to be slaughtered, because there was nothing to fatten it on." No cow for the rent could mean eviction, and hunger was soon compounded by scurvy, failing eyesight, even dementia, from vitamin deficiency. Nearly a million Irish men and women died as a result of the blight. Another million immigrated to the United States. They were, in a way, the New World's harvest from those first potato exports 300 years earlier.

—**Mary Talbot**

Corn - Builder of Cities

Were it not for corn, archeologists say, the Spaniards would have been mightily disappointed when they arrived in the Americas. There would have been no Aztecs with floating cities and carved pyramids to conquer, no vast Indian armies with whom to do battle. The conquistadors likely would have left Peru empty-handed, for there would have been no Incan empire offering temples paneled in gold and stocked with jeweled icons. Corn was what made the great civilizations of Central and South America possible: it supplied the calories that nourished the thriving populations required to build complex societies.

Christopher Columbus first sampled corn in Cuba. He was impressed, declaring it "most tasty boiled, roasted, or ground into flour." When he returned to Spain, he took along a few specimen Indians, some handfuls of gold dust and a packet of corn kernels. Those first seeds may not have made a big impression on Ferdinand and Isabella, but they quickly proved their value. Within a few years the Spaniards had introduced maize around the Mediterranean. By the mid-16th century corn was so familiar in the Southern European diet that it formed the basis of such national dishes as Italian polenta and the Romanian staple mamaliga (a sort of cornmeal must). Corn also traveled to the Philippines and the rest of Asia; by 1560 it was a fixture in Chinese cooking, in everything from porridge to stir-fry.

Portuguese traders, who used corn as slave-ship stores, carried the grain to Africa. It was an instant success there: corn grew more rapidly than other grains, and it needed very little cultivation. You could plant it and then pretty much ignore it until harvest time. Corn weathered drought and the harsh African sun better than other staple foods. But its advent in Africa was not an unmixed blessing. It produced something of a population boom, which may in turn have feed the slave trade. In addition, says historian Robert Hall, "Europeans used slave labor in Africa for cultivating New World crops like corn, yams and cassava to provision the slave ships." And it led to a serious imbalance in the African diet. But by the late 18th century, many Africans ate almost nothing but corn, and suffered from vitamin deficiency as a result. Africans today are still afflicted by pellagra or "mealie disease," a sickness related to malnutrition from overreliance on corn.

In the Americas, Indians who depended on maize combined it with tomatoes, capsicum peppers and sometimes fish-all of which contain the necessary vitamins to make up for the deficit in corn. In fact, corn on its own provided only about a third the calories of Old World staples like sorghum and millet. In Europe, humans never really took to corn, but it became a major source of fodder for animals and helped improve nutrition by making meat cheaper.

Today, corn continues to relieve the planet's hunger-and slake its thirst. Any portrayal of the Pilgrim's first Thanksgiving would be incomplete without the requisite display of Indian maize, but what probably made the meal so jolly was a native brew of fermented corn. Later, less puritan immigrants took the process a few steps further to make that most American of liquors, bourbon whisky. Corn is the staple food of 200 million people in Africa and Latin America, and Americans consume an average of three pounds of corn a day in the form of meat, poultry and dairy products. And it's not just food: corn is used in products from baby powder to embalming fluid-the cradle to the grave.

—Mary Talbot

Slavery: How It Built the New World

T "*I now saw myself deprived of all chance of returning to my native country,*" Olaudah wrote, "*and my present situation…was filled with horrors of every kind…The stench of the hold, while we were on the coast, was so intolerably loathsome that it was dangerous to remain there for any time…. The closeness of the place, and the heat of the climate, added to the number in the ship, being so crowded that each had scarcely room to turn himself, almost suffocated us….*

"*The shrieks of the women, and the groans of the dying, rendered it a scene of horror almost inconceivable…. I expected every hour to share the fate of my companions, some of whom were almost daily brought upon deck at the point of death, and I began to hope that death would soon put an end to my miseries.*"

Olaudah—plucky, resourceful and highly intelligent—was a remarkable young man who became an even more remarkable man. Shipped to Barbados, sold at auction and renamed Gustavus Vassa by his first master, he eventually earned the money to buy his freedom. He sailed the world with the British Navy and later became a leader in the English antislavery movement of the 1780s. His memoir, "The Interesting Narrative of the Life of Olaudah Equiano, or Gustavus Vassa, the African," was published in England in 1789. It is a compelling account of a young slave's survival against the odds and a vivid description of human bondage in the late 18th century, the heyday of the "peculiar institution" that built the New World.

African slavery is fundamental to the history of the Americas. It began earlier, lasted longer and played a larger role in shaping modern societies than most Americans realize. The conquistadors brought African bondsmen to the island of Hispaniola as early as 1505, and slavery was not finally abolished, in Brazil, until 1888. Between 1505 and 1870, when the last vestiges of the Atlantic slave trade were finally suppressed, at least 10 million Africans were shipped to the Americas in chains. Prior to 1820, the number of Africans crossing the ocean outstripped the combined total of all European immigrants by a ratio of 5 to 1. Through 350 years of continuous operation along both coasts of Africa, European and American slavers brought about one of the largest forced migrations in recorded history—the African diaspora, whose result today is an African-American population of hundreds of millions of people distributed throughout the Western Hemisphere.

Slavery is sometimes regarded as a tragic anomaly of history—a dark cloud, threatening but small, on the receding horizon of the past. But it was no anomaly, and its legacies are with us still. The form of slavery that sprang up in the Americas was vastly unlike serfdom in medieval Europe or slavery anywhere else in the world. It was a mainspring of early economic development and the source of enormous wealth, in the form of unpaid labor, for white colonists and their political masters in Europe. The colonizing powers recognized almost from the beginning that African slaves were the only possible remedy for the labor shortages that plagued their New World dominions; slaves mined the precious metals and harvested the sugar, indigo and tobacco that made colonization worthwhile. The golden age of exploration, says Columbia University historian Eric Foner, was in reality a commercial enterprise, and slave labor made it profitable. "The centrality of slavery in the development of the New World can't be stressed enough," Foner says. "Most people believe that slavery was an aberration. Actually, *free* labor was the aberration. Without slavery, the New World would not have been developed."

Slavery thus became a vast, highly regimented labor system that stripped captive Africans of their dignity and personal identities, subjected them to merciless deprivation and brutality and sent them to die by the millions from disease, malnutrition, injury and abuse. The average survival rate of a mining slave during the great 18th-century gold rush in Minas Gerais, Brazil, was no more than two years; the survival rate of a field hand in the sugar plantations of northeastern Brazil was only about seven years. Prior to 1800, slave-mortality rates in the Portuguese, British, French and Dutch colonies of Latin America and the Caribbean were so high that only the continued importation of more and more Africans kept the colonial economies thriving. An 18th-century Jamaican document offers a glimpse of the tremendous human cost. Of 676,276 Africans who arrived in Jamaica between 1655 and 1787, a legislative committee found, 31,181 died on board ships waiting to unload in Jamaican ports. This total—for only one sugar colony—does not include the loss of life during the Atlantic crossing, nor does it include the huge numbers of slaves who died during what was quaintly known as seasoning.

Uncovering the whole truth about slavery is a difficult task for scholars even today. The slaves themselves left relatively few accounts of their lives in captivity, and slaveholders tended for obvious reasons to be reticent about the realities of the system they controlled. The conditions of slavery varied dramatically from place to place and from century to century: depending on circumstances and the attitudes of white colonials, the treatment of slaves ranged from relatively benign paternalism to almost unimaginable brutality. John Gabriel Stedman, a young British adventurer who went to Surinam in 1771 to help suppress one of many slave revolts there, was appalled by the Dutch planters' casual use of torture to discipline their slaves. In his book "Narrative of a Five Years Expedition against the Revolted Negroes of Surinam," Stedman quotes a white colonist who described the torture-execution of a slave:

"Not long ago," this colonist told Stedman, *"I saw a black man hang'd alive by the ribs, between which with a knife was first made an incision, and then clinch'd an Iron hook with a chain. In this manner, he kept living three days, hanging with head and feet downwards and catching with his tongue the drops of water, it being the rainy season, that were flowing down his bloated breast, while the vultures were picking in the putrid wound."*

Is it any wonder, Stedman mused, "that the negro Slaves rise up in rebellion against their masters? Assuredly, it is not." As Stedman knew, slave uprisings were a continual threat not only in Surinam, where black rebels eventually overthrew the Dutch, but in almost every slaveholding colony and region of the Americas. Brazilian authorities repeatedly sent military expeditions to attack huge settlements of runaway slaves called *quilombres*, and they were forced to suppress three major slave revolts in Bahia during the 1830s. Spectacular insurrections—like the ones in Haiti in 1794, Guyana in 1823 and Jamaica in 1831—alarmed slaveholders everywhere. The historian Eugene Genovese quotes a white Southerner, Mary Boykin Chesnut, to make the point. "What a thrill of terror ran through me as those yellow and black brutes came jumping over the parapets," Mrs. Chesnut wrote in her diary, after seeing a play about the 1857 Sepoy mutiny in India. "Their faces were like so many of the same sort at home. To be sure, John Brown had failed to fire their hearts here, and they saw no cause to rise and burn and murder us all. . . . But how long would they resist the seductive and irresistible call: `Rise, kill and be free!'"

Mrs. Chesnut was wrong: slaves in the United States saw many reasons to rise up, and they did so on several memorable occasions. What is remarkable about slavery in the United States, however, is that slave revolts were relatively rare and never successful. That fact has engendered considerable debate among historians, and it has led (or misled) some scholars to talk of a "Sambo" slave personality—the stereotypical, happy-go-lucky slave. Simply put, the Sambo theory maintains that slaves were "infantilized" by systematic oppression and selective brutality and that, more often than not, they were psychological accomplices in their own subjugation. In recent years this theory has prompted sharp dissents from scholars who argue that slaves fought back in myriad subtle ways. "Slave resistance included carelessness, feigned stupidity, insolence, satire, deliberate evasion and refusal to work," says historian David Barry Gaspar of Duke University. "Slaves handled some of these forms with such finesse that whites tended to accept them as part of the black stereotype."

Frederick Douglass, the great American abolitionist, was not inclined to finesse. As a young slave in Maryland, Douglass rebelled one day and fought his master, a Mr. Covey, to a bloody standstill. "At this moment ...I resolved to fight," Douglass wrote in his autobiography. "I seized Covey hard by the throat and as I did so, I rose…. My resistance was so entirely unexpected that Covey seemed taken aback." Covey called another white man for help, but Douglass disabled the second man with a kick to the ribs. Then he and Covey fought for nearly two hours until Covey, "saying that if I had not resisted, he would not have whipped me half so much," finally let him go. "The truth was,"

Douglass observed laconically, "he had not whipped me at all" —and Covey never again "laid the weight of his finger on me in anger."

Like Olaudah Equiano, Frederick Douglass escaped bondage to become a crusader in the antislavery cause. By the 1840s, when Douglass took up his political and literary career, slavery seemed to be a dying institution. Great Britain and the United States outlawed the Atlantic slave trade in 1808, and Parliament formally abolished slavery in Britain's Caribbean colonies in 1833. France and Denmark followed suit in 1848; the Dutch in 1863. In the United States, Lincoln and his generals drove the slave-owning South to ruin through five years of civil war—and America's bloody example, combined with British diplomatic and economic pressure, ultimately led to abolition in Cuba, Puerto Rico and Brazil. Slavery, as old as mankind, was virtually eradicated less than a century after the founding of the first antislavery societies in the United States and Britain. It was, in all probability, the first example in history of a morally committed minority reversing an entrenched social judgment with propaganda and political pressure.

The economic legacy of slavery has been blight—a pattern of chronic underdevelopment that even today retards social progress through much of Latin America and the Caribbean. "There is a permanent inverse relationship between slavery and economic development," says Foner. "Even in the United States, in the South, slavery permanently distorted the economy." In much of the rural South, for example, the end of slavery meant the rise of sharecropping, a new form of peonage. "We are landless and homeless," the freedmen of Edisto Island, S.C., protested during the Reconstruction Era. "We can only do one of three things: Step into the public road or the sea or remain on [the plantations), working as in former time and subject to [the white man's] will ... We can not resist it in any way without being driven out homeless upon the road. You will see this is not the condition of really free men."

The worst was yet to come. The end of Reconstruction saw the abrupt termination of nearly every form of political progress for freed slaves-the passage of "Jim Crow" laws, the denial of the right to vote, the rise of the Ku Klux Klan and the revival of nightrider terror. The most malign legacy of slavery, in short, was racism. Slavery and racism are chicken and egg. Racism contributed much to Europe's willingness to enslave Africans, and the need to rationalize and defend the institution of slavery played a very large part in the growth of modern racism. From slavery times onward—from Stepin' Fetchit stereotypes to the rise of "scientific" racism—millions of white Americans have clung to the notion that blacks are inferior as a group. The persistence of that belief may well be the central tragedy of American history, and its bitterness surely contaminates the national dialogue today.

If there is any redemptive meaning in the history of slavery, it lies in the idea of freedom. To say the struggle over abolition led Americans to a deeper understanding of freedom is perhaps too simple: it took 100 years, and the passion of Martin Luther King Jr., to hold the nation to the promise of the Bill of Rights. But it is nevertheless true, as David Brion Davis observes, that 18th-century political thinkers generally saw no contradiction in espousing a radical view of liberty for whites while denying it to blacks and Indians. By 1865, Americans and Europeans alike accepted the premise that freedom could not be restricted to the few. This turnabout reversed a tradition in Western moral philosophy dating back to the Greeks—its implications affect all of us today.

Slavery: The High Price of Sugar

Right from the start, Columbus had a plan: to establish a sugar industry on Hispaniola much like the ones back home on the Canary and Madeira islands. So on his second voyage to the New World, he brought along several stalks of sugar cane. The Spanish hidalgos couldn't be bothered with the broiling, backbreaking task of growing and making the sweetener; so they forced the locals to do it for them. When the Indians started dropping from disease, the Spaniards turned to Africa. By the mid-16th century a nascent sugar industry completely dependent on black slave labor had taken hold in the Spanish Caribbean. The dramatic change on Hispaniola prompted a Spanish historian to write: "There are so many Negroes in this island, as a result of the sugar factories, that the land seems an effigy or an image of Ethiopia itself." Thus began a relationship between sugar production and African slavery that was to dominate Caribbean life for nearly four centuries.

This relationship had already existed in the Old World for hundreds of years. The first reference to sugar dates back to 350 B.C., with the report that people in India were eating rice pudding with milk and sugar and sipping drinks flavored with the sweetener. A little later, in 327 B.C., Alexander the Great's general, Nearchus, sailing from the mouth of the Indus River to the Euphrates, asserted that "a reed in India brings forth honey without the help of bees, from which an intoxicating drink is made though the plant bears no fruit." But not until about A.D. 500 is there unmistakable written evidence of sugar *making*; the technology didn't spread westward until the Moorish invasion of Europe in the seventh century. Sugar, according to anthropologist Sidney Mintz, followed the Koran.

The first Africans were enslaved soon afterward. Mintz reports that a slave revolt involving thousands of East African laborers took place in the Tigris-Euphrates delta as early as the mid-ninth century. Slavery grew more important as European crusaders seized the sugar plantations of the eastern Mediterranean from their Arab predecessors. By the 15th century, African slaves supplied the labor for the Spanish and Portuguese plantations on the Atlantic islands off the coast of Africa. To the Spanish way of thinking, then, African slaves were the logical solution to the labor shortages in the New World.

While Spaniards in the Caribbean were the first to produce and export sugar, their pioneering efforts were soon outstripped by developments on the American mainland. Sugar cane prospered in the Spanish territories of Mexico, Paraguay and Peru. By 1526, the Portuguese had begun shipping sugar from Brazil to Lisbon in commercial quantities.

By the end of the 17th century, the British had also established stakes in the Caribbean, and slavery became an integral part of their newly settled colonies almost from the start. Dutch traders, who had a foothold in Brazil, first introduced sugar making to English colonists on the island of Barbados in the 1630s. From humble beginnings, the British sugar industry spread north to the Leeward Islands, where it soon wrought a social, economic and political transformation so sweeping and rapid that historians have called it the Sugar Revolution. "England fought the most, conquered the most colonies, imported the most slaves and went furthest and fastest in creating a plantation system," writes Mintz in "Sweetness and Power." In 1655, when Britain conquered Jamaica—an island nearly 30 times the size of Barbados—she came to dominate the north European sugar trade.

The sugar industry was a messy business. Planters, clearing huge tracts of forested land, devastated the environment. In 1690, trees covered more than two thirds of the British colony of Antigua. By 1751 planters had stripped every acre suitable for cultivation. Antiguan John Luffman, writing in 1786, observed that even the largest hills were "clothed with the luxuriant verdure of the sugar cane to their very summits." The rapid deforestation only heightened the region's propensity for drought and erosion.

It was also extremely lucrative. In the 18th century, Antigua rivaled Barbados as one of the leading producers in the Caribbean, although neither could compete with Jamaica or French Saint Domingue (Haiti). "Barbados, in one period, and Antigua, in another, were producing more wealth than the entire North American continent," says Conrad Goodwin, an anthropologist who (along with geographer Lydia Pulsipher) has spent more than a decade excavating and studying sugar plantations on Antigua and the neighboring island of Montserrat.

The production of sugar—from holing, planting and harvesting to crushing, boiling and curing—depended on a large work force. To meet the demand for labor, Antiguan planters imported tens of thousands of slaves from Africa. In 1678 there were 2,308 whites and 2,172 blacks on the island. By the mid-18th century, Antigua's population had grown to nearly 40,000, and blacks outnumbered whites 10 to 1. David Barry Gaspar, an historian at Duke University, speculates that the ratio of blacks to whites would have been even higher if thousands hadn't committed suicide or died as the result of accidents, disease, poor diet, hard labor and mistreatment at the hands of their masters. "Because of the general oppressive environment of slavery, the slave population was not self-reproducing," says Gaspar. Their ranks had to he constantly replenished with imports from Africa.

A slave's life was grim beyond our capacity to imagine and sometimes beyond their capacity to endure. The workday was endless, and beatings were common for the smallest infraction. Mary Prince, a slave who lived on a number of different Caribbean islands in the early 19th century, describes her treatment by one particularly cruel owner: "To strip me naked—to hang me up by the wrists and lay my flesh open with the cow-skin, was an ordinary punishment for even a slight offence."

The conditions on plantations drove some slaves to suicide and infanticide. Others fought back with insubordination, malingering and feigned illnesses. Running away was virtually impossible since by the mid-18th century the forests had been cleared and most of the smaller islands afforded no place to hide. But, as recent scholars have begun to see, the slaves were often resourceful in adapting to their plight.

"I'm not saying that slavery wasn't bad, because it was," says Pulsipher. "But slaves were not just victims. We should give them credit for being able to seize a bad situation and make the best of it."

On most plantations slaves managed to carve out a degree of autonomy by insisting on certain rights, such as a weekly day off and the right to sell, at Sunday market, food they had grown in their own gardens. "One of the forms of both accommodation and resistance, especially on Montserrat, was through these slave gardens up in the hills," says Goodwin. "Because they could escape white eyes, these gardens had connotations of freedom and self-worth. But the gardens were also advantageous to slave owners because they relieved them of some of the responsibility of supplying food to slaves."

Sunday, market day, had little religious significance for slaves who, at least in the early years, didn't attend church. Because slavery did not square with their religious teachings, Anglican planters had little interest in converting their labor force. It was not until the late 1700s, when the Moravians and Methodists arrived and opened their doors to slaves, that Sunday became important as a day of worship. In the meantime, they quietly practiced the religious traditions they had brought over from Africa. Islam had some influence, but it's not known how much.

But even after the introduction of Christianity, Sunday remained one of the few days that slaves found free time to enjoy themselves. John Luffman offered this description of a musical afternoon: "Negroes are very fond of the discordant notes of the banjar and the hollow sound of the toombah . . . The banjar is the invention of and was brought here by the African Negroes, who are most expert in the performance thereon, which are principally their own country tunes. To this music I have seen 100 or more dancing at a time . . . The principal dancing time is on Sunday afternoons, when the great market is over. In fact, Sunday is their day of trade, their day of relaxation, their day of pleasure, and may be called the Negroes' holiday."

Slaves seized an opportunity that was given them by the western European calendar and, quickly and entrepreneurially, started the markets. "Slaves used this time to socialize, reaffirm cultural links, meet their mates and sell whatever it was they had for sale: the baskets they'd woven, the food they'd made or the vegetables they'd grown. It was a time to improve their economic status, in small but significant ways." In excavating Galways Plantation on Montserrat, Pulsipher and Goodwin unearthed an unusual abundance of artifacts from the plantation's slave village, including imported porcelain dishes, clay pipes, buttons, clothing fasteners, beads and coins. "These people were into a material culture," says Pulsipher. "Our theory is that their wealth was a result of their gardens up on the hillsides." Judging by the artifacts, Goodwin suspects slaves on Galways Plantation possessed maybe twice the material wealth of slaves on typical plantations in the southern United States.

In other parts of the Caribbean, however, slaves were not so fortunate. On Antigua, slaves had trouble finding space to plant their gardens because nearly every acre was in cane. Despite laws ordering slave owners to provide plantations with provision grounds, many wouldn't spare the land to ensure that slaves were adequately fed.

Throughout the Caribbean, sugar plantations were a curious blend of farming and factory work because so much of the industrial processing of the sugar was carried out on the spot. Mintz has dubbed the plantations "precocious cases of industrialization," and even the planters themselves recognized their industrial elements. In "An Essay Upon Plantership," Samuel Martin, an Antiguan planter writing in 1773, described the plantation as a machine with many moving parts: if one part broke, the machine broke. "Even that early, labor was very important, filling many cogs in the machine," says Goodwin.

The "sugar" cycle began in August or September, when the laborers prepared the fields for planting. Slaves, wielding hoes under a mercilessly hot sun, dug holes about five or six inches deep and about five feet square, into which they placed cane cuttings, covered them with a layer of mold and prayed for rain. The slaves tended the new cane shoots as they grew; the crop was harvested, one field at a time, 15 months later.

When it came to the harvest, timing was everything. As soon as the sugar cane was ripe it had to be cut and ground, often within 24 hours to keep it from spoiling. Black overseers, called drivers, would stand behind a line of slaves, crack their whips and give the order to start cutting. From the break of dawn until after dusk, the slaves toiled in the hot, sticky fields—cutting the cane, gathering up the stalks, stripping off the leaves and loading the 100-pound bundles onto ox carts bound for the mill. The pace was so frenzied that pregnant women were sometimes obliged to give birth in the field and then continue working.

For the slaves who fed the mill, the work was less physically demanding but posed different dangers. The feeders, as they were called, were liable, especially when tired, to get their fingers caught between the vertical rollers that crushed the cane. A watchman stood ready with a hatchet to sever an arm before it could be drawn into the machine. As terrible as this must have been, the alternative was worse. The rollers couldn't be stopped by flipping a switch. "If the limb wasn't chopped off, the slave would be crushed to death," says Goodwin.

The boilermen had a less exacting but hotter and heavier task. Juice from the sugar cane would enter the boiling house by a pipe that ran from the mill, and workers would siphon it into a great copper basin. After several hours of boiling and skimming, the slaves would ladle the steamy liquid into a number of successively smaller coppers until it was ready to crystallize. The sugar then cooled, packed into barrels rolled into the curing room. Holes were drilled in the bottoms of the barrels, allowing the molasses to drain into separate containers.

Laboring in temperatures above 100 degrees, the boilermen often worked through the night, and the darkness increased the likelihood of serious burns from the scalding, sugary liquid. But because their job required a high degree of knowledge and skill, the boilermen were among the most valued slaves on the plantation.

Slaves used the molasses and skimmings from the boiling house to make rum. Water, molasses, yeast and lees were combined in a fermenting cistern and left for a week to 10 days. The fermented liquid was distilled into rum and decanted in wooden barrels. The rum, as well as sugar and molasses, was stored in a warehouse until a ship arrived to carry it either to Europe or to one of the North American colonies.

In the 17th century, there emerged two so-called triangles of trade. The first and most famous of these linked Europe to Africa and the West Indies. European goods, such as trinkets, arms, gunpowder and gin, were exchanged for slaves in West Africa. The slaves were shipped to the West Indies and sold for sugar, coffee, indigo and other tropical products, which were then sent to the European mother country. The second triangle wasn't vital to world trade until the mid-18th century. In this scenario, New England merchants shipped rum to Africa, exchanged the rum for slaves and sailed to the West Indies, where they sold the slaves. bought molasses for rum-making and returned home.

As several scholars have pointed out, trade was not limited to these two triangles; more often than not, it moved in several directions.

"Some of the trade did actually flow in legal channels as it was supposed to do, within a single imperial system"' notes Philip D. Curtin, author of "The Rise and Fall of the Plantation Complex." "Much of it flowed outside those channels."

The sugar industry—so prosperous for nearly two centuries—had started to decline by the mid-19th century. Several factors contributed to its downward spiral: emancipation of the slaves, falling sugar prices and the development of alternative sweeteners. Still, on some islands—Puerto Rico, Barbados, Cuba and the Dominican Republic—sugar remains the main export today. On Antigua, the only reminders of the sugar heyday are the ruins of countless plantations, the Cavalier rum factory (which must import its molasses from the Dominican Republic) and a population that traces its roots to Africa. On Antigua, as with so many islands, one monoculture has simply been exchanged for another: tourism is now virtually the only industry.

Despite the changes wrought by 500 years of contact with the Old World, the people of the West Indies have managed to build a vibrant culture, mixing European elements with those of Africa and the Americas. In the British West Indies, for example, cricket has long been the most popular sport. Before a recent match between Montserrat and Antigua, the Montserratian team, which hadn't won a game all season, performed an old African rite to increase its chances: rising at dawn, they gathered on the playing field and started dancing...to drive away the evil spirits.